# Advance Praise for the Book

"There is no one greater than the Guru, and there is no power greater than faith. *Samarpan Yog of the Himalayas* (Part-1) penned by his Holiness Shivkrupanand Swamiji narrates the extraordinary journey of a young person on the path of inner search. This book is not about turning pages, but about turning lives.

"After reading this book, the search for the Guru and Paramatma will end for many sadhaks, because the source of inner knowledge is in this book."—*Nitin Gadkari, minister of road transport and highways, Government of India*

"Five years ago, I read this book for the first time. I thought, 'Wow! What an adventure story!' It transported me to the Himalayas as if on a magic carpet and gave me a very intimate view into the Himalayan spiritual practices that helped to make Swamiji ready to share with us.

"I continued reading with great enthusiasm, but what I couldn't have known at that time was how powerful this book is, and how it is being used as a medium to bring the teachings of the Himalayan Gurus to us normal people, so beautifully and easily.

"By now, I have read this book countless times and each time it is like the first time ... only deeper, more profound. It seems to be true that this book is really alive. It seems to change with my own ability to understand. As I become more open, deeper teachings from the book are reaching me."—*Sohamji, spiritual teacher, Germany*

# SAMARPAN YOG
## OF THE
# HIMALAYAS
#### PART - 1

# SAMARPAN YOG OF THE HIMALAYAS

PART - 1

An Autobiography of a Realized Sage
A Spiritual Journey

**SHREE SHIVKRUPANAND SWAMI**

An imprint of HarperCollins *Publishers*

First published in Hindi by Harper Hindi 2023
First published in English by HarperVantage 2024
An imprint of HarperCollins *Publishers* India
4th Floor, Tower A, Building No. 10, DLF Cyber City,
DLF Phase II, Gurugram, Haryana – 122002
www.harpercollins.co.in

2 4 6 8 10 9 7 5 3 1

Copyright © Shree Shivkrupanand Swami 2024
Translated by Krupa Kavadia
Illustrations by Shri Prabhakar Sharma

P-ISBN: 978-93-6213-188-1
E-ISBN: 978-93-6213-704-3

The views and opinions expressed in this book are the author's own and the facts are as reported by him, and the publishers are not in any way liable for the same.

Shree Shivkrupanand Swami asserts his moral right to be identified as the author of this book.

All rights reserved. No part of this publication may be reproduced, stored in a retrieval system, or transmitted, in any form or by any means, electronic, mechanical, photocopying, recording or otherwise, without the prior permission of the publishers.

Typeset in 11/15 Garamond Premier Pro at
SŪRYA, New Delhi

Printed and bound at
Thomson Press (India) Ltd.

# Contents

Introduction to His Holiness Shree Shivkrupanand Swami    vii
A Request    xi
Preface    xiii

**Episode 1: With Shree Brahmanand Swami**    1
Practice of Placing One's Chitta on Water    6
Importance of Chitta Purification    15
Eyes of the Soul    28
'Who Am I?'    39
Correct Meaning of Celibacy    56
Importance of Guru-charan    67

**Episode 2: With the Third Guru**    79
U-Tube-Like Relation between Husband and Wife    92
Importance of Mantra    104
Process of Attaining Inner Knowledge    129
Importance of the Word 'Samarpan'    141
Unknown Journey on the Brahmaputra River    153

| | |
|---|---|
| **Episode 3: With Shreenath Baba** | 155 |
| Kundalini Shakti | 170 |
| Mountainous Journey with Gurudev | 198 |
| Importance of the Naming Ceremony | 204 |
| Satguru | 217 |
| Types of Death | 253 |
| Subtle Body | 326 |
| Process of Child Conception and Values of Conception | 330 |
| *Glossary* | 401 |

# Introduction to His Holiness Shree Shivkrupanand Swamiji

His Holiness Shree Shivkrupanand Swamiji is a 'Bhagirath' (one who performs a stupendous task) who brought Himalayan Meditation (earlier known as Samarpan Meditation) from the caverns of the Himalayas to society, just like Bhagirath—the great mythological king—who, by his austere devotion, had brought down river Ganga ('Bhaagirathi') for humanity.

The knowledge of Himalayan Meditation was confined only to the meditating sages, ascetics and Kaivalya Kumbhak yogis in the Himalayas. How did Swamiji reach them? Let us go back to Swamiji's childhood to know about it.

Swamiji was born in a lower middle class Maharashtrian Brahmin family. His mother was a religious, gentle and quiet lady of few words. Swamiji received his religious orientation from his maternal grandparents and his mother. However, his quest took him in a different direction ... he wished to 'meet' God ... and to attain the ultimate spiritual experience.

Due to his father's limited income, Swamiji had to finance his own education, right from matriculation to post-graduation in commerce. He used to tutor students in his free time and earned money to pay for his fees and other educational material.

Right from his childhood, he was very fond of travelling. As a child, he would walk along the railway tracks and observe the villages and agricultural fields in the vicinity. As he grew a little older, he would travel on his friends' bicycles to far-off jungles and mountains. Then, in the course of his job, he travelled to almost all the places in India. While travelling, he would visit places of scenic beauty and, at the same time, he would also have spiritual discussions with the spiritual people of that particular place.

Whenever he went into a deep meditative trance while chanting mantras, he would get the vision of three images consecutively. In his meditation, he saw: 1. Pashupatinath Temple (Nepal) 2. An ascetic who was six-feet-tall, fair-skinned with blue eyes and had a long white beard 3. A temple of Lord Shiva on a hillock.

Once when he had gone to Kanpur for some job-related work, he found that due to some reason the banks there were on strike and this situation was expected to continue for some time. Then Swamiji thought to himself, *Why not go to Nepal and get darshan of Lord Pashupatinath?* So, he left for Nepal and got the darshan of Lord Pashupatinath. There he met an old gentleman who had come from a faraway village called Shibu and who said to Swamiji, "Shiv Baba is waiting for you, come along!" When Swamiji met Shiv Baba, he realized that it was the same ascetic whose darshan he often used to get during meditation. Shiv Baba transferred all his spiritual energies to Swamiji and paved the way for his spiritual progress. Then Swamiji returned from Nepal and continued with his job.

Soon he got married and he also had a son. When his son was eighteen months old, another Guru came to his house and took Swamiji away to the Himalayas after obtaining permission from his wife. Over there, Swamiji met and accepted several sages, ascetics and kaivalya kumbhak yogis as his Gurus and served them. While performing service to the Gurus, he also attained (spiritual) knowledge from them.

Each Guru bestowed him with all his knowledge and sent him to another Guru. While obtaining knowledge from each Guru, Swamiji came to know about the meditation values that paves the way for every soul's path to moksha. These meditation values are beyond religion, race, language and gender, which means that all the souls in the world can meditate using these meditation values.

Swamiji brought these meditation values to society as instructed by his Gurus. Swamiji could learn this meditation only because he surrendered completely to his Gurus. Thus, it was named 'Samarpan Meditation' (Samarpan means complete surrender). Every human being in the world who surrenders completely can obtain the knowledge of this meditation. Today, this prasad bestowed by the Himalayan Gurus is being appreciated worldwide in the name of 'Himalayan Meditation'.

The objective of Swamiji's life is the spiritual development of all the souls in the world and bestowing the state of liberation on them while they are living. That's why he is distributing this priceless knowledge free of cost all over the world through free camps and centres. Swamiji himself is an ocean of consciousness but always considers himself to be only a medium of the Guru-energy. We bow a thousand times before his gentleness and simplicity!

His Holiness Swamiji's wife

*Gursuma*

# A Request

*Samarpan Yog of the Himalayas*, written by His Holiness Shree Shivkrupanand Swamiji, is the chronicle of his spiritual journey. This is not an ordinary book but a living and holy scripture which bestows a spiritual experience as you read it. Through this book, the future generations will easily be able to attain the live spiritual experience for which His Holiness Swamiji performed severe penance for several years.

The energies of His Holiness Swamiji's Gurus flow easily through the medium of this book. Therefore, it is my loving request to readers that they should read it with due respect and maintain its dignity.

Jai Baba Swami!

Yours

*Guruma*

# Preface

My Salutations to all Pious Souls!

After performing the Deep Meditation Practicum (Gahan Dhyan Anushthan) in the ashram, some process was happening within me. I felt as if something was going to be written. But I could not understand it. What was going to be written? When is it going to be written? I could not even understand where it would begin. I felt terribly uneasy this way for three continuous days.

I wanted the beginning of this book to take place according to Gurudev's wishes; that he should introduce himself to society from whichever point (of time and place) he wished, because he was the one who was inspiring me to write all this. Therefore, *he* should begin this book. Some sadhaks from Junagadh Centre came to meet me at the ashram on 15 April 2007, and the work on this book started on that same day and ended after five months on 15 September 2007.

Thus, this work was accomplished through the grace of the Guru-energies in the year 2007. This knowledge is being given to you very easily through me, but I have not received it easily and not from one place either. The Guru-energies wish to pass on this information through the medium of this book. This is not an ordinary book but a distillation of the mystical knowledge of the Guru-energies which are reaching you through the medium of this book. It has been possible to write this book only after reaching a special meditative state. Once, when I was very busy and could not reach that special state, then the writing stopped. Then Guru Purnima was celebrated at Junagadh and I was able to reach the higher state once again; and the process of writing started was resumed. Everything was written after that and is being written today too. Now it can be written continuously for at least three years. That's why this book is presented to you as the first volume.

Actually, all this (knowledge) should have appeared in my discourses. But perhaps it did not manifest because it is more appropriate that it should appear through the medium of the book. One reaches a meditative state just by reading this book. One cannot read a lot at a time. In fact, through the medium of the book one gets the vision of Siddha (Perfected) yogis. The sadhak's chitta goes to their energies and he receives the blessings of these Guru-energies. This book has been written immediately after *Spiritual Truth* (2007) but it's so different; you will experience that after reading it.

I had returned (mentally) to the natural ravines of the Himalayas, and the proximity of the enlightened saints through the medium of this book. I am an ordinary human just like you. I too had to face various problems in my life and I've written about these personal experiences.

I could become the medium of Guru-karya only because I attained the proximity to my Gurus. Samarpan meditation is an 800-year-old technique of meditation but it has been made accessible to the society now, and this book is a description of how the River of Knowledge like river Ganga has descended from the Himalayas.

It is my belief that the Guru-energies have made me write

this book because of your love. I pray at Paramatma's feet that this book may bring new energy and new divine consciousness into your lives.

Yours,

*Babaswami*

Shree Shivkrupanand Swami
15 September 2007 (Ganesh Chaturthi),
Navsari, Gujarat

# Episode One

*With Shree Brahmanand Swami*

It was dawn. A small, clean rivulet flowed near where I sat. It wasn't very deep; mountain rivulets usually aren't. Such rivulets were common in these mountain ranges. As the water was flowing it was very clean, I sat on one side of the river, and Shree Brahmanand Swami sat on the opposite bank. We had been travelling on foot for the last three days and I was naturally tired. My feet were aching, and the sole of my shoe had split open at the front on the right side. This was a common occurrence because of the raised bone on my right foot, but this time it happened right at the beginning of the journey; I was worried about what would happen later. Not used to this kind of walking, my knees had started to hurt. I was also anxious about how I would fare in the future if this was how I felt after just three days. I didn't know where he was taking me.

I didn't know where I was supposed to go. I didn't know till when I was supposed to walk like this. I didn't know why. I just carried on. I was going towards an unknown destination, and I didn't know my way back; I didn't even know whether I would be able to get back. The last three nights had been spent in the jungle, without any bed or blanket; I hadn't been able to sleep. My eyes were burning because I hadn't slept for three nights. We had reached a very isolated spot, and I hadn't seen a single human since the previous day. I didn't know if I would ever see anyone again. There was no trace of civilization. As the jungle thickened, I doubted whether we would come across any human habitation. That day I realized that man is basically a social animal, which is why he chooses to live in a community, preferring small groups and villages.

Gurudev sat peacefully on the other bank with both his feet dipped into the rivulet. Behind him sprawled the Blue Hills mountain range. There was a cover of blue clouds over those hills, making us aware as to why these hills are called the 'Blue Hills.' We were in the midst of a thick forest, so thick that it obscured the river ahead. Gurudev was calmly observing the mountains. He must have been about six feet tall, with big shapely eyes. Even in old age, his body seemed to be robust. He was clad only in a loincloth and carried a heavy branch like a stick in his hand, which he used to support himself. He was dark-skinned and charismatic. I had never seen such an attractive dark-complexioned person before this. His whole bearing reflected purity; I couldn't help but wonder if his soul was holy; that's why the inner purity was so visible in every pore of his body. I don't know why, but from time to time he would just sit with his eyes closed.

Whenever he sat like that, I felt that he was looking deep into me, and I could feel something stirring within me. He spoke very little, but whatever he said seemed like a revelation, a divine communication. He spoke with great seriousness. There was depth in his words, and every word he spoke sounded like the truth. Whatever he said, my ears felt that his words should be absorbed with the words' aura. The last three days, he spoke very little, but whatever he said was to offer me encouragement. His voice always had a perceptible note of certainty. He definitely knew where we were going. He also knew with complete certainty why we were going there. In his eyes, everything about the future was certain. He knew it and I didn't. He was the very embodiment of certainty whereas I was filled with uncertainty.

I can't say why, but I could only look at him from a distance. On coming closer to him my eyes just couldn't rise above his feet, as if my own mind was cutting me off and saying, "You're only worthy to look at the Guru-charan, and no higher."

My joy was tinged with fear. The fear probably was due to my own impure chitta which was filled with impurities of past memories. My impure chitta induced within me this respectful fear of him. Gurudev suddenly opened his eyes and said, "Do you know, a day will come when hundreds of thousands of people will yearn for your divine darshan. There will be long queues of people waiting to meet you. People will come from all corners of the world just to get a glimpse of you. If someone just manages to get a glimpse of you, he'll feel that his life was worthwhile. They'll keep hoping that your glance falls on them at least once! You'll become the medium for them to reach Paramatma. Do you know how extensive your world is! Due to your ignorance, you had thought of your family as your world. Now just see, I'll introduce you to your world."

I looked around me. There was no one—not even a stray dog. And I thought to myself, "On the one hand he's taking me to a deserted place, and on the other he's saying that he will introduce me to millions of people! Perhaps he's talking about my next birth." I said, a little foolishly, "Gurudev, there's not even a stray dog here! You're taking me to an uninhabited place and you're saying, 'millions of people will yearn for your sight.'" Gurudev answered calmly, "The path to reach those millions of people passes through this uninhabited place. I'm aware that you may find this false under today's circumstances, but tomorrow it will come true. However, when this happens, I won't be here in this world because my work will have been completed. I can foresee the future because of my inner vision, but you can't. There is a big interval of time between us. The day this interval is bridged, the 'sun of truth' will be visible to both of us."

Truth is always the same: it is certain. Some people realize it early in life, whereas most others need more time to understand the truth. This is the only difference between us. The Guru speaks at his spiritual level, but the disciple listens at his own level. That's why there's no scope for meaningful dialogue between the two; that is why the disciple can't understand what the Guru tells him at that time. The disciple's vision cannot equal the sweeping immensity of his Guru's. The Guru is aware of both the disciple's past and his future. There is an interval, a gap of time between the two, and until that time elapses, the disciple can't understand what the Guru tells him. That's why I couldn't understand what he was telling me at that time. But he was sure that, one day, I would.

After a while, both of us started walking northward. We went round the hills and climbed, and then we went down the other side. After travelling for five days, we arrived at his dwelling. It was already evening by then. A stream was flowing down the hill. I followed Gurudev as he descended. After carrying on for some distance, we came to a small pool of water. His cave stood beside it. Upon going inside, I saw that water was continuously falling drop by drop from the hill into the cave, and since it had been dripping in the same place for several years, a deep pit had formed there. The water that collected there was used for drinking. When the level of water increased, it would overflow into the pool outside the cave. That same water would flow forwards, fall and join the stream. It was a beautiful scene in front of the cave.

If one sat near the pool outside the cave, one could witness the sunrise. On the right side of the cave, there was a high, milky, foamy waterfall. Gurudev used to pluck and bring tubers and roots. I gratefully ate whatever he gave me. For the first eight or ten days, he taught me how to connect with nature (at a deep level). He would say, "Look at this water flowing in the stream; look at it carefully. It flows according to a definite pattern; watch how it falls in the beginning, how it falls later. Study it with full concentration. Nature is giving a message through it. There is a steady rhythm in the flow of the water. Pay attention on it. There is a tune in the flowing stream; recognize it. Listen to that music, listen to its message and experience the sound of the flowing stream within yourself. Then when you go deeper inside, you'll become aware that the stream, the water, is not external, but is flowing somewhere within you. What effect does that sound have on your mind? Experience it. Now think about where this water must have originated, and the path it must have taken to get here, and the jungles it must have passed through. Which paths will this water follow as it flows further, and what is its final destination? You'll realize that not only the stream but every drop of water will finally reach and join the sea. Every drop has to finally reach the sea. Now slowly imagine that you have drunk that water and try to feel the taste of that water, and you'll find that you can taste it without even bringing it to your lips.

"Now imagine that you have jumped into the water and are bathing in it. Now you'll also feel the touch of the water and its closeness. Now try to imagine how you feel. Experience the feeling of water on your head, on the back of your neck, on your chest, experience it on your stomach, experience it on your feet, and imagine that the water is entering your body from the top and coming out through the soles of your feet."

In this way, he kept my attention on the flow of the water for several days. During those days I became aware that I had stopped having any errant thoughts, I had slowly forgotten the rest of the world; this stream had become my world, and that stream was flowing with new particles every day, and by focusing on the new particles of water, my chitta was gradually getting purified. Or you could say in the proximity of the stream my chitta was getting washed and getting purer day by day.

Some days later, when Gurudev went to the jungle to collect

tubers and roots, he took me along and told me about various trees. He told me about their fruits and leaves, he would explain about their special properties. I couldn't understand everything that he explained to me, but when he did explain, I felt like listening to him for the rest of my life. There was a hypnotic rhythm in his speech, a musicality that reminded me of the stream. I just loved it. Sometimes I felt that what he said and what he was saying without speaking were two different things.

It felt like all of his talk was intended to keep my attention on himself, continually. I loved being in his presence. I felt a deeper connection with nature because of the information he gave me. He explained the mystery of nature's cycle: "A tree absorbs energy through its roots and then conveys the energy to the bigger branches; the bigger branches pass on that living energy to smaller branches; then the smaller branches convey the same energy to the bigger twigs, which in turn pass it onto the smaller twigs. These small twigs receive the energy and give birth to a new bud. And the bud, which continuously receives the living energy, unfolds and blooms into a flower. The same flower later grows into a fruit.

"In this way, on the one hand, the fruit transforms further into a seed and reaches the pinnacle of its growth, and on the other hand the small twigs that nourish the fruit and make it grow give birth to tiny new and tender leaves. These tiny tender leaves have a beautiful reddish hue. The leaves grow bigger and become deep green. After some time, they turn yellow. When they realize after turning yellow that they are of no use anymore, they fall. They don't wish to be a burden on the tree, and they remain on the tree only as long as they can be of help to it.

"When they fall from the tree, they surrender their existence to the roots of the tree, and because they have surrendered their existence, they are transformed into compost. Thus, even when they are separated from the tree, they think about benefiting the tree until their last breath. Every part of the tree is involved in taking the energy forward. No part holds on to or stores the energy it has received. It always shares the energy with other parts.

"Similarly, a sadhak should also act only as a medium and do the work. He should, like the tree, absorb to his full capacity whatever knowledge he has received by being connected to Paramatma; and after absorbing it completely, he should distribute it, because whatever knowledge he has received is meant for distribution. Knowledge is always meant to be distributed. To accept and to absorb knowledge has meaning only if it is shared. By distributing knowledge, our attention is always on giving it to others; we are always 'givers' and not 'takers,' and this capacity to 'give' helps us to make progress in life. Every sadhak should think of himself as a small twig of the tree-like form of Paramatma, and he should distribute whatever he gets from that tree. In truth, to distribute and to share is the life of a sadhak in the true sense. One who distributes is genuinely connected, and one who is connected is truly alive. The entire mystery of human life is hidden in this act of distribution.

"It is not the responsibility of the sadhak to see who is receiving your distribution, how much he is receiving, who uses the knowledge properly or not, whether the person who accepts it is suitable or not. The sadhak is not distributing the knowledge for the progress of that person. He is giving that knowledge to others because the more he distributes, the more he himself receives in return. The sadhak gives it for his own spiritual progress, and by sharing the knowledge the sadhak isn't doing that person a favour; he is doing himself a favour.

"A tree is connected to nature—and therefore it is absolutely necessary that the sadhak should first understand the tree, if he wishes to understand nature. The entire mystery of nature is hidden in a single tree. A twig requires energy only up to a particular limit and, after that predetermined limit, it distributes the remaining energy. This gives the tree a lot of joy, and by distributing its energy to small twigs and leaves, it expands its personal relationship to thousands of leaves. Thus, the number of recipients that are ready to absorb the energy increases, and many of them accept it as a medium. When hundreds of small twigs and thousands of tiny leaves consider that twig as a medium and absorb the life-force energy from it, then it becomes necessary for the tree to provide living energy to the twig as the lives of hundreds of twigs and thousands of leaves depend on that twig. "The sadhak should also develop like the twig of the tree-like Paramatma, on which hundreds of twigs and thousands of leaves depend. You should act as a medium and convey the knowledge you have acquired from Paramatma to thousands of people.

I also felt that this was true. Man's desires are limited. If he wants to be happier, he'll get it only by distributing what he has received. For example, a person's meal includes four rotis. He won't be happy even if you give him hundred rotis, although he should get twenty-five times more joy if he has been given twenty-five times more rotis. Thus, happiness isn't possible only through more rotis. Together with the rotis, when you meet other mediums and distribute the rotis to those other medium-like people, you'll be happier after distributing and feeding others. Rotis are non-living; human hunger is living. If you don't find hungry people, lifeless rotis can't give you happiness. It isn't enough for you to meet other people, it's necessary to meet hungry people. The hungry people will eat your food, and you'll feel happy."

I also thought on that day, "If I ever get a large quantity of rotis in the form of knowledge from Paramatma, I'll search for those people in my life who are hungry; I'll find them and lovingly feed them the rotis (in the form of knowledge from Paramatma) and experience inner joy. I don't need more knowledge than is necessary for me. To reiterate: Knowledge is meaningful only if it is shared."

When I understood this basic truth in the presence of my Gurudev and received the secret of Paramatma's life cycle through a tree, then that tree itself became Paramatma for me. I sat and pondered over this. Gurudev asked me what I was thinking; then he told me not to think about it but to *assimilate* it. Then, while he was speaking, he gave me some gum (resin) that he had taken from a tree, and said, "Eat this." I didn't know what it was, but I quickly ate it. I would have been happy even to eat poison from his hands; what he offered wasn't important. The gum tasted a little bitter, but I ate it regardless. And the satisfaction I saw on Gurudev's face when he saw me eating it made the bitter gum taste sweet. Dusk fell, and both of us slowly returned to our cave. I was completely exhausted by the time we arrived there. My appetite had gone after eating the gum, and I went straight to bed. In fact, I didn't feel hungry at all for the next four days.

I don't remember where those four days went. I felt as if only a moment had passed, and the daily routine continued. We would get up in the morning and go to the jungle. We walked around during the day and returned in the evening. There are several similarly thick jungles in Assam. They are so large and thick that one can't feel the heat of the sun, even if one wanders around all day.

One day, while sitting near a tree, Gurudev explained the difference between a jungle and man-made woods. According to him, a jungle is created by nature. It is nature's own creation. That's why nature creates trees that bear juicy fruits and at the same time also creates thorny trees nearby. It doesn't discriminate between the two types of trees and develops both. There is equality in nature. It treats everything the same. Therefore, there are good trees in the jungle as well as bad trees. Nature provides all of them with the same chance to grow. Which tree grows in which direction depends on that particular tree. Paramatma gives all men the same chance to progress spiritually, but different people are in different states of receptivity. Every person is provided with an equal opportunity in life.

"Nature is Paramatma's own creation. That's why one always finds different types of trees in the jungle. Since the jungle is a creation of nature, it maintains a balance in the environment. It takes hundreds of years for a jungle to develop. But it can be destroyed in a very short time. The 'jungle' is a unique gift of nature to man. Jungles provide man with balance in the environment. On the other hand, 'woodlands' are always created by man. Man is selfish. He creates such woodlands that benefit him. That's why woodlands always have trees that are lucrative, bearing fruits and providing him with good timber. Man always plants these kinds of woodlands. Woodlands can bring greenery (to the environment) but can't maintain a balance in nature. That's why they can't create a balance in nature. Man's intellect and his selfishness are reflected by woodlands.

"There are several trees that are not useful from man's point of view, but are very useful to maintain environmental balance. These trees can only be found in the jungle. When all kinds of trees grow together, naturally, without being planted by anyone, man experiences inner peace in such jungles. That's why man prefers and enjoys being in the jungle much more than in the woodlands. Such a natural atmosphere that comprises similarity, diversity, naturalness and collectivity, is only found in the 'jungle' and not in the 'woodlands'."

In this way, Gurudev explained to me the difference between jungles and woodlands. I enjoyed listening to all this new information. Gurudev went on to say, "This was the reason why sages and ascetics always preferred to live in the jungle and meditate on Paramatma during their spiritual practices. There is a natural atmosphere in the jungle, and no particular person owns the jungle. The jungle is therefore suitable for spiritual practice.

"Similar is the case with land. Productivity of the land depends on its ownership. If a saint happens to own some barren land, even that land becomes fertile. Ownership of land by people is destroying its fertility because the 'owner' doesn't have the capacity to absorb anything. The landlord is unable to absorb anything from his land, and since the landlord can't absorb anything, the land can't give anything. Someone must be available to absorb the surplus (energy). That's why, when practising meditation, the sadhak must always be careful at all times about the place (where he meditates). All places are not suitable for meditating. There are several places that prove to be dangerous for the sadhak to meditate in.

"Man performs bad deeds for selfish reasons, but because of the bad deeds man becomes bad and also infects the place where he performed the bad deed. When a person sits at a particular place and performs bad deeds with selfish motives, a bad influence is formed in that place and, at exactly above the same place in the sky, an aura of the bad deed is created.

"When a good person reaches such a place, then because of the bad effect of the place and its bad aura, the good person also becomes affected. Therefore, not all places are suitable for meditation.

"Once a king attacked his neighbouring kingdom and defeated its army, and after that he attacked its capital and killed all the unarmed villagers. After some time, the king passed away, but an evil effect was created in the place where he had killed the innocent people; and the evil aura got created exactly above that place. Today, even after hundreds of years, innocent people still die mysteriously in the vicinity. Sometimes, there is an accident, sometimes there is a fire, sometimes an earthquake, or sometimes there are floods. Thus, there may be different reasons, but even today innocent people keep dying. That's why you shouldn't just sit anywhere for meditation. Meditation practised in the presence of the Satguru is always best, because the Satguru's influence makes the place holy, pure, and more receptive to spiritual energy. It is always useful to sit and meditate in such a place. I remained at this location because this was where my own Gurudev was, and his aura is always present.

"Not only do I feel the deepest joy, but birds and animals also seem to revel in the aura of this place. That's why there are more birds and animals here than in the rest of the jungle. The effect of a good aura attracts all kinds of birds and animals. All creatures experience a sense of security under the influence of a good aura and feel like staying longer in such a place, and so birds always build nests wherever they feel safe. But they avoid places where they don't sense a good influence." Days with Gurudev passed quickly, as if time had grown wings.

There was a pool of water in the front of Gurudev's cave, and the sunrise happened right in front of it. There was a waterfall on the right side. It made such a loud noise no one could be heard properly if they spoke outside the cave. Various kinds of birds and animals came there to drink water. On one such morning, Gurudev said, "I asked you to concentrate on this waterfall because water not only purifies the physical body, but also purifies one's mind. And purification of one's mind is absolutely essential for spiritual progress. Chitta's purity is the foundation stone of one's spiritual mansion. Spiritual progress can't start without such purity. If our mind is impure, we are useless both to ourselves and to others.

"We become pure and empty by purifying the mind. Our

mind is generally full of expectations. It is human nature to have desires. Man is never satisfied with the conditions around him—it is like this, this should not have happened, it would have been better if it had happened like this—man always tries to get more than he has; and man's mind runs even faster than his efforts. Man's mind is always racing ahead; and because the mind is always racing, it is restless. Spiritual progress is impossible unless the constantly racing mind is stable.

"Man's mind moves from one place to another, instantly. Despite its power, the mind is also fragile. Like a strong horse, it will go in the wrong direction and mislead us if left uncontrolled. Man must have full control over this 'horse,' otherwise it can mislead him. That's why the rider (symbolizing one's desire) of the horse (symbolizing the mind), can only be kept in check by the bridle of 'satisfaction.' Be satisfied in your life, otherwise you'll say that we haven't obtained everything we wanted, so how can we be satisfied? My dear! No one has ever got satisfaction in life or will ever get it! We always have to accept this and be satisfied, because satisfaction is a pure feeling of one's soul. How can one get it externally?

"Are you going to be satisfied after obtaining whatever you desire? After you get whatever you want, the fire of expectation will flare up even more and the desire for 'more and more' will grow unchecked. We have to stop the desires with satisfaction. The expectation of this restless mind takes us into the future. When we say 'we should get this,' it means 'we have not got it.' And 'we have not got it' implies that discontent and dissatisfaction are always simmering within us. That's why we should thank Paramatma for whatever we have received and not have any expectation or desire to receive something. Whenever we think that we should get something as a reward or a gift, we are not fully immersed in the present; spiritual progress can only happen in the present.

"Just as one's mind goes into the future because of anxiety, it also goes into the past because of dissatisfaction and regret. When a child is born, he is able to remember his previous birth till he is five years old, and he lives till that time with the memory of his previous birth. Then, slowly, the layers of experience in this life start covering up memories of his past life, and he stops remembering them, just as we leave our house wearing 'white clothes' that gradually become dirty as we travel. Similarly, as a child sets forth on the journey of his life, his mind gets dirty like the white clothes. The dirtier the white clothes become, the more difficult it will be to clean them. And like these clothes, the mind of the child, always recalling the past, remains dirty. This is because the child is adding more layers on the stains of his past by remembering it. Thus, man's mind is destabilized by his past regrets and his future desires, as he can't engage with the present when both of these aberrations occur together. The mind unconnected to the present is unstable, and an unstable mind is weak. So then, how can one attain the power of Paramatma through an unstable mind? It is impossible."

Just then the sun rose, and Gurudev saluted the sun God and continued with his narration, "Man can neither forget his past nor control his desires. Until today, no man has been able to do so, nor will he ever be able to in the future, because man's mind is stronger than his life-power. That's why a man's life-power can never control his mind-power. Man will have to increase his life-power to have control over his mind-power. The power he has over his life can only be increased in the 'collectivity of life-power' (living energies), and the collectivity of this 'life-power' is present with the Satguru. The Satguru is connected to the lives of millions of souls. And these millions of souls have been connected for several births with their Satguru. That's why the Satguru is the nurturer of these millions of souls and there is a collectivity of those souls with him.

"We can get connected to those millions of souls through the medium of the Satguru, which is how we connect to the 'collectivity of souls' who dwell at a high level. The collectivity of souls of this high level is present at the Satguru's feet. That's why the Guru-charan are spiritually important. The more you surrender (at the Guru-charan), the more your capacity to receive and absorb spiritual energy will increase. The lowest extremity of the medium in the form of the Satguru is the Guru-charan. That's why one needs to surrender more in order to absorb more. When a person bows, it reduces his ego; as the ego decreases, so does his awareness of being a separate entity. The more this awareness of being a separate entity decreases, the more will be the increased awareness of collective energy. That's why Guru-charan is where man can surrender his past and his desires in the form of flowers and attain liberation."

In this way, just as Gurudev had explained, I mentally surrendered my past and my desires in the form of flowers at my Guru-charan. My eyes closed as I contemplated on his purity in the temple of my mind. When I opened my eyes, Gurudev had a smile on his face.

One morning, a strange noise jolted me out of sleep. It was dark outside, but Gurudev was not in his bed; in fact, he was nowhere in sight. There was a large slab of stone, leaning against the inner side of the hill. It was higher at one end, as if nature had fashioned a headrest for Gurudev. There was a lot of grass on it; Gurudev used to sleep on it. I don't know why, but every time he slept on that bed, I enjoyed pressing his feet. I would wait eagerly for him to lie down so that I could press his feet. As night approached, I kept hovering around him, and my whole attention was on his feet. That's why I couldn't move away from his body. When his feet were in my hands, I would be overwhelmed by a feeling of stillness, a sense of peace. I would feel that I had achieved everything in life, and that my life should end in that very condition. I would get the feeling that my whole life had suddenly become worthwhile.

That morning, as I've said, Gurudev was not in his bed, and it was after dawn. I came out of the cave and couldn't see anything, but I could make out from the noise that a herd of elephants had come to the stream to drink water, and one could hear their cries as they played with each other. As the day grew brighter, I could see that they had their young calves with them. Suddenly, a calf slid from the side of the bank and fell into the water. A nearby elephant pushed the calf out with its trunk, and its mother pushed it further to safety with its leg. The baby elephant was delighted to get out of the water, and it immediately started playing with the other baby elephants. I saw that the elephants always lived as a collective, protecting their group, helping each other. One could learn a lesson in communal living from these elephants. I enjoyed watching them playing and rolling in the water as much as they seemed to enjoy doing it.

Gurudev appeared on the scene after a while. He carried a big fruit that looked like a guava but wasn't. He said it was called a 'squash.' He gave me two of these fruits to eat, but they were so large that I was satisfied after eating only one. One can see lots of these fruits growing in the surrounding areas, but I wasn't aware until then that they were edible. They tasted like raw guavas. There were several wild banana trees, too. These bananas were big and fat and had black seeds at the centre. They were not as sweet as regular bananas; in fact, they had a pungent taste. One could find several such banana trees around there. It was entirely free of human beings, but we saw many birds and animals.

Gurudev sat outside the cave near the waterfall, and our discussion resumed. He said, "No man can ever control his mind through his life-power (his own energy), because man's mind-power is several times more powerful than his life-power. That is why man needs the support of collective living energy.

"Once man's mind becomes pure and holy, it starts getting stronger; and a strong mind is very effective. A powerful mind becomes the medium of Paramatma's energy, and a person with a powerful mind benefits society. People with such powerful minds achieve an exceptional state, and due to this state, whenever such a person prays for something with a pure mind, Paramatma answers his prayers. Such individuals have full faith in Paramatma's power, and this total faith fills the soul with positivity. This individual knows the true form of Paramatma, and therefore there is complete trust and faith in his prayer.

"It is absolutely necessary to know the true form of Paramatma before trusting His absolute form. Just like finding the path is more difficult when one is not aware of one's destination, similarly if one is not aware of the form or place of Paramatma, then to whom should one pray, and in which direction? The direction of one's prayer is not clear. Till the prayer is not in the right direction, there won't be complete faith, and when there is no faith one can't pray from the depth of one's heart. Till one prays from the depth of one's heart, how will any prayer be answered? The heart has a very important place in prayer. The emotion in one's heart is the strength of one's prayer and this emotion is a result of one's faith.

"In spiritual matters, the mind is supremely important. That's why a symbolic puja of Lord Ganesh is performed in every religious activity to purify one's mind. Lord Ganesh is considered the symbol of purity. Holiness and purity strengthen the mind, but one's past weakens it, and man's desires don't allow his mind to remain steady. That's why when one keeps away from both (past regrets and future desires), then his mind will become pure and strong, and one's prayers will be answered.

"Any type of desire is destructive; and the desire for a woman causes double harm to one's mind. Before one understands what desire for a woman means, it's necessary to understand the term 'woman'. Paramatma has created woman in the form of Shakti; Paramatma has created woman in order to activate man's energy. Thus, woman is energy, and you have to accept her as Shakti. A woman has unlimited power to absorb (energy); she can fully develop the energy she has absorbed. She can develop it and bestow completeness to it. This creation is not only at the physical level; she can do so in everything and at every level. Man and woman are like the two wheels of a chariot that is society, and society can't develop without these two. Man understood the powers possessed by women even before woman herself. Therefore, men started suppressing women in order to prevent them from dominating men with their powers. Until today, women have been subjugated for thousands of years, and this oppression has created a pervasive social imbalance.

"It is not possible to develop a balanced society until 'woman-power' is balanced. A woman is less a man's wife and more a mother, because her basic nature is to be a mother. There has always been a woman somewhere in the lives of every saint or great personage, who has inspired them either directly or indirectly. That's why, even among gods and goddesses, women have been given special respect.

"Thus, a woman is 'energy.' On the one hand, physical desire for that energy destroys one's mind; on the other hand, it also destroys the constitution of energy within us. Feelings of desire for women cause a lot of harm to the mind. Women are not an object of sexual pleasure and enjoyment. Woman-power is a place from where one can obtain energy. When we consider a woman as an object of pleasure and enjoyment, we are spoiling the place from which we can absorb energy. And when the place from where we can absorb energy itself becomes polluted, how can one absorb energy? What meaning will one's life have if one doesn't absorb energy? We are cutting off our feet by spoiling the place from which our body can absorb energy. That's why amongst all other attachments, the longing for a woman can cause double damage. Lust is even more dangerous than desire. Lust can destroy both the mind and the body.

"The body of a woman has been constructed in such a way that she can quickly reach a state of satisfaction, whereas a man takes longer to reach that state. This is not only at the physical level but at the mental level, too. A woman enjoys distributing things much more than using them. A woman has a greater capacity of absorption; she has a greater capacity for nurturing and sharing. But women have greater expectations from men. All these are the special qualities of women. The more pure and holy the woman-element, the more these special qualities will be visible in a woman.

"The capacity to take risks is inherent in women. While giving birth to a child a woman gives everything she possesses to the child, even when it is in her womb. That's why, whenever a spiritual revolution takes place in the world in future, it will be woman power that will activate it. This comes naturally to a woman; in her life she has an affinity for, and is connected simultaneously to, several relationships. She may have just one physical body, but she has the capability to live in several forms (to play several roles). While on one hand she is the mother of a child when she is pregnant, she is at the same time a wife to her husband; whereas a man plays the role of a husband to his wife but is not simultaneously a father to his child (in the womb). He is detached from his child.

"For as long as women are not given equal status (with men), there is no chance of any spiritual revolution in society; society will be crippled until then, and a crippled society can't ever progress.

"We are not doing women any favours by showing them respect; we are balancing human society by empowering women. And balance is necessary for the progress of any society. Man will have to control his ego to be able to honour and respect women's energy. Men are arrogant about their gender, even though all men have been given birth by women. By insulting women and relegating them to secondary status, man forgets his own birth. Meaning, he is attacking his own roots and forgetting his mother. A man who has love and affection for his mother can never insult a woman.

"Many saints have understood this fact. That's why they have tried again and again in this direction (granting equal status to women) and are still trying. Future saints will also keep trying because this imbalance is so prevalent between men and women. It will take many years to rectify the situation. All saints are aware that this imbalance can't be rectified through their own efforts. Even then each saint tries to reduce this huge imbalance between men and women in his life and will continue to do so."

After saying all this, Gurudev closed his eyes, and I felt as if his message had penetrated me deeply.

Gurudev's cave was situated deep in a trench. That's why no one could even imagine that there would be a cave deep down in such a big trench. There was a narrow path on the northern side, which one descended into the cave, and after going fairly deep inside, one had to turn right, and as one neared the waterfall, the sound of water grew louder. The trench was so wide and deep that from above one could see the water falling, but couldn't make out where it was falling. If one looked down, one could see the thick and dark forest. One could see the sun rising in the morning; but as the sun rose higher, the sunlight couldn't reach the ground. There was always a mist, and very little light reached there even during the day. Since there was very little direct sunlight, there wasn't much heat there and the atmosphere was very cool. The waterfall enlivened the atmosphere.

Birds were seen there only in the morning and evening, because they had built beautiful nests. All the birds used to leave in the morning to peck grains and would return in the evening. There were very few trees with thick foliage; there were fewer big and wide trees. But there were many tall trees growing close to each other. In fact, they were so close that if a tree got uprooted and fell, it would fall onto the nearby tree and remain leaning on it. Small bushy plants grew under the trees. Also, small plants with special yellow and white flowers grew there. Once while I was there, all the plants were in full bloom, and Gurudev could count the number of years through the number of flowers and get information about the seasons. Gurudev had been staying there right from his childhood with his Guru. I never asked him much, but he himself would tell me whenever some incident occurred. I understood through his conversations that he had been living there for several years, but in-between he had also travelled frequently to the Himalayas.

Sometimes he would narrate incidents from the Himalayas, but I don't know why I didn't ever feel like asking him anything; my mind was blissful in his presence, mostly free of thought. He seemed to be very serious and introverted, and it seemed as if I learned very little about him. But he was of course very knowledgeable and shared his knowledge with me. He had studied the area in minute detail and knew about water, the seasons, trees, birds and animals of the surrounding area. He had a slow, languid gait. He walked with a stick, but never seemed to stumble or stagger; the way he walked reflected the equilibrium of his soul. He took very measured steps; and whenever I looked at his feet, I felt that his feet weren't touching the ground at all. If any green leaf was crushed underfoot, then the moment he lifted his foot it would resume its normal shape, as if it had a spring which made it stand upright again.

My attention was always on his feet, as if my whole world was confined there. In the beginning I felt that there was a contradiction here—on the one hand, he was telling me that thousands of people (in the future) will be eagerly waiting to see me, and that there would be long queues of people awaiting me; on the other hand, he had brought me to this big trench (in the jungle)! Maybe he was talking about my next birth. In short, it all seemed impossible! I felt, at that time, that I would always have to live in this trench like him and would never be able to go home again; that it was impossible to get out of that trench because if my foot slipped even once I would slide straight down into the trench and my life would end! Why did he have to bring me to this place? I don't know why in the beginning I used to get such negative thoughts. Later slowly they reduced, and then they stopped completely, and my whole world got contracted and shrivelled up into that place. Initially, I use to be scared when I heard the cries of animals.

The cave didn't have a door, so any animal could easily have come in. but the fear slowly decreased. Then I felt afraid from within because the only light there came was from the burning logs in the pit for the fire ceremony. My imagination conjured up unknown animals in the dark. Sometimes I would think—what if spirits and ghosts turned up! Then I would immediately tell myself—Gurudev is here with me; no spirit or ghost can come near him. Gurudev was aware of all my thoughts, and while talking he would purposely bring up such frightening subjects and indirectly try to get rid of my fears.

Sometimes, I would get the thought that all this turmoil was created because of Shiv Baba. If he had not entered my life, Gurudev wouldn't have found me and brought me into this trench. I didn't know whether this was a trench or the very pits of hell. I had read stories about the nether world in my childhood. Sometimes I felt that that this must be the nether world that people talked about! Who knew how deep down we had descended! From where we were down below, we couldn't see anything above us! I thought that hardly any human being would have ventured into this ditch. But it was otherwise a beautiful and peaceful place, suitable for connecting with nature.

There was not a single human around; therefore, there were no thoughts from any humans, nor was there any kind of thought pollution. Thoughts are unnatural; they separate us from nature. But as soon as we go close to nature, thoughts automatically stop. Gurudev kept me so busy that I didn't have time to think at all. As all the tasks had to be performed in the midst of nature, I unknowingly got the chance to be close to nature and learn a lot. Sometimes I felt that it was the law of nature that only the strong can survive and the weaker animal gets killed. But I witnessed several incidents where even the weaker animals created problems for the stronger animals if they were working together. Therefore collective energy can create problems even for stronger animals.

There were several cassia (bay leaf) trees near our cave. We used to pick those leaves and use them as spices for seasoning. One day, when I had climbed one of these trees and was picking some leaves, I saw that a pair of sparrows had built a nest, and there were three eggs in it. The male sparrow would go out and the female would stay in the nest. Later that nest became a centre of attention for me. The female sparrow would fly nearby and quickly return. The male would go in the morning and not return until the evening. Then I don't know what happened, but one evening the male sparrow didn't return and the female was very sorrowful. She kept waiting for him, but he never turned up. The female sparrow was sad for a few days and then forgot her sorrow. After a few days, two of the eggs hatched; maybe the third one had fallen and broken. Then the sparrow went out every morning and when she returned in the evening, she would carry grains for her chicks in her beak and feed them very lovingly. As the time for her return drew near, the chicks eagerly waited for her.

One evening I saw the sparrow returning but she kept falling again and again and finally she fell right under the tree. I went up to her and saw that she had been hurt by a small arrow and was bleeding profusely. She glanced towards her young ones, almost as if she was asking them to forgive her since she wouldn't be able to protect them or bring food for them. Then she looked at me as if she hoped that now I would be the one to take care of her chicks. I kept giving her water to drink for quite some time, but she couldn't be saved, and died. As I was feeding her with water, four small grains of rice fell out of her beak. I took those grains and climbed up the tree and fed the chicks with the grains, saying that this was the last morsel from their mother that the poor thing had carried for them. They couldn't understand anything but were craning their necks looking for their mother; she would never return. I buried her under the tree and started thinking about that man who must have shot the arrow at her. Human beings can be so cruel! It's good that Gurudev kept me away from humans. That man who shot the arrow wasn't even aware that this was the mother of some babies, and that she was carrying some grains for them. Afterwards, I used to give something every day to those little ones to eat. They soon grew up and flew away. Then I felt that I had fulfilled the hopes of that sparrow. The incident with the sparrow made me aware of a mother's heart. I surmised that the sparrow must have gone towards the Nagaland border. Eating bird meat is part of the Adivasi culture there.

Giving birth to a child is strenuous and difficult, and even more difficult is the process of nurturing the child. And yet it takes just a moment to kill it! What right does man have to destroy what he can't create? Violence is always unnatural. We may be walking on the road, and unknowingly an ant may get crushed under our foot. This type of violence that takes place unintentionally is understandable. But killing someone on purpose is unnatural. Nature has given us this human form, and it is the basic nature of man to love all creatures. When we indulge in violence, we go against our basic nature. This is a decline in humanity.

That's why several religions have stressed the supremacy of non-violence. Any kind of violence is against the principles of religion; it opposes the religion of humanity. This is like cutting off one's own feet. On the one hand, we are awakening our power of humanity, and we are awakening the vital energy within us; on the other hand, we eat dead animals and consume dead energy. So how will the vital energy awaken within? How can it move forward?

Violence is a comprehensive word. One shouldn't cause hurt or sorrow even unknowingly to any creature. Using wrong words, or hurting someone through words, insulting someone with your eyes and causing offence, talking sarcastically and causing pain—all these acts are a kind of violence. When we cause pain and sorrow to someone, we go against our basic nature. Your spiritual progress can be judged by how many people are happy with you, how many people you can make happy, and to how many people you can give love! It is these things that lead to spiritual progress; and all these should occupy all the room within your heart.

※

One morning, I was seated with Gurudev near a large rock, and the thought entered my mind that Gurudev keeps asking me again and again to make my mind pure and holy, to make my mind powerful. But what exactly is this chitta? And how can we understand it? As these thoughts were passing through my mind,

Gurudev looked at me and asked what I was thinking. I hesitated to answer, because what was going through my mind was very deep, and I wasn't at such a high spiritual level that I could easily articulate what I had been pondering. I couldn't explain it easily to him because I wasn't aware that I'd been thinking about that subject. Gurudev seemed to look deep into my mind, as if trying to fathom my thoughts. And then he started speaking.

"We have eyes, and we can clearly see whatever is visible through them; we can see whatever is present inside the light; we can see whatever is bright and shining; our eyes themselves are not sufficient to see everything, they need light to be able to see. Without light, the eyes are useless, and even when light is present, eyes have their own limits and can only see whatever comes within their range. Beyond that the eyes can't see anything! Thus, when light is present, eyes can see objects that come within the range of their vision and transmit information about those objects to the brain. If the eyes have already seen the object earlier, the brain recognizes whatever it sees through the radiance the eyes receive. Sometimes the eyes also see some things never seen before, or they may get an entirely new experience.

"There is a soul within each human being's body. Think of it as a minor body that can't be seen. Chitta is the eye of that soul. The soul is more powerful than the body. That is why the energy of the soul is more powerful than that of the body. Just as the body has eyes, the soul also has eyes, and that is called the chitta. We can therefore call the chitta the 'Eyes of the soul.'

"The more inward this chitta goes, the steadier it will be. The steadier it is, the more powerful and effective it will be. The more effective it is, the more subtle it will be. And one can sit still in one place and instantly travel thousands of kilometres away through a subtle chitta at a speed faster than sound. In the same way as your eyes give you external information when a person comes in front of you, if you put your powerful chitta on that person, it will give you information about that person's past and future thoughts. One can obtain the power of inner guidance only through a powerful chitta.

"A person can gain control over his chitta and reach this state by meditating continuously for twelve years. Magnetic powers are created in a person with a powerful chitta and positive energy flows continuously from within him. He is always involved in constructive and creative work, and such work keeps happening through him. As a result of positive vibrations always flowing from his body, he gives positive energy to people with negative, despondent, and disheartened vibrations. Such people with negative vibrations are always strongly attracted towards people with positive vibrations, and a change is brought about in their negative vibrations.

"A person with a powerful chitta can easily merge with nature and can easily absorb energy from nature. Then he can cause the energy he has obtained to flow to others according to his will. He has control over his chitta, which is why he can also easily control the flow of that energy. The earlier ages were the ages of physical prowess, when there were great strong warriors with maces and powerful bodies. The ones with the powerful bodies were the best warriors, and so physical strength was a sign of supremacy. Today, however, we are in the age of intellect. An intelligent person may be physically weak, but he just needs to press a button to kill even the strongest person; the symbol of strength these days is the intellect.

"The future age will be that of chitta-shakti. A person whose chitta is powerful will be dominant over everyone through his chitta. Now the symbol of supremacy will be the chitta. The person who has a strong and powerful chitta will be considered the best in society. Thus, the symbol of superiority will be the chitta. This will happen in the future. The chitta will be a weapon of immense power; it will be the medium of Shakti.

"Our chitta should always be focused within us because the more inward it is, the steadier it will be, and the steadier it is, the more powerful it will be. The ordinary man destroys it by thinking about bad incidents and bad events from his past; or he wastes it by trying to find fault with others. Thus, the chitta-shakti is destroyed, and the chitta becomes weak. One has to constantly keep trying to control it or be a part of the collectivity of people who are trying to control it. The chitta can thus be made stronger by turning it inwards during one's daily routine."

Then for some days Gurudev continually took me to a jungle where there were several short bushes. Small pearl-shaped seeds, which were half-black and half-red in colour, were growing on the bushes. He would pick seeds every day, bring them and place them in a pit in front of the cave. This went on for several days. The leaves of those bushes tasted sweet and sour and were small like the leaves of the tamarind tree. The pit was about six feet long, nine feet deep, and three feet wide, and was slowly filled with the seeds.

Then, one day, he asked me to sleep in it and then stand in it every day for two to three hours. He told me that these seeds were called 'gunj' (seeds of the shrub Abrus presotorius). They have the ability to suck heat from one's body; and after the excess heat is removed from the body, one's chitta stays calm and peaceful. After a few days, I started enjoying my time in this pit. This exercise went on for several days.

He would ask me to eat the leaves of these bushes together with leaves from some other bushes, and then lie in the pit. This routine went on for some months. Along with this, he also gave me the juice of some herbs every morning, which I had to drink on an empty stomach. The juice didn't taste very good, and I didn't like drinking it. But he went through so much trouble to pick the leaves and grind them to extract the juice that I didn't have the heart to refuse him. He knew a lot about plants and herbs. Our lunch consisted of squash, bananas, some leaves from trees and some other fruits. We only had one meal a day. Sometimes we wouldn't eat for four or five days. We didn't really feel the need to eat regular meals there. Day after day he would keep trying out experiments on me. He used to insist more on keeping one's bowels and system clear. He said that if one has clear bowels, the stomach will be clean. And if the stomach was clear then anti-bodies wouldn't collect or be formed in one's body. For this purpose, he would sometimes give me some leaves and ask me to tie them to my navel. All the processes being carried out there didn't give me the impression that I was undergoing any spiritual practice at all. I used to feel as if he was a vaidya, a practitioner of Ayurvedic medicine, and I had come for an extended stay at some Nature Cure Clinic; perhaps that was his way of working. The whole thrust of his program was on getting me ready for some great spiritual practice. He was moving ahead day by day and wanted to take me to some definite physical level. He knew where he was heading but I wasn't aware. He was happy with my day-to-day progress, and I'd made it the sole purpose of my life to make him happy.

It seemed to me that he was preparing my body for some special spiritual sadhana through nature, and he was using nature for that purpose. He seemed always to be preparing the chitta to be positive. Then he taught me how to sit in the moonlight on the first day of the lunar month and meditate by concentrating on the moon. Day by day the duration of the study period kept increasing and on the Purnima night, he made me meditate till dawn. He asked me to concentrate my chitta on the moon and to establish a subtle relationship between myself and the moon; then he asked me to imagine that I had accepted the moon as my diety and to surrender myself completely to it, to imagine myself being showered by the cool, pure energy of the moon; that I was experiencing coolness in the light of the moon and that I could especially experience the coolness on my Surya Nadi; that my liver was slowly becoming cooler and I experienced inner peace through that spiritual practice.

One morning, Gurudev was sitting on the floor, and he made me sit there with him. He asked me to imagine that I was sitting in my mother's lap and asked me to sit on the floor with the same carefree feeling of belonging. He asked me to surrender completely to Mother Earth. "You will experience all the bad energy pulsating within you, and your chitta becoming pure and strong. There is a profound gravitational force within the earth, and when we establish oneness with the gravitational force through our prayers, our chitta is purified.

"Mother Earth is very helpful in purifying one's chitta, and when the chitta becomes strong, the body also becomes healthy. The gravitational force of the earth does the work of balancing one's chitta and one's body, provided we get ready for that balance. One can use the powers of nature if one so desires. You can't force someone to align with nature."

After practising for some days, I realized that my chitta concentrated faster after sitting on the floor and meditating for a short time. Later, I felt very calm and peaceful, and my body also felt light.

One morning, Gurudev started telling me about his travels in the Himalayas. He said, "There are small settlements and villages near the Himalayan mountain range. Villagers there use the earth element to cure their physical problems. When foreign elements enter our body, it becomes sick. That's why we should have clear bowels and our mind should be clean, so that we don't get bad or negative thoughts or sicknesses resulting from negative thoughts. That's why the tribal people take the help of the earth element. Our body comprises of the five basic elements—earth, sky, water, fire and air. We become pure and holy because of the earth element. The earth element purifies our body and mind and bestows us with physical and mental stability.

"First of all, one will have to accept the earth element as a great power, surrender completely to it and establish oneness with it. And, to establish that oneness, there is no better path than prayer. That's why the tribal people sit on the ground and first of all bow down to the earth. They bend down and bow their heads before it, and then they pray with full faith to the earth: 'We surrender ourselves completely to you. Please cure us of our sicknesses through your power of gravity.' Then, miraculously, they get cured. In reality, they get balanced by being close to earth. Earth bestows them with balance and stability. But, for that, one must acknowledge that 'earth' is an element. One must be able to bow humbly before the earth, and one must bow down with full faith. Only then will all this be possible.

"The tribal people also cure their sicknesses by applying mud-paste all over their body under a special tree. They are also able to cure themselves by bathing with mud. In several settlements the sick person is buried up to his neck in mud. He is made to stand in a deep vertical pit and the space around him is filled with mud. He stands buried like this all day, and for some sicknesses, even at night, sometimes for three days, and sometimes even for a whole week, he is kept covered with mud in that pit. And all this takes place under the guidance of an experienced elderly person, an expert. The elderly person studies the face of the sick person, observes the rhythm of his breathing, feels his pulse and then makes his decision. He can diagnose some diseases just by looking at the eyes of the sick person. There are no doctors or Ayurvedic practitioners in those colonies. It's a very backward area. They have neither medicines nor any instruments. They all depend on nature and the vibrations of nature. A mudpack is often applied to the forehead to bring down fever. But the patient must have faith in these kinds of natural treatments, and this faith ensures positive results. The tribal people have no other option apart from using this cure. That's why it has to be practised with faith; physical ailments can be cured though the earth element.

"If we take the palm of our right hand, place it flat on the ground, close our eyes, and fully concentrate on it, we can also learn about the activities within the earth; we can understand what is happening within the earth. We become aware of the sounds within the earth and its inner vibrations." Saying this, Gurudev placed his right palm fully on the ground, closed his eyes, focused his chitta totally on it, and asked me to do the same. I could actually feel mild vibrations in the beginning; I later became aware of the movement within the earth and could make out which layer beneath the ground was shifting and in which direction. I felt very calm and peaceful. In this way, my chitta became one with nature.

"This results in our chitta gaining immense focus," he said, "and we move away from the narrow limits of the 'I,' of the ego.

"In our endeavour to connect with the earth element, we connect with our roots at some level because the earth (dust) is an inseparable part of our lives. The earth element plays a very important role in our creation and our nurturing. The 'dust' doesn't have any reservations even when we try to establish a separate identity from it, and it accepts our physical body after our life ends. That's why man has been called 'an image made of dust.' This 'image of dust,' which is the body, is created out of dust and ultimately consigned to 'dust.' This dust is the final truth. Earth bestows the soul with this vehicle-like body, made out of dust to help it achieve liberation. If liberation is a destination, then this 'image of dust' is a vehicle that will take the soul to its destination. Earth bestows the soul with an instrument in the form of the image of dust, which will help it to reach its destination of liberation at its own time in its life. Several saints often incarnate on earth and purify some special place, and then vibrational power increases there. The influence of that place increases owing to the presence of the saints.

"No land is good or bad for saints. They don't look at the good or bad condition of the land. They are connected to the energy of the entire land, and therefore the saint may reside on any land or sit on any ground, and whichever place absorbs the presence of his body will become especially holy. This is because the vibrations received by his presence will remain forever in that land. A saint's body is perishable, but the energy of that body is eternal. Even after the saint's life comes to an end, it keeps bestowing spiritual experiences for hundreds of years. Not only that, but as time passes the level of vibrating energy will increase, because there is more consciousness than in nature at that place. As a result, consciousness from the surrounding atmosphere also starts collecting there in a natural form. Good consciousness accumulates at a good, holy place. It grows with time because the energy of that saint's power of resolution is present there. Due to that additional conscious energy, whenever any creature visits that place, it is affected by the consciousness of that place, as nature's energies become focused there.

"No land is either good or bad, but the inhabitants, their thoughts, and their deeds create a good or bad effect. The influence of a person who is connected to nature and has merged with it is always good. When one creates a separate identity apart from nature, it creates a bad influence. Man becomes insignificant when a separate identity is created. A person whose identity is separate from nature becomes weak; and because of his thoughts, the energy in his house becomes weak or strong. Plants also breathe in the same way that man breathes, and a place also breathes in the same way. If a place continually receives energy from every direction, then that place gets balanced.

Gurudev tried to explain this to me through an experiment. He took two seeds of the same tree, sowed one seed at one place and another seed at another special place. Gurudev gave energy every day to the seed at the special place from all directions. First, he would sit to the east of the seed, absorb energy, and pass it on to the seed. Then he would sit in a southerly direction and give energy to the seed. And then he would sit facing the west, absorb the energy, and pass it to the seed. Finally, he would sit facing the north and give his absorbed energy to the seed. After eight days, it was observed that the seed which he had been energizing regularly had sprouted leaves, whereas the other ordinary seed had not sprouted at all.

When Gurudev absorbed energy from all directions and passed on balanced energy to the seed, it progressed very fast. If the order of giving energy from the direction of the east, south, west and north is followed, it will be more effective. "Similarly," Gurudev said, "man should keep all four directions around his house open, so that his dwelling can get energy from all directions. Vastu Shastra has been devised from this very premise. Birds and animals also have knowledge of energy, which they receive from all directions. It is essential for a place to receive energy from all four directions. Man thinks all the time and creates bad energy around him, so it's impossible for him to absorb the external energy around him.

"What generally happens is that when we concentrate our chitta on a particular thing for some time, we start having thoughts about it, and the same thing happens with a place, too. If a person unknowingly stores something in his chitta, he sees the same thing even in his dreams. But what he sees in his dreams is a mixture of several things. That's why dreams fuse a variety of images from different periods in one's life.

"Man can purify his chitta in the collectivity of people who have a good connection with consciousness. The Satguru is a medium for harnessing such energy. If we wish to make our chitta more powerful, we should focus it on imperishable objects, since material things are always perishable. If we put our chitta on perishable things, the chitta will be destroyed along with them. It is therefore imperative for us to focus chitta only on eternal, everlasting things. We can call chitta one of our senses, in addition to the usual five. Just as we can see with our eyes and hear with our ears, we can also sense the world and acquire knowledge through our chitta. All this slowly becomes possible with practice. The purer our chitta becomes, the harder it is to control it. That is why we should purify our chitta only to the degree that we can control it; otherwise, a chitta that is pure but uncontrolled can prove fatal for us.

※

One day, Gurudev woke me up early in the morning, and led me out of the cave. He started walking northward. After a fairly long trek, we came across large rocks on either side of a path leading to a cave. We descended, deeper and deeper. I thought to myself, "We came from the land above us and have been staying in a deep trench, and now he's taking me even further down." I didn't know where Gurudev was taking me, but I didn't have the courage to ask. After descending for quite a long time, he stopped and said, "Rest for a while. I'm now taking you into a different world. This world will be beyond your imagination."

After a brief rest, we resumed our walk. For light, we had a tree trunk that would burn like a torch, like some big candle when lit. I found it difficult to walk on that path. I frequently had to stop and sit down to recover my breath. There was total darkness around us. Gurudev cut a path through the bushes and started walking further. There were several bushes and stones ahead, but he was unfazed. He created a path for me and walked on; I followed him. I was quite frightened; if we came across an animal, we wouldn't be able to see it. Walking behind Gurudev was the only choice; I certainly couldn't have turned around and gone back on my own. My situation was unequivocally 'do or die.'

Walking further down, I could hear the sound of flowing water. And as we went on walking, the sound grew louder and louder, and I understood that we were heading toward some kind of water body.

Several hours went by. Later, we came out of the cave, and the view outside was pristine, a wonderful, refreshing scene. There was a large waterfall near the cave we exited. I saw that the waterfall was flowing into another large cave, and we were walking into the cave along with the water. A variety of plants occupied the interior of the cave. Lines of deep orange had been etched in the walls. There was a lot of iron in the water; when the water level rose, the iron content in the water must have produced different colours on the walls—orange, yellow, white, green. It seemed as if someone had created paintings on both sides of the pool. As we moved on, we saw that the flow of water was decreasing because it spread out into different directions. Later, we saw that drops of water were falling from the roof, and they had apparently been falling for thousands of years. A small shape like a Shiva-ling had been formed there. We rested there for a while, then continued our walk. I was waiting to see when we would turn back, as we would have to walk the same distance to head home. The natural scene was of course lovely, but I was also frightened; where on earth were we?

Gurudev went ahead and sat on a rock and made me sit on another rock on the opposite side. He asked me to close my eyes for some time. He also closed his eyes. My eyes soon grew heavy, and I didn't even realize when I went into deep meditation.

When I came out of my trance, I found Gurudev staring at me. I felt very calm after having meditated. Our forlorn surroundings had made me somewhat anxious; I had been apprehensive about whether I would be able to get out of this place; in short, I wanted to go back. But now I was thinking: where will I go? Why do I want to go? The physical world isn't the truth. I have to leave this world one day! What will I do when I go to that world? Where have I come from? Where is my eternal place? Who am I? These ears are mine, this hair is mine, these hands are mine, and these feet are mine! But I am not the ears, I am not the hair, I am not the hands, I am not the feet! All these are mine, but what importance do they have without knowing who I am? Who is the master of all these ears, hair, hands, feet etc.? This body comprises all of these, but is this body *me*? No! This is my body—which means that I am not the body! I am not the body, and yet this body is mine. This means that this body is the medium of 'I.' But apart from this body, the identity of 'I' is definitely present somewhere. Ears, hair, hands, feet; all these are visible. But 'that' to which all this belongs is not visible. The body that has been created out of all these is also visible; but 'that' to which this body belongs is not visible. Am I the body? No! I am not even the body, but this body is mine.

How can this be possible? My life began to feel like some sort of cosmic riddle. I tried very hard to find out who I was, but I couldn't do so. Gurudev understood my state of mind. He said, "If you wish to know yourself, then ask yourself the question: 'Who am I?' Ask yourself three times in this manner and you'll understand who you are."

I shut my eyes and asked myself: Who am I? Who am I? Who am I? And I didn't even realize that my eyes had slowly closed. The moment we ask ourselves this question, our chitta goes within. We go around the world searching for everything; but we never search for our own self. We ignore what is necessary and keep searching externally for everything else. But the moment we try to understand this question (who am I?) our inner journey commences. And when the inner journey begins, we realize that the body and 'I' are separate. Then the 'I' separates from the body, and we undergo a spiritual revolution.

Gurudev explained further: "As soon as we ask ourselves this question, we realize that 'I and my body are separate; I am not the body.' Then the illusory ego falls away, and the feeling of guilt and disgust with oneself for having performed some wrong deed also ends, because one realizes that this wrong act has happened through the body. And when I have not committed any sin, the feeling of being a sinner ends automatically. There are two points where man's imbalance can occur. One is pride that 'I' have done it, and the second is a guilty feeling that one is a sinner; both are illusory. Man keeps swinging between these two positions. That's why you should understand that the good deeds that have happened through your body have not been performed by you; and that is why you should give up your sense of 'I.'

"Secondly, consider that whatever bad deeds you have performed must have been through the body; *you* have not performed them. Don't harbour feelings of guilt or disgust. You shouldn't be proud about your success and achievements in life, nor should you be guilty about a lack of material success. Think of yourself as a soul and that 'I am a soul' is the only truth. Everything else is an illusion. You will only get out of the web of 'Maya' in life if you remember this. Otherwise, you'll never be able to realize the truth and will continue to wander all your life. Always remember that you are a soul and practice this fact. Happiness and sorrow, passion and desire, hatred, jealousy, ignorance and delusion, fear and fear of death—all these emotions are present at the physical level. The soul is detached from all this. As soon as you accept yourself as a soul, you'll be free of all these concerns. All relationships and interactions are of the body. The soul is free of these physical ties. The first step to spiritual progress is the awareness that 'I am a soul.' Come on. Wake up! We are going back now." And he started walking towards the road.

On the journey to this place, I had found the road very long. I had found it strenuous, and I had gone unwillingly. But now, on the return journey, I felt light and free, and my fear was gone. Now I was accustomed to being here. Gurudev said, "You are only the second person to visit this place. Apart from you and me, no other person has been able to reach here for thousands of years." He bent down and picked a few leaves growing near the water and asked me to eat them. Then he started walking again. I looked around in all directions; my pace had slowed considerably because I was no longer scared. The distance between Gurudev and me had widened. I walked along, observing the bounty of nature. I don't know why, but in jungles one feels less hungry and thirsty, and even one's breathing slows down.

Really beautiful paintings had formed on the walls around the water. Sometimes the figures resembled an elephant while sometimes the painting appeared like a crocodile and many appeared like a fish. But there was no painting that looked like a human, as if there was no connection between nature and man or maybe nature was also influenced by its surroundings. The flowing water was very clean, so clean that the stones underneath could be seen clearly. The water was cold and pristine, of course, but it was hard water, therefore inappropriate for drinking. Gurudev and I slowly approached the waterfall, and we bathed there. The water wasn't very deep, but it flowed very fast. The flow was so strong that I couldn't even stand upright.

After our bath, we again started walking in the dark cave. I was looking at the caves around me on our return journey. How had these caves been formed? This soil, these cliffs could be a subject of investigation for researchers. As we carried on, we had to create our own path. In several places we had to cross flowing streams. In some places we found aquatic plants growing on some large rocks. Some of these plants also had white flowers growing on them. As we slowly emerged from between two big rocks, we felt as if we had returned to our own world. The whole journey felt like a dream. When we approached our cave, we saw that the plants on the opposite side were covered with flowers in full bloom, which indicated that we had been away for quite some time.

Time had no meaning in that place, and you weren't aware of how many days and nights had passed. The same thing happens in life, too. When one is having a good time in life, one doesn't realize how quickly time passes, how many days have passed, how many years have gone by! On the other hand, times of trouble are fleeting, but they stay with us for the rest of our lives. We may think that the bad times have gone, but they remain neatly arranged somewhere in our mind; and even after several years, the prick of that memory hurts and saddens us. Then the wounds open again and start bleeding. We are hurt not by the actual incidents but by constantly recalling them in memory. Problems in our childhood, misfortunes in our life, bad events, bad people we have come across in our childhood and their bad behaviour, etc., imprint themselves indelibly on our minds.

Some people even enjoy scratching their wounds again and again. They keep remembering bad incidents and making themselves unhappy. And they get a kind of peculiar joy out of their pain—they believe that they have progressed so much in their lives: "where we were in our past and where we reached today! We've gone from beggar to king!" Unknowingly, we keep feeding our ego; and thinking about our sorrows from the past and comparing them with how we are today, we feel happy within ourselves and even tell our children about what our childhood was like and how things have ultimately turned out! How bad our childhood was and what a good life they have!

Our mind enjoys this kind of constant comparison—we have made so much progress in life, we have reached the pinnacle of our life! This kind of comparison is especially noticeable at the economic level. First, a person notices that his financial condition has improved. But you were not happy then, and you aren't happy now! You were unhappy then because you didn't have money, but you are unhappy despite your current wealth because you keep reflecting on the relative poverty of your past. Until you recognize your unhappiness despite your wealth, how could you have been happy in your childhood even if you were rich then? Wealth is ultimately meaningless. No one can be happy because they have it, and no one can be sad because they don't have it!

Happiness and sadness are states of mind. They exist or don't exist based on your belief in them. If you accept the situation, there is happiness; and if you don't, there is sadness. Yesterday's sorrow was because of lack of wealth, and today's sorrow is because of problems with your body. Both are perishable. A person's wealth can neither give him joy, nor his body happiness, because you are neither wealth nor a body. Then how can both of these make one happy? They cannot. Both of these are fundamentally lifeless and illusory.

Because my existence is separate from them, I have realized that I am a soul. I am not a body or wealth. My physical body and wealth can't give me happiness; only my soul can give me joy, and only the joy that my soul gives me will be real happiness, which will finally be called 'Inner Joy.'

The happiness of one's soul does not involve hoarding or assimilating or collecting. The happiness of one's soul always comes through sharing. The wealth one has collected can give physical joy because both the body and wealth are perishable. One perishable thing can give happiness to another perishable thing. That's why donation is deemed important in various religions, so that you may accrue wealth and be happy at the physical level, and at the same time experience the true joy that comes from sharing. It is only donation that keeps your soul happy and joyful. That's why donation is so important to one's spiritual development. One should donate simply for the experience of inner joy. Spiritual progress is possible only through inner happiness, because one's soul can only be strong if it is happy; if the soul is strong it will be able to practice spirituality, and if it practices spirituality, it will of course make infinite spiritual progress.

When we ask ourselves the question, "Who am I?", the inner voice replies, "I am a soul", and one realizes that one is a soul; only then does one understand that whatever activity one performs through one's ego was in fact just at the bodily level. In reality, 'I' am a soul; a soul that exists but can't be seen; the soul that manages the body but can't be seen managing it. This body has no existence without the soul. If the soul leaves the body, then people will either bury the body or burn it, and it will be destroyed.

This body appears to be everything, but it isn't. And that which seems to be everything isn't anything at all. That means what is, that is not; and what is not, is everything. We can understand all of spirituality through our body, and if one understands a soul then one can understand Paramatma.

The power that runs the world, in the form of the body, is Paramatma, invisible but omnipresent. This world is dead without Paramatma, a corpse which is only meant to be destroyed. The day Paramatma moves away from this world, this world will also come to an end, and it will be a corpse. If you understand a soul, then you will be enlightened about Paramatma. One can't understand Paramatma without understanding the existence of one's own soul.

I heard the same facts from Gurudev that evening as if I had become one with him at that level; or it can be explained like this—that as a result of the influence of his aura, I was thinking according to his wishes. He said that whatever is present in the universe is similarly present in our bodies.

"If the body is a drop of water," he said, "then the universe is an ocean. But whether it's a drop of water or the ocean, it is water after all. There is no difference in the basic nature of water. In the same way, a small form of Paramatma exists within us in the form of our soul. How can one know Paramatma if he doesn't know his soul? And once one recognizes the Paramatma within, he will undoubtedly know Paramatma outside. There is only one Paramatma. Paramatma is present everywhere. There is Paramatma inside us and there is Paramatma outside. But it is easier to know the Paramatma within us because he is closer to us. He is yours and for you. He is present when you need him, according to what suits you and according to your level. He is within your grasp and within your reach. You and he are not separate. You have no identity without your soul. What you are thinking of as 'I' is merely the ego of one's body. As soon as you understand yourself, all the ego in your body will break down because you will have realized that you are a soul.

"Man is born with the covering of his body and lives inside this shell. Only after the covering falls off, does he realize that it was a covering, which is not there anymore. The body is a vehicle, and the soul is its driver. The driver can't go forward without the vehicle, but it is also true that the vehicle can't move forward without the driver. That's why one can never know who is going to need whom. Both are equally suitable in their own place, and both complement each other.

"That's why it is necessary to understand both in order to reach our destination. We'll only be able to reach our destination if we can maintain their rhythm and balance. Our body is an instrument-like vehicle. Just as the vehicle requires care and maintenance, the care of our body is also essential. In some religions the care and importance of one's body has been ignored right from the beginning, emphasizing the importance of the soul. This doesn't seem right, because if the soul didn't need the body, why would it have one at all? The soul has also realized the importance of the body, and that's why it has retained a body. There are several souls that have not found a useful, suitable body, and are therefore stuck and are awaiting a suitable body.

"When the soul waits for a suitable body, how can the body be useless or unimportant? The body, which the soul has acquired after a long wait, must be taken care of. This is not only our duty but the need of our soul. That's why one should pay attention to one's body. The body should be kept clean, holy, free of thoughts, and natural. It's not possible to attain liberation without a healthy body. What can the driver of a broken-down vehicle do? No matter how expert the driver is, he won't be able to do anything if the vehicle has broken down. Even an expert driver can't do anything without a vehicle. If one's body isn't healthy, having a driver (the soul) is useless. The vehicle and its driver are equally important. The vehicle can't move without a driver. And a vehicle that doesn't work becomes useless and has to be scrapped.

"In the same way, when the body is without a soul, it is a corpse—and of what use is a corpse? After some time, the corpse will begin to stink. No matter how beautiful the body, no matter how beloved it is, no one wants to live with a dead body. That's why one values the body, as a vehicle for the soul. Once the soul leaves the body, the body is destroyed. Thus, the body is useless without the soul. The body has been deemed important in many religions, and several rules have been drawn up to ensure the health, strength and purity of the body. This is also an extreme way of thinking. We should give equal importance to both body and soul. Both should be developed equally because a pure and holy soul resides in a pure and holy body. We should think of ourselves as a soul to save ourselves from the defects of the body. We have to live in the body but in the form of a soul. If we are able to live like that in the body, then through the medium of this body through our lifetime we'll be able to lead our soul to liberation, which is the final destination of every soul. The soul has taken on the covering of the body for this very purpose, and we should always remember this."

One day, Gurudev took me outside in an easterly direction where there was a large waterfall. There were several other smaller waterfalls near the main one. Lots of birds gathered there in the morning and warbled merrily in the fresh air. Different birds were making various sounds. Gurudev said, "Look at that tree and listen to what that group of sparrows is saying. Try to understand them." I looked in that direction and saw that hundreds of sparrows had assembled there and were chirping loudly. Gurudev said, "First of all, you should stop thinking that they are creating so much unnecessary noise and start thinking that they are in fact talking about something. Understand that you consider it noise only because you can't understand their language. Now try to understand what they're saying. Concentrate on what sounds they're making, and you'll realize that they are repeating the same sound several times. This means that they're saying something that is being ignored, and therefore they need to repeat it. Then study whether they are saying it happily or unhappily; study one particular sparrow. Study its mannerisms, study its aura. Study the bird's aura when it speaks. You will understand what it's saying from its aura. Look at how the sparrow is sitting on the upper branch, saying something loudly. No one is listening to her, so she's saying it forcefully.

"That sparrow is an experienced sparrow. She's telling them not to go to the place where all the sparrows went the previous day. There they found a lot of grains to eat, and that's why all the sparrows are talking about returning to the same place. This experienced sparrow isn't agreeing with them, and she's telling them that they've been going to the same place for the past eight days and the grains are secure there. They can easily go there any time and collect the grains. In a way that's their safe storage, and they shouldn't use up their secure store. They should keep it safe in case of any trouble. She's asking them to search for a new place as the rainy season is fast approaching. Then the store of grains will be useful as it's close by. Therefore, they should keep it safe. The other sparrows, who are not so experienced, are ignoring her. That's why the experienced sparrow is saying it repeatedly, and their argument continues about which direction to take to peck for grains that day. Finally, the experienced sparrow succeeds in convincing the other sparrows about her point of view, because together with her experience she also stresses her age and says that she's older than all of them, and they should take heed of her age as well as her experience. In reality, she was the oldest of them all. Everyone respected her age and decided to accept what she said, and later all the sparrows agreed with her and flew off together in a flock, following her lead."

Gurudev said further, "If someone wants to learn a language one should first study it. Establish a close relationship with the language, and only then can you learn. If we consider someone's language to be noisy or creating a racket, if we consider it to be insignificant or unpleasant, then forget the language of birds and animals—one won't even be able to learn the languages of humans. There are no words in the language of birds because they have no knowledge of words. In their language, there is a particular sound for a particular sentence; and through the medium of that distinguishing sound they talk and explain to each other. Man may not understand the language of animals, but birds and animals understand the language of humans. They study man's aura, the effect of man's consciousness, the effect of man's consciousness on his aura, and through it they understand the language of human beings. Just as birds and animals communicate without words, there are several languages of Adivasi tribal settlements that don't use words, either. One sound constitutes a sentence; then why speak such a long sentence when one sound can convey the meaning? For example, a mother calls out to her child—'where are you?' For this sentence the sparrow just makes a sound, *cheee*, and that sound conveys the question, 'where are you?' to her chick. And the chick makes a sound, *chooo*, which conveys the answer, 'I'm here.'

"One's language should be such that it promotes a sense of bonding. Just as a body is dead without a soul, a language is dead without a sense of bonding. There should be communication between the two (the speaker and the listener). If one's language doesn't lead to communication, it has no meaning or importance. The person who speaks should have a cordial relationship with the person who listens. A dialogue should be established between the two at some level; otherwise what often happens is that due to lack of closeness, or because it's happening at different spiritual levels, there's no meaningful dialogue. This situation usually comes about between a Guru and his disciple. The disciple must be close to the Guru, and this closeness can only be established through unwavering faith in him. If there's no faith, there won't be any closeness; if there's no closeness there won't be any faith. They're all interconnected. The Guru's talk will be understood in the right context only if there is a close relationship. The Guru speaks at a certain level, for as long as the disciple doesn't understand what the Guru is saying at the same level, the Guru himself will get stuck. The Guru will keep on repeating the same thing until the disciple understands. The disciple's age, his experience, his knowledge, his spiritual experience, his level—they're all different from that of the Guru. That's why there's no spiritual parity. The Guru speaks at a very high level and the disciple understands at a very low level. The wide gap between both their levels can only be bridged by a close relationship between them.

"You, too, may not understand all of what I'm telling you, as you don't have similar experiences, you have no prior knowledge. You'll understand what I'm saying only if you trust me. If you don't have faith in me, then it'll seem unbelievable to you, because there is a great gap between us; whatever I'm saying is from my vast experience, and you are listening to it at the level of your relatively limited experience. Whatever you're hearing is at the physical level. Have faith and trust in it because Gurudev is saying it. That's the right thing to do because whatever he is saying is for your benefit. It's only this faith that will enlighten you. Secondly, you may not have the same experiences in your life that I have had in my life, because there's bound to be a difference between the time in my life and the time in your life. But it may so happen that one experience we've received in our lives, without paying a price for it, may guide us. Man should always learn from experience. There's no need to be afraid of experiences. Such incidents don't just happen between a Guru and his disciple; they also happen between a father and his son. There's a difference of twenty-five or thirty years between the two. The time-gap between the two is also different. It isn't necessary for the bad experiences in the father's life to happen in the son's life. But the father's experiences are passed on to the son free of charge, and without payment of any price.

"Secondly, the son should respect the father's way of thinking. The father only wishes that his son shouldn't face the problems that he faced in his life, that he shouldn't experience the bad events and incidents that he had to go through in his life. He keeps explaining all this out of love for his son. His purpose is only to do something that'll benefit his son. It's also possible that because of being part of a new generation, the son may have to face new crises that were not around in his father's time. That's also possible! But the mistakes committed by his father in his life can at least be corrected. The father doesn't want his son to repeat the mistakes he committed in his life, either knowingly or unknowingly. If you look, in reality, the father lives his life a second time through his son. Therefore, it is natural that the father won't allow his mistakes to be repeated in the same way by his son. But it's possible that some misfortune may arise in the son's life, perhaps as a result of some new discoveries that didn't exist during his father's life. Misfortunes, problems, and their solutions also keep changing over time. From time-to-time man solves the problems that arise in his life. And it is this process of sunlight and shadow, of problems and solutions, that is called life. Thus, this game will go on continuously, and this continuous movement is 'life.'

"The same thing applies to vocal and instrumental music. If a singer or a musician absorbs knowledge from his Guru with faith, trust and surrender, if he has internalized it, then he'll be able to reach the souls of his listeners through his singing or music. Singing and music are only a medium for one soul to reach another. The voice of a singer will have the skills or tricks to impress his audience, not just because he has learnt music but because he has connected his soul to his Guru. That's why in Indian classical music, classical singing, a Guru–Shishya parampara, is followed. At the physical level, there is only a teacher, but when we talk about the soul level then one is not a teacher but a Guru. Body has a teacher; soul has a Guru. Knowledge of the soul can neither be taught nor learned; it can only be assimilated (internalized) by one soul from another. Playing classical music and classical singing are the type of art forms that are internalized and that have sustained themselves in the same way for thousands of years. They are as effective today as they were in the olden days. When a singer establishes contact with his Guru's soul and sings, he conveys the consciousness that he has acquired from his Guru's aura to his audience. He becomes only a medium; his own ego terminates. Then it's not a song but consciousness that he showers on his listeners when he sings. It is only through this connection that a singer becomes successful and creates a place for himself in life.

"The same thing applies to meditation, just like classical singing and playing music. The knowledge of meditation is the knowledge that has been conveyed from one soul to another. No one can teach meditation, nor can anyone learn it. This knowledge is above teaching. Learning generally happens either at the physical level or through one's intellect, but meditation is beyond both the body and the intellect. The Guru himself can't do anything to teach meditation as it is not in the Guru's control. No Guru in this world can teach meditation because the Guru himself hasn't learnt it from his Guru. The Guru doesn't have any importance on the path of meditation. The Guru is of no use on this path, because he doesn't do anything here. The Guru can't do anything even for himself, so what can he be expected to do for his disciple? The Guru is useless at the physical level. There is nothing one can learn from the Guru at the physical or intellectual level. In fact, the Guru is not well-versed with the ways of the social world or social dynamics. The Guru's demeanour is also not worth emulating.

He doesn't behave in a way that someone can learn from. His speech is inconsistent, and one generally can't understand what he is saying when he speaks. As a rule, what the Guru says can't be fully understood in his lifetime. This means that the Guru is of no use even when he gives discourses. Whoever hears him won't get any knowledge because he himself hasn't gained it from his Guru by listening.

"As long as you don't acquire the knowledge of meditation the way he acquired it, you'll find whatever he is saying nonsensical. He continues to fool you and will keep doing so as long as you're happy to be fooled. When you're tired of being fooled, then you'll think: 'What is this nonsense? He's saying the same thing over and over again! Why do we keep coming back to listen to it? Why do we like being near him? What kind of magnetism draws us to him? He's not beautiful, nor is his language beautiful! He doesn't walk well, nor does he have any intellect, and he's not a scholar. In fact, he's nothing! So why does one like being in his proximity! Why do we come to him again and again? Why? Why?' When you start thinking about 'why,' then your attention will automatically go beyond the Guru's body, to his energies, and in an instant the event will take place. It is this moment that every Guru eagerly awaits. The Guru's body is the instrument of consciousness. The moment you surrender to him, the path for consciousness is ready. After that, whether you wish for it or not, the nectar of consciousness keeps pouring on you. Until you bow and surrender before the Guru's soul, the Guru himself can't give anything at the physical level. The Guru can't give anything; one has to take it from the Guru by surrendering to him. One who learns to bow and surrender acquires everything automatically.

"Actually, 'bowing' means one soul expressing will power and desire in front of another soul, because inner knowledge can be obtained through meditation, and this shouldn't happen only be at the physical level. Just imagine that there's a very big water tank. A pipe has been put in that tank and someone is holding the other end of the pipe in his mouth. Even if the person keeps holding the end in his mouth all his life, he won't be able to drink the water in the tank. He'll have to hold the end in his mouth and suck on it and then the water will flow into his mouth. Secondly, the pipe itself doesn't contain any water so one won't get any water by just putting the pipe in one's mouth. The pipe is only a medium, and the water is in the tank. One must remember that it can flow through the pipe, but it isn't actually present in the pipe. Similarly, the Guru is always connected to consciousness, but there's no consciousness in the Guru; nor can the Guru give consciousness on his own. But one can gain consciousness through the medium of the Guru. Thus, one will have to go beyond the medium of the Guru's body so that one may meditate. However, one thing is certain: a person has more chance of getting water if he has a pipe in his mouth than a person who doesn't have a pipe in his mouth at all, because he won't have to search for a pipe. It has already been found and is being held. All that remains is for the pipe to be used. It isn't enough to hold on to a Guru. It's necessary to look beyond the physical body of the medium that is the form of the Guru.

"In the spiritual world, time spent close to the Guru is the best period of one's life. But the time a sadhak can spend with a Guru depends on the karma of his previous birth. This is the golden moment of a sadhak's life. It is often seen that there are few such golden moments in one's life. The remaining time has to be spent remembering those golden moments. This is why one needs to understand that meditation is the best knowledge that can be acquired by one soul from another. It's impossible to obtain this knowledge without purification of one's chitta."

Gurudev was an expert at lighting a fire. He did so by placing some grass and rubbing two flint stones near it. It would light up so easily that I would sometimes wonder whether there was actually a spark from the stones or whether he was making the stones a medium and using his power of consciousness to ignite them. There were two big stones that he rubbed together to light a fire. This normally happened only a few times as there was generally a fire burning in the cave. There was a pit in the cave, and the fire was kept burning in it like an oblation. Some dry logs that had been placed nearby would be fed to the fire. These were scented logs, and when they were put on the fire, the whole cave was filled with fragrance, and the whole atmosphere would turn happy and joyful.

※

Gurudev started talking about the 'chitta' while adding firewood to the fire. He said, 'sexual desire' is like this fire. The more fuel you add to it, the more it will grow; and sexual desire weakens the body the most. Sexual pleasure is a physical function, and the body needs it. But the joy one gets out of it is not lasting. It is momentary. But this can only be understood through experience. If it had been eternal, then all the people whose sexual desires were fulfilled would have been happy. But that is not the case. They, too, are not happy. But until one's sexual urge is satisfied, a person feels that the joy of satisfaction is everything in life. That's why those who haven't obtained it are dissatisfied. They feel that they haven't achieved sexual satisfaction; those who have received it, on the other hand, are dissatisfied because they have realized that there is no satisfaction in it. One should never try to progress in the spiritual field with this sexual dissatisfaction, as it will prove to be the reason for one's spiritual downfall. Imagine, for example, that there is only a small hole in a balloon; but when the balloon is blown up that small hole grows bigger, and eventually the balloon bursts. Similarly, there can't be spiritual progress with sexual dissatisfaction. It isn't right to force oneself to control the sexual urge because then desire comes out in a wrong way.

"It often happens that a sadhak forcibly controls his sexual urge all his life, and then in old age he commits the sin of raping some young girl. Thus, the impulse that he had suppressed comes out in the wrong way, and the forced control proves destructive. When a sadhak crosses the physical level and moves to the spiritual level, he develops natural control over his sexual desires. This control must come naturally; it can never be forced, as that would be the suppression of sexual desire, which is wrong and potentially dangerous. Whatever is forced is always at the physical level and whatever is natural is everlasting. Several people observe fasts in the name of Paramatma for spiritual progress. That is also wrong. A sadhak shouldn't eat too much, and he shouldn't fast either. Stay on the middle path. When we fast in order to remove our attention from food, then instead of taking our mind away from food, our attention goes even more towards food. Then we keep seeing food all the time, everywhere. This is also wrong and will harm one's mind. When you become so immersed in meditation that you don't have any sense of food or eating left, that is fasting. Fasting takes place automatically. If you force yourself not to eat, that is not fasting. Therefore, one should not undertake these kinds of forced fasts. Fasting is only acceptable if it happens naturally. Food is necessary for one's body.

"Just as food is necessary for one's physical body, fulfilment of one's sexual desires is also a necessity. One shouldn't suppress one's sexual desires. People think that celibacy means semen-control. In reality, semen is a creation of nature. It can't remain within and will come out in some form or the other. Celibacy doesn't mean controlling one's sexual urges at the physical level. Celibacy also means being celibate in one's thoughts, when one doesn't even think about sex. It is necessary to raise celibacy to an even higher level. The release of semen can be likened to monthly menstruation for men. This is a natural flow, which is similar to the monthly menstrual flow experienced by women. It isn't proper to suppress it unnaturally, otherwise it will lead to distortion of the natural process. Some sadhaks try to deal with sexual urges on a war-footing; others use drugs like cannabis to try and suppress their desire. They consume herbs as well, but there's no need to do all this at the physical level. A woman finds her sexual contentment, but a man can't, and this is because of the way their physical bodies are structured. After some years, a woman becomes free of her sexual desire. But a man can't be free of it even when he has one foot in his grave. That's why, compared to men, freedom from sexual desire is easier for women. It should happen on its own and shouldn't be forced."

In the jungle, I didn't know when it was morning and when it was evening. I didn't even know how long I had been there. I had brought a small calendar with me and had made a habit of marking the day as soon as the sun rose. This went on for several days. But when I visited the large cave with Gurudev, my calculations went wrong. I felt as if many more days had passed; at least that was how it appeared to me. Now my fears of darkness, death, animals in the jungle, having to stay in these woods—all of it had ended.

Now I would keep watching the water falling for hours at a time. Sometimes, Gurudev would be in meditation for several days. I used to do tasks such as cleaning the cave, collecting firewood, picking fruits, keeping the surroundings clean and making sure that the fire was always burning. I felt strongly connected to fire. I made friends with several birds and animals, and they would come regularly to meet me. I would talk to them as I wanted to know their language, and I tried to understand the meaning of the sounds they made. I studied their aura and realized that their aura basically remained natural as they didn't have any thoughts. They undertook certain activities at a particular time, but those were also done in a state of thoughtlessness. I got used to the place and started to like it. I enjoyed living in the environment and I gradually got used to the food there.

There was no set time for eating; I just ate something whenever I felt hungry. I don't know why, but I never felt very hungry there. Pure drinking water was also available. I had a lungi, which also served as a bedsheet. Sometimes, I would cover myself with it like a blanket or use it like a towel to dry myself. I'd also brought with me a tunic and a shoulder bag made out of cloth. I'd brought a torch, but its batteries had run out. I had a white dhoti, which I would roll up and wear like a loincloth. I would tie a cloth string around my waist to hold up the loincloth. I had other clothes in my bag, but I didn't wear them. I didn't really have much luggage. My beard, moustache and hair had grown quite long. I had a pair of shoes that I never wore, and they just lay unused as I was afraid of slipping in them. I had a small calendar and marked the date every morning on it. Later, when the ink in my pen ran out, I used to make a hole in it with the pen. I had a small knife that I used to make a cut in my nails, and then had to peel them. I would rub my teeth with ashes to clean them. I had brought a bar of soap, but it had been used up long ago. I rubbed myself with leaves while bathing, but even bathing was infrequent.

I hadn't seen a human being for several days. In fact, I hadn't seen anyone except Gurudev, which was why all my attention was on him. My attention would be on every little detail about him, on even the smallest activity. He had a tremendous power of attraction. I had never seen him laughing, but his face was gentle and pleasant. He used a stick for walking, mainly more out of habit than need, it seemed. He would sometimes look into the void, as if he could glimpse the future. One day, while gazing into the void, he said to me, "Your container is very big. That's why Shiv Baba has placed his energy in you. And I'm also putting my energies into you. One birth is not enough for the spiritual practice of meditation. One has to meditate devotedly birth after birth. It's never possible to do both—accept Chaitanya as well as pass it on to others in one birth. And it's extremely difficult to absorb and pass on more consciousness and more experience simultaneously. One requires a very large heart and great generosity for that.

"How is it that one can so easily pass on knowledge that one has acquired through so much hard work! It can never be given. Giving this knowledge is like giving up everything one possesses. Only a mother can do it in this world. In this universe, it is only a mother who can put her whole life at risk and give birth to a child. You are a mother; you have a mother's heart within you. You have in you the capacity to give up everything you possess. You are capable of giving up everything to anyone! You can offer a new life to someone; you can give a new birth to someone! You can become a 'mother.' It's completely possible for you to become a 'mother.' Awaken that possibility. Awaken the capacity of becoming a mother. That capacity is the one ray of hope in our world of Gurus. Awaken that ray, awaken the ray within you; awaken that desire within you that 'I wish to give up everything.' If you wish for it, you can give it, as the emotion of motherhood is innate in you. Awaken the emotion of motherhood! There is an emotion of motherhood in you—awaken it! A man can obtain something, but he can't give it, whereas a woman can obtain something and give it, too. That's why knowledge can be obtained in society through women and not from men. Therefore, awaken the femininity lying dormant within you. The feminine element can give a new life to the human race!"

I couldn't understand what Gurudev was trying to tell me. How could I become a woman when I was a man? And why was he asking me to become a woman? Can a man become a woman just like that? What was he saying? I couldn't understand anything. What does he mean by saying that my container is big? What is big? What does 'become a woman' mean? What does become a 'mother' mean? What does it mean to awaken one's feelings of 'motherhood'? I couldn't understand what he was saying. I had realized in his proximity that he wasn't joking, and after realizing that I became more serious. Does he want to turn me into a woman? Why does he want to turn me into a woman? I mulled over it relentlessly that day, but understood nothing at all. The next morning, after meditation, I asked Gurudev to explain what he had said the previous day; I hadn't understood even a fraction of what he was telling me. I was ready to become a woman and do whatever he expected of me; I wanted his blessings so that I could fulfil all his expectations. I kept thinking about what Gurudev had said at that time—the Guru speaks at his level and the disciple listens at his level, and therefore no meaningful dialogue can take place between them.

The same thing was happening here—he was speaking at his level, but I could only understand it at mine; and that was why there was no conversation between us. I had come with the purpose of receiving some knowledge from him, and instead of passing it on to me it seemed as if he was trying to awaken some latent knowledge within myself. So, what was it within me that he was trying to bring out?

I did my own introspection. I had a fierce desire to know Paramatma, and I also had a strong desire to pass on the knowledge of the path of Paramatma to others. But I hadn't found Paramatma as yet, so how could I pass on the knowledge to others? I had a strong desire to share the divine knowledge with others. But the question of sharing it didn't arise as I hadn't received it. How can one share something that one hasn't received? Secondly, Gurudev was also not talking about giving anything. My concern grew as I kept thinking that there was definitely something within me that needed to be brought out and distributed. What could it be? This question remained unanswered. But because of what Gurudev said, my external wandering and searching ended, and I started looking within. My inner journey had commenced. Something was hidden within me, and I had to reach it. What had I received in life that could exist within me? I had not received anything at all!

Then, suddenly, I had a flash, and I started recalling Shiv Baba's words. He had said, "I have handed over everything I possess to you." Maybe Gurudev was referring to that, because Shiv Baba had said that he was giving me everything he possessed, whereas I had never felt that I had received anything. Shiv Baba had said that he had passed on everything he possessed to me, and this Gurudev was saying that I had to distribute everything that was within me. There appeared to be a link between both. Both were saying something at their level. Both knew it and both of them had understood it; only I was in the dark about it; I was the fool who couldn't understand. I felt that it was appropriate to wait for the future since that was what Gurudev wanted, that whatever was within me should come out and reach people. I didn't know whether he was referring to this birth or my next birth since I hadn't seen any people around for several days now.

Gurudev sounded as if he spoke with great depth, but I remained uncomprehending. I realized that when one can't understand anything the best thing to do is to surrender completely to the Guru-energies. If one acknowledges and prays saying, "I can't understand anything; may everything be done according to your understanding and wishes," then your ego fades away, which allows you to truly understand. For example, when we used to go for a long walk with our mother as children and our feet started aching, we would leave everything to our mother and say, "now I can't walk anymore, carry me!" Similarly, one should say, "I don't know what you are saying; you can understand it, let everything happen according to your wishes," and surrender completely. But with surrender it's also necessary to have complete faith and trust, because complete surrender is not possible without faith and trust.

After surrendering to him in this way, I slowly started understanding him. He was inspiring me to go inwards, and his purpose was to take me within myself and make me realize and become aware of Shiv Baba's treasure of energies that had been placed within me. Gurudev was reminding me of the treasure that Shiv Baba had obtained from his Guru after forty years of devoted spiritual practice, and which he had diligently preserved. It was a collection of energies, which are collected only to be shared.

The Guru-element always goes to nature and establishes oneness with it, and after acquiring the dormant knowledge, the living knowledge of spiritual experiences, from nature, the Guru element absorbs it. Then they distribute the priceless treasure to ordinary people. Since their nature is to distribute everything, nature's energies are drawn towards them. I suddenly remembered Gurudev's words: "What you obtain from Paramatma is determined by your capacity to give."

And, truly, if you look at nature, you'll realize that it keeps giving to everyone. Clouds give water; small streams give water to rivers and rivers to the ocean. Some clouds give water to the earth, the earth gives it to the trees, which give flowers and then fruits to the birds. The basic nature of earth is to give, and that's why a person who has merged with nature learns to give on his own.

Nature gives equally to everyone. It doesn't discriminate; all are equal. If you go to a river, it gives water equally to people of all races, people of all colours, all religions, and all languages. It gives water equally to both the virtuous and the vicious. Maybe all these differences have been created by man. Man distances himself from nature by creating such differences. A person becomes one with nature by being in its proximity, and he who is one with nature can't discriminate between anyone. Even those who meditate get close to nature, and so their thoughts are above any inequalities.

I had been away from society for some time, and so I started feeling a kind of isolation within me. I was enjoying nature's company. I felt that the normal routine of my life should stop here, and I should keep enjoying this natural beauty forever. There was no human around, so it was only natural that I had developed an attachment with the trees, the creepers, the stones and the mud. I spoke to the trees. Several birds and animals had become my friends, and I built a close relationship with them and would recognize their needs without being told. This was like a mother knowing why her child is crying without the child explaining.

That day, my peaceful life was struck by a thunderbolt when Gurudev said, "Your education with me is complete. Now I'm sending you to another Guru for further education. We leave from here tomorrow morning."

I was very disturbed when I heard this. I had thought that I would be spending my life at this Guru-charan. That night while I was pressing his feet, I thought that I would never have this opportunity again. Why had he done this? Had I done something wrong? I don't know how, but Gurudev fathomed my feelings and started explaining to me: "The Guru is like a gardener. He plants a small seed in a nursery. He waits for the seed to grow into a plant. He fertilizes the plant and waters it. When the seed grows into a plant, he takes it to some new place where the plant can develop into a tree. He transfers the tree to a new place and hopes that the tree will do well. When the gardener trims the plant, then it's with the same aim that the plant may grow well and progress. Thus, no matter what the gardener does, his purpose is always to develop the plant. Several gardeners often develop a variety of plants over their lifetime, but it isn't important to them to see the fruits of the plants they have developed in their lives. Someone in the next generation eats the fruits. The gardener can never damage his plant.

"The same is the case with the Guru. The Guru puts the seed of his energies in his disciples and hopes that the seed of those energies will develop. Some of the Guru's disciples are able to develop that seed and some aren't, but the Guru's efforts are always to develop the seeds in the form of his disciples. A Guru has several disciples. You are my only disciple and therefore all my future hopes rest on you. Now I have put into your container whatever I had acquired and preserved in my lifetime from my Guru, because there isn't a better container than yours. I'm aware of your future life. I feel at peace after passing on my Guru's energies to you because I feel that the spiritual work of my life has been accomplished. Now I'll be able to end my life peacefully in this cave. A person who is born is sure to die. The wheel of life moves along with the wheel of death. This is my last birth because my Guru gave me the task of passing on these energies to you, and he told me, 'Complete this spiritual work and achieve liberation.' Several years ago, my Guru bestowed on me the state of liberation, and he had asked me to complete this task as Guru dakshina for it. Today, I am relieved of this work, too.

"I was tied up in the bonds of my Guru's soul and now my soul is free of that, too. Just as the life of a river has only one purpose of reaching the ocean, I also had only the aim of reaching the ocean. Hey, you silly boy! Why are you crying? *You* are my ocean! I am not considering you *an* ocean; you are *the* ocean. You don't know how many rivers will merge into you. I can see that happening in the future and you can't. That's the only difference between us."

I couldn't understand what Gurudev was saying. I was holding his feet very tightly. I was afraid of losing my grip on his feet, and he kept explaining to me while I cried.

He said, "Hey, you silly boy! Whoever has come into this world must go one day. A human being comes here with the sole purpose of going, but very few people are fortunate to reach their goal of achieving liberation. The purpose of the birth of every soul is to attain liberation. That's why the soul takes birth in different forms. And finally, through the process of evolution, the soul takes birth in the form of a human being. The human birth is the only birth in whose form liberation can be attained. This is a form between Paramatma and other creatures, (for example, birds, animals, and insects). This human form is an important link between Paramatma and other forms. We can understand it like this—the human form is the bridge that must be crossed before one can reach Paramatma.

"Man takes birth in this form and believes that this bridge, which is his body, is the final destination. But whosoever believes this, gets stuck on the bridge itself, and continues to stay there until he sees someone else crossing the bridge. Up to that point, he isn't even aware that there's something beyond the bridge. When he sees someone attaining liberation, then he realizes that he had accepted the human body itself as his home, which in fact was only a rest house; his home is different. But for that to happen, it's necessary for a soul who has moved from the rest house to their home, to come close to him. That soul will make him realize that a rest house is only an inn after all, and a home is the final destination.

"When a soul takes birth as a human being and uses the human body as a bridge to reach Paramatma and attains liberation after crossing the bridge, then that soul awakens several other souls stuck on the bridge. The souls sleeping on the bridge awaken and try to attain liberation by going across the bridge. Thus, not only does that soul achieve liberation, but also becomes a role-model for others. You are that soul who is going to help several other souls to cross the bridge. Recognize yourself, try to understand all the knowledge within you.

"Right now, your state is like that of the musk deer that keeps getting the scent of musk from the musk lying within itself, but runs around madly, trying to find out where the scent is coming from. I have reached liberation, and I wish to help thousands of souls do the same. Always remember this—you will now come across thousands of people stuck on this bridge represented by the human body. But I won't be present to witness that scene! How does it matter that I wasn't able to eat the fruits of my tree! Someone at least can benefit from the fruits of my tree. Isn't that enough? The work of Guru-energies is very vast. No Guru gets to eat the fruits of trees he has planted, because good coconut-bearing trees always take several years to bear fruit. In the same way, I won't be able to see the fruits of the trees I planted in my lifetime. And the same thing is going to happen in your life, too. You also won't be able to see the fruits of the trees you have planted in your lifetime; the fruit orchards you have planted will only blossom after your life.

"Therefore, get up and get ready, and don't even think about the fruits. Carry on with your spiritual work because it is in your hands today.

"The fruits you are eating today didn't come from trees that you had planted! You, too, are eating the fruits of trees that were planted by someone else. This is the natural wheel of Guru-energy through which we have to pass. This spiritual work of Guru-energies has been going on in the same way and will continue in the future. After you achieve liberation, a whole era of 800 years of Guru-energy will come to an end. The souls that had been stuck on the bridge for the last 800 years will all cross the bridge together in collectivity. Collectivity is your energy. The purpose of your life is collectivity. You are an infinite sea. You are going to be an ocean! Thousands of small rivers come together and create a great ocean. I know everything clearly! I won't be present at that time but today I'm able to see everything with my divine foresight. I'm very happy today because my Gurudev gave me a chance to contribute to the creation of a great ocean. I'm grateful to my Guru for that." My Gurudev was saying something more, but perhaps it wasn't appropriate for me to hear it at that time—and I fell asleep! I don't know what he said after that.

✤

When I awoke, I found that I had slept near Gurudev's bed, and Gurudev was not there. After some time, he returned after having taken a bath. I went for my own bath soon after, and I was very unhappy that morning. I was leaving these stones and going away; I was leaving the Guru-sthan and going away. I was dejected, and so that morning I went around and met all the trees; I met all the birds and animals I used to meet every day, and they also seemed to be stunned! That morning, I left that beautiful nature's heaven with a heavy heart and followed Gurudev.

We went north, and after reaching a particular place, Gurudev started climbing upwards. I realized that this was the big turn from where the road led out of the valley. Then, after climbing up for some time, we reached the top and found that it was already evening. We stopped in the shade of a big stone ridge, and that night I prayed to Gurudev, "Gurudev, you must be tired. I wish to press your feet. It is said that Heaven is at the Guru-charan." Gurudev nodded his head and gave me permission, and I started pressing his feet as he began to speak.

"In Indian culture," he said, "the Guru-charan are very important. But the Guru-charan are symbolic. I don't want to displease you, so I'm allowing you to press my feet. We have to surrender everything before the diety-like guru whom we worship. All this is our inner feeling. You will surrender everything and bow completely. If Gurudev is standing on the ground, imagine that you have bowed down completely in front of him. At this point, your head and his feet are in the same place. In reality, bowing completely means connecting your existence with that of your Gurudev, and in this way, we extinguish our ego. Once our ego, which separates us from Paramatma, is extinguished, we become natural and return to our original state because we were not born with this ego. The Guru-charan are a symbolic place for us to bow. What is important is that we should surrender somewhere. It's easy for us to bow before someone we love, someone whom we trust completely; and bowing is a way of wiping out our own existence. Whoever masters this art will cross the ocean of life. This can't be acquired. It's an art that is natural and can only be achieved naturally." Afterwards I fell asleep, because my feet were aching after having climbed the hill.

The next morning, we walked northwards and continued all day. When we reached a tribal settlement by the evening, we found that as we approached, two people from the tribe had already seen us climbing the hill from afar. We looked further and saw the king of the tribe coming forward to welcome Gurudev with seven or eight people. With great reverence, he brought Gurudev into the village. Exquisite arrangements had been made for Gurudev's stay in a large hut, and I was accommodated in another outer hut. It had been a long time since I had seen other humans, and the humans I now saw were very strange. But it was enough for me that they were humans. We had a meal of fruits, and I didn't notice when I had fallen asleep.

When I woke up in the morning, I found that the tribal people were saying their prayers. That day I watched a wonderful scene.

The tribal people, dressed in colourful costumes, came with small bamboo baskets adorned with leaves and flowers. They placed their bouquets in front of Gurudev and, sitting with both their hands tied behind their backs, they touched their foreheads to the ground. They were sitting in a row in Vajrasan or 'diamond pose' while performing this ritual, and I thought it was lovely. Everyone here respected Gurudev very much, and since I had come with Gurudev, they treated me with great respect, too.

I couldn't understand their language, nor had I ever seen such attires. The ladies wore a lungi over which they wore a big blouse with several beaded chains. The men wore only a short lungi and had tied a special kind of cloth on their heads. They knew Gurudev from the beginning and considered him to be God. Whenever they were in trouble or faced problems, they would pray to God through the medium of Gurudev. They had glasses made of bamboo, which were prepared by cutting the bamboo near the knotted part. They cut the bamboo about eight to ten inches above the knot and used the glass for drinking water or any other drink. They had a drink that was like tea, to which they added bay leaves and ginger. It had a very pungent flavour, and I thought it was similar to a decoction. They gave it to me, and I drank it, or rather pretended to drink it; the flavour didn't appeal to me. As it was given with great reverence, I accepted it out of deference for their feelings, but threw it away when they weren't looking.

They used various herbs to cure illnesses. They also used some special leaves for exorcism. When I carefully observed their method of exorcism, I realized that they were using the leaves of a particular tree and were cleaning the aura of the person before them. When a person has thoughts, especially negative thoughts, his aura gets polluted and he therefore can't absorb the required energy, which leads to illness.

These people used the method of exorcism to clear the aura of the person who had polluted it through negative thoughts. They would twirl special herbal plants around the person and then throw them in the fire. They said that they had cleared the person of the effect of the evil eye, of bad spirits, and the person would start feeling perfectly fine. When I was a child, my maternal grandmother used to clear me similarly of the bad effects of an evil eye, by twirling big red chilies and mustard seeds around me and then putting them in the fire. This was especially done where there were many people around at some function and they would lift and carry me. After that, if I got a fever, my grandmother would say that it was because of the number of people around; someone's evil glance must have fallen on me. She would then make me sit on the floor, take red chilies and mustard seeds in her hands and move them from left to right once, and then from right to left. She did this seven times. She didn't know about the seven chakras, but doing this was a tradition, and I felt that the method of exorcism used by these tribal people was similar. There was a special person in the village who was quite old. He had a special hut for doing all this, and this ritual was carried out there. He was called Dondai and throughout the year he would perform exorcism on everyone in the village and pray for them. In return, the people used to give him grains after the harvest, which he lived off. This person is also called 'ojha' or witch-doctor among some communities.

According to these people's way of thinking, the effect of evil spirits pollutes a person's aura, and he becomes ill. These people believed in spirits and ghosts. They were very pure and simple-minded and depended more on natural methods for curing sicknesses. Or one could say that they were forced to depend on nature because of their situation, where they had no modern medical facilities. While wandering in the jungles, I used to feel that the earth is vast, so huge, and man has developed only a small part of it and thinks that the human race has developed! In reality, it is man's ignorance that makes him think this way. Even now there are several settlements, several undiscovered places that people from the modern world have not yet found. There are places where one can't even imagine human habitation. These tribal people were simple, sincere and believed in rebirth. They believed that if they performed some karma in this life, and didn't surrender them, then they would have to take another birth to endure the effects of those acts.

There was a particular incident. That tribal king was staying on top of a hill. He invited Gurudev and me for a meal to his house. There were vast plantations of ginger around his house. At eleven in the morning, an old tribal woman passed in front of the king's house; she was carrying a whole basketful of firewood tied to her back. The king bought all the wood from her and paid her with bamboo glasses full of rice. This way of bartering had been decided in advance. The woman had asked for four glassfuls of rice in return for the wood, and afterwards she went on her way.

I asked the king, "You already have so much wood, why did you buy more from the old woman?" The king replied, "If I hadn't bought the wood from her, she would have had to cross this hill to get to her village, which she would have found too troublesome. That's why I bought the wood from her. Buying the wood was just an excuse. Actually, I just wanted to help." Later we had lunch, and afterwards we sat outside and chatted. While we were absorbed in conversation, the old woman returned and gave some rice back to the king. She said, "After going home, I saw that you had made a mistake and given me five glassfuls instead of four glassfuls of rice, so I have come to return the extra rice." The king replied, "Hey, so what if I gave you a little more rice? I wouldn't have missed it." The old woman gave him a rather enlightened reply: "You may not have any need for it, but I will have to take another birth to pay you for that extra rice! I desire liberation in this life and don't want to take another birth. Therefore, I don't want the debt of that rice on myself, and I don't want to take another birth for a handful of your rice. Therefore, I'm returning it. Man has to pay for obligations, murder, and revenge at some time or the other."

After that, the woman returned the rice and left. I found this incident deeply meaningful, and said to Gurudev, "We consider these tribal people backward, but their thoughts are so pure and progressive." The exchange really impressed me. This community, which was supposedly backward and undeveloped, didn't want to take anything from anyone. Later the king said, "I had purposely given her more rice because I wanted to help her, but I took the rice back so she could maintain her self-respect." That night, one question kept popping up again and again in my mind—is this community more developed, or is our modern society? Who are the backward ones? As I was pondering over this question, I fell asleep.

The next morning, I woke up to the sound of goats bleating. I saw that two kids were crying for their mother and the mother (nanny) goat was calling out to them. The kids were pure white with some black spots here and there. They looked very sweet. They were still small but were quite agile. I tried to catch them but couldn't. Later, with great difficulty, I managed to catch one of them. These goats were very small compared with other ordinary goats. The kids were tiny, and their mother was also short. Later, I took the kids one by one to their mother. The mother was happy, and so were the kids. They started suckling her. They were sucking so hard that the poor little nanny goat was shaking and couldn't stand still.

When I went to freshen up, I found that there was a well in the yard in front of the hut. The well was very small and shaped like a big drum, and the water was just ten to twelve feet deep. I drew the water with a bucket and rope and then saw that someone had already drawn the water for me in a nearby bucket. It was an earthen bucket like the flowerpots in a garden, but because of the water the colour on the edge of the bucket had turned yellow and red. This showed that this was heavy water, and the iron content was very high. It looked a little oily and was difficult to digest.

These people farmed ginger and sold it in nearby settlements where they bought other commodities. No one had any knowledge of money or currency. The ancient barter system was practised, rice and vegetables were grown; everyone was happy and satisfied. Dancing and singing were the main forms of entertainment. They used to make thread out of cotton and weave cloth. They had no connection with the outside world, and they lived thinking that their world was the whole world. They didn't have any knowledge of my life and I didn't want to tell them about it. They thought I belonged to Gurudev's world and I didn't disillusion them, nor did I tell them much about myself. We slowly established a dialogue through facial expressions and sign language. They could speak a little broken Assamese and I replied in a little broken Assamese.

Their king's name was Jhinga. He appeared to be the richest and most progressive person in the settlement. He spoke very little but listened with interest to everything that was said. He was short and stocky, but his eyes looked very serious. His wife was just the opposite: she seemed to be very jolly. Both were old, and the wife was a compassionate woman. They took good care of me. Most of the time Gurudev used to be in meditation and no one had the courage to go near him. Everyone used to look at him with a feeling of awe. Gurudev's accommodation had been prepared outside the village among large trees. I couldn't understand everything that they said but I was happy to be among humans. In the evening, their children would surround me; I was a different kind of creature to them. Most of the children used to look at me with curiosity. Maybe they saw me as an alien from outer space. They were very strong. Each child used to carry a coconut in one hand and bring it to me. A coconut filled with water is a fairly heavy thing, and the children used to bring me tender green coconuts. Perhaps as a result of living in nature, these children had also become a part of nature! The hut that had been allotted to me was constructed from mud and had a roof made out of fine grass. The king told me that the same roof had lasted since his childhood, despite being almost hundred years old. It was just the same, and when it rained it didn't absorb any water. This showed that even a grass roof could last for more than a century. I found this really surprising. The grass was very fine and there was a layer (of about a foot) of it on the hut. It had been constructed in such a way that no water could drip from it, nor would it be blown away during a storm. The hut had been built like a strong, protective fort.

They would take me to the lake to bathe even on cold mornings. The lake had been formed from a small river, and its water was surprisingly warm even though the weather outside was very cold. My time in the water was pleasant because of how warm it was, but I bathed quickly and got out, since Gurudev was going to come out of his deep meditation that day, and he had called me in the morning. I quickly got ready and went and sat in front of Gurudev's hut. After a while Gurudev came out and took me up to the top of the hill. He pointed in the direction of the hill on the opposite side, and said, "A sage lives on the opposite hill. He is always in a state of meditation. I have spoken to him today. I'm sending you to his ashram for further sadhana. His ashram is on the hill where you can see a small rivulet. To get there you'll have to descend across this entire range of hills and then cross the small hill on the opposite side. After that you will have to climb up again. It may take you eight to ten days to reach there, and you should take with you all the essential stuff that you need as you have to leave tomorrow morning."

He said all this so quickly that I was suddenly shaken. "All this time I have been preparing you and now you are ready to go to him. I am old now. I'm passing the flame of my devoted spiritual practice into your safekeeping. Don't ever allow this flame to die. From today I will remain alive only in your form. The purpose of my life has been fulfilled. After bidding you farewell tomorrow, I'll return to my cave. My Guru gave me this responsibility and said, 'The values of spiritual practice are important, and they should remain alive. Humans come and go, that's not important. It is we who help in conveying the good values of devoted spiritual practice to the next generation.'" We know the fact that the time is not right for future generations but the next generation isn't and that's why the flame of spiritual practice should continue to burn eternally; this is the only support for those who are wandering in darkness and searching for the right path.

After saying this, my Gurudev passed on to me the values of spiritual practice: "I am now passing them on to you for safekeeping, and I feel satisfied that I have completed the task in accordance with the assurance I had given my Gurudev. Now there is no purpose left, nor any reason for me to remain alive. I'll return to my cave and give up my physical body. My Gurudev resides in that cave. I'll go to his lap and tell him, 'Gurudev, I have obeyed your orders and have passed on the flame of the values of spiritual practice into suitable hands. Now please give me permission to enter the sacred abode of liberation.' That's what I'm going to tell him."

I shuddered at the very thought of being separated from my Gurudev, and I soon started crying. He told me: "Life is not important; what is important is what you have achieved in life.

How long you have lived is not important, what is important is what you have received. Every person has only one purpose in life, that is, liberation of the soul in the presence of the body. It is for this very reason that man is born. I had also obtained the state of liberation in my life, but I couldn't give up my physical body without my Gurudev's permission. Now the purpose of this physical body has been accomplished, and the spiritual work of handing over the flame of the values of spiritual practice has also been completed. I trust you completely. You'll never allow this flame to die. I can see tomorrow, the future. Thousands of rivers will come and meet you, and you'll become the ocean of the values of spiritual practice."

The next morning, I was collecting fruits and other items to be taken with us, when the Queen gifted me a lungi with blue and green checks and said, "This king rules over seventy-two villages. He is revered by people from seventy-two clans. This is a symbol of the royal family. It indicates that the person who is wearing it is the Guru of the royal family. There are several clans of cannibals ahead. I'm therefore giving you this gift for protection. This gift reflects my feelings for you, so please accept it. With this lungi you'll get help from other settlements ahead. The type and shape of this lungi will identify you to them." It was an ordinary lungi made of thick material, but its weave was different and didn't seem extraordinary to me. But I accepted it to please her.

I said to Gurudev, "He doesn't know me. How will he recognize me?" Gurudev said, "They will know you and recognize you, too. You'll feel good when you go there. Do whatever he asks of you. He will show you the future path of welfare. Listen! The path to man's liberation is in collectivity. This path can't unfold if one doesn't do something for others.

"It is said that man can't achieve liberation without a son. This has a much deeper meaning. Liberation is a matter of soul level. Therefore, this statement is made completely at the soul level. When man is at the physical level, he accepts everything at the physical level. In reality, the true meaning of this is not at the physical level. It means giving birth to a soul, awakening a soul in your lifetime. When one soul gives birth to another soul, then that's his son, isn't he? It's necessary for a soul to be born from another soul. The secret of your spiritual progress is hidden in the number of souls you awaken by becoming a medium. That's why sages and ascetics didn't physically have sons but used to give birth to several sons in the form of souls and achieve liberation. Liberation is a state that man obtains by awakening the souls of human beings. As soon as we become mediums for awakening souls, our soul starts developing."

All the villagers gave me a tearful farewell, and two villagers came right up to the slope of the hill with me. When I bent down to touch Gurudev's feet before leaving, he stopped me and started scolding me, "Hey! You silly boy! Why are you touching my feet? My status is not even equal to your toenails! I just became the medium to bring you here." After saying this, he bid me farewell.

# Episode Two
*With the Third Guru*

I kept mulling over his words. Why had he said that? He was ninety-five years old. He was so old, a great saint who had reached such a high spiritual level, a realized soul. I was an ordinary person, so why did he say that to me? The question that kept coming to my mind was, "Who am I?" It was imperative to find out who I was. His words echoed within me: "Hey! You fool! My status is not even equal to your toenails!"

I wasn't even aware of when I'd finished descending the hill. The two tribals who'd been accompanying me wished me well and returned home. I ate two fruits near a rocky ridge and then decided to rest for the night because I had to climb the hill the next day. The whole area was very new to me. I slowly climbed the small hill and kept climbing for the whole day. Then it was sunset time, and I rested near a big tree. I lit a small fire and slept near it. I was so tired that I fell asleep as soon as I lay down.

The next day, I awoke to the chirping of sparrows. They were assembling to go to a special place. I had also eaten the last of my fruits, so I started looking around the nearby jungle; I saw a few banana trees, but they were in a very inaccessible place, so I would have spent too much time and energy trying to get them. And so, I changed my mind and carried on.

My goal was to reach the hill before nightfall. I would walk, then rest, and then walk again. I got used to the jungle after having lived there for so long. I was in a completely thoughtless state of mind. It was as if I was just walking mechanically. If there was a steep climb, I would rest for some time and then continue walking. It was a bizarre situation. The place where I was going had been identified but was unknown to me. I was going to an unfamiliar place, and at the same time I was trying to understand myself. I was trying to find myself. The words at the time of farewell still echoed in my head. If Gurudev knew everything about me, then why hadn't he said anything about it all that time? And what was the meaning of what he'd said? Did I really possess some unknown energies within myself that he knew about, but I didn't? But I hadn't ever undergone any spiritual practice nor tried to attain any energies! So how did these energies appear? Why did they come, and for what purpose? Why did the energies choose me as their medium? I had no answer. I was so absorbed in these musings that I didn't realize when I'd finished climbing the hill. That night I made a bed between two rocks and slept there.

Rain woke me in the morning. A large cloud had appeared and dashed against the hill, and I was soon drenched. Sunrise had already taken place, but I was enveloped by the cloud and didn't see it clearly. I thought it wiser to wait as one by one the clouds were being pulled towards the hill and soaking me. I couldn't see anything in front of me, so how could I go anywhere? I enjoyed the rain tremendously! After about two or three hours, the rain stopped, and I could now see a little, so I started to descend. When I looked back at the hill behind me, I couldn't see the settlement too clearly, but I could see the smoke rising out of some houses. The jungle was so thick that the village was hidden in it—the village I had left behind, where I'd stayed with my Gurudev—all habitation was hidden from me; all I could see was the smoke rising from the houses. That scene seemed to be telling me: just as the settlement has disappeared and only the smoke is left, one day this body will also come to an end; and what will remain are the karma that one has performed, and only the marks of those deeds will remain. I thought that a man who thirsts for every drop of water doesn't deserve to be bathed by the clouds, and here, in this place, the cloud is bathing me. Actually, if the clouds didn't bathe me that day, I would have gone without a bath. Man doesn't have enough status to be bathed by a cloud. This status belongs to eminence. It's due to his standing that man reached such a height that the clouds bathed him; and that eminence was bestowed on him by the hill. How could I have climbed so high if the hill didn't exist?

I don't know why but I felt that the hill was a form of Gurudev and through his support I had achieved the peak of spirituality. I had reached such a high point that Paramatma's grace in the form of vibrations had rained on me through the clouds. The role of the hill in all this activity was exactly like that of Gurudev. I mentally accepted the hill as my Gurudev and offered namaskar to it and felt the same sense of satisfaction as if I had offered Namaskar to my Gurudev. Again, the same words echoed in my ears: "Hey! You silly boy! Why are you offering Namaskar to me! My status is not even equal to your toenails ..." Then my mind, which had calmed down, once again became imbalanced—why did he say that? His words were creating a disturbance somewhere deep within me. They completely shook me. I hadn't acquired these energies. So, to whom do they belong? What are the energies that made an old sage of ninety-five bow to me? How could he spend so many years having this knowledge about me when he never explained anything like that to me even once?

I would walk all day, rest somewhere at night, and then walk again. On the days when the road was steep, I climbed less. When the road sloped downhill, I covered longer distances. I just kept walking. Day by day I progressed onwards. When I had to climb up, I looked forward to the downward slope, consoling myself that there was only a short distance to climb up after which the road would slope downhill again over a longer distance.

It seemed as if all this going up and downhill was a reflection of man's life. Man has good and bad days in his life. On the good days it appears that time passes at the same speed. The hands on the clock move at the same speed. However, on good days, man doesn't look at the clock very often, and when he does, he finds that time has flown by. The good times in one's life always pass quickly, as if time has grown wings. No matter how good the moment is in a person's life, and no matter how much he loves that moment, he can't hold on to it. Neither a king nor a pauper can hold on to it. Time has its own momentum, and it proceeds at that speed. Time also appears to be like Paramatma. It deals equally with everyone like Paramatma. It never discriminates between anyone. Time never stops; it keeps moving forward. Time has only one quality: continuously moving forward! No one has been able to catch it, nor will they ever be able to. No matter how many moments a person experiences in his life, not a single moment can be caught and be held, as if time is saying that even golden moments are an illusion. You think that these are golden moments, but there are actually none. No moment is either golden or bad. Man considers the moment to be good or bad depending on his state of mind, and it is his own thinking that makes it so. Every moment is a fixed moment in itself. It is neither golden nor bad. A moment is just a moment!

When a person is going through bad times in life, a moment seems like an hour and an hour like a day. Man's attention keeps returning again and again to the time of the bad moments of his life. Man keeps thinking: why isn't time moving more quickly?

Sometimes a person gets so angry with the clock that he feels like hanging on its hands and moving time forward on his own. Time appears to come to a standstill and just doesn't seem to budge. It's very difficult to pass through bad times. However, this bad period doesn't last, it moves on. Thus, nothing is in a person's hands. Neither can he imprison and hold on to golden moments, nor has he been able to push forward the bad moments. He can't do either. Man himself decides on the definition of every moment. It is he who defines that this is a good moment or a bad moment. Thus, the moment is not good or bad in itself. It all depends on the person's belief—how he lives his life. If he lives at the physical level, then the moments may seem good, or they can appear bad. The moments he considers to be good, he may consider them to be bad, too. Generally, there are fewer good moments in a man's life and more of bad. Thus, there are only losses in life if one keeps living at just the physical level.

Now it's necessary for man to rise above those moments and live at the soul level. He should stand apart from the moment and observe it. Then he'll realize that no moment is good or bad. All moments are equal. Life is also momentary. It is neither good nor bad, it just moves on. That is why no person's life is completely good or bad. Both good and bad are interwoven with a person's life; some more, some less. When there is a deficiency in one's life, then one has to pay for it with the surplus within oneself. Thus, one can say that plus and minus are always present. Whatever is 'minus' today will become 'plus' tomorrow, but what is 'plus' today will become 'minus' tomorrow. This means that today, too, we aren't completely plus, and neither will we be tomorrow. The situation will always remain the same, and therefore man will have to rise above these situations. Man can do this and will be able to keep himself safe only if he has the feeling that 'I am a soul'. Observe all moments in life. If it's a good moment, observe it; if it's a bad moment, observe it! Don't get attached to any moment thinking that this is a golden moment, or this is a sorrowful moment. Don't scrutinize that moment to see whether it's good or bad, just move on! I, too, had moved forward quite a lot while on the hill. This hill had explained the secret of man's life to me. I decided to observe myself, too. Gurudev told me that energies exist within me, and I know that I haven't acquired them. This means that it is someone else's legacy, and I'm only a porter carrying these energies.

I could see a lot of brightness on the opposite hill, and I didn't know why, but I also experienced a lot of brightness within me on seeing that radiance. I remembered that Shiv Baba had said, "I'm entrusting to you all my energies. I have handed over everything I possess to you." I hadn't understood at the time what he had entrusted to me, but Gurudev's statement reminded me of what he'd said. I don't know why but I felt as if I had been made the leader of some activity that was about to happen, something that was going to take place in the future. I didn't know what was going to happen. I also decided not to think about the future. Whatever happened in the future would be seen then. Now, today, I will live for the moment.

The days passed; morning followed night every day. But my journey went on and on. The only ray of hope was the river that Gurudev had pointed out to me, which was now visible like a shining line. Its water was also shining, and this indicated that now I was moving towards the bank of the river, which seemed to be quite near. Distances are quite short in hilly areas, but a lot of time is spent in climbing up and down the hills. Thus, it takes two to three days to go from one hill to another. Actually, the hill seems to be right in front, but even that can't be reached easily.

There were a lot of thick jungles on the way and there was always the lurking danger of disorientation and losing one's way. While crossing the jungle, if one went towards the hill in the front, then it was all right; otherwise one could go in the wrong direction. There are jungles of fir trees. These are the trees that are nicely decorated and displayed in the cities, and they were spread out here like a jungle. One had to cut the trees to make a path. There were large plantations of banana trees; there were also jungles of bay leaves that are used as spices. The tribal people here used to take a bunch of these leaves and hang them in their kitchen and whenever required they would just break them off and use them. The various food items they prepared were very tasty because of the bay leaves. The special quality of trees in this area was that there were fewer thick or wide trees—all the trees were very tall. There appeared to be some connection between the height of trees and the gravitational force—that wherever there was increased gravitation, the trees were shorter, and where there was less gravitation, the trees were thinner but taller. Perhaps the soil there wasn't very deep and therefore didn't have much grip.

Secondly, there were lots of creepers; there was hardly a tree without creepers. There were lots of creepers growing on every tree, but flowers would grow on only one or two of them. The creepers were very thick and only had leaves growing on them; generally, all the trees would be covered with them. The whole place was so quiet that even if one stepped on a dry leaf it made a loud sound. Water flowed out of the hills in several places and created small streams. Water was no problem as there was water everywhere. Then at one place I saw a plantation of wild bananas. I stopped there and bowed before the banana tree and prayed, "Oh, Tree-King, I am hungry so I'm asking you to give me alms of two bananas. Please give me two bananas." And with this prayer I picked two bananas. My Gurudev had taught me this, that every tree develops with great difficulty, and we don't have a right over the fruits of the mature tree. This doesn't fall under any authority in the jungle, nor does anyone take care of the trees. Thus, there is no caretaker for the trees. That's why we should only eat the fruits with permission from the trees themselves.

When a small seed falls on the ground, it feels happy that it has found a place to develop, and it considers its life to be blessed. As soon as it falls, the seed lies on the ground and starts dreaming—I'll really develop in my life; I, too, will grow into a big tree! It thinks in this way the moment it reaches the ground. These sentiments are crushed when some small stones fall on it during a storm; stones which have tumbled down the hill and have fallen on it accidentally. The seed has no idea about these stones. In the seed's dreams about its future there are no stones and neither has it thought about them. The seed is firstly startled by the stones that have suddenly landed on it. It is frightened. Its future appears to be full of darkness. The seed is very small and the stones which have fallen on it are very large. The seed gets buried under the weight of those stones and thinks—what has happened? Can something bad like this happen in one's life? I had never thought that something like this could happen. What do I do now? Everything turns dark before its eyes and its life is filled with sorrow. It starts thinking—maybe this is the end of my life. Now my life is over. I'm so small and these stones are so big! Even if I want to move them, how can I? I'll never be able to move them, they are so heavy. What have I done to them! Why did they have to fall on me? I'm so small and they are so big. Didn't they even feel ashamed of falling on such a small seed? Shameless stones! They're laughing at me! They have crushed me and are laughing at me. They're making fun of me and saying: Weren't you dreaming of being a big tree? Go on, show us how you can turn into a big tree! Dreaming of becoming a big tree!!! Look at your shape and size first.

The poor seed is small. It listens to whatever the stones say to him. The stones keep teasing it and there's nothing it can do. First of all, it is alone and small, and these stones are large and in such numbers that nothing can be done about it. This is my destiny (it thinks) and this is my end; thinking this, the poor seed lies there quietly. What is to be done? There is no clear way out of this. Now, perhaps, I'll never be able to grow into a tree in my life. Thus, the poor seed kept on thinking. Then after lying quietly for some time, it had a thought: there are so many trees around here; they, too, must have faced problems in their lives. They, too, must have been small seeds at some time, and stones must have fallen on them as well. So, how did they stay alive? I can at least take guidance from them.

Suddenly the seed's glance fell upon a big tree that was swaying majestically. It was a very heavy tree, and so huge that these stones were nothing at all in comparison. The seed decided that this was an ideal tree. "I'll make this tree my Guru and ask how it could develop so well. Stones must have fallen on it in its life, too, when it was a seed. What did it do then?" Now the problem was that the seed was so small and that tree was touching the sky! How could it talk to such a big tree? How could a dialogue be established with such an enormous tree? The seed thought, "What I have to say can never reach the tree because it's so big. I'm so small that I'll never be able to talk to it. What do I do? I am small, and this tree is large, and there's a big difference in our sizes. There can't be any dialogue between us based on our sizes. That's why the dialogue shouldn't be at this level. First, I should think about why I decided to take guidance from this tree. I took this decision because I am a seed, and this tree was once a seed. This is the only similarity between us. This is the only relationship between us. We were once both seeds. Now I'll have to understand from the tree's seed-element how it managed to develop—I had just looked at it and thought of developing myself when the stones fell upon me."

Then the seed contacted the seed of the tree that was still lying at ground level. This seed could easily reach the other because both were in the ground. No matter how big the tree had grown, its seed was still in the ground, though it had transformed into roots. That is why, as soon as the little seed prayed to the seed of the neighbouring tree, the seed of that huge tree came to meet the little seed in the form of a root. Then this little seed prayed to the seed of that big tree, "I, too, wish to grow big like you, but what can I do? All these big stones have fallen on me." The seed of the neighbouring tree came in the form of roots and gave the message saying, "There is only one difference between you and me. You are calling yourself a seed. End your ego of 'I am a seed' and finish with this 'I' sense. I surrendered myself completely to Paramatma and then the 'I' sense ended, and I wasn't a seed anymore and became a tree. You should also bring your ego of being a seed to an end and you'll also grow into a tree." Then the little seed said, "I accept that. I will also surrender it to Paramatma, but what about these stones? They are the problem in my life!" The big tree said, "These stones are also the problem of a little seed. Once you become a tree, this problem will go away. Look! I'm such a big tree and these small stones are tiny in front of me!" The little seed replied, "But I'm so small and these stones are so big. How will I be able to move them?" The roots of the big tree said, "Surrender yourself completely to Paramatma. Give up your ego of being a seed. It is the ego of being a seed that is giving you the feeling of being small. The moment you give up that ego, the road ahead will automatically open up."

The little seed accepted what the big tree had to say and relinquished its 'I' sense (of being a seed), and a strange incident took place. The seed was destroyed, and out of it a sprout was born. The sprout was fully immersed in Paramatma and started moving towards him. There were many stones in its path but the sprout's whole attention was on Paramatma, and it didn't pay any attention to those stones and went on making its way around them and slowly started developing. Then one day it grew into a big tree and the stones lying on the path remained as they were! When I saw all this in nature, I realized that I should consider the seed as my Guru. I had a darshan of Gurudev in the seed, as if Gurudev was guiding me in the form of the seed.

※

Night was approaching, it was getting dark, and there was a chance that I would lose my way. I therefore decided to take rest. Now the water in the river shone even at night, and this indicated that I had reached the bank of the river. Again, I decided to rest for the night in the shadow of the same rock. When I woke up in the morning, I found that I had actually reached the river. When I turned and looked back at the hill, it appeared far away. What a long distance I had travelled from the hill where I had started my journey! As I was in Gurudev's proximity on this long journey, I was unaware of how I crossed hills, where I slept at night or what problems I'd encountered! I didn't realize anything! Man's journey through life is similar. If one observes man's journey in general, one finds that he journeys alone in the form of a soul, all other people just accompany him. The people who are with him are present because of the relationship with the body. Some are together because of friendship, and one becomes close to some souls because of their previous birth. Also, some are together because of their relationship in their previous birth.

If one looks at it from the point of view of the age of one's body, then man spends the maximum time with his wife, because he can't spend his whole life with his parents owing to the generation gap. One spends time later with one's children because they are the future generation. But man's biggest companion is his wife. The success of man's whole life depends on this companionship. The secret of man's success or failure in life is hidden in this association, and the wife's company is also of importance in a man's life, because man has a close relationship with his wife at the physical level, too. There is also a special emotional relationship with his wife because of that internal relationship. There is a special love, too, and man achieves success or failure because of that love. Whether man gets success in his life or not depends on this relationship. The relationship between a husband and his wife is like a U-tube that is found in a laboratory. This means that if you pour hundred grams of water at one end of the U-tube, fifty grams will automatically go to the other end. One doesn't have to put it there; it goes there on its own. Just as the U-tube has separate ends on the outside but is joined at the bottom, similarly, the husband and wife, despite having two separate bodies, are one because of their physical relationship.

Now if you absorb some spiritual energies through your spiritual practice, then half of your energies will automatically go to your wife, and you won't be able to progress as long as she doesn't progress. Thus, both make progress spiritually together. That's why no man in this world can have a better friend than his wife or a greater enemy than his wife. Every man has to undertake a long journey in life with his wife. That's why a husband and wife are called life partners. As it is usually seen that this close relationship is not the same throughout one's life. It may be closer or more distanced depending on the time, but it always remains. For example, when a man gets married, the attraction for his wife is strong, and this is natural because he establishes an intimate relationship with his wife. Then it is natural that an emotional relationship will also be established. This close relationship is very intimate for the first ten to fifteen years, and after that the man doesn't get divided, but the woman is apportioned. The woman starts paying more attention to her children rather than the husband. On the other hand, the man is not as involved with the children as his wife is.

The man remains busy in his job or in his profession, and he is involved with his work in the interim ten to fifteen years. The distance between the man and his wife grows. Later the children grow up, they get married and start their own domestic life and, then again, the man comes closer to his wife. Now when he comes closer, it isn't because of physical attraction but due to the emotional attraction, because the man realizes that during the wide gap in their relationship, an emotional bond had developed. Then what is left is the old man for the old woman and the old woman for the old man. Both of them establish one unified world, and it has been seen that the wife once again has to take on the mother's role, and this time her old man becomes her child. Thus, it appears that a woman is a lover for a short time and a mother for a lifetime. Then in old age the husband and wife become very close to each other because again both the relationships come together. This is similar to a circle that is joined at the upper end and also joined at the lower end. It is only the middle portion where there is distance. That's why in a man's life his greatest companion is his wife, and I also feel that it is because of my wife's co-operation that I have been able to reach this stage, because if she had harboured negative sentiments against me, then problems would have arisen in my spiritual practice. It was good for me that she didn't oppose anything.

A man doesn't know how his life passes. We continually absorb energy from the place where our attention goes; it doesn't matter where we are present physically. It is our state of mind that makes us aware of happiness and sorrow; it creates an illusion. Once you go beyond that, there's neither happiness nor sorrow. We have one delusion that is not permanent. We are aware of happiness and sorrow depending on our level. Happiness and sorrow are present at the physical level and also at the soul level. We can obtain physical happiness through material things. But the material items also have a limit. They can't give happiness beyond a certain limit. Thus, to attain more happiness, we should use these articles only for distribution to others. For example, a man has hundred sweaters. If you present that person with another sweater, he won't be any happier with the extra one. He will take it and keep it with the hundred other sweaters. If he wants to have more happiness then he'll have to give the sweater to someone who needs it and who doesn't have a single sweater, and by doing so, he can be happy. This shows that, to be happier, we have to depend on someone else.

"Service is happiness of the soul." Provided there is no exhibition of the service, one finds a lot of inner happiness by serving others. This need to serve others is the pure emotion of one's pure soul, but one should take care that this act of service to others is not done to impress others; otherwise, it will increase one's ego, and that will be fatal. That's why a lot of importance is given to donation in every religion. If you attain inner joy by donating to others, your soul becomes stronger, and if your soul becomes stronger, you'll progress spiritually. Therefore, service is also a tool for spiritual progress. People offer service but don't understand its meaning. Service is not something to be done just at the physical level, but is also yogic food for the soul.

In order to understand all this, one really needs a suitable Guru. I thank Paramatma that he gave me such a Guru, through whom I could imbibe all this knowledge.

There are several languages that are not prevalent today because their written script is not in existence. These were spoken languages, and once the speakers passed away, the languages, too, passed away with them. There are some languages prevalent today that are spoken but don't have a written script. These languages are passed on and taught from one generation to another, and the medium for teaching them is only a living person because the language does not exist in a lifeless book. This language is called a living language because its mediums are living beings. Similarly, lifeless knowledge can be obtained through lifeless books. From a lifeless book one can understand what a cow looks like. One can see its picture and read the description, but fresh cow's milk can only be obtained from a living cow.

Lifeless books can give all knowledge except the knowledge of a live experience. A spiritual experience is a living process, which is why a lifeless book can't give it. Yes, one can become arrogant by reading too many books, and then the person will want to gain all knowledge only from books, because he can't imagine that there can be any knowledge beyond books. That's why such intellectual individuals want to meditate, as they have already analysed the benefits of meditation through their intellect. They want to meditate but they don't want a Satguru. That is, they want milk but they don't want the cow. They have no awareness of living knowledge, and that is why they fail to understand that when meditation is a living technique it is but natural that there will be a living Guru. The technique of living meditation is based on spiritual experience, and this living spiritual experience has also been carried forward like a living language from one living medium to another. This technique can't be found written in any book.

With all these thoughts I didn't realize when I had reached the riverbank. The water was flowing swiftly. This river was coming from the Himalayas, so the water was very cold but also very clean. Stones rolled around in it and became smooth and rounded. The water there wasn't very deep; it was a small river, but a good one. I sat on the bank of the river, dangling my feet while sitting on a rock, and I felt refreshed. All my tiredness disappeared, and my aching feet were also relieved. There were tiny fish in the water that had reached there in the current, and they fearlessly came up to me. When I went into the water to bathe, so many fish gathered around me that I feared some fish would get crushed under my feet. I had never seen so many fish so close to my body.

I came out of the water after my bath and sat near the fire I'd lit under the overhang of a rock. Then I slept for the night. I woke up in the morning and had a bath. When I came out of the water, I saw that a lot of crabs had gathered there. Generally, they live hidden under the rocks. I decided to resume climbing, and as I slowly started to climb, I suddenly reached a state of thoughtlessness. The energy within me increased, and before I knew it I had already climbed the hill. Just before reaching the summit, I saw a small hillock, and my new Gurudev's hut was sheltered in it.

The hut was quite big, and there was a place for performing the havan quite close to it. The place for performing the fire ceremony was also housed in a small hut. There was a third hut where firewood, fuel for the fire ceremony, herbs and other materials were stored. All three huts faced the east. They faced the east to the front and west to the back. There was a raised platform at the back. It was almost evening when I reached there, and the sun was about to set. Gurudev was performing a fire ceremony in the 'fire ceremony' hut. I waited outside, and after completing the ceremony he came towards me. I saw that he was of medium height and appeared quite old, but his body was full of radiance. He had tied his hair at the back, and he had very sharp, piercing eyes.

As soon as Gurudev came close to me I respectfully prostrated before him, and he said to me, "Come, first have a bath. There's a tank over there." He pointed towards a small pool that I hadn't noticed. I went to the pool, left my shoulder-bag there and bathed in it, thinking that this water must have come from the same hillock, when I noticed a small piece of bamboo. This piece had been pushed into the hill, and the hill-water was flowing out as if from a tap and flowing into the pool. Later, Gurudev gave me some fruits to eat, and made room for me to stay in the hut near the fire ceremony hut where the firewood was kept. That hut also was quite small. Gurudev said to me, "Take rest. You have travelled a long distance, and you must be tired. Now you must take some rest." I prepared a bed in the hut with some dry grass and went to sleep. I don't know when I fell asleep. My feet were aching very badly and I was very tired, so I slept.

I woke up in the morning to the sound of birds chirping in the ashram. The sun was about to rise in a reddening sky, and I could see the river before me. Just as I had seen the previous day, the sun was about to rise on the hill across the river. It was a beautiful scene. Gurudev was meditating in his hut. I got up, swept the whole ashram, cleaned it, and then went for my bath. By the time I returned, the sun had already risen, and Gurudev was busy preparing for the yagya. His ceremonies and other activities went on for some time. I watched everything from outside. Gurudev had a vast knowledge of mantras, and he chanted them in a clear, sweet voice. After completing the fire ceremony, he sat in the same room with me. There was an altar for performing the ceremony, which appeared to be built with mud and stones, but was quite nice and big.

Gurudev asked me, "I hope you didn't have any problems getting here." I said, "No." Then he said, "I know your Gurudev quite well. When he told me about you, I felt that I should call you here. We have never met physically, but at the aatmic (soul) level we follow the same path. Similarly, I have never met your Gurudev physically, but we have connected with each other through our minds. Meditation is a spiritual practice that has to be perfected through continual study, and one shouldn't desire anything while practising it. The spiritual practice should be undertaken in its purest form because impure spiritual practice won't lead to completion.

"The spiritual practice of meditation is similar to an art. An artist is a person who reaches a high state of thoughtlessness through the medium of art; the state of thoughtlessness through which one can reach Paramatma. Art is present in every human being through the grace of Paramatma. Art can't originate without his grace. That's why you'll find every artist close to Paramatma. It may be any form of art—singing, playing musical instruments, sketching, sculpture—all artists are special mediums of Paramatma. They are not tied down by any race, religion, language or colour. They are only mediums of Paramatma, and He bestows all these special qualities in every human in some form or the other. Some people may be able to raise it while others may not, and those who are able to do so are the blessed ones. That's why these artists are completely surrendered to their art. When someone surrenders through the medium of his art, he can easily reach Paramatma. For an artist his art is everything. Every human loves his own life more than anything else, but an artist loves his art more than his life. Every artist has the desire that his art should remain alive, and the artist always lives for his art.

"Every artist wishes that his art should remain alive even after his lifetime. He loves his art more than his life. Generally, every artist, during his lifetime, practises his art and passes on the legacy of the art he has acquired through continual practice to some deserving suitable disciple, and only then can he die peacefully. Otherwise, there are several artists who can't find peace even after death because they did not find anybody who loved their art. The dissatisfied artist's soul wanders around in the form of a spirit. As long as their art doesn't develop further, such artists remain in the form of spirits for several years, and they keep on wandering in that form. Only an artist can give liberation to another artist. That's why every artist makes sure that he passes on his legacy to someone before he passes away. He is not obliging anyone by passing on his legacy, he is opening the path for his own liberation by creating a path for his art's future. Today also the spirits of many artists are wandering around in the form of ghosts. For as long as they don't find a suitable disciple, they will keep wandering. The full attention of these ghosts is on their art, and without taking their art forward they neither want to take a birth again, nor do they wish to achieve liberation. They are stuck because of their art. Every true artist desires his art to remain alive, whether he lives or not, because an artist loves his art more than life.

"An artist is a unique creation of Paramatma. An artist can bring joy and happiness to several souls through his art. An audience can be spellbound after listening to a singer or instrumental music being played. He forgets himself and reaches a thoughtless state. This isn't possible without the special grace of Paramatma. An artist is created under special conditions. When an artist develops the art which he has obtained from his Guru, he takes it forward, and then bestows it on some suitable disciple before the end of his life—it is called Guru-dakshina, an honorarium or offering to his Guru. When you pass on to your disciple whatever you have obtained from your Guru in his name, that is Guru-dakshina in the real sense. Liberation is not possible without offering repayment to the Guru, as otherwise the soul keeps wandering as it owes a debt to the Guru. Every artist is impelled to give an offering of repayment to his Guru. The offering of repayment is always at the inner soul level. When the Guru has handed over everything that he possesses to you, then you should also hand over everything of yours to him. What your Guru gives you is Guru-krupa and what you hand over to him as repayment of the debt is Guru-dakshina. One's life exists between Guru-krupa and offering Guru-dakshina. In society, people think that an offering to the Guru-dakshina means money. Actually, it is not an offering of money. Money is a medium for one's feelings. It is only a way for the disciple to express his emotions.

"The death of art is the death of an artist. If art is alive in an artist, then he is alive; otherwise, the death of art is like his own death. A true artist will prefer to die, but he'll never allow his art to die. Art is Paramatma's grace. That's why one has to become a soul to receive it. A disciple has to become a soul, and only after establishing contact with his Guru's soul will he be able to gain Paramatma's grace for the art. When an artist accepts his Guru as his 'Guru,' that is when he bows before his Guru with the reverent feeling that he is Paramatma, and only then will be able to receive the art that is lying in a dormant form in his Guru. Then, if the Guru wants to give or not to give his knowledge, it is not in the Guru's control. We have the story of Dronacharya and Eklavya as an example before us. If you think of the Guru as an ordinary person, then he'll give you all ordinary knowledge at the physical level; if an artist thinks of the Guru as a normal person, he can never obtain his Guru's knowledge, which has made him famous all over the world. In order to obtain the basic elements of knowledge, one will have to accept the Guru as Paramatma, and only then will he be able to obtain the art that he has acquired through his grace. It makes no difference to the Guru whether you accept him as Paramatma or as a human being—it is we who are affected.

"Thus, first of all, the feeling that we have attained Paramatma gives us satisfaction, and this feeling of satisfaction increases our capacity to absorb. It completely opens up our capacity to absorb. That's why we see a feeling of deep reverence in all great artists towards their Guru. Artists have developed their art and grown because of this feeling towards their Guru, by perceiving him to be Paramatma. Art is always a special grace of Paramatma. It can only be acquired through Him. That's why every artist should consider his Guru to be Paramatma, and only then can his grace be obtained. Just as art is a grace of Paramatma, similarly, the spiritual practice of meditation is also an art. For as long as this art is not handed over to someone as an offering of repayment to the Guru, I, too, can't achieve liberation. That is why I needed you and was searching for you. Now I can pass on the legacy of the 'spiritual practice of meditation to you,' and I wish to open up my path for liberation. Your Gurudev has helped me a lot by placing you in my care."

I didn't realize how much time had passed, and the sun was about to set. It was again time for Gurudev's fire ceremony, and Gurudev started preparing for it. I sat there motionless, like a statue. I could see everything, but I was not able to move.

The discussion that took place with Gurudev the previous day made me suddenly realize that only living knowledge is the knowledge of spiritual experience, and this is the only true knowledge. "This knowledge can't be bought because it has been acquired through the grace of Paramatma, and one can't attain his grace through one's own efforts. Thus, it can neither be bought nor paid for. It is always free, and to find this living knowledge is to attain his grace, and distributing this living knowledge is an offering of repayment to the Guru in the right sense of the term. The 'spiritual practice of meditation' is also a type of art which can be acquired spontaneously. Paramatma's grace can never be obtained through one's efforts. One can only obtain it when He showers his compassion, and one must be suitable at the inner soul level to become a suitable receiver. One can't be a suitable soul, nor can one attain purity of the soul through one's efforts, as this effort will only be at the physical level, and Paramatma's grace is not possible through efforts at the physical level. Paramatma's grace is divine energy. This will come to you only if your soul is worthy of it.

"Several sadhaks take up Guru-karya to make their souls worthy while undergoing spiritual practice, but they do so only at the physical level. Guru-karya is work carried out at the physical level, but the purpose of doing so is actually the purification of one's soul. One should only perform Guru-karya after understanding its deeper meaning. Work that is taken up only at the physical level can never be Guru-karya. That is why Guru-karya should happen at the physical level but should be experienced at the soul level. Work that takes place at the physical level, but with a complete feeling of surrender at the soul level, becomes work at the soul level. Several people undertake work for the Guru, but they still don't understand the meaning of it. First of all, spiritual work is that work which is performed through one's soul for the soul; and the task which is performed through one's soul is the best work. That's why Guru-karya is that which should be the best because we perform the task with full feeling and emotions and with full concentration. Secondly, this work shouldn't be done in order to show off to someone, because showing off is related to one's ego, and the ego is a fault of the physical body.

"Guru-karya should be undertaken quietly because it can lead to negative results if one performs it in order to show off. First of all, it leads to the creation of one's ego, and secondly, we lose an important chance to develop at the soul level. Thus, when one makes a show of one's spiritual work, it harms a person in two ways. We can therefore understand that the body is only a medium or is symbolic for performing Guru-karya. The sadhak can progress in his 'spiritual practice of meditation' through this path, too. Guru-karya should only be performed with a complete feeling of surrender. When one does spiritual work, one purifies the soul, and as the soul gets purified it becomes stronger. A strong soul becomes worthy of Guru-krupa, and when a soul becomes worthy, then the Guru's blessings are showered upon him. The worthiness of the soul is related to the showering of Guru-krupa. That is why a sadhak who undertakes spiritual practice should be a worthy person."

I didn't have much information about that ashram, and Gurudev generally performed his own tasks because he knew where everything was kept; and that was why I did the work of sweeping and watering the plants at the ashram. I used to go to the nearby jungles and get firewood, pick and pull out herbs; and while performing these tasks I felt that I was serving my Guru. His hut was surrounded by a big, thick jungle, and one couldn't even see it until one was quite close to it. The hut was situated on a slope close to the main peak of the hill.

Gurudev's daily routine was quite ordinary, but he was fully occupied with it. He continually looked at the sky every day for a long time, and as he looked at the sky he would say, "I get darshan of my Gurudev in the sky, and he keeps sending me messages. Secondly, the sky is not perishable; that's why when one looks at the sky one's mind is purified and becomes holy. That's why I keep looking regularly at the sky, which enables me to connect with my Guru. The sky is an enormous element, and when a person looks at the sky, his chitta gains enormity. If we keep the extent of our attention narrow, it becomes contracted. If we place it to a wider circle, then it will also widen. The expanse of the sky is vast, and I keep my chitta in the circle of the sky so that it should stay vast. The wider our chitta, the greater is our capacity of absorption. That's why a Guru with a developed chitta can talk about great things. His chitta is great because he has kept his chitta on the presence of greatness."

Gurudev used to gaze at the sky both in the morning and in the evening. He did this in the morning after sunrise and in the evening before sunset. He spoke very sweetly, and his pronunciation was very clear, as if he was a great scholar of Sanskrit. When he was performing the fire ceremony and chanting the mantras, I liked it very much. I wanted him to keep on chanting so that I could keep listening to him. He chanted the mantra from deep inside, and it seemed as if the sound was coming from the sky.

※

That day, I again asked Gurudev, "Gurudev, I have heard several people enunciating mantras and chanting them, but when you chant them I like it very much. I have heard the same mantras chanted by other people, too. Why is there so much difference when the mantras are similar?"

Gurudev replied, "Mantras have their own special knowledge. No mantra is just a particular collection of words. It is important who gave the mantra and what feeling it was given with. Imagine that a mantra is like clear water, which has its own special qualities and special properties. The clear water takes on the colour that is added to it and makes it powerful. The colour merges with its own identity, and then encourages the colour to manifest itself. Similarly, the mantra brings out the emotions and is filled with emotion. It represents the feelings with which the mantra is chanted. That's why there is a tradition of accepting the Guru-Mantra from the Guru in person. The Guru gives the mantra to his disciple with a feeling of complete surrender, and the disciple experiences the same feeling of surrender with which the Guru has given it to him. We understand that the mantra is a strong medium for expressing one's feelings. The disciple should be able to accept the Guru Mantra with the same feeling with which it is given, because it's very important for the disciple to accept it with the same level of emotion. One's feelings are very important in a mantra. A clear rhythm and a clear pronunciation also prove very helpful in making the mantra effective.

"There are some mantras that, when chanted, start producing a circuit of energy around the person chanting them. The shape of the circuits in their aura slowly starts changing, and it slowly gets established in a larger area, and whoever comes close to that area is affected by the mantra. The mantra that I was chanting just now was a similar type. The words of the mantra are only a medium, but they are important. The mantra will be effective depending on how much feeling you bring to it while chanting. Each mantra is created by some energy. Mantras are a medium of energy. If the mantra is chanted only at the physical level to make a show, then the effect of the mantra will only be at the physical level. In reality, every mantra is a blessing from Paramatma, which is obtained by man through the Guru-krupa. This means that it can't be obtained through one's efforts. Whatever is obtained through one's efforts can't be Paramatma's blessing because a blessing or prasad is only available through his grace. Similarly, the gift of energies that one has obtained through the mantra should be absorbed with great humility and a feeling of total surrender. Your power to absorb will depend on your feelings of surrender. The sound that has been created through the chanting of some mantras remains present in the atmosphere for several years. Whenever it comes across a person who can absorb the sound, it materializes; so that is why a mantra is given great importance in one's spiritual journey.

"The mantra becomes more effective when chanted close to the fire at the fire ceremony. It is the special quality of fire that it purifies the atmosphere and helps man to reach a thoughtless state, and the light that comes out of the fire spreads the power of mantra. That's why the mantras chanted in a specific yagya-shala are more powerful. The fire ceremony destroys man's negative thoughts and bestows positive thoughts on him. A person who is filled with positive feelings is more successful in life. In this way a person who is positive is also successful in his spiritual life. The ceremony that is performed in the morning is for absorbing energies. At sunrise all the energies in the atmosphere rise upwards. That's why the fire ceremony that is performed in their proximity bestows energy on us, and the ceremony that is performed before sunset is meant to make the atmosphere pure and holy before nightfall, so that we can be saved from negative feelings in the atmosphere at night. The effect of negativity prevails more at night than during the day, which is why the evening fire ceremony is performed before sunset to save oneself from negative feelings. This creates a positive atmosphere even after sunset. Fire relates to our thoughts and man gets more thoughts when the fire element decreases. Man shouldn't get any thoughts while worshipping Paramatma, and that is why in every practice of worship, fire is present in some form or the other. Even after a person's death, great importance is given to fire in the practice of cremation.

"The final rites are performed on a person after his death so that his soul may be liberated from the attractions of the physical body, and so fire is used to burn the body. Man's physical body is created through the five elements in which the fire element is also present, and this plays an important part in the human body." Gurudev would put the ashes that came out of the sacred fire of the fire ceremony into the plants, and because of that the plants would receive a lot of energy. This was why there were such beautiful flowers in his ashram. He was very quiet and did all the work very quietly. He said, "Why should I be in a hurry when I'm doing all this spiritual work? I'm doing all this work at the soul level, and I don't bring it to the physical level by doing it very fast. I do all the work peacefully and with complete feeling." I really found this very lovely, and I also learnt how to do my Guru-karya like him in a proper way. I was actually enjoying the work very much.

At the ashram, I didn't realize when it was dawn or when it was evening. One morning, after the fire ceremony, Gurudev started telling me about nature. He said, "There are no thoughts in nature; thoughts are unnatural. That's why, while practising meditation, man always wants to be close to nature. Whenever we go near nature, we realize that our thoughts have stopped. Thoughts are a creation of our body and therefore, because our body is perishable, the thoughts that are created by the body are also perishable. Nature has its own special cycle, and all nature is connected to this cycle. As the wheel of nature goes around, the natural atmosphere is created within it and also destroyed. Creation and destruction continue to take place within nature. Destruction is also a transformation that allows for creation. Both the states are connected to nature. In order for man to know himself, it is necessary for him to understand this mystery of nature. Nature also has its own musical sound, and one needs to know that sound, one has to listen to it. Once one starts hearing it then the same sound also starts playing inside. When your chitta is turned within, that sound can be heard. That sound is called Brahmanaad. This is the sound of the energy that moves nature. When we are connected to this celestial music, we are in a completely natural form. When we are in a secluded place, we can hear this sound within ourselves. This sound is similar to the sound one hears when one puts one's ear close to an empty metal pipe. It is the same kind of sound.

※

"It is the basic quality of nature to be connected to the natural cycle. We can call this the religion or dharma of nature. When someone was connected with the religion of nature and narrated his experiences to others, then that became a religion for society. But the basic foundation of all these religions is the religion of nature, and all religions have started from this religion of nature. Creation and destruction keep taking place within this natural cycle, and destruction is also a process of creation. External religions were created from the religion of nature, and now they'll also be destroyed. All created religions will end and then finally only one religion will remain, which is the religion of nature, man's own dharma of nature that is inner religion: Atma-dharma.

"In future, only one's inner dharma will be everlasting; that will be the only religion—the religion that man is born into. With each birth, the inner religion is with him. That inner religion never changes. It is permanent. The external religion is not constant. It doesn't last. With every birth, the external religion is different. Actually, these are not religions at all but methods of worship, and man through his ignorance thinks they are religions. There is only one dharma, and that is inner religion, and this always stays with man. One can discover one's inner religion through self-knowledge. All the religions have manifested from this inner dharma. And now all religions will dissolve into this inner religion. The process that is going on at present is not destruction. It is the creation of inner religion. That's why man should obtain self-knowledge and get to know his inner religion. The saints who attain self-knowledge and realize their inner dharma talk only about the inner dharma. They never talk about external religions, nor do they give importance to external religions. Why should one give importance to external religions that keep changing with every birth? That's why people who have reached the spiritual level speak only about inner dharma. I'm not talking about some new religion. I'm talking about the inner dharma that is always present with man in every birth. The religion of one's soul is only inner religion. For as long as this inner religion is not awakened, spiritual progress cannot take place. You may change any number of religions at the external level—all are illusions! Does religion change by changing one's method of worship? There is only one religion—inner religion. And if one says it in simple words—the religion of humanity. Every man is first and foremost a human being, and then he becomes an individual who follows a particular way of worship.

"External religions change with each birth. It is only the human religion that stays with man in every birth. That's why the religion of humanity is the only natural religion. Only this religion is eternal, and saints who have acquired self-knowledge only talk about the religion of humanity. The inner religion is always present even with an individual who doesn't believe in any external religions or any method of worship. You may give up your life, but you can't give up your inner religion. That is permanent. That is the only one. You can neither change it nor leave it. That religion is eternal. It will always remain. People who have acquired self-knowledge continue to awaken that inner religion inside. The person in whom the sun of inner religion rises, the light of knowledge is lit within the person. That's why Saint Gnyaneshwar, in his lifetime, prayed that the sun of inner religion should arise in every human being, and that every man's inner religion should awaken. The time that he spoke about, that right time is approaching now. Due to this right time, it has been possible for you to get to this stage, since I, too, have gone through several births, and you have also been wandering for the last 800 years. We have never met before, but this meeting itself was the end of all this, and it has happened in this lifetime. It is man's nature to immediately hold on to weaker things. One needs patience to propagate self-knowledge; one has to be patient in everything because self-knowledge is inner knowledge.

"For as long as man doesn't introspect, he won't be able to understand anything. Man takes time to introspect, and when he doesn't go within, he wont't be able to understand what you say. Therefore, a lot of patience is needed to make this knowledge understood. If we want to be patient, we will have to give up our expectations. It is these expectations that destroy our patience. If we work without expectations, only then can we keep our patience while working. Patience comes automatically if we execute each task by going in-depth."

After sunset, Gurudev would ask me to sit with a calm mind and study the sky. One day, he said, "First of all, one should sit quietly and look at the sky, and then one should study the redness that spreads in the sky after sunset. One should study the splendour of brilliant forms that spread out in the sky after sunset. Study continually—where have those clouds come from, and where are they going? Study the colour of the clouds and see what shapes are being created through them. Observe it. This 'study of the sky' is a continual spiritual practice. We have to learn as we study it. We have to observe every event that occurs in the sky. We have to watch the changes that occur. We have to study what the state of the clouds was before and what it is now. Slowly, we have to take our chitta deep within. We have to experience what is beyond the clouds, because that is beyond our sight, and hold on to whatever spiritual experience is taking place, which can be seen when you look beyond the clouds. Now hold on to that spiritual experience, keep your attention on it, and slowly take the experience inside and feel it inside through your eyes, then close your eyes and experience the sky element within you. Then, experience what spiritual experience is happening within yourself, and slowly a state of void will be created. You won't realize when the sky disappears from your chitta and the chitta becomes connected to the universal consciousness, because the consciousness inside you and the consciousness outside will become one. The 'I' sense of the body will automatically end, and your personal identity will also come to an end.

"This is the spiritual practice of 'the study of the sky.' Practice this every evening, and after a few days the study of this spiritual practice will be completed through your chitta." Actually, after studying this for a few days, I started to get different experiences in my body. After a few days of doing this spiritual practice, I started enjoying it. I also started wandering in the sky through my chitta. I felt as if my entire body had suddenly become very light and I was flying in the quiet blue sky. There were different types of clouds around me. Some clouds were white while some were blue. Some were of a deeper shade of blue, and gradually I started coming down, and later returned to my body. I experienced this not once but several times, and I could also look down at my body when I was up in the sky. I could experience myself as a holy and pure soul, my body is separate, I am not a body, I am a soul, and that both the soul and the body are separate.

I started getting this awareness every day, and I enjoyed this spiritual practice. Going upwards in this manner, then looking down at the body, and then returning to the body—I understood that all this was happening due to Gurudev's grace. This act of returning to the body so easily was happening because of his presence. In the beginning, this troubled me, but slowly, as my study increased, the path started becoming easier, and I later became steady in it. Such an interest was created in me that I started waiting for the spiritual practice. One requires continual practice of all progress that happens in the presence of the Guru, because at that time the effect of Gurudev's aura is present, and we have to practise spirituality not with his physical body but with his subtle body. This only happens if we continually study the spiritual practice.

I had become very attached to Gurudev in a very short time. He had the habit of stroking his beard repeatedly. He would sit very quietly and stroke his beard, and that scene captivates me even today. I liked the way he stroked his beard. His beard was completely white and very long. He kept combing it with a wooden comb. There wasn't a single black hair in his beard; all the hair had turned white. When I stood close to him, the red rays of the sun during sunset fell on his beard, and for that single moment his beard would turn orange in colour. I liked watching that scene. I had a great attraction for his beard, and I felt that whatever energies he had acquired were all stored there. When sitting on the floor his beard seemed to be trying to touch the ground; that is, it was so bushy and long, and because it was so white it appeared like silver. When we went to the neighbouring hill at the time of sunset, there would be a strong wind blowing, and Gurudev's long white beard would fly in the wind. I enjoyed watching the beard flying. The white beard suited him very much, and perhaps he loved it, too.

One morning, Gurudev started a new type of spiritual practice. He sat in a large open space like a playground and made a circle around him with some sticks, and then he told me that he was going to sit within the circle and meditate. He asked me to keep feeding wood to the fire around him, saying that the fire should be kept burning continuously for the next three days, and that I should stay around that area so that I could ensure that the fire was kept alight. That morning, he turned his face towards the sun and started his meditation at sunrise. I had collected a lot of firewood from the nearby areas that I fed to the fire from time to time and kept the fire burning. Only he knew what his spiritual practice was; I was only obeying his order. My duty here was to obey his orders, and I was doing my job. I had to keep adding sticks to the fire from time to time.

Evening was approaching, and I took proper care of my work. At the same time, I took care to see that the fire didn't spread outside the circle, because Gurudev had already cleaned the ground completely within the circle. He was sitting quietly and meditating, and I had no problem finding more sticks. My problem was the strong wind that sometimes blew towards the river and because of which the fire could potentially blow out. I kept big logs for this reason so that the fire should keep burning continuously. I had to keep a watch over the fast-blowing wind;

sometimes I used dry sticks to make the fire burn more brightly.

I got through the night somehow, but in the morning, I started to feel sleepy. I kept walking around the circle so that I shouldn't fall asleep. Then the sun rose after a while, and now somehow one day of spiritual practice had been completed. Then, as the sun slowly started to climb, the wind started to blow, and again there was the increased possibility of the fire going out or the fire spreading outside, so I had to remain alert. From the second day onwards, I started experiencing some changes within me.

The effect of whatever we see with our eyes is felt on our mind. If we see something good then the effect is good, and if we see something bad then the effect is bad because its subtle effect stays in our mind. This is because our mind keeps absorbing things through our eyes, and then our mind reflects it. That's why it has been seen that wherever there are violent scenes, murderous scenes like bullfights, cockfights, human fights—wherever these fights take place, this violence also affects society and society becomes violent. Increased crimes like killing and murder also take place in such a society. If one concentrates on this violence collectively then violence will affect society, too, and it will have a very deep and fatal effect. That's why saints and sages have opposed violence, and that's why, whenever we see something with our eyes, our mind absorbs everything and reflects it. Therefore, we keep experiencing the same effect, too.

My attention was on ensuring that the fire wasn't put out, because fire is a sacred element. I was keeping my attention on a sacred element like fire, and therefore my mind also started becoming pure, and I was getting the continuous presence of my Guru. That day, I felt that man can achieve everything in life through his efforts; only the presence of the Guru can't be obtained through one's own efforts. Proximity of the Guru can only be obtained through Guru-krupa, and Guru-krupa is never possible through one's efforts. In reality, Guru-krupa is Paramatma's grace, which is showered through some medium. Proximity of a Guru is also very rare because there is nothing greater in this world than that proximity. Whether you utilize that presence you have experienced for your physical body or the future development of your soul is dependent on this proximity. I felt as if I was blessed to obtain the presence of Gurudev. I felt as if I had been born only for the purpose of experiencing his proximity.

This proximity can't be described. One can only experience it. Only those who have achieved the spiritual experience of this proximity can understand its joy. Only the one who has experienced the taste of nectar can understand this grace. One has to taste this to know what it is. One can't fathom what it is just by looking at it from a distance. This is similar to the one who has tasted a mango knowing the taste of a juicy mango. That taste is momentary, but this is the taste of an eternal mango. Once one has tasted it, he won't ever be able to forget that for life. There are no words that can be used to compare the taste of that proximity. No form of words can describe it. I felt very happy in the presence of my Satguru. Waves of consciousness of his proximity arose in me, just as waves arise in an ocean; and every wave arose due to Gurudev's grace. With every wave of consciousness my soul would say: "Gurudev, all this is because of your compassion, all this is the nectar of your grace. Gurudev, you are an ocean of compassion, and I am only a conch-shell lying on the shore." My soul bowed down with every wave, and the more I bowed, the more I realized that the waves increased, as if they were being pulled towards me.

There was a shower of so much consciousness that my eyes started closing, and at the same time I also had to pay attention to the fire. It was causing me a lot of problems, and this was a very difficult test for me. On the one hand, I had to keep my attention on the fire, and on the other my soul was riding each wave and travelling inwards and then outwards, and my soul was pulling my attention inwards. The physical body was pulling my attention outside because I had to tend to the fire. Then I decided that it was difficult to keep my attention on the fire while I was sitting, so I decided to move around. I went around Gurudev, and my decision took me more inwards. Instead of coming outside, my state went more inward, and at night I started getting such experiences that Gurudev was also within the circle of fire and a golden ball of fire was encircling him. That ball was even more radiant than the fire, but the fire had coolness in it. There was a kind of attraction in that ball of fire. I was going around the circle of fire, but my attention was on that ball of fire encircling Gurudev in an area of ten to fifteen feet. Before that ball of fire, the fire that I had lit seemed pale and faded. It seemed as if the sun had come down to earth. This ball of fire looked like the sun that looks attractive as it rises in the morning.

The light of that ball of fire increased and decreased from moment to moment, and waves of consciousness were also swaying together with the light. The waves of consciousness also increased and decreased with the light. Then, from the third day onwards, I had spiritual experiences of a different world altogether. On the third night, the light that was moving around Gurudev and the light of the outside fire took on the same form. Actually, there was a great distance between the two, but there was no difference in the fire. The light of both had become one, and it seemed as if the sun had come down to earth. There was bright light everywhere, and because there was no other light in the jungle this collective light appeared very powerful. Then, something started moving slowly within me. I started getting vibrations below my spine, and the pulsations slowly started to move upwards. There was considerable heat around me, so much fire, and someone seemed to be pouring consciousness within me on my spine, which was completely cold. I couldn't believe that such an experience was happening.

I touched my back again and again to see whether there was something actually cold there, similar to the experience I was feeling inside, but when I touched my back there was nothing there, and cool vibrations continuously flowed towards the back of my neck. I experienced this for the first time. Until today, despite all the knowledge I had, nothing could tell me what this was, what was happening, what was actually taking place, or why it was taking place. These pulsations were moving from the back of my neck to the crown of my head. Now even the crown of my head started pulsating, and I got an exciting experience of consciousness all over my body. I experienced this for the first time; there is no experience in the encyclopaedia of intellectual knowledge that could compare with this. The experience was incomparable.

I felt that I had lost control over my body, but in spite of all this I went around the fire and kept a watch over it and made sure that it was burning properly. This was a kind of "test by fire" for me. There was testing by fire outside and also testing by fire inside. There was a test by fire on both sides. I had been close to the fire all the time, but I wasn't aware of its heat, and I found this very surprising. Then next morning, during sunrise, Gurudev slowly completed his samadhi and slowly opened his eyes. As soon as Gurudev came out of the Samadhi, as soon as he crossed the fire and came out of the ball of fire, I bent down and touched his feet and said, "By your grace I felt great divine experiences for three days. I've never had such experiences in my life." He just smiled and said, "I took you along in my mind during the three days of Samadhi. You were with me through your mind. I had assigned the task of keeping the fire burning during these three days to you so that, with the excuse of keeping the fire alive, your mind would remain on the fire, not wander elsewhere, and remain pure like the fire. I did all this so that your attention wouldn't wander outside.

"It was possible for me to give this spiritual experience to only one person in my lifetime because, through this spiritual experience, I have handed over to you the legacy of life-force that I had received through my spiritual practice and had preserved. I handed it over to you because I found you to be the most suitable for keeping it safe."

I said, "I'm just an ordinary person."

He replied, "That itself is your greatness. No matter how good a seed may be, as long as it doesn't find good fertile soil, it'll be useless. In the same way, no matter how powerful my life-energy is, as long as it doesn't find someone to keep it alive and someone who can make it grow, it will be lying useless with me. You are the fertile ground for my energy. I'm blessed after handing it over to you. You have obliged me greatly by accepting it. My life has now become meaningful, and my spiritual practice has borne fruit. Today the energy has spread from one to many. You don't know who you are; I'm aware of it, but I am also bound by certain limits. That's why, in spite of knowing everything, I can't tell you about it. You'll understand when the time is ripe. There's still some time left for the sun of knowledge to rise. Once the sun rises the whole world will know about the sun."

Gurudev was expressing his joy; he was very happy today. He told me happily, "I, too, had acquired this spiritual experience from my Gurudev, and he received it from his Gurudev. In this way the tradition progressed. One can achieve a spiritual experience only through the Guru-krupa; and to hold on to the grace that is in the form of a wave is most difficult in life because it takes only a moment to obtain grace. But to keep that grace safely needs a lifetime of spiritual practice. We have to go through several sacrifices for that and give up several things in life, or we can say that they leave you automatically, because to keep that grace safely becomes the main desire in your life.

"Thus, it's only natural that, before reaching this goal in your life, all other things have no meaning. It becomes possible to hold on to one point all your life because one's whole world shrinks. One's whole world dissolves into that one dot. One has no identity outside that point, and it becomes everything for man. And the person for whom the Guru-krupa becomes everything won't even realize that. However, the person from the outside world can stay away from Guru-krupa and think: 'How can Guru-krupa become everything for a person?' For the person who has reached within, his whole world is only at that level. He doesn't want to see the outside world at all, and the person who is outside isn't aware of the world within; therefore, the inner world has no importance for him. That's why the person who hasn't gone within can't know anything about the world that exists within. Such a paradox exists, but the person who goes within has gone there from the outside world. He knows about the world outside and also knows about the world within, because he's already inside and has knowledge of both worlds.

"The person who is within went within from the outside world and then remained there; he didn't come out into the outer world at all. Thus, we can imagine that the inner world must be superior, more likeable, more peace giving—that's why the person who went inside from the outside world doesn't want to return. The outside world is vast, but the inner world is even deeper, and there's no way out into the outer world from there. This is because man can progress only when he closes the path of return, so that he may progress more inside. I, too, had the same experience. Once I went within, then with the help of my Guru-krupa I kept going deeper inside; I kept going deeper and deeper.

"Shaktipaat or initiation can only happen through Guru-krupa. But it's very difficult to maintain the energy one receives. One has to carry on with continuous spiritual practice. Maintaining it continually is a very important factor because when someone has surrendered everything to us, then it has been done with full trust that this person will keep it safe. It is not our business to decide who to pass this Shakti on to. That task is only possible through Guru-krupa. Until a suitable sadhak comes forward, this energy won't come out at all. This energy is firmly entrenched within. Even when we try to give it to some suitable sadhak, the act of giving won't be possible until the suitable sadhak absorbs it. The energy has to be obtained and then passed on. These activities are amazing and this has been my experience. I get more joy out of giving than receiving.

"In reality, you may try fervently to pass it on to someone, but it has to come out, at least (from within). If it doesn't come out, then how can you pass it on? Neither giving nor receiving it is in our hands. Both the processes are possible only through Paramatma's grace. This is a living experience. It can neither be attained through one's own efforts nor can it be given through one's efforts. This grows only in its own proximity; and by constantly staying in its proximity, we fulfil Gurudev's trust in us, who had put divine energy in us with full faith. I acquired it in my lifetime through my Gurudev; and now you have come into my life and acquired it. I couldn't go anywhere to pass it on. Therefore, I just kept waiting in the hope that there must be someone for whom my Gurudev had handed this energy to me. I kept waiting for you in this ashram. I'm very happy after passing on this energy to you because today I'm free from my debt to my Guru. Today, I have given Guru-dakshina to my Guru. There's no meaning in life without giving Guru-dakshina, and this wouldn't be possible without your help. Today, I feel very light."

I asked him without any fear, "Gurudev, will I, too, have to wait for the coming of some sadhak like you?"

Gurudev laughed and said, "You are not a river; I was a

river. You are an ocean. Several rivers will come and join you; your vessel, your container is very big. I have only given a small offering in your atma-yagya or yagya at the level of the soul. You won't have a problem about whom to give the energy. Hundreds and thousands of souls will come to you solely for the purpose of obtaining self-knowledge."

I was scared by all this, and asked, "How will I recognize whether a person is suitable or not?"

Gurudev became serious and replied, "That's not your concern. Deciding which soul is suitable and which soul isn't, doesn't fall in your jurisdiction. Your concern is only to distribute inner knowledge. Now the question is—who is a suitable soul? This is the final place for those souls. After this, they don't have to pass on the spiritual experience to anyone. The spiritual experience that they receive is only for their benefit; it is for their liberation. Now the concern for those souls is: how many births will they need to give you an offering of repayment after receiving liberation, because this is also their last birth! But how many souls are aware of this fact? Who knows!

"Three types of souls will accept this inner knowledge from you. The first type of soul will acquire self-knowledge and will keep it safely in this birth itself and, with the help of this knowledge, the soul will reach liberation in this life itself. After obtaining liberation in this life, the soul will be free of debt of Guru-krupa by achieving liberation and making an offering of repayment in this life. The second type of soul will be the one who will absorb inner knowledge, but won't meditate, and will obtain liberation only in the next birth because it will get involved in worldly illusions; it won't be able to meditate in this birth, but will take another birth to meditate, achieving liberation only in the next birth. After attaining liberation in the next birth, the soul will make an offering of repayment to you. The third type of soul will be the one who will absorb all the experiences in this birth. It will absorb all knowledge in your presence but will be stuck in the worldly illusions and won't meditate.

"However, the soul will absorb the complete divine knowledge, and its situation will be strange. It won't be able to take another birth because it wants to obtain liberation in this life itself, but the soul hasn't prepared its spiritual state to achieve liberation in this life, and that's why it can't obtain liberation; neither does it want to take a new birth. That's why it can't get a new birth. Such souls will become ghosts, because they have obtained the entire divine knowledge in their lifetime but didn't undertake suitable spiritual practice. Several such souls will become ghosts in your lifetime. Then when some Satguru prays for them and showers his grace on them, they'll obtain liberation. Until then, they'll wander for several years.

"Several souls that have been wandering like this will obtain liberation in this life through you. These are the souls who are now ghosts because they had obtained spiritual knowledge but didn't engage in spiritual practice. Several souls will become ghosts through you and several souls will obtain liberation through you. This is the cycle of nature, where one person plants a tree and another eats the fruit. This happens continually, and no one can do anything about it. We can bear witness to it, but we can't do anything. Satguru is only a medium for liberation, a reason for liberation, but actually every soul has to obtain liberation by itself. A Satguru can only guide a soul towards liberation but can't give liberation because liberation is a higher state of meditation. Everyone has to meditate regularly to attain it. Liberation is a high state of meditation in which faults of the physical body dissipate in a subtle manner, and only the physical body remains. Existence of the physical body comes to an end, and what remains is the soul. Now the soul is a part of Paramatma, or one can say that the sense of the physical body completely ends, and the soul merges with Paramatma. The soul becomes one with Paramatma.

"Just understand that to die while being alive is liberation. Now there are no desires, and the body becomes free of desires. The biggest desire—to live longer—also ends. Thus, one attains the state of liberation while one is alive. Now it makes no difference when the physical body reaches death. Several people say that we don't want liberation; we want to serve more people. This shows that their feelings are still alive. No one can serve another person, because the one who performs the service and the one who makes you perform it is one and the same. Whom will you serve? Why are you holding on to the feeling of being the doer because of the desire to serve? Actually, the wish to serve someone is also a ladder, and you are holding on to that. In reality, serving someone is a ladder that one has to climb to reach one's destination in the form of liberation. However, several souls get stuck serving others. No matter what spiritual work we take up, we can't escape the feeling of being the doer. That's why the sadhak should keep himself safe from the feeling of being the doer.

"Sometimes, a sadhak gets a chance to serve a Satguru because of the circumstances or because of his good karma. One should consider that as one's great fortune because every soul tries to get a chance to serve the Satguru. The soul may be encased in the body or may be without a body, but both the souls continue to do the Satguru's work. That's why the Satguru's work can never stop. Yes, it is possible that the Satguru himself may not wish for it, but that is different. Otherwise, several dead spirits are eager to obey even the smallest order of the Satguru. They wait for a chance—when will the Satguru give an order? When can they perform that work? By doing Guru-karya, they continue to clear the path for their liberation. Then those spirits may get the work done by making some person their medium. That is why, in a short period of time, a considerable work can be accomplished at the hands of a Satguru. If one thinks that I must be a special pious soul, because I'm getting the chance to serve such a Gurudev and creates an ego of the 'I' sense, then he'll never get such a chance in the future. Whenever one gets a chance, one should realize that it is the fruit of that Satguru's compassion and hold on to the compassion, because he got the chance only through the Satguru, and only through his medium will he get the next chance. I'm telling you all this on the basis of the knowledge that I have received through spiritual experience. You'll get spiritual experiences depending on your life and the situations, according to your time. Spiritual experiences are always different according to the time and situation. You'll get your own separate experience."

There were several plantations of wild bananas in the jungle that the animals there would eat, especially monkeys etc. The bananas were bigger than ordinary bananas, and they had seeds with long black points, and tasted a little different from ordinary bananas. In general, we would peel them and dry them in the sun and store them. Later, we would eat them like roots. There was a lai or mustard leaf that was available everywhere in large quantities, which we boiled in a stone vessel. Sometimes we filled large bamboos with water and leaves, sealed the ends and put them in the fire. When the water inside the bamboo started to boil, the leaves cooked in the juice of the bamboo. Everybody would eat the vegetable there. The bamboos were used from morning to night in different ways. We boiled and ate the bamboo leaves, which had a nice sweet and sour taste. The part above the knotted part of the bamboo was cut and a glass for drinking water was created. It was cut again and then used for cooking. Roots were put in the bamboo pieces, and they would be closed with banana leaves, and then the part that was tied with banana leaves would be placed on the fire and cooked. One bamboo piece could be used only once because, while cooking in this way, the juice of the bamboo got mixed with the root, and it would be shaped into a long roll that could be removed by cutting open the bamboo vertically. This also had a sweet and sour taste. Sometimes the bananas would be cooked in the bamboos with bay leaves. The bamboo was also used like a water-tap.

Where the water came down the hill, a bamboo would be cut and both ends made pointed. Then one end would be pushed into the hill and the other end, because it was pointed, would help the water to fall in the shape of a stream, and this piece of bamboo did the work of a tap. Tender bamboo pieces were crushed and used in the morning to brush one's teeth. Big quantities of bamboo were used for constructing a kutir. The bamboos were also used in the fire ceremony, but they were not put in the fire or burnt. When the bamboo was used to make a mat, it served the purpose of a meditation aasan. A basket made of bamboo could be used like an umbrella in the rain. Actually, bamboo jungles were everywhere and in large numbers. Bamboos last for several years, and their trees have a very long life.

Gurudev once took me to a bamboo jungle and pointed towards a special type of bamboo tree and said, "In my lifetime, I have seen several bamboos, but this is the first time I've seen flowers on this bamboo. Lots of flowers were blooming on that bamboo tree and the whole tree was covered with flowers. A bamboo tree starts flowering once it is over fifty years old. Generally, man can see this blooming only once in his lifetime."

I found that scene very rare and thought to myself that perhaps I won't see the second flowering of this tree. It is said that if these flowers are eaten by a wild rat, then their numbers will suddenly grow. These flowers increase one's feeling of lust. They stimulate one's feelings of lust and increase one's sexual prowess.

The bamboo is ordinarily used as a walking stick, but here

sharp stones are tied in front of it, and the stick is also used as a weapon for cutting leaves, fruits, etc., from trees. Slivers of bamboo served as nails. The size of the bamboos in these jungles was much larger than ordinary bamboos, and a good variety was found there. The bamboo trees grew in clusters. During the rainy season, they would suddenly be covered with greenery. Each bamboo wants to grow taller and taller. A bamboo always wants to grow as tall as possible in life, and there's competition among bamboos to attain this height. If one bamboo grows tall then the second one wants to grow taller, and then the third one wants to grow even taller.

It's really enjoyable to see them growing daily. Their daily progress is visible, although slow. When the bamboos are green and tender, they can be heated in fire and cooled in the water, and then they're bent. The special quality of a good bamboo is that it is very tall and also very flexible. A secretion resembling milk comes out of it, and this is called the juice of the bamboo. It tastes sour like buttermilk. Generally, bamboo groves are homes to snakes. A pointed bamboo can also wound a person. The dry stumps of the tree, after the bamboo has been cut, are also dangerous. One finds jungles of a good variety of bamboos in Assam. Perhaps the environment and atmosphere of the place are more suitable for bamboo trees. There are more bamboo trees here than other ordinary trees. The secret of their height is due to their flexibility and their nature of bending.

The art of bending is the secret of their progress. No matter how many storms or strong winds they face, they never break, because they have learnt the art of bending right from birth. They are very humble in the face of every storm. They bend so much that the storm also forgives them. The storm forgives them and dosen't uproot them, and as a result of their humility they succeed in maintaining their existence even through the most severe storms. After observing this virtuous quality in them, I, too, bowed before them. I prostrated before the bamboo trees because I glimpsed Shiv Baba in them, and he was telling me: "Learn to be humble in life, and you'll automatically reach great heights."

A large number of monkeys would come near my Gurudev. They didn't come every day, but whenever they came, they stayed for about eight or ten days. I got a great chance to observe them. I didn't notice any special difference between a man and a monkey. I understood that man's brain is more developed, and therefore he goes into the past in a moment to retrieve his memories, and in a moment, he can dream about the future; but monkeys can't do that. Their attention is only on whatever is in front of them in the present. They forget everything quickly. Man has progressed as a result of the development of his brain, but the same brain has also proved to be the reason for his dissatisfaction, because he can't forget the bad experiences of his past. He doesn't realize how much time he is wasting in the present by remembering his past.

"Remembering his past isn't appropriate for man under any circumstance," Gurudev said, "because the past refers to time that has already passed. Why should we remember what has already passed, and which isn't ours anymore? If the memories of one's past are bad, they'll make us unhappy even in the present. Then what is the need to keep opening such wounds? It's better if one forgets the bad incidents in one's life. Several people keep spoiling the 'nectar of the present with the poison of the past.' On the other hand, if your past was good, then (in comparison) one feels that the present is bad. This is apparent. And such feelings also cause guilt and disgust in oneself—I was on such a high peak yesterday, how much I have fallen today! So why do you also remember your good past? One only progresses by remaining in the present. A person should always remain in the present because the present is that time which, if used judiciously, can create a better future.

"This developed brain has helped human society to progress, but this brain is also troubling mankind at the individual level. The poor animals have no idea about their past or future and are not caught up in them. They always remain in the present. It is said: 'anything in excess is not good.' Everything should be in moderation because the present is between the past and the future. The present is the period of creation."

I noticed that a baby monkey has to cling to its mother, and she keeps the baby with her for several days. The male monkey doesn't have any special role to play in nurturing the baby, but the female monkey loves its baby very much.

One day, I witnessed a scene where the baby monkey died because of some illness, but its mother kept wandering around for several days carrying the dead baby. She wasn't ready to let the baby go. Thus, that female monkey gave me a glimpse of her motherly feelings.

If there is any relationship in this world that is most sacred and superior, that is the relationship of the mother and child. To give someone a place in one's womb, to develop it and bear pain while giving birth to it, is something only a mother can do. The mother risks everything she possesses; she risks her very existence and gives birth to a child. That's why no other relationship is greater than that of the mother. That is what I felt after witnessing that event of the female monkey. The monkeys stayed around the ashram for some days and then left. The area surrounding the ashram was very small, but there was a thick jungle around it. There were huge trees of different varieties and several types of herbal plants. There was one herbal plant that could keep on burning continuously like a candle. It was a great help in lighting the path at night. While walking, we would light it like a torch. There were lots of fireflies at night in the jungle. Sometimes they filled the hut to such an extent that it seemed that we were sleeping under the moonlit sky.

The fireflies were quite big, and when eight or ten of them got together they would shine brightly like a night lamp. They could be seen only at night when it was dark, and they used to illuminate the area. That was why one could see things clearly. They had a very short lifespan but kept giving light during their lifetime. Like these fireflies, there used to be a glowing caterpillar, which also used to glow brightly. It would climb on a tree or a stone and could be clearly seen at night because it would be illuminated. It never entered the hut and would always stay in the jungle.

❧

Gurudev spent most of his time in meditation and in performing fire ceremonies. He was very knowledgeable about mantras as well. The evening scene was very beautiful, and after completing his fire ceremony etc., he took me to the top of the hill. I also loved that place very much because, while sitting there, I got a chance to talk to him at leisure. consciousness seemed to be showering through his eyes, and his whole body seemed to speak. Whenever he closed his eyes, I, too, would go somewhere inside myself. Every day brought a new communication, a new message. One day, as we were sitting at the top of the hill, he started speaking. It felt as if some divine sound was coming from the sky. "Every disciple can attain spiritual experience from his Guru only through Gurukrupa. The Satguru takes birth especially for the disciple, and the disciple takes birth for that Guru. Both these are connected for a purpose. Both complement each other. The Guru doesn't oblige the disciple by giving him the spiritual experience of inner knowledge, and the disciple, too, doesn't oblige the Guru by receiving it. Both are like two ends of nature's cycle. Neither end is either big or small. Both are appropriate in their own place. This is similar to the event when milk pours out of a mother's breast only for her child, and the child gives satisfaction to its mother by accepting the milk. However, if the child doesn't drink the milk, then the mother is troubled.

"The Guru-disciple relationship is also similar to that of a mother and her child. Once this relationship has been formed, then the Guru is troubled if the disciple doesn't absorb the inner knowledge. That's why the Guru keeps searching for a suitable disciple throughout his life. This is because no matter how much inner knowledge the Guru attains and persuades the disciple, and how much he desires to give it to the disciple, if the disciple doesn't have the desire to accept it, the Guru can't give it. This is the Guru's helplessness. One can only clap with both hands in this situation. This is not a process that can happen with one hand. The Guru has to start the process and the disciple completes it. It's like this: a mother grinds wheat into flour, then prepares the dough, makes small balls out of it, rolls out the rotis with a wooden rolling pin and then roasts it on the griddle; then at the risk of burning her hands she lifts it from the griddle and breaks it into small pieces. Then, with each small piece, she takes a bit of vegetable curry and puts a morsel into her child's mouth. She completes her task and hopes that her son will now chew the morsel and then swallow it. But the act of swallowing depends on the child. She can only hope for it but she can't do it for him. This act will always have to be done by the child as it's their task. Now what can the poor mother do if the child doesn't swallow it and spits it out!

"No matter how great the mother's care, no matter how hard she works, completing the whole action depends only on the child—though it isn't necessary for the child to complete the process. The same is the case with the Guru and his disciple. First of all, the ease with which the Guru gives isn't simple. The process of receiving is simple, but the process of giving is very complicated. But because the Guru gives it easily to the disciple, the disciple isn't even aware of the complicated process involved. This is the only difference between the two. Every disciple accepts it in the same way, and when he becomes a Guru, he also bestows it in the same way.

"The main barrier in this whole process is 'the physical body.' What is important is the parents from whom one has received one's physical body, and what values and ethics the foetus has absorbed in the mother's womb. The effect of both the parents' thoughts and values can therefore prove to be a barrier as well as an opportunity, because the body is made up of all these things. Now the soul wishes to gain inner knowledge, but the path to the soul can't open until the body has undergone all the sufferings and pleasures it is destined to experience. The capacity of the body to absorb the inner knowledge also decreases due to physical experiences. But the soul keeps on making the person aware of what a priceless gift he is receiving from the other soul because of its good (spiritual) state. When the awareness of the soul rises above one's physical experiences, then the soul slowly starts controlling the body and its activities. Then the soul succeeds in making the sadhak aware of what a priceless gift he's receiving, and the event of gaining inner knowledge takes place.

"Sometimes it happens that due to some circumstances a sadhak accepts inner knowledge without realizing its importance, and then, after accepting the knowledge of spiritual experience, the sadhak has to face a lot of problems in life. Problems keep on coming one after another. All difficulties come together at once, and problems come to him like a storm. This happens because the problems that he was destined to face throughout his life he is forced to face all at once; he has to undergo this because, after his union with the universal soul, nothing more remains to be experienced. Thus, he has to suddenly undergo all the sufferings that he is destined to face in his lifetime. Later on, his life becomes quiet and without any problems. From one point of view, this is good because if you undergo difficulties in your youth when you have a lot of life-force in your body, then you can spend the rest of your life without problems. The body starts declining slowly, and it's appropriate for this association to take place together with the physical process.

"The body becomes weak; the body becomes old. But one's sexual urge doesn't age. The sexual urge of a young man and that of a weak old man is the same. The obstacle of lust is more than an obstacle of the physical body. When it comes to lust, one doesn't think, 'I have become old, now I'm not capable, now that time has passed.' Whether the body is in a state to endure anything or not, lust can still predominate. While attaining inner knowledge, lust arises in the form of a predominant obstacle. That's why, until one goes beyond this obstacle, one can't reach the path ahead. Secondly, several people suppress it and move on, but it is merely suppressed, not removed from the root. When a favourable situation arises it will rise once again, because its roots exist within, but it hadn't grown earlier because it didn't get any water (a favourable situation). The moment it gets water, it'll develop once again. That is why it isn't proper to suppress one's sexual desire, as one uses up a lot of mental energy while suppressing it. Secondly, there is always a danger that the sexual desire will rise again. There's always a danger that the desire may arise, and it can arise at any time. Thus, suppression doesn't seem appropriate.

"Imagine that an ascetic suppresses his sexual desire and practises meditation all his life, and when he becomes old, when he gets the chance, he rapes a sixteen-year-old girl. This means that all these years the sexual urge that he had forcefully suppressed came out in his old age in a distorted form. Similarly, when we try to suppress sexual desire or any other type of desire, it is very small and therefore we can suppress it. But when it comes out later, it comes out at great speed because it has been suppressed for so many years, and as a result, great speed is created.

"Therefore, one should not go on in the spiritual world with any desire, as the main reason is that it affects your total and overall development; so if there is any sexual desire within you or any other desire, then that, too, will develop in the same proportion that you are developing. That is why one shouldn't enter this (spiritual) area until one is completely pure, because if you enter with even a small desire then that one desire will become the cause of your downfall. There's a way of freeing oneself from desires—one way is to experience it so that your mind never goes towards it. Move out of it after you have experienced it or understand what it is through inner knowledge. When you understand what it is, then it helps you to overcome that desire. Once you understand that desire, you'll realize that there is no everlasting happiness in it, and this is only a momentary physical joy. You thus move forward and start searching for everlasting happiness, and your desire leaves you. This is how one gets rid of one's desires, and this happens at the soul level. You become a pure and holy soul, a soul without any desires. Thus, if any Guru finds a totally pure disciple, he feels that his spiritual practice is completed and his life is successful, that the purpose of his life has been achieved. Today, my state is similar. I became a medium to pass it on to you. You were always the rightful person to attain the inner knowledge, otherwise I couldn't have given it at all. Today, I'm very happy that I've been able to pass on my treasure of inner knowledge to the right hands during my lifetime."

I said, "You're very generous. You are an ocean of compassion. All that you have made me understand indicates the greatness and generosity of your knowledge. You have given me priceless knowledge. Now I request you to bless me so that I, too, can pass it on to pure souls, because my purpose of acquiring all this was to give it to souls who have been waiting for it."

Gurudev said, "This is the only purpose that gives you a status that is different from others. Your greatest special quality is that you have been born only to give to others. This is the secret of your life, which I'm revealing to you today. You have been created for the purpose of distributing this knowledge. Several souls have wished for your birth. Thousands of souls have been awaiting your birth. They have been waiting impatiently for several years for the giver of liberation to arrive and give them liberation. You have taken birth through the efforts of thousands of souls, their prayers and their wishes. Your birth has taken place in collectivity. You will become the leader of a very big ocean of souls; millions of souls will come and join you; millions of souls will dive into your reservoir of inner knowledge to get liberation.

"You are the Yug-purush because a spiritual era will come to an end with your life. You will be the torch-bearer of a great spiritual revolution. All this is going to happen because you have taken birth due to the prayers of these millions of souls, but you have no knowledge about them. When the right time comes, all this knowledge will come to you automatically, because everything is within; everything is inside you but isn't available to you (at present). You have no knowledge of it, and this is the only difference between you and me." Gurudev went on speaking, and I listened with my bowed head. I was absorbing it as if Gurudev wished that all this should happen; and I absorbed it because these were blessings from Gurudev that I should absorb, and so I absorbed them.

One morning, Gurudev took me down to the river, and when we reached the river, we had a bath and returned to the ashram. On returning, Gurudev cupped his hands together and carried water. He wanted to take the water to the ashram and pour it on the Shiva-ling, but by the time we reached the ashram, all the water had slipped through his fingers. So, he returned to the river, bathed there, and carried water in his hands and reached the ashram, and on the way the water ebbed away. So, he again went to the river. I, too, would go to the river; and when he returned to the ashram, I would also return with him. He did this several times a day, and I couldn't understand why he was doing it, and I didn't have the courage to ask him why he was doing it over and over again. I felt that there must be some purpose behind it, and I would follow him because even an ordinary person can understand that water can't stay in one's hands for such a long time. So, what was the justification to carry water in this way?

I didn't deem it fit to ask him, and I gave myself a simple explanation that this must be some process that he is carrying out for my benefit. Gurudev was an auspicious personage, and I was going to benefit a lot at his hands. When there was no place in his life for anything inauspicious then this incident must also be some auspicious event, some auspicious activity. That's what I thought, and so I followed him to the river and back to the ashram. I didn't pay attention to what he was doing. I was happy that I was in the proximity of Gurudev because of this activity. During the day, I got a chance to bathe in the clean flowing river. There was a pool of water in the ashram, and because of that there were very few occasions on which we went to the river for bathing. Now, for the past three days, this process was being repeated.

At the start, I studied this process in minute detail in the hope that I could understand it, but I couldn't understand anything, and later I stopped paying attention to it. In this whole process, what I liked best was going to the river and bathing because I could be with Gurudev. Three days passed like this, and on the fourth morning Gurudev again took me to the river, and we bathed there. Then he filled his cupped hands with water and said to me, "I'm also aware that the cup formed with my hands will never be able to hold water for the time it takes us to reach the ashram. By the time we reach the ashram, my hands are completely dry. Thus, there is no question of retaining the water through the return journey. I was just testing your patience, to see how much patience there is within you, and I thought that you would ask me about this process, but you have passed the test. For the last three days, I was performing this strange activity, yet you never asked me what I was doing or whether such a thing was possible. By not asking, you have revealed that you have great patience. I'm very happy with you."

After saying that, he poured the water from his hands back into the river. Gurudev looked very happy at that time, and I asked for permission to wash his feet, which he happily gave. I went nearby and picked some leaves and flowers. Gurudev was sitting on a rock. and I sat on the ground. I brought water from the river and washed his feet. As a result of walking for my test, his feet had also become dusty. I put the dust from his feet on my forehead and washed his feet until I was satisfied. I applied the juice of the leaves to his feet and cleaned them, and I also put some crushed leaves on his feet to reduce the heat. There is a continuous process going on through the Guru's body, and that's the process of purifying the disciple's mind. The Guru always absorbs the impurities of the disciple's mind, and due to those impurities, a lot of heat is created in the Guru's body, and that heat can be felt in the soles of the Guru-charan. This happens automatically when clearing the disciple's mind. That's why it is the disciple's duty to help his Guru in clearing the heat and faults that have reached the Guru because of him.

That is also the reason why during Guru Purnima the programme of pad-puja—worship of the Guru-charan—is held. The Guru has cleansed the disciple's mind throughout the year and the disciple can never repay the debt, but he performs pad-puja to express his feelings of gratitude. That's why the Guru's pad-puja has been given a lot of importance in the spiritual field. This is a type of activity to express one's gratitude. With a similar feeling in my mind, I, too, performed my Gurudev's pad-puja on the banks of the river. I felt as if that day was the best day of my life, and time should stop there and then, but such things don't happen. That golden moment had also passed. I had picked and brought some wildflowers, which I offered at his lotus feet. I had picked some fruits, which I offered him, and asked for his blessings. "Let me be true, Gurudev, to the trust that you have placed in me. I have surrendered this life to you; let my life pass according to your wishes. Please bless me that, from today onwards, you may live through me by accepting me as your medium, so that I may prove to be a pure and holy medium for your thoughts, for your goal, for your project, and for your movement of spiritual revolution. From today, I have no separate existence from you. Let me wipe myself out completely, and only you and you should remain everywhere."

On hearing my emotional outpouring, Gurudev felt overwhelmed and said, "The Guru-element is a flow of Paramatma's energy, which flows continuously, which has come down to earth and which has been flowing from time immemorial. This flow of Guru-element existed in the past ages and also exists in the present age, and will continue to flow in the future generations, too. This flow is a true and everlasting flow. Truth is always one. Truth is immortal. This truth has to flow continuously. The Guru-element is not a physical body, which is perishable. The Guru-element is everlasting and keeps changing its medium from time to time depending on the situation. The Guru-element doesn't choose the medium, but the medium chooses the Guru-element. The Guru-element is happy to flow through the soul that has acquired a physical body and wishes to lose its identity, and through the person who is ready to give up his ego.

"The Guru-element is ready and waiting to flow through the

medium—which soul with a physical body is ready for it? The Guru-element wants a soul that has a physical body, because it has to manifest in the present. The Guru-element is the energy of Paramatma, which is always ready to descend to earth, just as the sun is always ready to give its light and keeps giving equally to everyone. It doesn't discriminate between anyone. Paramatma also has the same special qualities. He is available for everyone, but someone should be ready to accept Him. If we keep the doors and windows of our house closed, there will be darkness in our house, and then we complain to the sun—you give light to our neighbour but not to our house! What can the sun do? The sun also has its limitations; it can't break the door and enter the house forcibly. If you want to have light in your house, then open the doors of your house. You'll have to open the doors, and when you open your doors, you'll find that the sun is waiting at your door. Similarly, the Guru-element is also the energy of Paramatma, which is lit up equally for every human. Yes, there's much more light in the house of those people who open their doors and windows. The extent to which a sadhak loses his identity determines the chances of him becoming a medium of Paramatma. A disciple surrenders himself completely at the Guru-charan. In reality, he's not surrendering at the feet of the Guru's physical body but to the energy that is flowing through the Guru.

"Actually, the Guru-charan are only a medium to invite the Guru-element because the Guru slowly moves his feet away and connects the soul to Paramatma. The greatest barrier to the relationship between the soul and Paramatma is the human body. The end of one's ego is samarpan, because as soon as Samarpan takes place that person becomes empty; he becomes void, and as a result the Guru-element merges with him. That's why no Guru is only a physical body. The meaning of Guru is that which is in the physical body but is not the 'I' of the body. Such a physical body without the 'I' is a Guru. The one who is present in the physical body and has become the medium of the Guru-element is a Guru. So how can the Guru's body become the Guru? This is why the mediums of Guru-element keep on changing, and those who keep on changing are only mediums; that which doesn't change is the Guru-element. A Guru can't exist without the Guru-element, but the Guru-element exists without a Guru."

My complete attention was centred on my Guru-charan, whose light I could also experience inside. I felt as if I was going into samadhi and didn't want to come out of it. I understood what happiness was while experiencing the joy of that soul. Gurudev continued to speak. I felt that he was speaking from an elevated state. He said, "Every human being can become a Guru. The yoni is a form from where one can undertake the journey from nar to narayan, i.e., from man to God. This human birth is a birth in which any man can become a Guru. Any human, meaning any human, can empty himself, and this opportunity is available to all humans; it's available equally to all humans, free of charge.

"This is a special quality of Paramatma. He gives to everyone equally. There is no discrimination of religion or country, and Paramatma bestows it free of charge because there is no place for commerce in Paramatma's kingdom. It is also free of charge because Paramatma is priceless, and therefore Paramatma's grace is also priceless. This grace can't be bought with money; one has to diminish one's identity and make a place for it within oneself. The more you reduce your ego, your 'I' sense, the more the Paramatma will enter within you. I, too, have become a medium between you and the Guru-element. Actually, you were already empty and innocent. I was waiting for the time when the spiritual work could begin. A lot of work remains to be achieved. After that work has been completed, your field of work will change completely. No boundaries can delay you because your area of work is in every human's heart, and you will have to reach that point.

"My Gurudev was behaving as if he hadn't done anything even after doing everything. I was full of gratitude after staying in the presence of such a Gurudev. He was doing everything himself, and everything was happening due to his grace and compassion, and yet he didn't have the feeling that he was the doer. He had merged with Paramatma to such an extent that they didn't seem to be separate at all. For me he was Paramatma. He used to recite the Ganapati Atharvashirsh or verses in praise of Lord Ganesha every morning. He possessed a very good voice, and his pronunciation of Sanskrit words was equally good. Every morning, I heard the sound of his recitation, and whenever he recited the verses, I felt like listening to him forever. I learnt the verses by heart by listening every day. He didn't teach me these verses. I had wanted to learn them in my childhood, but no Brahmin was ready to teach me, and I realized why after reading a book in which the verses were written. The book said that if one taught the verses to an unsuitable person, he would be committing a sin; and because of that fear, no one taught me the verses. Here, I managed to learn them easily in Gurudev's presence. One morning, I asked him about the verses, and he said, "One's chitta is purified on reciting the verses. That's why I recite them every morning, so that my chitta gets purified early in the morning and all the tasks can be performed throughout the day with a pure and holy mind. I learnt this from my Guru by listening to him. Purification of one's chitta is very important in the spiritual field because we absorb everything through our chitta. This chitta can be called 'the eyes of one's soul.'

"Just as the body sees with the eyes, the soul sees with the chitta. The chitta should be purified slowly because, along with with purification of chitta, it is extremely important to have control over one's mind; otherwise, it is damaging, because if we purify our chitta on a big scale and there is no control over it, then significant problems can be created. The purer one's chitta, the stronger it will be, and the stronger it is, the more subtle it will be. And the more subtle it is, the more necessary it gets to control it. When we purify our chitta too much and we don't have control over our normal human behaviour—for instance, looking at the faults of others—we will knowingly or unknowingly absorb the faults in others like dirt, and the chitta will be polluted.

"Astrayed yogis who have deviated from their paths are created this way. There are a large number of yogis who deviated from their paths in the world of dead spirits for the same reason. Everyone likes wearing white clothes very much, but it's very difficult to keep white clothes clean, because any stain on white cloth can be easily seen. That's why, before wearing white clothes, it is necessary for one to learn how to keep oneself safe from dirtying those clothes; and that's why more than purification of one's chitta it is necessary to have control over it, as then we won't see any faults. That's why meditating ascetics would think that 'one can't have a flute when there is no bamboo to create it,' and lived in isolation. They didn't see any humans, so there was no question of seeing their faults."

I was afraid after hearing this, and said, "Gurudev, this will become even more difficult. I am an ordinary human being, so how can I control my chitta?"

Gurudev replied, "The easiest way is Samarpan. If you surrender to your Guru, then purification and control over one's chitta will both take place together. You won't have to do anything because if you have to do something and you do it, then the 'I' will appear, and when the 'I' appears, control won't be possible.

"We put ourselves in the care of a doctor when we are ill, and then the doctor gives us medicines depending on the sickness; after taking the medicines we become all right despite not having any knowledge about medicines. In the same way, we should know how to surrender ourselves. Everything can't be learnt in life because there are too many things to learn, and life is very short. Thus, to learn greater knowledge in our short lives, we should know how to handover ourselves and how to surrender, which is essential. What is necessary, we learn automatically. Instead of saying we learn automatically, we must say it comes automatically."

When I heard this, I decided in my mind that I, too, would surrender myself and keep control over my chitta. I also made a rule for myself at that time and decided that every morning after my bath I would recite 'Shree Ganpati Atharvashirsh' once, keeping my chitta on my Gurudev.

※

Gurudev carried forward the previous day's discussion in the morning and said, "Everything is contained in the word 'Samarpan.' But people can't understand the meaning of Samarpan properly. 'Arpan' means giving up something out of whatever good things you have, and that too with good feelings. This is arpan. And the meaning of Samarpan is to surrender everything that you have. People think that to surrender everything means to give up all your wealth, to give up your physical body for work, or to take a vow to undertake Guru-karya throughout your life. This is what people think.

"But this meaning is wrong. The word 'Guru' is at the soul level, and wealth is at the material level. Thus, wealth has no connection with Samarpan. Working for the Guru all your life with your body or surrendering your body for Guru-karya is also not Samarpan, because the word Guru is at the soul level, and you are talking about handing over your physical body. When surrendering your wealth is not Samarpan, then surrendering your body is also not Samarpan. Then what is Samarpan and how can it be done? First of all, it's necessary to understand the meaning of the word. Samarpan is aatmic. The word 'Guru' is of the soul. Thus, the feeling of Samarpan should also be at the level of the soul. The meaning of Samarpan is that you should destroy yourself completely in the physical form and should merge yourself in the aatmic form of your Guru's energies. When you dissolve sugar in milk it doesn't have a separate identity, but the milk starts tasting sweet because of the dissolved sugar, and the taste changes.

"Similarly, when the disciple surrenders before the Guru, his identity is wiped out. How can the disciple hand over his wealth or his physical body to his Guru when he doesn't have a separate identity? There's no question of handing it over when it doesn't belong to him anymore. 'I' am surrendering my wealth means that the 'I' is still alive; 'I' am handing over my wealth means that the 'I' is still alive. It's very easy to give up one's wealth and one's physical body, because even after handing it over one's 'I' remains alive— 'I' surrendered my body, 'I' handed over my wealth! Samarpan doesn't mean surrendering one's body or wealth. The meaning of Samarpan is to hand over your 'I' sense. This 'I' in a person is very deceiving. It asks you to hand over your wealth but keeps itself safe and asks you to surrender your body. Thus the 'I' remains safe. We shouldn't get caught in the deception of the 'I.' We must hand it over, and to surrender the 'I' is the real surrender. Samarpan means to destroy our identity and make it void; to empty it, so that, through the Guru-krupa, Paramatma's energy can descend. When we surrender before someone, the Guru to whom we surrender is also a medium. Actually, we keep surrendering to Paramatma only through the medium of the Guru. Then we, too, become one with Paramatma. But this surrender should take place at the soul level, otherwise 'I' can bring about your downfall at any time, from any level.

"The feeling of surrender towards the Guru can be created just by bowing down, provided the bowing isn't at the physical level but from within oneself, because we become pure with the act of bowing. The Guru is just a medium for us to bow before Paramatma. One has to make a study of all this and then undertake spiritual practice. Just by creating a feeling of surrender once within ourselves, we can't bring about surrender. This is a process that must be practised continually, so that the Samarpan may be maintained. For example, we scrub a vessel that is dirty and stained. We have to scrub it over and over again to clean it, and if after cleaning the silver vessel we put it on one side and say that it is now clean enough, then after a while it will get dirty again. This means that even after scrubbing a silver vessel clean, one must keep scrubbing it from time to time to maintain its cleanliness.

"Similarly, even after a person has surrendered completely, he must maintain the feeling so that the feeling of surrender may always remain the same and the dust of time won't settle over it. Thus, to surrender and then to maintain the feeling of surrender are both important tasks. But maintaining it is more important because one may lose whatever one has achieved. That's why maintaining it is more important, and this is a process that has to be practised everyday like a 'devoted spiritual practice.'

"A stone will also get covered with dust and dirt if it remains lying in one place, but Samarpan is the feeling of a living individual's soul. The bad influence of people around us can also fall on it. That's why it becomes necessary for a 'samarpit' sadhak to maintain his feeling of Samarpan, because the bad effect of people around us falls on us, and the effect of those who are not samarpit is felt. Their feelings of 'I,' which contains the feelings of jealousy, haven't been surrendered completely—how can that be surrendered completely? Jealousy is present even in the spiritual field. Therefore, it's good that here there is no one to be jealous of you and to pollute you. You should take your chitta inside because you are alone here, and all the treasure has been kept within you.

That treasure can't be obtained without you journeying inwards because, if you succeed in obtaining it, then the doorway of a new possibility will open for the truth-loving souls. Go inwards, go deeper inside and search for your identity. Once you go inwards, you'll find it. The entire sea of knowledge is lying inside you. Your state is like that of a musk deer. The scent of musk spreads from the musk deer's navel, and everyone enjoys it. Only the deer doesn't know that the scent of musk is coming from its own navel and wanders around the entire jungle in search of that scent. You, too, are like a musk deer that isn't aware that the scent is not coming from outside but from within you."

I became very serious—what knowledge was filled within me? This Gurudev was asking me to go inside myself like the previous Gurudev. There was definitely some mystery in this. I began thinking of myself as a mysterious person, and suddenly realized that the Guru-element appears to be separate from outside but is not so. Both the Gurudevs were talking about the same thing—look within yourself, go within—the previous Gurudev had also said the same thing. I don't know why but I felt as if both Gurudevs were asking me to solve the mathematical problem whose answer they knew; and there was a definite answer that they knew and I didn't know. I didn't think it proper to look into the future when they didn't want to tell me about it. Perhaps this wasn't the right time for me to understand. Then I stopped thinking about the subject; whatever the future held would appear before me. Why should I lose what I have today by thinking about tomorrow? This appeared to be true. I was happy with the present. I was in Gurudev's presence.

Night was approaching, and I thought that it was better to sleep, and went to bed. I couldn't speak to Gurudev the next day because he was busy, but in the evening, I went with him to the top of the hill, and we both sat there for some time. Suddenly,

Gurudev said, "If a person's attention goes to something then the chitta isn't much affected. But if the chitta goes again and again to the same thing, then it has a greater effect, and if it goes to a person then also it has even more effect. But if it goes to the same person again and again, then the chitta definitely gets destroyed. Wherever one's attention goes, it should be momentary. Just as a bubble of water rises in a moment and then breaks, if the chitta goes somewhere it should move away the next moment. The chitta should be controlled in this manner.

"The medium of the chitta is one's eyes. When you look at a person and don't look into his eyes then your chitta won't go to that person, and if the chitta doesn't go there, then it won't be destroyed. One has to study how to control one's chitta. This isn't something that can happen overnight. That day, I purposely tested you to find out how much patience you have, because the responsibility of planting this seed of inner knowledge is in my hands. But making the seed sprout is not in my hands. It is like a farmer who sows seeds in the soil, then waits for rain, and then prays to Paramatma to send the rains soon, so that the seed he has sowed should germinate. The farmer can't do anything beyond praying. In the same way the Guru can also give the seed of inner knowledge to the disciple and pray to Paramatma that it should germinate like the seed. But the Guru himself can't do anything. Just as the possibility of every seed growing into a tree is hidden in the seed, similarly the possibility of every disciple becoming a Guru is hidden in the disciple. That is why the Guru has to work patiently after sowing the seed of inner knowledge in him, and until now one Guru used to give inner knowledge only to one disciple. Thus, he needed less patience because he had only one disciple. Inner knowledge is going to spread in your lifetime, and this self-knowledge is going to reach millions of people through the medium of spiritual experiences.

"That's why you need to be very patient. What has actually been said is, 'Do your work but don't desire its fruits.' But the act of giving self-knowledge doesn't happen while spreading inner knowledge. The reason for this is that one obtains this state of giving only when the feeling, that one is the doer, has been destroyed completely. Secondly, self-knowledge can't be given when suitable disciples are not available. Thus here, too, it can't be given. It leaves on its own, and that is also the reason why the feeling of being the doer is not present. This work will happen in your lifetime in collectivity. Millions of people will obtain it through you as a medium; the path of liberation for millions of people will open through you! You'll be the medium for such a big event and that's why patience has a lot of importance in your life.

"Millions of people will receive inner knowledge through you. That's why it is necessary to understand how it happens. First of all, remember that the person who has come to you must be suitable, otherwise he wouldn't have come before you, and even if he does come to you, he won't last long. That is why it isn't in your purview to decide whether someone is suitable or not. You are an ocean. Both a saint and a sinner can reach the ocean, and it heartily accepts both of them because it is so vast that it can't have control over whom to accept and whom not to accept. Your form is also vast like this ocean.

"You will also acquire the vastness, and then there won't be any question of whom to accept and whom not to accept. Therefore, the question of suitability or unsuitability doesn't arise. The person who comes to you and stays must be suitable. Why will an unsuitable soul reach you at all? That soul has reached you because it is definitely worthy of receiving the seed of self-knowledge from you. It takes a long time to obtain the seed of self-knowledge and to germinate it. Sometimes, it may even take three to four births. Several souls manage to acquire the seed of inner knowledge because the present situation is suitable, but their chitta is not inside them: it's somewhere else. Thus, the soul manages to receive the seed of self-knowledge but can't germinate it. The seed will stay in the same state until it finds a suitable atmosphere within the soul. Now it is up to the soul's own ability to create a suitable atmosphere within the soul. What can you do in this situation? This isn't your concern at all. Several souls are going to come into your life, which are suitable only to obtain the seed in this birth but aren't suitable for germination. Thus, that soul will obtain the seed in this birth and the seed will germinate in the next birth. This is generally what happens. It takes several births for the tree of self-knowledge to be created. That is why you have to perform only the work of sowing the seeds. Don't think that those seeds must germinate and don't be discouraged if they don't. They will definitely germinate because they are seeds of a good quality.

"These seeds will definitely germinate. Yes, it's not clear when they'll germinate. Such a process takes place because these are souls who have accepted the seed of inner knowledge unwittingly. These souls will be so entangled in the social web of illusion that they won't be aware of the seed at all. They have no knowledge at all about the importance of that seed of inner knowledge. Thus, it is natural for them to accept whatever they receive easily, because the event of your giving it to them and their acceptance of it will be a very joyful occasion. They'll be very happy to accept it easily, whether they know about it or not, and it isn't necessary for them to know who you are.

"This is similar to the situation when a poor man is given a priceless diamond. The poor man accepts the diamond when he sees it shining, along with the attractive form of the Paramatma who gives it to him. But he isn't aware that it's a priceless diamond. He takes it and keeps it. But the diamond that he has put aside won't have any value for him until a person comes and makes him aware that what he has is a diamond. The same thing will also happen with people because the same thing has happened to you. You are not aware of the treasure of inner knowledge that your Guru has given you and you don't even know that the one who gave it to you was Paramatma incarnate. You neither know the person who gave it to you, nor do you know what Shiv Baba has given you. Here you don't even know yourself, and my situation is that today 'the well itself has approached the thirsty person.'

"Whatever you are searching for outside is all inside you. All of us Gurus are doing only one work. Only if you know what Shree Shiv Baba has given you will you understand what he has given you. You'll be able to know yourself only when you understand that. The entire secret is inside you. Go inside and get to know your Guru. All of us Gurus know what is within you. Birds and animals also know it. Only you are not aware of what is within you."

I prayed to Gurudev, "Gurudev, you told me that one should germinate the seed of self-knowledge by keeping one's chitta on one's Guru. Then please guide those souls who are going to acquire the seed from me but won't be able to germinate it in this birth, so that they may be able to germinate their seed of self-knowledge in this life itself. You are an ocean of compassion. If you reveal this secret to me, you'll shower me with your grace. Those souls won't be able to reach here and benefit from you as I have done. That is why I'm asking you to please show me the path for the progress of those souls." Gurudev had tears in his eyes; he became very emotional and said, "Hey! You silly boy, it's because of your desire that others should receive the inner knowledge that Shree Shiv Baba has made you his medium. Shree Shiv Baba was Paramatma incarnate. You are really very fortunate that you were in his presence.

"There is only one path for progress in self-knowledge. Show them the same path that I'm showing you. Do you think there's a different path for each soul? There's only one path for achieving liberation through self-knowledge. I'm asking you to recognize Shiv Baba so that you'll understand what he has given you; when you keep your chitta on him, he'll surely shower you with compassion. Similarly, if the souls who have obtained the seed from you get connected to you by keeping their chitta on you, they'll easily reach the same state as you. You have to wipe out your existence and dissolve yourself in the Guru. Similarly, those souls have to merge into you. You are the Guru of all Gurus, you are a Satguru. It'll be easy to get connected to you because there will be a collectivity of hundreds of thousands of people who'll be connected to you. The seed won't know when it germinated and turned into a tree. Everything takes place through Paramatma's grace. What happens in our lives and what we do, it is much larger than that. This also happens because we think within our limitations, but when Paramatma gives, there are no limitations.

"Thus, you can show people the same path of self-knowledge that I've shown you. There is only one path to know the truth and to acquire it, only one path. Generally, where a person is, or at what place he is, doesn't have much importance in his life. What is important is where his chitta is; he'll absorb energy from the place where his chitta is focused. A disciple who has received a seed through his Guru-krupa, the seed will get energy from the same place (Guru-krupa) to grow into a tree. This is because, while sowing the seed, the Guru does so with the positive thought that this seed, which he has sown, should definitely grow into a tree. If one doesn't have such a generous attitude, then the process of sowing the seed can't happen, and only a Guru who sows the seed can have such an emotion. That same emotion must be made the medium. The same emotion that has given the soul the seed of inner knowledge will clear the path and transform the seed into a tree.

"The disciple will have to hold on to his Guru's feeling of compassion. When the wave of compassion comes, then one will have to wipe out his identity. If one has a separate identity, he won't be able to establish oneness with that wave of compassion. The soul will have to forget its identity as a droplet and dissolve its identity into the ocean. This has to be done by the disciple himself. This work is very private and has to be performed by each person alone. Sometimes it seems as if this is the only work that has to be performed; all other work in one's life will happen through the Guru-krupa.

"This is the only work that has to be performed. A seed destroys its identity and performs this work through its own wish, and this is the only work it does. The remaining work to transform the seed into a tree is performed by Paramatma himself through the medium of nature. Paramatma is a universal energy that manages nature. It is omnipresent. All that is required to experience the universal energy is for the soul to be in an appropriate state." With these words, Gurudev concluded the discussion.

Many tapioca trees grow in that jungle. If one of the trees was uprooted, then one could get tuber roots weighing around twenty-five or thirty kgs under it. These tuber roots could always be stored. When a tree was cut and then again cut into four pieces, those four pieces were pushed into the ground; six inches would be pushed in the following way—they would be pushed six inches underground, leaving twelve inches above. They would be pushed at an angle, and later they would grow into four trees. There were a large number of trees, and their tuber roots were used for food. The leaves of these trees were palm-shaped, and they were boiled and eaten. I loved the work involved in cutting these trees, then planting the four pieces, then collecting the tuber roots and roasting them over the fire and serving them to Gurudev on banana leaves. A bamboo would be cut below the knotted part, and this tuber would be filled in the upper part and then roasted in the fire. The bamboo didn't get burnt as it was green and tender, but it would get nicely roasted from inside, and the tuber inside the bamboo was mixed with the juice from it. While roasting it, some ginger, bay leaves and a special pod of a leguminous plant were added to it. After a while, it was taken out of the fire. The bamboo would be slit open and the tapioca from within it would be extracted. Sometimes the tapioca would be eaten roasted and sometimes boiled. This was the main diet there and it tasted good with the bamboo juice.

One morning, after completing the fire ceremony and other duties, Gurudev said, "Your life is like an Ashwamedh Yagya. You have taken birth on earth with the purpose of performing a very sacred and great spiritual work. Your family is very large. I won't get the proximity of this kind of collective family in my lifetime, and after this life I don't have another birth. In order to be a part of your great work, I've passed on to you whatever I possessed. Now the time has come for you to go ahead with this work. I am telling you this because I don't wish to keep you tied down or be a hindrance to your duties. We have stayed together for a very short time, but we've done it to take this sacred spiritual work forward.

"Always remember: thoughts are unnatural. We move away from nature because of our thoughts, and thoughts come to an end in the proximity of nature. The more we stay in the proximity of nature, the more we stay in the presence of Paramatma. People spread pollution in the atmosphere by thinking too much, and due to this thought pollution, the atmosphere starts getting hot and becomes polluted. This hot polluted atmosphere is the biggest danger to the new world because it will become difficult to even breathe. Always keep your chitta inside because all knowledge is within yourself. Living knowledge can never be written in books; that can only keep flowing through experiences. The work of spreading the living knowledge always happens like this—from one Guru to one disciple and from one disciple to another disciple. This always happens in this traditional manner. This is divine knowledge, which can't be written down because the person who receives the spiritual experience is not in a position to write. When he is in the state of receiving the spiritual experiences, he can't even open his eyes, let alone write about it. Actually, writing and speaking are physical acts. When the process of divine living knowledge happens, all physical activities stop at that point; they end. So how will the act of writing be possible then? That's why, until today, one's spiritual experience of Paramatma hasn't been written down.

"But these spiritual experiences will be written down in your lifetime, and you will write about all this because your capacity to give is much more than your capacity to receive. You always think about giving, and because of this limitless desire to keep giving you will become a medium for spiritual experiences, and Paramatma will get this work of (giving) experiences done through you. I don't know how he will get it done, but this work will definitely take place. Your ability to acquire it is inevitable because of your capacity to give; and because of your capacity to give, several Gurus chose you as their medium, and you will become a suitable and appropriate pure medium, because you don't have any identity of your own. It becomes very easy to make someone a medium, who doesn't have any identity of his own. It is easy because the flow of energy starts to flow quickly through him so that he can pass it on as fast as possible.

"The purpose of knowledge is to spread that knowledge. Your purpose of getting living knowledge is to spread the living knowledge, and for that very reason each and every one is handing over their knowledge of spiritual experiences to you. My dear! No one pours oil in a broken earthen lamp. Oil is always poured into the lamp that is ready to burn, one which is suitable to accept the oil. The container of your lamp is huge; it can hold a lot of oil. I believe that it is my good fortune that I had the chance to pour oil into your container during my lifetime, because the darkness of ignorance in this world is going to be removed by the illumination of your lamp.

"You have to leave from here tomorrow morning. Tomorrow, I will come with you till the river. There you will make a boat out of bamboos and begin your journey. This same river meets the river Brahmaputra ahead. The banks of the Brahmaputra will now be the area for your next spiritual practice. Just as you are going to move from a small river to a large river, I, too am a small river in the river of knowledge; now I am sending you to an even bigger river, and I have been preparing you to send you to that Guru. That Guru lives on the banks of the river Brahmaputra, and you have to go to him next."

When I woke up the next morning, I wondered why Paramatma sent me to such beautiful places where I couldn't stay for long. I became very sad and emotional. I had become attached to that ashram in a very short time. I told Gurudev, "I have become very attached to your ashram. I like staying here and I don't want to leave this place."

"My state is also similar," Gurudev replied. "I have also started to love you in this short period of time. I have also become attached to you. I have been greatly influenced by your humility and your desire to distribute knowledge. But Guru-karya is greater than our feelings. The Gurus have entrusted you to me with the faith that you will spread this knowledge and convey it to every human being. Finally, regarding the ashram, I give you my blessings that you will have your own large and grand ashram, from where millions of souls will absorb knowledge. Come, let's go. I have to drop you near the river and then return." And I, who was tied to my Guru-karya, started off with a heavy heart. Later, after walking for some time we reached the river, which was flowing down the hill. There, Gurudev had already prepared a boat with four layers of bamboos and made it ready. What a boat it was! It was just like a wall made from four layers of bamboo, which had to be put in the water, and then one had to sit on it. It kept on moving. I had seen ordinary tribal people using this kind of boat.

I told Gurudev, "I don't know how to make this boat float and I don't even know where I have to go." He laughed and said, "You just get into the boat without worrying. At your next location, there is a great sage. His subtle body will properly guide you to his place because he has sent for you. Even now he is with you. I can see him, but you can't, and that is the difference between us."

Gurudev wished me a very emotional farewell. I bowed and touched his feet, and he happily blessed me, "May you be successful!" Then he gave me some fruits and made me sit on that raft-like boat, and then gave me a long bamboo to help me move the raft in case it got stuck somewhere. Then he wished me farewell, and I started out on a journey into the unknown ...

# Episode Three

*With Shreenath Baba*

I was going towards an unknown place. When I looked back, I saw that Gurudev was climbing the hill. I was moving forward, the water was flowing slowly, so the raft began to move ahead slowly.

This was my first journey on this kind of boat. The entire boat was made of bamboo—there was a vertical bamboo, and over that a horizontal bamboo, and then again, a vertical bamboo and another horizontal bamboo. In this way, there were four layers one above the other, and there was a square-shaped wall-like base that was twelve feet wide and twelve feet long and about one foot thick. All these bamboos had been tied together by rope made of bamboo bark. They had been tied very tightly. The flow of water was good in the river, and therefore there was no question of the boat getting stuck anywhere. I had fastened the bamboo oar and was sitting at ease. The boat was moving easily with the flow of the river. Soon, it would be evening, and my boat was slowly moving in the middle of the river. The sun was setting, and the rays of the sun reflected in the water. There was a thick forest on either side, and I hadn't seen any habitation so far. I passed grove after grove of banana trees.

Night had almost fallen, and I lay down on the raft-like boat. I thought, whatever happens, we will see at the time it happens; Gurudev had said that Gurudev himself is present with me in his subtle form, so why should I worry about what will happen? And so, in that state, I fell asleep.

When I woke up in the morning, I found that the boat had slowed down. It was still moving but moving slowly. Gurudev had given me two bamboos, which I had tied and put on one side. I had some fruits and my shoulder bag, which I had also tied securely. I went to the edge of the raft and washed my hands and face and drank some water and felt refreshed. The scenery was still the same. There were jungles in the surrounding hills, but there was no sign of any human beings. And so, my journey continued. In the afternoon, I found that different coloured fish were moving around the boat fearlessly. The water was not very deep here, and so the speed of the boat had decreased. But the water was so clear that the fish could be seen swimming beneath the surface, and stones of various shapes and colours also looked very beautiful. The afternoon heat was really intense. It was cloudy yesterday, so I did not feel the heat, but today it was very sunny.

It felt that this is like life, which changes like light and shadow. Man should learn to live under both circumstances. I had been travelling alone since yesterday, and I don't know why, but I never felt I was alone. I felt as if Gurudev was constantly travelling with me and saying, "Hey! Every soul comes alone into this world and travels alone in the same way. The soul always travels alone. It is never with anybody. What goes along with it is the physical body. All these are experiences of the body, all these are relationships of the body, and the body is perishable. That is why the relationships of this body are also perishable. Sometimes new relationships are formed, and sometimes old relationships end. Several old relatives leave you and move on, and several new relatives enter your life. All relationships continue moving in life—like at an inn. The relationships that are formed through one's body are perishable like the body. All relationships of human beings are temporary.

"There is only one everlasting relationship of the soul, and that is the relationship with Paramatma, because the soul has been created through Paramatma. Paramatma is the Satguru of one's soul, which creates the soul. Satguru is the mother who gives birth to the soul. This relationship between the soul and Satguru lasts birth after birth. This relationship is everlasting because, without the Satguru, the birth of a soul is not possible. That is why a lot of importance is placed on this relationship in life, and such an everlasting relationship is now present with you. So, what difference does it make whether someone is with you or not with you?"

Absorbed in these thoughts, I didn't realize when afternoon had passed. I hadn't seen any other boat or any other village or anything at all throughout the day, and the boat was moving forward. Again, it was evening. Today, I saw the sunset taking place behind the hills, between two hillocks. That was a very attractive scene where the sun was slowly setting between these two hills. Now I could easily look towards the sun. I prayed and bowed before the sun God and suddenly remembered how I used to sit with Gurudev on top of the hill and watch the sunset. For quite some time after sunset the redness remained spread out in the sky, which created a red glow everywhere in the sky, and then again night slowly fell.

This was my second night on this boat. I wondered how far I had to go; and the river Brahmaputra, on whose banks Gurudev's ashram is situated, had not yet arrived. His name was Shreenath Baba. He was a great ascetic, and very knowledgeable in the spiritual field. Gurudev had said that my spiritual knowledge would start only after I reached Shreenath Baba. He was a great yogi and had acquired several divine energies. Gurudev had told me quite a lot about him, and so the desire to meet Shreenath Baba was getting stronger in my mind. It was because of that strong desire that I was prepared to embark on such a daring journey. I sometimes felt that Gurudev had become the medium for pushing me into the water in this boat and sending me on this journey, because I was not really ready, and it was he who had pushed the boat out.

It seemed as if his only purpose was to push me. Do you think I would have been ready to go on such a journey if he had not forcibly pushed me? I would never have been ready on my own. Never! Yes, after pushing the boat into the water, I sat right in the middle of the boat; because if I sat on the edge the boat would have started rocking due to my weight, and its direction would also be altered. Thus, I was forced to sit, and I sat on the boat, and I also learnt to manage it, something completely new to me. So, even in the spiritual field, once a person takes up that path, he can create the path to liberation on his own through practice, and then achieve liberation. This means that the Satguru does not do anything. We ourselves have to accomplish everything on our own through practice. Yes, the Satguru has to give you a push in order to enter this spiritual field. And that push is the push of spiritual experience. If one doesn't get that push, then no one can reach the spiritual field on his own. Thus, the Satguru doesn't do anything on the spiritual path, but it is also true that without a Satguru a person can't do anything on his own in the spiritual field. In order to dive into this field one definitely requires a push, and the spiritual push is also very important, and equally not important. Today was a full moon night, and the moonlight was proving to be very helpful since the water was highly turbulent. Several fish were jumping and dancing in the water around my boat and creating a loud noise. Because of the competition of those jumping fish, I could constantly hear various sounds.

The sounds made by the jumping fish sounded very loud as the rest of the atmosphere was totally silent. Over a long distance, as far as the eyes could see, the whole river seemed to be lit up in the moonlight, and the water was shining. I stayed awake until midnight, and later I didn't even realize that I had fallen asleep.

In the morning, the boat started shaking a lot, and so I woke up. The river was flowing downwards, and it was flowing very fast.

The boat was also moving forward very fast. The sun was about to rise when I saw that, suddenly, there was a greater flow in the river, and I was looking at a sea. I thought that I had lost my way, and instead of reaching the Bramhaputra I had reached the sea by mistake. Waves of water were rising in all directions, and the boat didn't stop but also jumped quite a bit. The boat jumped especially when the water rose and fell. Several times I jumped at least two feet on the boat. I held on tightly to the rope with which I had tied the bamboos so that I shouldn't fall off the boat. Several times the boat tilted sideways up to ten feet at a time, and it was going very fast. I couldn't see any bank nearby. Suddenly, there was a big wave, and my boat turned turtle. I was underneath and the boat was above me. I went to the side of the boat and tried to hold on to the rope at the edge and managed to catch hold of a slightly loose rope.

The river water was ice-cold, and I was flowing along with the help of the rope. There was water everywhere, and I thought for a moment that the time had arrived for me to take Jal Samadhi. I thought maybe I was supposed to do only so much spiritual work in this lifetime, and that I would reach Shreenath Baba in my next life; there was such a flood of water that it was difficult to continue holding on to the rope. I suddenly remembered that Gurudev had said that Shreenath Baba was with me in a subtle form and he would show me the way; astonishingly, as soon as I remembered what Gurudev had said, with a forceful push from the water, the boat became upright once again, and I sat on the raft. Now the current was flowing very fast. All the fruits I had with me were washed away, and only my cloth bag, which had got caught in the bamboo, was saved.

When I sat a little more comfortably, I saw that it wasn't a sea but the river; but it was so vast that it looked like the sea. Then I could see the riverbank on my right hand, but the river was so wide that I couldn't see the riverbank on my left. Then I remembered Gurudev's words that the river Brahmaputra was of the male gender. All the other rivers are female—river Ganga, river Narmada, river Godavari, river Yamuna—but Brahmaputra is the only river that is male. That is why it is quite wide and appears vast. Gurudev had also said that there is such a strong current in the water that even if an elephant falls in it, it will be swept away. The current was really very strong, and it was only because of Gurudev's grace that I was not swept away.

I don't know how, but the river appeared to be getting closer, and the boat was slowly sliding away from the main river on its own towards the right-hand side. I wasn't doing anything, but this was happening as if someone was taking the boat towards the right-hand side. What was that invisible energy? By now I had moved away from the main current of the river towards the right. There was a small island, and it was covered with a thick forest. This island was in the middle of the river Brahmaputra because water was flowing behind the island, too. The boat slowly started moving towards the island on its own, and I took out the bamboo and gave support to the boat so that it could get to the shore. I got out of the boat and tied it to a tree. By then it was already evening. I wondered whether I should spend the night under that tree or do something else. I didn't know what to do.

I wrung out my wet clothes and, after sitting quietly for some time, I prayed to Shreenath Baba that according to his wishes, through his compassion, I had arrived here. "I pray to you that the road ahead should also be guided by you and with your compassion." I prayed and sat down quietly, and I felt someone coming towards me. It seemed to me that perhaps there was a shadow in the jungle on the other side. I didn't know if that was just my feeling or if it was true. I decided to stay there because it would be dangerous to search for anything in such a thick jungle.

I didn't know anything about the place, so I quietly sat down under the tree.

I couldn't see anything in the jungle on the other side, but it seemed as if someone was coming. The whole atmosphere appeared very enjoyable. A fresh earthy scent was spreading through the air, and it seemed as if someone was approaching from the other side; but no one was visible. I was not at all afraid despite the sound of the footsteps, but I was curious to know if someone was really coming or if it only seemed so. I wasn't delusional; someone was really approaching. The sound of footsteps could be heard coming closer, and my attention slowly focused on those footsteps, as if they were the footsteps of someone I knew. Slowly, easily, my chitta started going within, and my body became as cold as ice, and my eyes grew heavy. I wanted to keep my eyes open, but I just couldn't, and I felt as if a cloud had appeared in front of me. There was bright light everywhere, and for a moment I felt as if it was the light of the moon. But no, that was something quite different. I had never experienced anything like this in my life. The hair on my body stood on end as if it had also become alert and awake, and I didn't notice when my eyes had closed, and I went into meditation.

When I returned to my senses, I heard the following words, "Wake up, my child, open your eyes. I have arrived." I felt someone lightly touching the crown of my head. A shiver ran through my body, and his hand was so cold that it seemed as if someone had placed a block of ice on top of my head. When I slowly opened my eyes, Gurudev said, "I am Shreenath Baba. Wake up."

I saw that a very old ascetic was standing in front of me. He had a tall but weak body. He had practised a lot of penance, and its effect was clearly visible on his body. His whole body was wrinkled, and his hands were trembling, but there was a divine radiance on his face. He seemed to be very old. I prostrated before him. Gurudev lifted me up and said laughingly, "So, you had to keep diving again and again in the Brahmaputra to reach me, didn't you? Come on, come to my hut." I realized that he had understood through his chitta-shakti how I had travelled. I went along with him. It was a barren place. I don't know how far I walked with him, but it had grown dark by the time we reached his hut. He gave me some fruits to eat, and there was a small hut on the outer side in which some fruits had been placed, and he asked me to take rest there. He said, "You must be very tired. Go to sleep and take rest. We'll talk tomorrow morning." I was so tired that I didn't notice when I had fallen asleep.

When I woke up the next morning, I sat up, and for some time I couldn't make out where I was and who I was with, or even in which ashram. Then, slowly, I remembered that Gurudev had made me sit in the boat; I had reached the banks of the river Brahmaputra, and Shreenath Baba had met me there and had brought me to his hut. Yes, so now I was in his hut. After some time, I came out and sat outside the hut. I looked around me and saw that in the vicinity there was a thick jungle. It was at a slightly higher level, like a hillock, and there was thick foliage all around. This place was right in the middle of the river Brahmaputra, and perhaps Gurudev lived alone on this island because no one else was visible. After some time, I saw Gurudev returning from the river after taking his bath. I saw him and greeted him with folded hands. He told me to go and take my bath.

I saw that my lungi had dried during the night, and my cloth bag and other clothes had also dried. I took the lungi that served as my towel and went to the river. The bank of the river was down below, though it was not very wide. There were big rocks nearby, and as a result the flow of water was a little slower. My boat was still tied up there. I looked at the boat fondly. It had been my companion during my journey. Then I bathed in the river Brahmaputra. I was beginning to realize why this river Brahmaputra is a masculine river. Its expanse was as immense as the sea. I sat on a large rock for a while after my bath. I could see the effect of Gurudev's vibrations and energy on every tree and stone. I returned to the hut, and Gurudev said, "Eat some fruits etc., and we'll talk later."

I had some fruits, and later Gurudev said, "My name is Shreenath Baba. I have been doing penance here for several years. You are the first person to come here, and no one has been able to get here until today, because I don't want anyone else here. That is why this whole island isn't visible to anyone, and there is no question of anyone coming here. I have brought you here, and it was I who guided your boat and brought it here. There is a purpose in bringing you here."

I very humbly told Gurudev, "I surrender myself before you at your feet. Please make use of my body in whichever way you can for your purpose. It is my great fortune that I have got a chance to help you in your work in whichever way you desire."

He spoke very seriously as he said, "Nature has its own cycle, and it is within this cycle that we are born and within this cycle that we die. Every soul must respect this cycle and I, too, wish to respect this cycle. I wish to give up my body, and it is my final wish, that after I die, you should perform my last rites. I wish that after I take samadhi, you should cremate my body with your hands so that I can attain liberation. It is the son's duty to cremate his father. I don't have a son, and I accept you in the form of my manas-putra, and just as a son receives all his father's wealth, similarly I, too, wish to hand over to you the legacy of all the knowledge that I have obtained."

I was thunderstruck by this unbelievable talk. Expressing my fear, I said, "I have never performed cremation on anyone all by myself. I don't even know how the ceremony has to be performed."

He said, "Don't worry about that. I will arrange all of that. Did you know how to ride a boat? But you managed to reach here, didn't you? In the same way, I will assist you in my cremation.

"My Gurudev had also called me here in the same way, and after accepting me as his son, he asked me to cremate him. His purpose was to convey that knowledge to you. I am only a medium for my Guru. This area of inner knowledge is very vast. A single birth is not enough for it. It can't be attained in one birth. If one attains it in one birth, then that can only happen with the Guru-krupa. But it is one thing to acquire it through the Guru-krupa; to be a suitable candidate to obtain it is a very different state. Man is tied down in the bonds of his karma, and this feeling of karma is connected to his body. The Guru's nature is to keep on giving continuously. The Guru's nature is like this holy river Brahmaputra. It will give to whoever comes before it, just as the river will quench the thirst of whoever comes to its shore. But the river will quench the thirst of the person regardless of whether he is a sage or an ascetic or a thief, because it has become its nature to quench the thirst of whoever comes to its shore. The river performs this duty free of charge and equally with everyone. These are two special qualities of Paramatma: he loves everyone equally, and he is equally compassionate towards everyone without any discrimination. Paramatma is available to everyone. If someone is ready to meet Paramatma, then Paramatma is also ready to meet him. Yes, Paramatma will love equally, even an atheist who doesn't believe in Him. There isn't even a little bit of deficiency in Paramatma's compassion.

"That is why believers live comfortably in Paramatma's world, and non-believers also live comfortably in His world. Both are the same for Paramatma. Thus, these are the two special qualities of Paramatma—one, that it is free of charge and secondly, that it is equal. In this way, the Guru wipes out his existence in meditation and merges himself with nature. Thus, the special qualities of nature become a part of the Guru. He bestows knowledge free of charge and bestows it equally to everyone. He is exactly like this river. Now just imagine that because of the good karma of his previous birth, some person gets the proximity of some Guru, then the Guru bestows knowledge on him according to his nature. He will not see whether that person is suitable or not. Now it is up to this person to decide when he will take advantage of this knowledge. Inner knowledge is present within this person. But it is the personal affair of that person, whether to behave according to that inner knowledge, or whether to believe in that inner knowledge. It is not necessary for you to behave according to inner knowledge in this birth or not. It is possible that a person may behave according to this inner knowledge in his next birth or in the birth after that, because the existence of 'I' in every person is his personal affair. If you don't give up this 'I' sense, the inner knowledge will not germinate. When it doesn't germinate at all, there is no question of the tree of inner knowledge rising.

"The feeling of 'I' exists as a personal attachment in every physical body. The feeling of 'I' is an illusion, but the soul realizes it only after it leaves the body. Nothing can be done after that because the body is left behind, and spiritual progress is not possible without the physical body. This means that a person will be able to achieve it only if he gives up the feelings and emotions connected to the physical body, before he gives up the body (before he dies). But this doesn't happen, and man keeps wandering for several births in spite of obtaining the proximity of a Guru, and after getting inner knowledge through the Guru-krupa. One has to make a study of the feelings and emotions of the physical body before one gives up the body. Only then can one give up the feelings of the body. This is similar to the example that the land receives a good quality seed through the grace of some tree; but it is the job of the land to decide when to germinate that seed. The seed keeps the possibility of a tree within itself, but the seed won't germinate as long as it doesn't give up its outer skin. The condition of the land determines when the seed should shed its outer skin. The tree gives the seed because of its nature to give, but it can't make the seed grow into a tree. It is the seed that will have to transform itself into a tree, and the timing of this will be decided by the seed itself. In this matter, the tree can't force the seed. In the case of inner knowledge also it is the same. To obtain inner knowledge and to behave according to it are two different things.

"Once the soul receives inner knowledge, then again it starts developing whenever it finds an appropriate atmosphere after taking another birth. The atmosphere and proximity around a person are either good or bad conductors for it. It all depends on the proximity and when the atmosphere around it will be suitable; and who knows when this proximity in life will be available, in which birth, and when it will be possible to accept that proximity positively? Nothing is pre-determined. There are seven energy centres in our body. The sadhak has to activate these centres. Only after that is it possible to circulate the entire energy throughout the whole body.

"Before explaining all these things, it is imperative to know the secret of human birth. There is a holy atma-lok and all souls have come to the earth from there. The situation of this atma-lok is like a different earth, and all souls live there in collectivity. It has its own limit. Sometimes, when its grip on the collectivity weakens, then that soul leaves this place; and after leaving it, it realizes that there is nothing at all outside. It thinks: 'I came out unnecessarily because of my curiosity,' but after leaving, its collective energy ends. Then, based on its desires, the soul chooses a physical body. One can understand the capacity for spiritual work of a physical body from its composition and the state of the chakras. The soul knows how suitable that body is; and after realizing this, it takes on some physical body with the purpose of attaining liberation. Thus, the soul itself makes the choice of the body in which it wishes to be born.

"When the parents live together, then, their aura is created according to their thoughts and their mental state. If they come close to each other only out of lust, then their aura will be of the physical level; if they have come closer with a Soulful feeling, then it will be at the soul level; and if they have come close to each other in order to invite some spiritual pious soul, then that aura will be of a very high level. Thus, their aura affects their life, and conception takes place under its effect. The foetus will be formed at the level at which conception takes place, and a soul of that level will arrive in that body. This is the reason why the same parents may have two children, one of whom is good, and the other is bad. This is the only reason why there is such a great difference between them. Then the soul takes birth through that body, and after taking birth a lot depends on the kind of company it gets. Quite a lot also depends on that. Several times the soul forgets its purpose for taking birth after it has taken birth, and at the end of his life, when it leaves the body, it realizes the purpose of his life. But by then it is too late. At the time of each birth, the soul leads towards evolution. Evolution keeps on taking place at all levels—material, physical and mental levels. In the course of this evolution, the soul gets inner knowledge in some birth. To get the inner knowledge, to understand the inner knowledge and to internalize it—all this takes place birth after birth. This is not an event that can take place in one birth. Man has to take several births for this.

"With every birth that man takes, one more energy gets connected to it. This energy is called Kundalini Shakti. This Shakti carries the records of every birth that the soul takes; its account is maintained. And according to what is written, the soul moves in the direction of evolution in every birth. This Kundalini Shakti enters the body in every birth with the soul and leaves the body at the time of death. This is the same Shakti with whose support the soul can progress spiritually. The body is a tool of the soul, and the tool of Kundalini is the soul. The body is a tool of the soul and without it the soul can't obtain liberation. We may call the body a bag of flesh and bones, or we may attach less importance to the body, but the truth is that without this perishable body, obtaining liberation is impossible. It would be a mistake from any perspective to consider the human body to be less important. The body is the vehicle for every soul. Without the vehicle we ourselves will make the journey go on for years at a time.

"There are several dead spirits that have been wandering about for hundreds of years in the form of ghosts because they don't have a body. When they existed in the body, they didn't make proper use of the body, and now they are wandering about without the body. If a saintly person with a physical body doesn't pray for their liberation, they will keep on wandering, and because you have come to me with the desire to get inner knowledge, the first lesson is that you should realize the importance of the physical body and understand the life of the body. The human life as such appears to be quite long. But man spends most of his lifetime sleeping, and he wastes the remaining time focused on useless things. He tries to understand everyone except himself, but he doesn't know that his life is running out with all this activity. Each and every moment of a man's life is important. But it is his nature to live with negativities. He should know how to live every moment positively." Quite a lot of time had passed, and we ended our discussion there.

In the state of Assam, the river Brahmaputra has a lot of importance attached to it. Even in Assamese literature, references to this river can be found in poems and stories. I had never imagined that this river would be so large. When I went for my bath in the morning, I used to sit on the large rocks there. Several hours passed by, and I would not even be aware of it. I had become attached to this river in the time I stayed there. The special quality of the river was that its flow was never stable at the same level. One flow was always fast and kept changing. The water used to be clean and very cold, like ice. The atmosphere around was also quite cold. This river had a wide basin; it was so wide that the other bank couldn't be seen at all. It was vast, and in spite of having such a wide basin, its flow was quite fast. I went to Gurudev's hut after my bath. Gurudev did not have any fixed routine. Sometimes he kept meditating and sometimes he kept talking. Today, when I arrived there, I found that Gurudev was seated in his hut, meditating. I stood there watching him. He had tied dry banana leaves around his waist, and there was no other clothing on his body. His body looked dark and weak. Each bone was visible. His countenance was very peaceful but, behind this aged body, his energies were present; energies in the quest for which his body had become decrepit.

There was a very strong aura behind this weak body. When I tried to look beyond his weakened body, I experienced a very powerful light there. Whatever I was seeing through my eyes was external, but one requires inner eyes to be able to look within. Suddenly, I don't know what happened—a golden fiery radiance came out of his crown! And it slowly increased. It came out of his crown and started falling on the top of my crown; it felt as if nectar was being showered on me. In this way, I experienced nectar for the first time in my life. The words of Gurudev could be very clearly heard like Celestial sounds from the sky: "A pure and holy chitta has great importance in the spiritual field. Any negative thought can make the chitta impure. A pure chitta can only reside in a pure and holy body. A weak body weakens the chitta, too. The chitta is related to the muladhar or root chakra. The muladhar chakra is situated in the body in the small stretch between the urinary passage and the anal passage. The bad energy that has entered one's body can be expelled into the earth element from here. The work of this chakra is to remove the extraneous elements that have been created by the body. The control of this chakra is at the place from where the body discharges its waste. This chakra does the work of excreting the waste from one's body, and also of throwing out the dirt of one's bad thoughts. This chakra does the work of purifying one's body and chitta.

"This place is a seat of power. It is absolutely essential to purify the body before absorbing any new energy in one's body. This chakra is purified after seven years of continual spiritual practice. I had to perform spiritual practice for seven years on every chakra, and forty-nine years of my life have been spent only in purifying my chakras. This is not meant for an ordinary person. Only a person who is completely devoted and for whom spiritual progress is the only purpose in his life can be successful in this spiritual endeavour."

Gurudev was talking to me about it, and I started feeling vibrations in my muladhar chakra. I suddenly felt as if the temperature in my body had increased; and it was so hot that I felt as if I was sitting on hot coals. But, at the same time, I didn't feel like getting up from there. It was a very strange situation.

Slowly, those vibrations started to rotate, and I felt as if all the heat was passing out from the place of the muladhar chakra into the earth, and then I went into meditation. When I came out of the meditation, I saw that a lot of time had passed. Gurudev was arranging some wood to light a fire, and so I started to help him. Gurudev said, "As a result of constant spiritual practice, unknown divine powers have developed within me. Now I have grown old, and these energies that I have obtained are of no use to me. I have fulfilled the purpose of my life, and during the period of my spiritual practice, these inner Shaktis have developed. There are several divine energies in our body; there are several positive energies, but as long as our chitta is outside, they cannot develop. Every human being has the potential to grow from a human being to a super being, and this opportunity is equally available to everyone. When we meditate, our chitta goes inwards, and only when it goes inwards, then those energies start appearing one by one. One birth does not seem to be sufficient to develop all those energies. This is a process of spiritual evolution, and everything takes place slowly.

"I wish that I could go even further than the level I have achieved, with you as a medium; through you I can reach that high peak, after attaining which there is nothing more to achieve. I could not reach that place in my life as I ran out of time, but it is my desire that you should reach that peak. Will you fulfil this final wish for me?"

I became very emotional and replied, "Gurudev, which high peak are you talking about reaching? I can't understand it. You want me to reach the place that you couldn't. I want my ego to disintegrate here, and I want you to reach that high peak, and wish that the life of my 'I' should come to an end, not yours. Please give me your blessings Gurudev, that from today I may live not as 'I' but as you. Today, I am surrendering my total existence at your feet. From today, let each breath that I take be according to your wish, and that every moment of my life is spent in your presence. From today onwards, I should die, and you should remain alive. From now onwards, only you should remain in life. Please end my 'I' sense. From today, I will live my entire life in your form. Today, I am surrendering my 'I' sense to you. People offer flowers to Paramatma, but I'm surrendering my ego to you. Please accept everything." And, with that, I started weeping.

When I awoke in the morning, I found that my whole body had become very light. The whole morning was full of joy, and there was a sense of peace around me. Gurudev was sitting in meditation, and so I went to the river to bathe. These days, the riverbank was my favourite place. On the way from the riverbank to the river, I had to cross a path on which there were big and small rounded stones. They were beautiful stones formed from years of water flowing over them, so they had become smooth and rounded. As a result of constantly being in the flowing water, the level of their energies had also increased. There were some yellow-coloured stones, as well as white ones, some black ones, red ones and some green ones. Some stones even shone like glass. I collected some black and white smooth rounded shaligram there, and every day I used them as decoration by placing them in different shapes; everyday, this was my game. These stones were my only companions, they were my friends and I used to like being with them. I would play the whole day with them and bathe there. I didn't even realize when a whole day passed. Several fish also became my friends, and I used to bring some special seeds for them to eat, and they would eat those seeds. I had learned through this experiment that they liked eating the seeds.

Everything had to be learned here through experiments. When I went into the water, a lot of fish gathered there; and when I bathed in the water, they bit me, and this tickled me a lot. They kept playing like this. When I got tired, I would sit in the shadow of some big rock because there wasn't even a tree in the vicinity of the water. I had three or four fixed places for my bath. I used to go to the same fixed places for my bath. I would decide on the place according to the time I had available. When Gurudev was meditating, then I used to go off to faraway places for my bath. When he was not meditating, I would go to someplace nearby. Whenever I went to a far-off place, I would only return to the hut in the evening. A yellow grass used to grow on the stones of the river along the bank. It didn't grow everywhere, and wherever I found it, I would eat it.

I would take a small bamboo, fill it with small stones, and then tie one end of it and close it with some leaves. This would thus be turned into a wonderful musical instrument. That bamboo used to become a rattle. I had prepared several such instruments and had fixed them into the ground in several places. There were no other humans around, and therefore anything that was put in one place remained there for days at a time. Whenever I looked east, I saw great snow-covered mountains. In the afternoon, the snow shone so brightly that one couldn't look at it. There were also some crabs in the river, which could be seen sometimes together with the fish. There were more black-coloured fish. It felt good to be in the water, and I didn't notice that a whole day had passed. I would talk to the fishes; I would talk to the stones and get great joy from that. As a result of being in the water for a long time, I would feel very hungry. It was a completely isolated and lonely place. It was filled with natural beauty, and one lost track of time immersed in nature. I got some idea of the time of the day by observing the sun; and the other way I could guess the time was by looking at the shadow of the tree—the shadow of this tree falling here means it is going to be afternoon, or it is going to be evening.

In this way, I could guess what the approximate time was. There was no need to know the exact time, and during the night one could gauge the time by looking at the moon. But one had also to keep the shape of the moon in mind because there is a difference in the time of the moon rising during amavasya and purnima. The riverbank looked beautiful on the full moon night.

One morning, Gurudev suddenly said, "There are countless energies within our body, but we are not able to develop them. If our mind is pure, then we get to know in advance about incidents that are going to happen. We can, therefore, make the necessary preparations to face such situations, if we know about them in advance. Because we get to know about the incidents before they take place, and all the energies that give us the information are natural, we don't need to perform any special spiritual practice for that. We need to only keep our mind pure, because if our mind is pure then whatever event is going to happen in nature, or if there is a possibility of it happening, can be discovered through one's chitta. One can get advance information about an earthquake or an approaching storm or floods, so, through proper study, it is possible to guess the right time when these calamities will happen. This is because earthquakes, floods, storms—all of these don't come suddenly. A certain type of atmosphere is created before they occur, and man can't guess about that atmosphere in nature. That's why it seems as if the storm has come suddenly, or the earthquake has occurred suddenly or that the flood has come suddenly. In reality, nothing happens suddenly.

"Before an earthquake occurs, there is a change in the vibrations of energy. This change also affects the gravitational force of the earth. Exactly the same thing happens before a storm approaches. It affects the wind pattern, and similarly, it rains heavily before the floods. One can make a guess about rain also from the clouds and one can get a lot of help from the study of clouds. Animals like elephants, mice, etc., are more sensitive than we are. That is why they become aware in advance about the changes that are going to take place in nature. They also increase their knowledge through spiritual experience. This is the only difference between human beings and animals—human beings think, and animals do not. Man needlessly wastes all his energy in thoughts about the past and the future. That is why meditation is that state in which man conserves his energy and uses the energy to awaken the Shaktis lying dormant within himself. Kundalini Shakti is an energy present in the human body, but man is not aware of it. This is the Shakti of Paramatma, and after it is awakened, all the Shaktis within man start to awaken, or we can say that the birth-giving Shakti that is within man is the Kundalini Shakti. This is Paramatma's energy, and it can't be awakened if one doesn't get the presence of Paramatma. This Shakti carries several other Shaktis along with it, and it awakens only in the collectivity of Paramatma. It can't be awakened (through one's efforts). Paramatma has a very special quality—Paramatma can't be obtained through one's efforts because whatever efforts we put will be at the physical level, whereas Paramatma is the name of collectivity at the soul level. So how can it be obtained through efforts at the physical level?

"You can reach Paramatma only through your pure desire. The stronger your desire, the easier will be the path to reach Paramatma. Pure desire, good desire, is always created through a pure chitta. There is a written account of man's karma in this Kundalini Shakti. It is influenced by man's karma. Several times it so happens that, when something is created, the fault of creation is inherent in the created object. Similarly, at the time of the birth of a person, when the human body is being created, some faults are passed on by the child's parents due to their thoughts and values. That's why the soul can't progress until these faults are removed, and that is why the life of several people in their early years is filled with difficulties and failures. But the latter part of their life is good. After the Kundalini has been awakened, first of all one's fault-filled karma are destroyed. One's spiritual journey commences after enduring them. This Kundalini Shakti can only be awakened in the presence of a Satguru who has the authority to awaken it through his grace. Whether the blessings happen or not depends on the capacity of a person to absorb them, because one can't obtain the grace of any Satguru through one's own efforts. Blessings are after all blessings—they just happen automatically.

"Your desire to give is more than your desire to gain, and as a result the collective desire of millions of souls has been created automatically within you; and, therefore, your capacity to absorb is millions of times more than that of an ordinary man. One can therefore understand that millions of souls will obtain the spiritual experiences of the soul through you, but that time is still to come. Your limitless capacity to absorb has increased manifold as a result of your limitless capacity to give, and this is the purpose of your life. It is because of your desire that you have reached me, and because of this desire that I wish to entrust you with the Shaktis I have obtained through my spiritual practice. When you reach millions of people, those Shaktis will reach the people through your medium. Just as every gardener desires the progress of his plants, in the same manner every ascetic, every sage hopes that the energies that he has acquired should reach every human being. He is connected to the entire human race, and not only to one person. That is why the Gurus always live in a vast circle, a vast area, and always try to uplift the human race; and only those who try to uplift the human race get the golden opportunity to do so. Such a chance is not available to an ordinary man. You have been given such a chance, and through your medium I am also getting this chance.

"Your pure desire to give to others has increased your suitability. There is no place for efforts at the physical level, and everything depends on the suitability of the person. The more open and generous a person's heart, the greater his ability to think; that person will have great opportunities in his life. That is why we should always keep our way of thinking pure and holy, and our chitta will also develop equally. The Guru-element is the Shakti of

Paramatma. We call the body of the soul that dissolves its body in the Guru-element a Guru. Guru is not a physical body; Guru is the medium of Guru-energies. And the easiest way of obtaining energy from the Guru is to surrender oneself to the Guru, because our ego breaks down as soon as we surrender ourselves. Then, as our capacity to absorb increases, we start experiencing the Guru. The Guru is a power to be experienced. Experience the Guru in whose presence we are present. It won't be enough only to be with the Guru—one will have to experience the Guru. And after experiencing the Guru, one will be able to understand the Guru-element within the Guru; one will be able to recognize it. This can only be possible when the connection between both the souls has been established. When this happens, the knowledge of the spiritual experience itself makes one aware of all other knowledge. It makes us aware of knowledge that we never even imagined could exist within us.

"Generally, man tries to hold on to external information, but in order to do so his chitta goes outside, and when the chitta goes outside it becomes weak. One can go within oneself and obtain knowledge about the outside world, but this is only possible through the medium of experiencing feelings, because this is the only way to go within oneself and know about the outside world. One can obtain all types of information through the chitta.

"At every energy centre of the body, man gets experiences of different types of feelings. But to experience the feelings, there is a need to be pure and holy. The body plays a very important role in spiritual practice. Many people don't give importance to the body because they think that the body is perishable, but this is not correct. In reality, it is due to the body that you possess the chitta, and yoga takes place because of the chitta. The meaning of yoga is to get connected. In getting connected, the whole role is of the chitta. We get connected to Paramatma through the medium of this chitta, and this chitta is a gift of the physical body. The chitta is the guide on the spiritual path. Just as the body has two eyes, the eyes of the soul are the chitta. Till now, the spiritual path has been very narrow. One Guru could transfer the sensitivities that he had developed through his spiritual practices to only one disciple during his lifetime, because after this transfer the Guru would give up his body. Till now this transfer happened at the physical level, because that was the prevalent practice.

"Now a new age is beginning from your tenure. This process of transfer of subtle sensitivities will happen in a subtle form during your lifetime. The physical body will have no role to play in that transfer. This will happen only through the subtle body. As a result of the subtle body performing the transfer, millions of people will be able to accept its benefit, and the physical body will also continue to exist. The body will continue to exist because in this process the body will have no role to play. Whether the physical body remains or not, the subtle body will carry on with this process. This body has been created because of special prayers by the Guru-energies. Therefore, you are the 'father,' the originator of this era, and I'm blessed to have you as my disciple.

"This work will take place through the subtle body, and that's why it will happen very smoothly and easily. But this very simplicity is a barrier in this path, and because they'll get it very easily, sadhaks won't be aware of what they have received, and they'll never know what it is that they have received. This is the biggest fault of this path, because the basic nature of man is that when he receives any knowledge without any effort, without wishing for it, then he doesn't appreciate or value that knowledge. He won't care for it because the web of illusion of the physical body won't allow his attention to go to that knowledge. When the body perishes, the illusory web of the body will also break.

"When the web of illusion breaks, then only the subtle body

remains; that's why your physical body is a barrier in your work. It won't be possible for any sadhak to break out of this illusion, and therefore you won't be able to see the harvest of success of your work in your lifetime. You are planting trees whose fruits you won't be able to see. Your work will begin only after you give up your physical body. Don't feel sad after hearing all this and don't have any desire for the fruits of your work. Just continue performing your work, as that is your sphere of action."

The next morning Gurudev said, "Today is purnima and tonight we'll bathe and undertake meditative spiritual practice or anushthan."

In the evening, he took me to the banks of the river Brahmaputra. There was a fork in the river because of some large boulders that were lying there. There was a smaller flow of water on the inner side, and its speed was also slower. It wasn't possible to stand in the water, but in spite of that Gurudev went into the water where it was deeper, and asked to me to join him there. The water reached up to my chest; he asked me to concentrate my chitta on my navel. I concentrated my chitta on my navel. He said, "Stand with your chitta focused on your navel. I am transferring my energy through my navel to your navel. Accept it with a complete feeling of surrender. This will develop your nabhi chakra.

"Spiritual progress always begins from this nabhi chakra. First of all, there should be physical progress, then one should obtain inner peace and then one should have control over one's thoughts. Only after that can one reach this chakra." As Gurudev was speaking, I started experiencing coolness around my navel. I felt as if a fish had got stuck there. I even touched the place with my hand, but there was no fish there—and even then, it felt cold. Spiritual progress takes place from this chakra. An unsatisfied person can never cross this chakra. A dissatisfied sadhak can never get beyond this chakra. That is why, as long as a sadhak is not content, meditation cannot start. The sadhak will first have to become contented. Contentment is always a spiritual experience within one's soul, and this can be acquired when one goes inwards. This can never be obtained externally; foolish sadhaks keep searching for contentment outside. This is a type of inner feeling. This feeling is like that of a beggar on the one hand, who doesn't possess anything and yet can experience everything; and on the other hand, it's like that of a king, who has everything and yet can't create this feeling (of contentment). A person whose chitta is outside won't be able to establish this. To establish it, one's chitta has to be within oneself because this is an inner process, and when a person's chitta is within, this process happens on its own.

"This ocean of existence can't be crossed without the Guru's blessings, because if you don't find an authoritative Guru, you won't ever obtain this feeling, as you need at least someone to tell you that contentment can't exist externally. It is within, and one should search for it within; go within yourself, because if we don't get a great man who can guide us in our life we won't ever find out about it."

I screamed suddenly, "Gurudev, something is going round and round in my navel!" Gurudev said, "This is the chakra being activated. Let it happen.

"Contentment is not something that one can acquire from outside. Sadhaks search for contentment in perishable objects; some people get satisfaction by getting intoxicated. But, in reality, any experience of contentment can be obtained only through subtle sensitivities. This sensitivity can't be created as long as the 'I' sense is present. 'I' is always ambitious; 'I' is never satisfied and never contented. That's why it is very difficult to come out of the illusion of 'I,' which keeps taking on new forms and new layers; it keeps taking the support of the intellect, and attacks by stealth. 'I' is the enemy that we have nurtured within ourselves, and which is hidden within us in the form of a friend.

"It won't ever allow satisfaction to be established within us, because if satisfaction is established then the death of the 'I' sense will certainly take place." Gurudev went on talking, and perhaps he was talking so that I could become thoughtless, because vibrations were being showered through his speech. I still remember that night. It was a full-moon night. The river water was very cold. This was my first experience of standing in such deep water, but there was no fear at all. There was certainly a curiosity about what sort of process was taking place. The full moon of Purnima had lit up the river water. The water was shining, and the river seemed to be made of silver. From time to time, the fish became excited and jumped out of the water, up to six feet, as if all of them had suddenly become very satisfied. There were lots and lots of fish all around me; sometimes when they came and touched my body, they tickled me.

It occurred to me that fishermen move here and there in search of fish, but they still can't find them. I don't have any expectations of finding fish; instead, I don't want the fish to come so close to me, and even then, they are there. It seemed as if Gurudev was teaching me a lesson of satisfaction through the fish. He was saying, "If you wander outside, search for contentment outside; you will never find it. If you don't search for contentment outside and go inwards, there will be a shower of contentment." I thanked him in my mind for his grace. Something was moving slowly near my navel from right to left, and its circle kept widening. In the beginning, there was only a subtle feeling, but later on it seemed as if a big wheel was moving on my stomach. Its circle slowly widened so much that my whole body was enfolded in it, and its effect kept growing continually.

A bright radiance like the moonlight was being created around me, and that radiance slowly advanced towards Gurudev, and then both Gurudev and I were enveloped by that radiance. I couldn't keep my eyes open even though I wanted to, because now the radiance was outside my limit of endurance. I was experiencing a kind of weariness. I felt as if I would not even be able to continue standing in the river, and on the other hand the fish seemed to be having a jumping competition. They were not afraid of me at all. Slowly, my eyes closed, and I didn't know what happened after that, but I seemed to be in a wheel that was rotating very fast. My whole body had turned to ice, and all bodily feelings seemed to have stopped. A state of void had been created.

I don't know how long that state of void lasted; when I came out of it, I saw that it was almost morning, and Gurudev was bathing in the river. The night had passed, and it was morning, and now the vibrations in my nabhi chakra had also stopped. It was Gurudev's greatness that he never had the feeling of being a 'doer,' because he had risen above this feeling of being the 'doer' of any work. I realized that Gurudev had wiped out his identity; he had merged himself in the collective universal consciousness. That was why he was not doing anything, and yet was a complete medium of universal consciousness.

Whatever living knowledge I received last night had been acquired through his medium. He was my universal consciousness, my Paramatma, because I had attained Paramatma only through him as a medium. How could I forget the ladder of Paramatma? I was fortunate to be given the chance to stay with him for a few days. I don't know why, but I kept feeling that all these Gurus are separate from their physical bodies. They had neither met each other, nor was there any similarity between them in their colour, or their appearance, their behaviour or their spiritual practice, and yet they all appeared to be connected from within. All of them had a certain purpose, and they all knew what they were doing. All of them were at the topmost spiritual levels in their lives, and all of them had the desire to distribute the living knowledge. Despite following different paths, they could reach the same place. All of them had attained that level after undergoing very difficult and rigorous spiritual practices.

I found the presence of all of them quite similar. I never felt that I had come from one Guru to another Guru. I found all of them similar. Everyone knew about me and was also aware of what my role was going to be in the future. I didn't have any knowledge about myself, but all the others knew me. My state was such that I was walking on some unknown path on which all the other travellers knew where they were going, and I was the only one who was walking towards some unknown peak. One day, Gurudev suddenly addressed this topic and said, "You are the path. A path doesn't come from anyone, nor does it go anywhere. The path remains steady in its own place. You, too, have not come from anywhere, nor do you have to go anywhere. You don't begin from anywhere, nor do you end anywhere. You are a stationary path that was created more than 800 years ago. This path has been created because of man's desire for spiritual progress. Man expressed a desire for spiritual progress in collectivity, and this path has been created because of that desire. The continuous devotion of thousands and thousands of pious souls has been instrumental in this creation. It was only because of their spiritual devotion that this simple and straightforward path could be created. This path has been created because of a good collective energy, but today this royal path can be used by anyone who wishes to progress spiritually. This is an open road. There are no restrictions here; there is no discrimination here. It is meant for everyone.

"This path is for all those people who wish to walk on it. All they require is their soul's desire for spiritual progress because it is only due to these desiring souls that this path has been created.

You have been born because of the wish of millions of souls. One's inner progress always happens in collectivity. Only those souls who understand this secret can find it in collectivity; you have taken birth only because of the collective efforts of those souls. For example, if a diamond has fallen in the dirt, then some dirt will stick to the diamond, too. Similarly, the karma you have to endure through the body has also come along with the body through which you have been born. Only after enduring all the karma can you perform Guru-karya. Each one has to endure the pleasures and sufferings of one's body. The soul is liberated after enduring them, and after that it becomes strong through the Guru-krupa. Right now, you are under the influence of the body, which is why you won't be able to understand all that I'm telling you. When you have gone beyond the influence of this body, then you'll reach the area of the soul. The area of the soul only is everlasting, because Paramatma resides in the soul. The body is perishable, and that's why the sphere of the body is also perishable. Change is the gift of nature. No two bodies are ever alike. The secret of nature is hidden in the changes that take place in nature. Changes keep happening in everything that is connected to nature. Man also takes birth under the influence of a determined sphere of nature. That is why it keeps on changing from time to time. To change is the basic quality of nature, and changes keep on happening in nature.

"You are an ancient path that was created 800 years ago, whose aim is to help in the progress of the soul. Only those souls who wish for the progress of their soul are able to accept you. It is the personal sphere of every soul to desire the progress of one's own self. It is possible when the soul wishes for it. This can't happen under normal circumstances. When that soul wishes for its own progress, then it happens through the Guru-krupa. The Guru through whom this progress of the Self takes place doesn't do anything, but it occurs through him because he, too, is only a medium. Similarly, you, too, are only a medium. You yourselves won't do anything, but this spiritual work will be completed through you. You won't do anything, but without you this spiritual work won't happen. I'm able to tell you all this because I have moved away from the influence of the physical body. One day you, too, will leave it, and then you will understand the influence of the body to know oneself. When we move inwards, then our journey also moves inwards. All of us Gurus wish to give you the direction on the inward journey, because you will acquire knowledge only when you go inwards. Spiritual progress is not possible without knowing yourself, without knowing who you are. Everything has been determined in your life; everything will happen at the right time. Wait for that right time because it can neither take place before it nor after it."

I was thinking about the same thing the next day. I couldn't understand what Gurudev wanted to tell me yesterday. I couldn't understand what he was referring to, and I prayed in my mind, "Gurudev, let me understand through your grace all that you wish to make me understand." Then again today was the full moon day, and during the full moon night, Gurudev used to have a special programme of an all-night meditation. In the evening, I again went to the river with Gurudev. Today he had come out late from his hut, which was why it got dark while we were on our way. On the way to the river, we had to cross a path of large, rounded stones. We could see the river water shining at a distance, but we hadn't yet reached it. Our feet were sliding noisily over the rounded stones, and the sound disturbed the peaceful atmosphere. By the time we reached the river, night had already fallen, and the moonlight was shining all over the water as if the river was made of silver. The water was quite cold, and as we started moving into the river, the water started to become colder. Then, after a while, when the cold started to increase, Gurudev went and stood in the middle of the water; I went and stood with him. One had to be careful while standing there, otherwise the flow of the water would push one forward. It was only with great difficulty that I could stand steady, but as soon as I stood still, the fish in the water started gathering around us.

Gurudev was saying, "Don't pay attention to the fish, don't pay attention to the cold; try to move your attention within your body." Then he continued, "First, put the palm of your left hand on your navel. Then place the palm of your right hand on it, and through the medium of your hands, concentrate your chitta on your navel." Then I found that some vibrations slowly started at my navel. In the spiritual experience this time, I could feel a cold touch; I could feel a cold ball of ice rotating on my navel. Slowly, these vibrations started increasing, and when I opened my eyes, I found outside that a ring was coming out of Gurudev's navel and was ending at my navel. Then another ring would come out and end on my navel. The ring was moving very slowly, and its subtle sensitivity could be experienced. This process was going on continually, and by now I couldn't even feel the cold as I myself had become completely cold. The whole body seemed to have turned into ice, and therefore I couldn't experience the outside cold. The fish were still gathered around my feet, and I could feel that, but I wasn't in a state to do anything about it. This same process continued throughout the night. The moonlight was shining all over the river and looked very beautiful. Perhaps I was getting a beautiful spiritual experience both inside and outside and experiencing happiness.

It was going to be morning; even then, Gurudev was still standing in the river. He was not clearly visible, and only the light of his aura indicated his presence; then, as it started getting brighter, his aura started to become cloudy. Later, he came out of meditation and said, "Come on, have your bath." Then both of us bathed there. After bathing, Gurudev offered arghya, and I also did the same. I felt very happy and experienced inner peace. I felt now that I had acquired everything in life. I was experiencing a kind of satisfaction. Gurudev was quiet. Then we started back towards the hut. Gurudev was silent on the way. Here I was, remembering the spiritual experience I had last night—how difficult it is to give up one's identity, and how easily Gurudev performed that difficult task! It is really a reflection of Gurudev's greatness that he could perform this task so easily. He must have acquired this after undergoing so much spiritual practice, and since then he had preserved the spiritual experience for so many years! He entrusted to me so easily and smoothly the spiritual experience that he had preserved with so much care. I found myself blessed to have had the presence of such a Gurudev. I was very happy.

Next morning, I was sitting on the riverbank. I was thinking about yesterday's experience, which I had gone through in Gurudev's presence. Spirituality is a very special subject. People have taken up the subject of the soul for many years, and those who have worked on this subject continually have studied it and gained considerable knowledge. They have chosen this subject and studied it, and by studying it and attaining spiritual experience they have also obtained living knowledge. Then they have distributed the knowledge of their spiritual experiences to others, and the knowledge has grown because they have distributed it. Thus, there are three steps: first, to obtain knowledge from one's Guru and practise it; secondly, after practising it, to attain the spiritual experience of that living knowledge for oneself; and thirdly, to distribute the spiritual experience. Those who perform all these three tasks are called 'spiritual gurus'.

This is a subject for (inner) soul knowledge. That is why one will have to become a soul in order to obtain this knowledge; one will have to reach the level of the soul and accept the medium before us, as a soul. The person who gives knowledge at the physical level is called a teacher—but the one who gives knowledge at the soul level is called a Guru. The work of both is similar. The teacher gives knowledge at the intellectual level, at the physical level. The Guru is also a teacher, but he bestows inner soul knowledge. That is why one has to accept him as a soul in order to absorb that soul knowledge, and that is why he is called a Guru.

Just as there is a Mathematics teacher to teach you Mathematics, there is a Language teacher to teach you Languages, and a Science teacher to teach you the Sciences; similarly, there is a Spiritual teacher to acquire Spiritual knowledge. He is called a Guru. Spiritual knowledge is that knowledge from which man gets a spiritual experience. After man has obtained physical and intellectual knowledge, he desires to obtain soul knowledge. This is the best type of knowledge. As long as one doesn't gain physical and intellectual knowledge, one dosen't even have the desire to obtain Spiritual knowledge. All this is at the level of human beings; it takes place at the physical level, mental level and then at the spiritual level.

Knowledge that has been obtained at the physical level can be exhibited, and the knowledge one has obtained at the intellectual level can also be displayed. But spiritual knowledge can't be displayed, as it's not possible to exhibit it. It can only be experienced. One can develop an ego because of knowledge that one has obtained at the physical level, because that knowledge is at the physical level, and ego is also at the physical level. That is why the knowledge one has obtained at the physical level nourishes one's ego. Similarly, knowledge one has obtained at the intellectual level also nourishes one's ego, because the ego is present along with one's intellect. A person obtains knowledge at the physical level and then displays it; he similarly obtains knowledge at the intellectual level and displays it; and after doing both acts, he doesn't find complete joy. When he expresses a desire to obtain knowledge not for display but to know himself, then he goes within himself. Then his journey for inner knowledge commences, and only then does his journey towards the soul begins. Thus, because of his desire to know himself, man begins the journey of his life; and then he finds his path—that path is the Spiritual Guru. That is the path which is stationary; and when the time comes for souls to attain spiritual happiness, they reach that path.

That is why Gurudev must have called me a 'path' the previous day; a path that is 800 years old. Yesterday, he explained the purpose of my life to me. He introduced me to 'myself'. He gave me a vision of my soul. But this could only happen in my life after I had found knowledge at the physical level and had displayed it, when I had obtained knowledge at the intellectual level and displayed it, but I didn't find satisfaction in my life. I still had the feeling that I wanted to acquire something, and I realized that it could only happen at the inner level. Therefore, this inner journey commenced. I felt as if there was a hidden feeling of ego behind the display of each kind of knowledge. Somewhere, deep in a corner within myself, there was a desire to tell someone, to display it before someone. I started to feel that my life itself was like a movie.

In my childhood, I had an interest in wrestling, and for that I also had got a ganda tied on my wrist from the master wrestler. According to the instructor's guidance, I learned various strategies and tricks in wrestling; and, according to his instructions, I improved my diet and exercise.

Every day, my instructor made me carry out the exercise of digging out soil in the wrestling arena and then levelling it. The soil in the wrestling pit used to be red-coloured, and after I undertook these tasks, my attention would go to my body—how sinewy my thighs have become; how strong my arms are becoming; and I was able to finish the tasks in such a short time! On my way home from the wrestling centre, if someone noticed the red mud on my face and asked me, "Have you just left the wrestling pit?" I would feel very proud. Several years passed, and I made my body strong and symmetrical. I used to exhibit my body either knowingly or unknowingly from time to time, and that display inflated my ego. When I crossed over to the side of the opposing team while playing kabaddi, the players from that team would run scared on seeing my muscular thighs, and seeing their fear made me feel very joyful. Later, the instructor told me, "Now that you are trained and ready, try wrestling, too." Then I enjoyed going to different wrestling pits with my instructor and wrestle with different champions. On purpose, my instructor made me wrestle with champions who were bigger and stronger than I was. That was why I had to work very hard in order to win, and I slowly found a way out of that, too. I had become an expert in two techniques of wrestling—the scissor hold and the Langi. In those bouts, I would catch hold of the wrestler in front of me and manage to win the match. At that time, my instructor used to take me to different wrestling competitions.

At that time, my goal in life was to become the best wrestling champion ever. My instructor also had great faith in me. He used to tell me, "One day you will become a great wrestling champion in this country." In this way, behind the physical level of knowledge, was the hidden purpose of exhibiting it. When I obtained this physical knowledge and scaled the topmost peak, I suddenly started feeling: "This is not your path. You have to go elsewhere." Then I felt if this is not my path and I shouldn't carry on with it, what was the point of continuing? But then I heard a voice telling me from within: "Search for that path on which you have to walk."

Thus, the knowledge I had obtained at the physical level was not the final knowledge. Then I slowly started paying more attention to my studies; I graduated and completed my post-graduation. I took up a job and used my intellectual knowledge in my job. At my workplace I was called honest but lacking in experience. My employers used to tell me, "One can get experience with time, but a person should be basically honest. Getting the work done through people who are better than oneself is the art of management." I had discovered that art, and I used to take care of even the most junior people working under me. I remember that once I had gone with a peon named Ramprasad to a factory to conduct an audit. That factory had actually closed down, but I had to take a look at the old accounts. Around lunchtime, I took the car and reached the city, and on returning from the city to the factory, I bought a new lunch box and carried lunch in it for Ramprasad. He never forgot that meal in his life; he said, "That day, you remembered to bring lunch for me in that barren place." That was why every worker was very happy whenever I arrived.

I obtained experience in my job with honesty. I was always ready to do all types of work. Even when I was working, my search continued. I used to visit temples, to search for someone; I was searching for some living Guru. I still remember that, after office hours in Kolkata, I would go down to the various ghats. For hours at a time, I would stare at the river water and think—sometime, somewhere, this water will meet the ocean. Somewhere there must be an ocean; when will some ocean-like Guru enter my life? I can go to him and find peace.

On the bank of the river, a holy man used to sit with a lighted fire in front of him. In the evening, labourers would gather around him and sing devotional songs. I kept watching those holy men. Sometimes they would look at me, but that was our only acquaintance.

Several parties were also held during that time by the office in various hotels. The purpose of these parties was business-related. I used to accept the expenses for arranging the parties, but I would never take part in them because there was always non-vegetarian food and alcohol. In the beginning, my fellow organizers urged me to drink alcohol, but when I didn't accept it after being repeatedly asked and cajoled, they called me Pundit Maharaj; but after that they never insisted on it. I became aware that they respected me. They used to say that I was not like everyone else, that I was different. I remember that at this time, the state of my mind had become very strange. I always used to think about my Guru. Who would he be? What would he be like and how would I be able to reach him? Once, I had been to the Dakshineshwar Temple near Shree Ramakrishna's place (in Kolkata), and was sitting thinking, "You were a Guru in the past, but of what use are you to me? I want a Guru of the present time who will be able to give me spiritual experiences."

If I had only been living during your lifetime! But now I am not in your lifetime. You were not a physical body; you were a medium of Shakti. Energy used to flow through your body, and Shakti is everlasting and must also be present even today. In what form will the present Shakti be, which body will be its medium, through which medium would the energy be flowing, which body would obtain the highest peaks of physical and mental levels and reach its soul level? Who would be alive at the physical level but whose purpose of life would not be to live; who would it be whose desire for life would have come to an end? If one's desires come to an end during one's lifetime, then that is a state of liberation, and one who obtains the state of liberation must have already become the medium of universal consciousness. Who would it be and when would he meet me? I was consumed by this curiosity.

I sat there and prayed, "Thakurji, please help me to find my

Guru." At that time, I felt like a child who gets separated from his mother at a fair and then wanders here and there in search of her. You may try to console the child with chocolates, by giving biscuits, but he won't accept anything. He'll just keep yelling—Mother, Mother, Mother! My state was somewhat similar. I had no interest left in my life. My condition was like that of a madman. I was searching for a Guru everywhere.

One evening, I was sitting on the banks of the river Ganga, listening to devotional songs sung by the labourers. The holy man who was sitting there told me, "Now your time has come. Go on a journey to Tarkeshwar, and the path ahead for you will open from there." The very next day, I went from Kolkata to Tarkeshwar. There was a small village there, a small Shiva Temple. I prayed at the temple and returned from there. I didn't feel I had found anything after the trip. There was an ordinary temple, and it was an ordinary village. I didn't meet anyone there, and I felt that I hadn't gained anything. Sometimes, I used to feel that after coming into this world we become so insensitive that even if we find something at the soul level we won't be aware of what we have found. Something similar had happened there, too. One needs to be very sensitive in order to have a spiritual experience. One can obtain a high level of sensitivity only when one's mind is at a very subtle level. One can attain a very subtle level of mind through a state of thoughtlessness. Man weakens his mind by useless thoughts of the past and the future, and as a result his sensitivity decreases. I returned to Kolkata from that place, and after that my days just passed by. I had a strong desire to meet some living Guru who would bring my search to an end. The year prior to getting a vision of Shiv Baba was spent with a lot of uneasiness. First, the severe thirst for a vision of my Guru was awakened, and only then was it satisfied.

I was sitting on the bank of the river, and I didn't even realize that a whole day had gone by, and it was evening. It was going to be dark. I started walking towards Gurudev's hut, and it had become quite dark by the time I reached the hut. The jungle was very thick, and I could hear the sounds of the dense forest. I sometimes felt as if some peaceful sweet music was being played in the jungle, and I should keep my mouth shut and my ears completely open to hear it, and that I shouldn't make any sound while walking. I reached Gurudev's hut, taking care that the peace of the jungle was not disturbed by the sound of my walking. When one listens to that music in the jungle, the sensitivity of one's ears also increases, and even small distant sounds can be heard. Gurudev was almost always in a meditative state, and he would meet for a very short time when he came out of the meditative state. He used to meet me in both the states—in the meditative state, he used to meet me through his subtle chitta; there was a terrific attraction in his body. Once one looked at him, one would feel like staring at him forever. It wasn't as if his body was particularly beautiful and symmetrical. It was his soul that was very beautiful and attractive. His body had become weak from continual meditation for several years, but his soul was pure and holy. That is why the inner radiance of his soul could be mirrored on his body, and that was the reason why a magnetic energy had been created in his body, and one could feel inner peace in his presence.

Sometimes, it would seem that a Satguru becomes so immersed in meditating on Paramatma that he doesn't have any identity of his own. When his own existence comes to an end, then Paramatma's energy arises automatically. Then the Satguru's physical body ceases to exist; he becomes the medium of Paramatma's energy and Paramatma's energy starts flowing through that medium. Then our soul is filled with joy in the presence of Paramatma's energy; we rejoice, and we can experience that joy only because of our soul. It can neither be seen, nor can one write about the joy one has experienced. The happiness of that soul can only be experienced.

Thus, it seemed as if the Satguru doesn't give anything because he has gone beyond giving, and neither do we obtain anything in his presence because all this is only at the material level, whereas the Satguru's presence has to be experienced. These Satgurus do not expose themselves, and because of that it is difficult to reach them. It is only the purity of our soul that takes us close to them. consciousness would keep on flowing from every pore of Gurudev's body. When he walked, the ground on which he placed his feet, the stones on which his hand rested while walking—all these inert substances also would experience his vibrations. All this was the miracle of a moment's closeness to him. Sometimes it seems that Paramatma gives everyone a chance; some people are able to catch hold of Paramatma's vibrations, while some are not. Everything depends on where our chitta is focused, when consciousness is being showered.

※

One morning, Gurudev came out from his meditation and, taking me along with him, started walking towards the river to bathe. He walked ahead, and I followed behind him. I was always very careful not to place my foot in the place where Gurudev had stepped, because the soil there where Gurudev had walked had become vibrated, so how could I step on it? I was being pulled along behind him, and I kept bowing to those sacred places. My whole attention was on the places where Gurudev placed his feet, and after some practice it became possible to walk behind him in this way. We both bathed together in the river. I stayed very close to the riverbank but Gurudev went into the deeper water and bathed there. Near the riverbank some baby crabs were moving about; perhaps they had just been born. They were all moving towards the water. After his bath, Gurudev started moving towards the hill opposite our hill, but I didn't have the courage to ask him why he was going there. I also started walking behind him. There wasn't a path at all, one had to prepare it, and one had to move the stones and bushes aside while climbing up, but as we started climbing higher, I found it difficult to walk. We were climbing higher and there seemed to be so much consciousness, so much energy on the whole hill, that I kept going into a meditative state again and again.

By now, we had reached quite a height. The scene on the river looked good from the top. We could see the opposite hill. That hill was much smaller than this hill, and Gurudev's hut was on that hill, but there was such a thick forest that the hut couldn't be seen at all. We had climbed quite high, but we had been walking for such a long time that we didn't realize that it was almost sunset. This meant that we had been walking all day and had reached this hill. The path for walking on this hill wasn't there; one had to make the path and then move ahead. There were several beautiful bird nests, and as it was near evening that all the birds were returning to their nests. By the time it was evening, we succeeded in reaching the peak of the hill. On reaching the peak, we saw that there was a large flat stone, like a platform.

Gurudev went and sat on that flat stone and indicated that I should also sit next to him, and I, too, went and sat there. As soon as I sat down, a cold wave emitted from the stone and passed from my muladhar or root chakra towards my sahasrara or crown chakra, as if a cold electric flow of vibrations were streaming through me. Later, I felt as if vibrations were flowing out of my whole body. The whole body was filled with vibrations, and I lost sense of the body.

Night had fallen by now, and Gurudev's body was turning into a divine glow of golden light, and then his body slowly stopped being visible. All this was a totally different experience for me. I had never experienced anything like this before in my life, and that black slab of stone was so cold that it seemed to be made of ice. My consciousness was slowly fading away. I didn't realize when the tiredness of climbing that hill all day disappeared, and I slowly felt my consciousness leaving me. I felt as if I was coming to an end. The 'I' sense within me ended completely, and then the existence of 'I' left me and became 'Him'. After that, I don't know what happened; I lost consciousness.

I woke up one morning and found that I was sitting with Gurudev on that big stone slab. I didn't know how many days had passed. My consciousness had returned, but I still didn't have any control over my body. The whole body was numb. After some time, I felt some movement in my toe, and then in my fingers. After some time, I could control my body and move my hands and feet. Then I saw that flat slab of stone again in the bright light and realized that it was very big. One part of it was completely flat, and its lower portion was also flat and looked like a platform. It was amazing how such a stone could have got to such a great height. While sitting on the stone one could look down and see the scene of the river. There was a thick forest around the stone, too, and it was a very quiet place. After a while, Gurudev said, "I have done my penance sitting on this stone, and for years at a time I have sat here and done my penance. This place was chosen by my Guru, and my Gurudev gave up his physical body at this very place. After he passed away, I performed his last rites in this very place, and from that time onwards I seem to be tied to this place. I can never leave this place. I built a hut on the opposite hill to meet you, and I have been waiting there for you.

"Paramatma creates everyone in a similar form and gives everyone equal chances for spiritual progress. Some souls take advantage of that chance, and some don't. Every soul has an equal possibility of obtaining liberation. There is no difference between you and me. Paramatma has created both similarly. No soul is superior or inferior. This is exactly similar to a drop of water that comes from the sky equally pure and holy. Later, it depends on where the drop lands and which form it takes. Therefore, you should also awaken the self-confidence within you, that you, too, can reach the meditative state like me. Paramatma has created the basic form of every soul in the same way, and with every birth the effect of that presence keeps connecting to that soul, and his journey depends on that effect. This is similar to the fact that we are affected by the company we keep.

"Paramatma is that energy which manages the whole universe, and that Shakti doesn't show favours to anyone or any bias. Everyone has equal right to that Shakti. Every soul has the full possibility of evolution, but that evolution depends upon the collectivity around us. Everything depends on the type of collectivity we get. Several years ago, my Gurudev sat on this very stone and gave me this same knowledge; and because of this very knowledge I became self-confident, so that I, too, can become a Guru one day. Today, I, too, am giving you this knowledge in the same place, so that your self-confidence can awaken, and you, too, can become a Guru like me. My Gurudev had passed away on this very stone, and it was his wish that I should pray for his liberation and cremate his body. According to his wishes, I prayed for him and then cremated him.

"I also wish that when I give up my body, my cremation should take place on this stone, and that you should pray for me and cremate me. The Guru-element is a Shakti that keeps on flowing in the universe in a positive form. Individuals who are its medium keep changing with time. The Guru-element never dies. It always remains alive in the form of its disciples. What dies is the body. Then why should one get attached to a body that dies? When my Gurudev passed away, the flow of that Guru-element remained alive in the present, in my form; and tomorrow, when

I pass away, that Guru-element will remain alive in your form. Oh, my dear! This universe will continue to exist only as long as the Guru-element is alive, because it is that Guru-element which maintains a positive balance in the whole universe. The Guru-element is a good collectivity of positive energies and the medium of the Guru-element is the Satguru's body. That's why it is difficult to hold on to the Guru-element but easy to catch hold of the Satguru's body. By the term 'to catch hold of Satguru's body,' I don't mean actually catching hold of his physical body. My interpretation is towards catching hold of the aura that is formed around him. This is also possible through the chanting of his name. Even if we chant the Satguru's name we can get the collectivity of his energies of the Guru-element. The Satguru doesn't have any identity of his own. He gives up his identity, and that is why he becomes a medium of the Guru-element. Guru-tattva is the flow of collective positive energies."

Gurudev suddenly stopped speaking, and he gazed at the sky. I couldn't understand what he was looking at. I was looking at the immensity of that stone slab. Who could have brought such an immense stone to the peak of this hill? This stone didn't appear to have originated on this hill. The stone was like a throne, and one could sit leaning against a part of it. The stones around us on this hill were light red in colour. Only this stone was of a deep black colour. So, it was definitely not from this hill. Then where had such an immense stone come from, and how was it carried up to such a great height? Everything seemed to be beyond imagination; and this peak was at such a height that it had taken us a whole day to climb it. So, how could anyone possibly have climbed up carrying that stone? This stone was the size of ten elephants, and the hills around us didn't have any similar black stones anywhere. Yes, there were black-coloured stones in the river, but they were very small. I thought about all the possibilities, but for a long time

I couldn't understand how such a large stone could be placed on such a high peak.

My Gurudev recognized my confusion and said, "This stone was lifted to this peak by the Gurus of my Gurus for their disciples through the power of mantra. A 'mantra' is not only a collection of words; it is an assemblage of Guru-energies. There is a great power in the mantra. There is a great power in the Satguru's words.

That is why in our ancient times the 'naming ceremony' of a newborn child would take place through some Satguru. The Satguru would name that child, and with this excuse of naming the child the Satguru's chitta would go to that child. Together with the given name were his blessings, which would remain with the child all his life. When a child receives the proximity of good collectivity right from birth, then that child grows up in the company and therefore in the proximity of good collective energy. That collectivity used to be very helpful in balancing the child. That's why this tradition of naming is very important. What is required is that it should be accepted with full faith and trust after understanding its importance, because only faith and trust develop our capacity to receive. In order to obtain knowledge from any Guru, it is essential to have faith and trust in the Guru. The Satguru is aware of the child's future, and he also knows what events are going to take place in that child's life; he also knows which energies are required to balance the child to face those events, and only after knowing all this the Satguru names the child.

"The Satguru bestows on the child the necessary elements that will be required to improve the child's requirements and his personality. There is great meaning in the name that has been given to the child, but the significance of that name can only be understood after that child goes through life. There is a different collective energy with every name, and the Satguru knows everything about what is required by which child; and according to the requirements of that child the Satguru connects those Shaktis to the child. Thus, that child goes through his life in a balanced manner and becomes a balanced and successful person. We can also say that the Satguru gives protection to the child's future through the act of naming him. Thus, in ancient times, in order that their child may lead a secure life, and in order to obtain good wishes for their child, people asked the Satguru to name their child.

"The Satguru doesn't name the child after looking at his colour or his good looks or his shape; he looks at the child's soul and recognizes it. What is the level of that soul? What was the karma in that child's previous birth? He looks at the records of his karma and understands the purpose of that soul in this birth and which direction that soul will take. The Satguru knows that direction, and he wishes that the child may travel in that determined direction, and remain pure and safe from the web of illusion and attain the goals of his life. That is why he addresses the child by his given name and passes on his blessings with the name. Every name has its own aura; and to recognize that aura and connect it to a suitable body in the form of a name is a very important event. The purpose of every life is different; and each name has a different aura. To know and understand both these things and to connect both with a suitable body is an important act, and following their conjunction he makes his collective energy flow through that bond—thus, a threefold union takes place through the Satguru during the naming of the child.

"The naming ceremony is a very important rite that shapes the child's future. But people see someone doing it and merely copy it without understanding its deeper meaning. Children who have been named in this way by the Satguru have grown up to be strong and successful people. Not only have these children themselves become balanced, but they have done the work of balancing society, too. The gardener knows how much water he should give to the trees that he has planted; and he waters the small plants according to their requirements, because he knows that he can only keep them alive if he waters them according to their requirements. If he waters the plant more than is necessary, then the plant may die.

"Thus, the same water is life-giving for the plant, and it can also be the cause of its death. That's why only the gardener knows about the amount of water required by the tree. Similarly, the Satguru knows which child requires what type of balancing, which energy, and connects him to those energies, to that positive energy. The Satguru also knows about that child's future only after he connects with the universal energy and then bestows the name on him accordingly. It often happens that, due to the wrong name given by parents to their child, the child's life is ruined as they are not able to connect the right name with the right body. What happens is that by giving the wrong name, the wrong aura gets connected to the child; and as a result of the wrong aura getting connected, a wrong influence is created, and the child may have to suffer the damaging consequences in his life. Thus, a child's name can make him or break him.

"Every name has an aura with it. No aura is good or bad. But the effect of every aura is different; and no effect should be extreme. The effect should also be balanced. This balance can only be created by someone who is acquainted with its influence. Children often have to keep on fighting all their lives against this imbalance. They are troubled all their lives, and they also have shorter lives. One should not give a name to a child without understanding its effect on the child. The name determines success or failure in the child's life. The child's name should therefore be according to his suitability and necessity.

"People often name their children after great saints. But it doesn't necessarily mean that the particular name is necessary for the child. The child's requirement may be quite different. When the Satguru gives a name, then it is according to the child's requirement. Through the medium of that given name he transfers his energies to the child. The Satguru has the energy of a vast collectivity. It often happens that the entire life of an unsuccessful individual has been changed just by changing his name. There is great power in a name. A mixed aura is created through the words of a name. For example, the word 'Rama' has the aura of the letters 'ra' and 'ma'; and the word 'Rampal' has the aura of the four letters, 'ra,' 'ma,' 'pa,' 'la.' Actually, letters are the beej or seed mantras of energy, and each of them has a different influence. It is necessary to find out which influence is required for your child. The child becomes successful in his life just by connecting with the proper influence that is suitable for that child's life.

"I'm explaining all this to you because I can foresee your future. Thousands of people are going to come to you to name their child, and through your medium the Guru-energy is going to give them names. Thus, you should be aware of the importance of the work that is going to happen through you as a medium, and therefore I'm giving you all this information."

I prayed to Gurudev, "I present myself before you as your medium. You may make whatever use you wish of my body. Today, I am surrendering my complete existence at your feet. It is my pure wish that every breath that I now take in my life may be according to your wishes." After saying this, I bowed before him with folded hands. Then he raised me and, putting his hand on my shoulder, he said, "Only you are my future. Now I'll remain alive only through your medium. You are not aware of how big your container is. Millions of souls are going to obtain liberation through you in this world. You are the doorway to obtaining liberation in collectivity. You are not aware of 'who' you are, and I'm blessed to have you as my disciple. My whole life has become worthwhile because I have found you. Now I have no other desire left in my life. The purpose of my life has been served. Now I'll spend the rest of my life in your proximity. I couldn't help anyone reach liberation in my lifetime; but I have no regrets about it. I'm very fortunate to have become the Guru of the 'Giver of Liberation' to millions of souls. Today, my heart is overpowered by love. Today, I feel completely satisfied in my life.

Now I understand why my Guru made me stay here for so many years—it was because you were going to come here; because I was going to get the opportunity to take part in your yagya of giving liberation. My Guru was aware of everything, but I didn't know about it. A Great Yagya of salvation or liberation is going to be organized through your medium, and I am fortunate that I have been given a golden opportunity to make an 'offering' in that Great Yagya (by having you as my disciple).

I was sitting open-mouthed, listening to what Gurudev was saying—Medium! Great Yagya! Giving Liberation! I couldn't understand the meaning of all these words! On noticing my confusion, Gurudev said, "I can see all this in the future! All this is going to happen in the future. You will understand all these things only after some time. Come on, we have spent quite a lot of time here. Now we'll go to our hut." And then we got up and started walking back.

I turned back to look at that great stone slab, and it appeared to be a throne; it was the highest peak of nature in that place. It seemed as if the king was sitting on his throne and surveying his kingdom. Sitting there on that high peak, one could see the river flowing below, and the surrounding scenery stretched far away for miles. There was such a thick forest around there, that no open space could be seen; and there seemed to be a blanket of trees spread out everywhere. Gurudev started climbing down the hill with me. We had to climb halfway down the hill, and then turn towards the hill on the opposite side and climb up. Night was falling by the time we reached our hut. Later, I said to Gurudev, "Gurudev, we managed to come down the hill very fast, but climbing up was very difficult." Gurudev smiled and said, "My dear! It is always very difficult to climb the hill of one's life as one evolves and progresses towards one's summit. There are fewer opportunities in life for climbing up, and more occasions for falling. People are not focused on how far one has climbed; they pay more attention to how far one has fallen! This negative attitude is always present in human society. We should keep away from it." Then we entered our hut. I was so tired that I fell asleep at once.

I woke up next morning on hearing the chirping of birds. Today, I was feeling very fresh and happy. The previous day's tiredness had disappeared. I observed that the nails on my fingers and toes had grown very long, and realized after seeing them that I must have stayed for a number of days with Gurudev on that great platform-like stone on the opposite hill. I had stayed with Gurudev for several days, but I wasn't aware for how long. As I was in a good meditative state, I was neither aware of the time nor of the number of days. The same thing happens in life, too. The good period in one's life passes very quickly.

I had planted some seeds, lai leaves, which we used for our meals, and they had grown into big plants. I used to boil and eat these leaves there. They were similar to spinach leaves, but they were four times bigger. These leaves were my main diet. I had made small beds (in which I had planted the seeds), and I used to pick the bigger leaves very gently from the plant. I liked these leaves, and I used to feed the birds with the stems of the leaves. The birds enjoyed eating the stems, and they soon became my friends. There was a black bird that had laid eggs in front of me. That bird had come with both her chicks to eat the stems, but now the chicks had grown up. However, they had not learnt to peck grains on their own yet, and therefore the bird used to peck on the stems with her beak and feed her young ones. I had spent many days on the opposite hill; I realized how much time had passed from looking at the birds that had grown up after hatching, and the size of the lai-producing trees, which had grown from the seeds I had planted. Even now, I didn't know how many days I spent there. It felt like we must have spent months. My Gurudev was very old and quite weak. He had reduced his needs considerably. One day he said, "As man grows older, he should reduce his needs, because in reality his needs automatically decrease. Man should leave all attachments systematically, otherwise he'll have to face problems in his old age.

"He should reduce his needs with age because excessive needs make his mind unstable. Man shouldn't be afraid of death as death is a certainty, and man shouldn't forget it. Death is inevitable, and one should keep in mind that death will surely occur. The thought of death always inspires man to do good deeds and stops him from performing bad deeds. Death saves man from greed and desires and makes him realize that everything will be left behind here. Death is a boon that has been given to every creature. Death keeps reminding man that this life is momentary. Man assesses himself to be great, and he's always worried about what will happen after he passes away—what will happen to my wife, what will happen to my children, what will happen to my work—whereas all this is a play of illusion and attachments. Man's state in this world is like that of an insect. What difference does it make whether it lives or dies? It makes no difference. People around him are unhappy for a few days and then carry on with their lives because one can't die with the person who dies. One who is alive has to keep on living,

दादागुरुदेव श्री शिवबाबा (भावनगरवाले)

Dada Guru Shree Shiv Baba of Bhavnagar

Shree Gurudev tells Guruma, "Hand over your husband to me. Spiritual work will happen through him on a global scale."

(Refer to page viii)

Gurudev Shree Brahmanand Swami and Swamiji
sitting with their feet dipped in the rivulet.

(Refer to page 1)

Swamiji lying in the pit full of gunj seeds in front of the cave.

(Refer to page 30)

Gurudev Shree Brahmanand Swami and Swamiji
meditating inside a cave full of beautiful natural
forms made from iron-rich water.

(Refer to page 38)

"I will never get this opportunity again…"
Swamiji's thoughts while pressing the feet of his
Gurudev Shree Brahmanand Swami.

(Refer to page 67)

While bidding farewell when Swamiji fell at the feet of Gurudev Shree Brahmanand Swami, the latter stopped him and admonished him, "Hey! You silly boy! Why are you touching my feet? My status is not even equal to your toenails!"

(Refer to page 77)

Swamiji sitting in the yagyashala with
his third Gurudev.

(Refer to page 97)

During sunset Gurudev's white beard would look
orange to Swamiji.

(Refer to page 111)

The glowing ball of light around Gurudev was
even more radiant than the fire burning in front
of him and yet there was coolness in it.

(Refer to page 115)

Gurudev and Swamiji carrying the river water to the ashram in their cupped hands.

(Refer to page 134)

Swamiji glancing back at his Gurudev as he sets
off on an unknown voyage.

(Refer to page 154)

When Swamiji came to his senses, he heard the words, "Wake up, my child, open your eyes. I have arrived," and he felt someone lightly touching his head.

(Refer to page 163)

Swamiji meditating with Gurudev on a full-moon night in the cold water of the Brahmaputra River.

(Refer to page 181)

Swamiji carrying Gurudev Shreenath Baba to the
mountain peak in a leaf-lined basket.

(Refer to page 317)

Gurudev Shreenath Baba paying his salutations
to Swamiji before giving up his mortal body.

(Refer to page 350)

and in order to keep on living one has to remain in the present.

"One can't live one's life in the past, and the person who dies becomes the past. How long can one keep on remembering him? That is why every human being should understand his status in this world and stop worrying about what will happen after his death. It is this worry that doesn't allow man to die in peace. He never realizes when he is alive that all this worrying is an illusion. He realizes after his death that nothing changes even after he dies. The sun rises every morning as usual, and the whole world keeps moving. Sunset takes place, and the whole world moves on in a very systematic manner. He realizes that he was unnecessarily holding on to the world in his life. We realize after death that no matter how great a person is, no matter how important he is, no one is indispensable. There is a certain pace to this world, and every living being has to flow with that pace.

"It is generally believed that man doesn't lie at the time of his death, and this is quite true. Therefore, the person who is about to die should be made aware that he is going to die now, and he should speak the truth. It is the basic nature of man to speak the truth, and man himself never realizes that his death is approaching. Right until the end, he never realizes that death is approaching, and someone else has to make him aware of it to acknowledge that he is dying, which is beyond his thought process. This is because no man thinks that he can ever die. Man is afraid of death but doesn't accept it. Death is the reality of life, and this is a natural event. No one knows who is going to die at what time. This is a subject that man should leave to Paramatma. He will die when he has to. Death itself is not so frightening or painful as much as the fear of death. Man doesn't even realize when death occurs."

Today, I understood that Gurudev had passed on the mystery of death to me, sitting in a meditative state. I had experienced several times that he stayed sitting in meditation, and through his aura he would reveal the knowledge of different mysteries of life to me. That's why, whether I was near him or not, in the jungle, I never felt that I was alone there. By living close to nature, I learned from nature that the tree that has more tolerance is able to progress. One day, during a great storm, I noticed that several big trees had been uprooted. There were very tall trees there, but they weren't very thick, and the soil wasn't very compacted around them; it was loose. If the soil under the tree was washed away during the rains, the ability of the trees to stay standing was weakened, and therefore the trees would fall. Thus, several big trees fell, but the forest was so thick that the tree couldn't even fall to the ground after it was uprooted. Before reaching the ground, the tree would get stuck on a nearby tree. During the storm, only those trees that had the capacity of tolerance, those trees that were flexible and could bend, would be saved. In the jungle, very few trees would break, and more trees would be uprooted, because the soil was washed away (with the water). I felt that man should also increase his level of tolerance with age, because lack of tolerance is leading to a growing dissatisfaction in the world today. The only reason for that is a lack of tolerance. The main support for a happy life in the future (for man) will be his level of tolerance, because intolerance is going to spread across human society.

There is a lack of tolerance in today's fast-paced world. I found a lot of tolerance and patience in people who lived with nature. I felt that this is a unique gift of nature, which is gained by man in the proximity of nature. Tolerance is the strength of one's soul. The stronger the soul, the more will be the tolerance level. Man merges with nature as he meditates, and so tolerance starts to be established in him. Due to this tolerance, man remains calm and peaceful even in the most difficult circumstances. Tolerance is the gift of a powerful soul to man. Tolerance is a power that develops within man when he meditates. Every human being has to develop himself on his own. This can't be obtained externally. Only those trees that possess tolerance can face even the most violent storms and succeed in preserving their existence.

I picked some lai leaves, and after stuffing them into a bamboo and filling it with water, I placed them for boiling in the fire; and when the green colour of the bamboo started changing, I realized that the juice of that bamboo had got mixed with the leaves and the leaves had been cooked. I took out the leaves and ate them and drank the water in the bamboo after it had cooled off. The water tasted sour because of the bamboo's flavour. This is how I usually cooked and ate my food.

These leaves grew here quite easily; they matured fast and cooked quickly. My mother always said that wherever you go, your food should be like the locals, because that food would have been prepared as per the natural atmosphere and environment of that place. Thus, these leaves proved to be suitable for meals, keeping in mind the natural atmosphere of the place. In order to remain alive in the jungle, one has to eat whatever is available, but food is not very important there. First of all, no one stuffs himself with food here, and secondly, this food is quickly digested. Gurudev ate even less. He used to eat less and speak less; but whenever he spoke, his words appeared to be divine, and nectar seemed to flow through them. Then I would go into meditation. Sometimes it seemed as if Paramatma himself was speaking through him.

It was very difficult to light a fire in the jungle. Two flint stones had to be rubbed together, and the resultant spark would be used to light dry grass, and then the dry grass to light the dry wood. But as I had no practice in doing this, I used to take hours to light a fire. Sometimes two dry bamboos could also be rubbed to light the fire, but compared to the bamboos it was easier to light a fire with stones. Sometimes the fire would go out when we stayed in meditation for a longer period, otherwise the fire would always be kept burning, so that we didn't have to go through the process of lighting it again and again. Thus, the fire would always be kept burning.

During the summer, two dry trees would often rub against each other, and a fire would start as a result of the friction. Then the fire would spread to the entire jungle because it would go with the direction of the wind. At such a time birds and animals had to run from the jungle to save their lives. During such a fire, it was their young ones who would get caught as they couldn't run with their parents. As they lived close to nature, the birds and animals could get all the knowledge and experience and keep on learning from nature.

A beautiful quiet music is always playing in the natural atmosphere, and even if a leaf falls in that quiet atmosphere the crackling sound can be heard till far. That silence also has its own music, and people who live in the proximity of nature enjoy this silence. That is why those who live close to nature are found to speak less and listen more. Listening is very important in the jungle. Birds and animals also keep listening, and as a result of their amplified hearing, they can judge any approaching danger. Listening is essential for birds and animals to stay alive, because it is due to their listening ability that they can save themselves from impending attacks. On the other hand, as a result of this listening process, they can also hunt for other birds and animals, as prey for their food. Thus, listening is a great protective activity in the life of the jungle.

The language of birds and animals in the jungle doesn't have any words; there are only special sounds at special times. There is a sound for calling someone, there is a sound for warning their companions of approaching danger, there is a sound to inform them that food is available, the sound of a mother calling out to its young ones, the sound of a mother searching for her young ones, the sound of a female trying to attract the male—and the sound of the male trying to woo a female—the combined sound of both of them when they meet, the sound made by young ones when they are hungry, the sound made by an animal while attacking its prey. Several hunting animals use a special sound to scare their prey, and when the prey faints with fear, they catch it. Quite often, when an animal is caught in the throes of death, that sound is the only sound in the jungle; there are no words.

This same habit is formed by various tribes living in the jungle. They make a special sound to say a sentence. If they want to call someone, there is one type of sound. The tribal people's songs are also a collection of special sounds. That's why tribal people don't have words, only sounds. Sometimes, it seemed that there was no need to choose words and make sentences when one sound was sufficient. It seemed that words are a creation of man's intellect as birds and animals don't use words, either, but even then, their life goes on. In every natural environment, Paramatma also speaks through the medium of nature. He gives us messages, but because we are not connected to nature, we are not able to understand them. There are no words in Paramatma's messages, only sounds. Those sounds can only be heard by one who is used to hearing them. One has to practice listening to those sounds. Paramatma speaks from within a human being, too, but we should make time to listen to Paramatma.

Man is occupied with his own thoughts. There is always a landfill of thoughts of the past within him. The remaining space in his mind is taken up by thoughts of the future. So, when does he have time to listen to Paramatma's voice? Neither does he see any necessity for it. Paramatma is our mother, and a mother wants to talk to her children, too; but the children have no time to talk to their mother. The mother's language is without words because the mother has to speak the language that every human being can understand, and all human beings are Paramatma's children. Paramatma is an energy that has given birth to man. Man's parents are just mediums to bestow him with a body. Actually, the mother and father of man is Paramatma, who wishes to have a dialogue and converse with the children he has produced. He wishes to pass on his messages to them. It is necessary for them to hear those messages. But only when you have the time to listen to those messages, when you are free from thoughts of the past and the future; from positive and negative thoughts, only when you are free from all these thoughts, then Paramatma's call will register. I, too, have experienced that the yoni is closer to Paramatma, but man never realizes it.

He never realizes this in his lifetime. Once the soul receives a human form, he becomes complacent, thinking that he has reached the destination of liberation; and he starts becoming lethargic in the human form. When he wakes up, he realizes that he had reached close to the destination of liberation in his previous birth; but now the destination seems to have receded far behind because all his life he kept thinking, and didn't listen to Paramatma's message, to what He had to say!

I have noticed a special quality about birds and animals. They never have any thoughts. They have contracted the humans to do all the thinking. Birds and animals don't think at all. Yes, when they are hungry, they go in search of prey, but they don't even think when they go in search of prey. The language of Paramatma is the language of vibrations, and there are no words in that language, there is only consciousness. There is such a large collectivity of human beings on this earth. All are the children of Paramatma. Paramatma has created everything, and Paramatma is everyone's mother. And when the mother wishes to speak to all her children then she'll use only one language, and that language is of vibrations.

This is understood by all human beings, they are aware of it, but by thinking too much, man has forgotten that language because he has only caught hold of the medium—the parents through whom man was born on this earth. He caught hold of the religion of those parents, he caught hold of the language of those parents, and he caught hold of the culture of those parents. These parents are not stable and therefore their religion isn't stable; their culture is also unstable, and thus man catches hold of all that is unstable, and he forgets those parents who are stable; he forgets their language. Man doesn't have living knowledge and all these things happen due to his ignorance of living knowledge. If man gains the living knowledge, then he'll realize that parents keep changing with each birth, and therefore their religion will change, their language will change, and then he'll try to understand the language of his stable mother that is Paramatma, and he'll want to listen only to the messages of Paramatma.

I realized that Gurudev was speaking. "Go into the society of man and remind them of their stable parents and free them from their thoughts and tell them to listen to what Paramatma is telling them, to listen to Paramatma's message; go and awaken the people in society."

I, too, decided that I would definitely go into society. I would go and help them to get in touch with their stable mother and tell them to listen to the messages of their mother. I'll create a society that is free of thoughts. It's possible that I may not be able to see such a (thought-free) society in my lifetime, but in future the coming generations will definitely create this type of society. The language of this society will be one; their religion will be one, their race will be one and their soul will be one. One day, such a world will definitely be created, and Gurudev has given me the Guru-karya of creating such a society. I sat listening quietly to the voices. Paramatma was speaking through the medium of

Gurudev, and Paramatma's language could be heard in the form of vibrations, and it sounded as if a conch-shell was being blown.

I prayed to Paramatma, "O Paramatma! I will definitely convey your message to all mankind that your mother is one and the same; that our mother's language is one and our mother has only one religion. All of you are children of the same mother. Recognize your mother and don't forget your mother's language. All of you have the same mother, and that is why your mother's language is the same. Remember that language and recognize that language—it is the same language because there is only one mother. It is you who have created these separate languages and these separate religions. Paramatma has only one language, and that is the language of vibrations. That is the only language in the whole world. There is only one religion in the whole world, and that is the religion of humanity, the religion of all mankind. Paramatma, I'll definitely convey your message to society, and I offer you heartfelt thanks because you have made me a medium to convey your message. Please give me your blessings so that I may be able to convey your message to as many people as possible in the world. You have given me charge of this work, so please give me the energy to complete it. According to your orders, I will spend the rest of my life engaged in this 'work.' I pray to you that you should keep on contacting me through your language of vibrations and keep giving me instructions. This is my prayer at your lotus feet."

That day, I realized that Paramatma is one. Paramatma is everyone's mother. The language of Paramatma is the language of vibrations and Paramatma's religion is the religion of humanity. Paramatma wishes to interact with all human beings but as long as man can't control the thoughts that arise in his mind, he won't be able to understand Paramatma's language of vibrations. Therefore, thoughtlessness is necessary, and meditation is necessary for that thoughtlessness. Meditation will awaken man and make him receptive to Paramatma's messages. Every human being receives Paramatma's messages equally. Some people are able to hear those messages, and some are not.

This is similar to the example of some children paying attention to what their parents tell them and some children disregarding it. Several people are so caught up in the web of their thoughts all their lives that they can't find the time to listen to Paramatma's messages and experience them. These messages have been sent for the soul that is present within man; and those people who listen to these messages in their lives, birth after birth, remain free from this web of thoughts. These people have formed a habit of listening to these messages because they have maintained a connection with them through several births, and their life is based on these messages. They take birth on earth based on these messages, live their lives according to the messages, and also die according to them. They always live in isolation during several of their births and are recognized in their final birth.

They are recognized in their final birth because their capacity to hear these messages increases to a large extent, and they have a close connection with Paramatma; and it is so close that their identity is merged with Paramatma as a result. Such people are called Satgurus. These Satgurus are recognized in their final birth because people become aware of Paramatma's messages in their proximity. Even an ordinary human begins to get spiritual experiences of those messages in his presence. These Gurus become the messengers of Paramatma. Very few fortunate souls are able to come close to them in their final birth, because they don't live long. They arrive on earth for Paramatma's messages, pass on the messages to society, and then they depart. It makes no difference to them whether someone listens to the messages they have passed on or not.

Birds and animals also experience the joy of the proximity of these Satgurus, because the spiritual experience of Paramatma's messages is very fulfilling and bestows happiness on the soul. Paramatma's messages keep flowing through their body. Birds and animals don't have any thoughts of their own, and therefore they can easily get the spiritual experience of these messages. When humans go close to them in a state of thoughtlessness, they are also able to experience Paramatma's messages through their medium. One should approach such Satgurus in a thoughtless state and observe silence, because only when they are silent will they be able to listen to Paramatma's messages.

The best thing is to remain silent in the Satguru's presence and experience his proximity. Several people try to tell him about their problems. Actually, there is no need to make him aware of their problems because he knows everything. What can one tell someone who already knows about it? By telling him about it, they miss Paramatma's messages that are flowing through him, because instead of experiencing Paramatma's messages in the Satguru's presence, their attention is on their own problems. The place where we can experience Paramatma's message in the Satguru's presence is our mind, but we keep our attention on the problem. Thus, because we don't recognize the Satguru's high level we feel that he isn't aware of our problem. In reality, he is aware of the problem, but it is we who are in his presence yet can't recognize him.

The same state is created by those people who sit in front of a temple begging for alms from people who have themselves come to beg from Paramatma. The people beg from such people who are themselves like beggars. The people who are begging, people who have an expectation of receiving alms, should beg from Paramatma, from whom those people are begging. Very few souls get the proximity of the Satguru in his final birth; very few souls get his auspicious sighting; very few souls are able to recognize the Satguru, and fewer still are able to believe in him. Man receives this proximity as a result of the karma of his previous birth, but because of his ignorance in this life, he doesn't realize the importance of that proximity.

Satgurus are messengers of Paramatma. They themselves don't say anything and, because they don't have any separate identity, Paramatma himself speaks through them.

Paramatma's messages can be experienced very clearly in their presence. That is why it is said that the Satguru is not someone to be seen but to be experienced. One should always experience the Satguru in one's life.

※

My Gurudev was passing on all this knowledge to me in a very subtle form through his messages. That was the reason why I didn't feel any difference whether he was with me or in a meditative trance. When he was meditating then my relationship with him was very close, because he used to meditate in his hut, and I wouldn't even see him for several days but felt his presence in every moment. I felt that he was very close to me in his meditative state, because he was close to me in his soul form. Satgurus obtain the state of liberation in their first birth, but they don't accept liberation, because they have to fulfil the promises and assurances they have given their disciples. As they are bound by their assurances, they accept their final birth and utilize the entire life of their final birth, for the spiritual progress of their disciples. They meditate in their final birth only for the spiritual progress of their disciples because they have obtained everything in their first birth, and nothing more remains to be achieved.

In their last birth, they generally live in isolation and meditate, taking all their disciples in their chitta. That's why all those disciples, who are connected to them during their spiritual practice, progress spiritually. This is because the Satguru can't ordinarily do what he does for his disciples during his practice of meditation. There is a direct connection between the Satguru and his disciples at the soul level during their practice of meditation, as the Satguru's is in isolation and his physical body is not seen at that time. Therefore, the Satguru dosen't want to meet often. They wish that the connection of their disciples is with their souls. Such Satgurus do not connect with their disciples at the physical level. They try to connect their disciples with the Guru-energies, and therefore they have been found to stay away from their disciples.

Their life gives only one message—don't hold on to the physical body as it is perishable. Keep your attention on the energies that are flowing through me as they are the energies of Paramatma. Thus, some Satguru can be found talking about some special form of Paramatma, or about his Guru or his powerful subtle body. He keeps making one aware that he is only a medium. Actually, he is a medium and also not a medium; both these states are present for the reason that if the disciple is at a lower level and looks at him on the physical level, then the Satguru's body is actually the medium for the energies. That's why the Satguru says that he is a medium. This is true. In the same way, it is not true, because when the Satguru himself doesn't have any identity, how can he be the medium of Paramatma? The medium has a separate identity, and that is why he is not a medium. He himself is Paramatma because he has merged his physical body with Paramatma. Thus, for the disciple, the Satguru is Paramatma.

He is a medium for the Satguru, because he can only stay alive as long as he calls himself a medium. When he stops thinking of himself as a medium, then he'll give up his life because Paramatma doesn't have any identity at all. So, how can he merge with Paramatma and keep his physical existence separate? This explains why the Satguru's lifespan is very short. Satgurus are one with Paramatma, and they are able to maintain their separate physical identity only for a short time. Life holds no attraction for them, and they eagerly wait to give up their physical body. But their physical body is tied to their disciples, and the disciples can keep them physically alive as long as they wish for their physical closeness through their desires and prayers. As they are bound to their disciples, their life depends on the prayers and desires of their disciples. In this way, the more these Satgurus stay in isolation, and the more they remain in a state of meditation, the longer they will keep on praying for the spiritual peace, the spiritual devotion and the spiritual progress of their disciples.

These Satgurus open the doors to liberation for their disciples through their practice of meditation. They make sure that they bestow the state of liberation to all their disciples who are connected with them before they give up their physical body. Thus, it is necessary that the disciples should give as much isolation as possible to their Satgurus, as much time as possible for their spiritual practice, and that at the time of their anushthan they remain connected to them through their chitta for all twenty-four hours. Now the Satguru has nothing left to be acquired; now he'll only distribute whatever he receives because it is his nature to distribute. He'll distribute it only when you allow him to acquire some consciousness. Thus, the spiritual progress of the disciples depends on how much the disciples allow him to acquire and how much their Satguru is able to obtain.

There is no place for physical effort in the spiritual field because the entire spiritual field depends on the purity and holiness of the soul. The more pure and holy the soul is, the stronger it will be; and the entire spiritual condition depends on one's close relationship at the soul level. One's efforts have no place because efforts take place at the physical level. On the other hand, these physical efforts prove to be a hindrance in the spiritual field because efforts that take place in the physical form will only take man up to the physical level. How can man get experiences at the soul level, when he is at the physical level? That's why there is no place for the physical level in relationships at the soul level between the Guru and his disciples. Any effort that man makes at the physical level to obtain a good spiritual level will bring about a subtle ego in him. Man will be imbalanced when ego exists within him.

So, how will he reach the soul level when he is imbalanced? That's why a person who desires spiritual progress should always remember this. There is no place here for physical effort. It is the disciple's feelings towards the Satguru that enlarges his container, and by container we mean our capacity to absorb. The more feeling a disciple has, the more will be the capacity of that disciple to absorb, and he'll be able to absorb according to his capacity. Until today, no one has been able to get anything more than his capacity to absorb. Thus, he'll be able to acquire Paramatma's blessings through the medium of the Satguru according to the volume of his container. Paramatma's grace never overflows or collects more than the container's volume, because it is acquired according to the size of the container.

During his lifetime, a disciple has to enlarge his container and wait for Paramatma's grace. He wonders whether the blessings have arrived or not, because Paramatma's grace is natural. It can't be acquired through one's efforts. Paramatma's grace can't be acquired, it can't be bought, nor can it be obtained through one's efforts. This is similar to the way that nature either gives showers in the form of rain or doesn't, because rain is dependent on nature. All phenomena are present in nature; no man can make an effort in this matter. Man should understand this secret right from the beginning, and this secret can be explained only by an experienced Satguru who has realized it. Several people can't progress spiritually because they have not understood this mystery, though they are interested in spirituality and wish to progress in it. In spite of their desire for it, they are not able to progress because feelings are given importance in this field, not one's efforts.

Everything in this field depends on the Guru-krupa. However, whether he showers nectar or not is also not in the Guru's hands, because the shower is from Paramatma and the Guru is only a medium. Thus, Paramatma's good qualities are received by the medium and he distributes them equally to everyone. He doesn't discriminate through race, religion or language. The feelings that the disciple has for his Guru are not for his physical body, because the disciple doesn't accept the Guru's physical body, but the energy of Paramatma. He acquires the spiritual experience of Paramatma through the medium of his Guru. The Guru's body is the medium for Paramatma's grace, and the medium can shower happiness only if he himself is happy. This is similar to the fact that if an artist is unhappy then he can't create a happy statue. The artist has to first experience happiness in order to create a happy and joyful statue, and then impart it to the statue. If there is no happiness in the artist, then how will he impart it to the statue? It isn't possible at all.

Similarly, as long as the Guru is not happy with the disciple, vibrations can't be showered through his medium. The showering of vibrations depends on the Guru's feeling of happiness. The Guru feels happy when there is a feeling of love, a feeling of closeness, as a result of collectivity. When he is happy, he becomes a suitable medium for the showering of consciousness; and only when he becomes a suitable medium, then Paramatma showers vibrations through him. The showering of vibrations takes place automatically when the Satguru is happy, because he has only been born for this purpose to distribute vibrations. He distributes them to whomever he meets; he can't keep anything with him. Distribution is the quality of feeling bestowed on the Guru by Paramatma.

The spiritual progress of the disciple depends on how happy he is able to keep his Guru in his life. Often, when the disciple is at the physical level, he tries to keep the Guru happy at the physical level by offering him material gifts. He offers the gifts of his feelings through the material objects. If the material gifts are offered with love and affection, then the Guru accepts those gifts because of his love and affection. The Guru prays for the disciple so that his feelings of love and affection for the Guru may increase; and as a result of the Guru's prayers the disciple's feelings increase. The feelings that have been expressed through the medium of the material gifts take on the form of a seed, and one day the disciple surrenders everything he possesses. Whenever any disciple surrenders a portion of whatever he has then that is not surrender; it is called an offering. Thus, the disciple holds something back for himself. But when the disciple doesn't keep anything for himself and surrenders everything, then that is called "total surrender".

The Guru always wants the complete surrender of the disciple's ego, but the surrender of the disciple's ego always happens last. A disciple surrenders everything he possesses but keeps his ego with himself, and the surrender of the ego happens after everything else. After the disciple surrenders his ego, he doesn't remain a disciple anymore but becomes a Guru, because the disciple doesn't have any separate identity left. The sooner this moment arrives in the disciple's life the better it is for him, because the disciple's journey of liberation commences only after this moment. The Guru, on his part, can only wait for the disciple to surrender his ego. He can pray for the disciple, but he can't pull him towards it; he can't pull the feeling of surrender towards himself.

This feeling of surrender is the disciple's personal business and will have to be offered by him. No one can make another person ready to surrender. Surrender of one's ego becomes possible only after that disciple's soul is completely purified, and this happens slowly, when one is constantly in the proximity of the Guru. Sometimes some incident becomes a medium for it, and the ego is surrendered, but this incident can't take place without the karma of one's previous birth, and this one incident can change the disciple into a Guru.

The final purpose of every Guru is to awaken the disciple's soul; and the Guru wishes that his disciple's soul should be awakened and should grow so powerful that the soul itself becomes his Guru. However, this is possible only when the disciple surrenders his ego. Every Guru who has come into the human society has experienced the same thing. Man surrenders before the Guru as a result of his problems and because of misfortunes. The Guru is aware that these misfortunes are a medium to bring the disciple to him. Actually, the right time for the disciple's spiritual progress has arrived, and then the disciple doesn't even realize the point at which his attention moves away from his problems and towards Paramatma in the Guru's presence. The problems in the disciple's life act as a bridge to help him cross the ocean of life. That's why man shouldn't be afraid of problems that come into his life. He should accept them as gifts from Paramatma and thank Paramatma for giving him so much in life. Thank him for what he has given you; and what he hasn't given you is so negligible that it isn't worth complaining about. Often, it is the problems in a person's life that free him from his ego. First of all, man tries to get rid of the problems that have come into his life due to his ego. Then he tries to free himself of the problems through prayers; and finally, when prayers also don't work, he starts begging and beseeching (Paramatma). It is this humble beseeching that breaks his ego, and then he starts weeping. Leaving the ego behind causes a lot of agony; it makes the disciple weep a lot, because the disciple's soul is purified through his weeping and the dirt is cleared from his soul. That's why the disciple cries in the presence of the Guru.

The Gurus have their own limits and always speak within that limit. The disciple therefore has to reach that soul level in order to understand what they are saying. Gurus often ask the disciple for his 'head'. By the word 'head' they don't mean his head in the physical sense, but his 'head' in the form of his ego. The Guru speaks at his level and the disciple understands it at his level. It's very difficult to understand what the Guru says during his lifetime, and therefore one shouldn't put one's attention at the level of the Guru's physical body, nor should one accept what he says at the physical level. Only then will the disciple be able to understand what the Guru is saying. The relationship between the Guru and his disciple is at the soul level. This is the only relationship in the world that is at the soul level, and it is unique because it is above physical relationships. The connection of souls is at the inner soul level, and the soul is connected to Paramatma. This is the only relationship in the disciple's life that brings about a spiritual change, because it is due to this relationship that Paramatma's grace is showered on humans. After that, there is nothing left to be attained in man's life, because man achieves Inner Peace.

Inner happiness is the greatest happiness in man's life. Both joy and sorrow are a part of man's life because these are states of mind in which man experiences both happiness and sorrow. Joy and sorrow keep on alternating for man in this state, and both are like two sides of the same coin. A person who can experience happiness can also experience sorrow and meditation in both of these states.

After doing meditation, man rises above the physical level and reaches the soul level. Then a stream of nectar flows from his soul, and he begins to experience inner joy in that stream. Whoever obtains this joy is always happy, and he is immersed in his own happiness. At such a time he is not affected by external situations, and his physical body is neither affected by external situations, nor is he affected by joy or sorrow. He observes the events that occur in his life like a witness; but he's not affected by them because he realizes that situations are temporary. They always keep changing, and external situations never remain static. He is never affected by those situations, and he observes each situation like a witness. He is not a part of any situation, and therefore he is not affected by it. As a result of looking at it as a witness, he realizes that all this is Paramatma's game.

He is always connected to Paramatma's energy, and he keeps obtaining happiness after experiencing inner peace. Once he learns how to do this, then, no matter what the external situation, this man always feels happy.

"Inner happiness is everlasting; it is eternal because one keeps on finding this happiness within oneself."

Today, I bowed my head before Gurudev, as Gurudev had revealed the secret of inner happiness to me. I thanked Gurudev once again in my mind for passing on this knowledge to me in his presence. I had often experienced that, when Gurudev was not visible, when he was not near me, then I used to get a lot of experiences. I always got experiences when he was in isolation, because when he remained alone in his hut I couldn't see him, and when I couldn't see him my attention would always go to his energies. Since I couldn't see his physical body, there was no question of my attention going to it. Therefore, when my attention reached his energies, his energies would give me new experiences every day. I would realize that he was close to me in the form of those energies. Actually, Gurudev used to stay in one place and his energies also were present in the same place. It was I who would get close to his energies through my mind.

I experienced that day that the Satguru is never nearby or far away from the disciple. He maintains a certain distance from the disciple and always maintains it, but it is the disciple who is sometimes close and sometimes away from him. The Satguru is always close to the disciple.

When the disciple's attention is on the aura of his Gurudev's energies, he automatically comes close to Gurudev. But it is true that when Gurudev was in front of me then my mind wouldn't be on his energies. This means that his body acted as a barrier. I felt that Gurudev wasn't an energy to be seen, but to be observed, and this is true because Gurudev is not a physical body—he is a medium of energies; and energies are never to be seen, but to be experienced with closed eyes. Take an example: if one wishes to touch a book, that is one thing; but if one wishes to *read* a book, then it can't be read by bringing it too close to one's eyes. We have to hold it one or two feet away from the eyes to read it. If the book touches our eyes, we can experience the touch of the book, but we can't read it; and a book is always meant for reading and not for touching. Similarly, I felt that my Gurudev was meant to be experienced and not to be seen. He should be experienced only from a distance. But I realized this only after a lot of study and practice. Gurudev is not an ordinary body, nor is he an ordinary human being for one to see and recognize.

My Gurudev is a medium for the energies. One will have to experience him and become aware of him after experiencing him. I felt that when one passes by a rose and automatically gets its fragrance, there is no need to pluck the flower and hold it in one's hands. What is necessary is that we should go close to the rose petals. Similarly, it isn't necessary that my Gurudev should be present in front of me. What is required of me is that I should be mentally close to him. This means that I should always keep my attention on him.

I sometimes feel that, as a result of several disciples being very close to their Gurudev's physical body, they can't get the spiritual experience of their Gurudev. This is because just as one can't read a book by bringing it too close to one's eyes, one can't get experiences in the presence of Gurudev's physical body. To get a spiritual experience, it is absolutely essential to maintain a distance from Gurudev. Gurudev is aware of the fact, whether the disciple realizes it or not. That's why Gurudev always keeps his disciples away from him.

I didn't realize how time had passed in all this talk, and by now it was quite dark; I decided to sleep. I had planned to get up next morning and clean the whole ashram. For that, I needed to get up early in the morning, and to get up early I needed to sleep early.

I woke up early next morning and got busy cleaning the ashram. First, I removed all the twigs that had fallen from the trees, then I removed the dry leaves that had fallen, and then I swept the place. I always swept a little later in the day so that it would be brighter. The birds were singing and also making plans about where they were going to peck for grains that day; I had realized this by observing their behaviour. I had been away from human habitation for a number of days. I didn't get any other thoughts as there was no human habitation for hundreds of miles around in the jungle. I was always in a state of thoughtlessness, in a state of void. I don't know why, but that day I felt as if Gurudev was saying, "Thinking is a contagious disease that is passed on from one body to another. This sickness is not visible. Every individual has a personal aura, but if that aura is influenced by the collective thought pollution around him, then as a result of that polluted Aura, we get thoughts. Then we are influenced by the thoughts of people around us, because every human pollutes the atmosphere through his thoughts. And when there is only one type of pollution in the atmosphere, we will definitely be affected by that bad atmosphere. Our identity diminishes in a crowd, and the identity of the crowd grows. We lose our identity in a crowded place. Then we ourselves can't identify who we are.

We think in the same way as the collectivity around us. Our thoughts are not different from theirs. We think like the crowd around us. All this happens because our aura is affected by the aura of other people, and under that influence our personal influence ends. That's the reason why 'good company' has been given a lot of importance here. This has been explained because the effect of the thoughts of people in whose company we stay is bound to affect those people, too, because there is a power of collectivity of thoughts. We start thinking what other people are thinking. That's why we find that, in some specific places, all people have similar thoughts. When one hears the same thoughts again and again, those thoughts get embedded within that person. Thus, we often find that success or failure in a person's life is the result of these thoughts. When a person thinks positively, then he performs good deeds, and when he performs good deeds, he'll be successful in life. Actually, when one thinks too much, or has useless thoughts, or thinks negatively—all these are illnesses caused by thoughts. These diseases are caused due to this specific company of thoughts. In reality, every thought reduces a man's energy. Man uses up most of his energy on these thoughts, but he's not even aware of it. This is the reason why sages and ascetics go into the jungle and meditate, so that their energy is not destroyed.

Man's thoughts are unnatural; therefore, whenever he goes into the lap of nature, his thoughts come to an end. Man becomes aware of his own thoughts only after going into the lap of nature. One's thoughts are reduced in nature, and then they slowly disappear. Just as scientists make discoveries externally by going to the moon, or by going to the planet Mars, some sages and ascetics journey inwards. But those who undertake the inward journey are not able to describe it. They can't narrate their spiritual experiences to others because they are no longer able to stay in a state to tell others.

Therefore, hardly anyone has any knowledge about this inner journey, and the ordinary man in society is unaware of this living knowledge. A treasure trove of living knowledge exists, but man is not aware of it. Once a person attains this living knowledge, then all his desire for physical activity ends. Therefore, both the activities of writing about the spiritual experience or telling others about it don't happen. That day, I realized that sages possess a great treasure of living knowledge. One day, they'll leave this world, taking the treasure with them, and the world won't even know about this inner journey.

I mentally prayed to Gurudev, "You are sitting in this thick jungle with so many energies. No one can enter this jungle against your wishes. When the ordinary human can't reach this place, how will he get this knowledge, because you will never leave this jungle and go out into society!

"Humans are very unhappy at present in society. Man is troubled; the whole human race is caught up in the web of these thoughts, and society is striving to come out of this vortex. Man is struggling to get relief from these sorrows and these problems, and he uses whatever means he possesses—some people perform puja or read scriptures, some people visit temples, some people perform havans, while some people chant mantras. Thus, man tries to go inwards. He wishes to go inwards and find everlasting happiness. Sometimes he achieves it momentarily while performing some great worship, or when he performs aarti, and he feels very happy. Someone else searches for this happiness differently, while others try to run away from this frightful situation. Often, he falls into bad habits or vices to escape this frightening condition—some people drink alcohol, some people smoke hashish, while others visit prostitutes for momentary pleasure, trying to forget themselves through sex. Thus, they want to forget their problems. But running away like this from circumstances is escapism, and this is not the way to overcome such situations. In society, man doesn't know how to find this everlasting happiness.

"Gurudev, you are aware of everything. I haven't run away from any situation to come to you, nor have I come to you in search of any everlasting happiness. I have been sent here. Some Satguru sent me to you. This means that I, too, am not qualified to reach you on my own, and neither am I suitable for it. It is my Guru-krupa that he kicked me, and I reached you. Now that I have arrived here, I have only one goal in life. Whatever I receive should be for distribution in society, or I should not receive it at all. I don't want any knowledge that I am not able to give to the human society. I don't want any such everlasting joy. What will I alone do with such everlasting joy? I don't have any desire to acquire it. Despite that, if you still wish to give me that knowledge, then give it with blessings that I may be able to convey this knowledge to those deserving souls who have been born on earth to acquire it.

"I wish to become a messenger of your living knowledge. Gurudev, please make me a medium for your messages. I have promised those souls that, when I realize the knowledge, I'll definitely pass it on to them. It is with this hope that these souls have been travelling with me for the last 800 years. The hopes of all these souls are dependent on me. They are not aware of the path and are wandering around, searching for the path. This is my final birth. I have achieved everything, but all that is for myself. I don't wish to carry all this alone and leave, and it is time now for me to leave, too. But I'm tied to my promises, and I can't achieve liberation without fulfilling those promises. Please bless me and show me the way to distribute this living knowledge. Gurudev, please understand my condition; my state is getting worse. I am stuck, too. My condition is like that of a mother whose breasts are filled with milk for her children, and she wishes to feed her child with milk. The child also wishes to drink the milk, but the mother doesn't know how to feed the child and the child doesn't know how to drink the milk. Gurudev, please give knowledge to the mother to feed the child with milk and to the child to drink it; otherwise, this milk, which has filled the breasts, will create problems for the mother.

"Gurudev, the human community can't reach here, and you can't go into society; how will the human community find out about this path? Gurudev, bless me." I was begging and pleading, I was weeping, and I don't remember when I went into a trance crying. But when I woke up, I found that Gurudev had placed his hand on my head, and I could experience Gurudev's pure touch, but my eyes were not able to open, and I felt that there was a flood of vibrations flowing from Gurudev's hand, as if a stream of cold water was flowing through my body. I wept and said, "Gurudev, please give me the knowledge for distribution; teach me how to distribute this knowledge. What use is this knowledge to me if I can't distribute it? I don't need it at all. I have achieved everything by reaching you. Now I don't even have any desire for liberation. I don't wish to give up your proximity to attain liberation, either. Gurudev, it's very difficult to distribute anything in life, but I have only been born to distribute, otherwise what was the need for me to take birth! Gurudev, the only purpose of my life is to distribute. If I don't get the chance to distribute (this knowledge) in my life, then I don't want anything because I don't need anything. This excessive knowledge is becoming a burden for me, and I am experiencing a lot of heaviness. This burden is going on increasing. What am I to do, Gurudev? Please show me the way." I spoke like this and started weeping.

Gurudev said, "Open your eyes. Look how beautiful this world is; you have come into this beautiful balanced world to maintain the balance of nature. All those who are close to nature are balanced; and those who are further from nature are facing the problem of imbalance. You have been born to remove their imbalance. Today, I'm revealing the mystery of your own birth to you. You have been born to guide those sacred souls who have been travelling along with you in each birth for the past 800 years, and you are their only ray of hope. Therefore, only those souls will reach you and will absorb the knowledge of how to achieve liberation from you, because this relationship is 800 years old. They have chosen you as their medium for attaining liberation. Thus, the purpose of this birth of yours is to pass on to them the knowledge of how to attain liberation. You enjoy distributing the knowledge because to distribute has become your basic nature, and you won't be able to exist without distributing. The very purpose of your life is to distribute. Your life will also end the moment this distribution ends. Only those holy souls for whom you have been born will be able to understand you, and only they will acquire knowledge from you. Therefore, you will distribute knowledge to human society because of your nature, but all the people to whom you distribute it won't be able to preserve it because their time has not arrived.

"In society, the people who receive this knowledge and who can keep it safe and preserve it will be few. While distributing, don't expect that man will preserve this knowledge. Actually, the question of preserving it arises when one is aware of what one has received and who is the giver. Both these things are very important, because without understanding both these things, it is impossible to preserve this knowledge. When man is not aware of the value of what he has received, why should he preserve it? One should have knowledge of what one has received and from whom one has received it. Giving knowledge is very easy, but receiving it is very difficult. One needs to reach a high spiritual level, to be very suitable, otherwise even after receiving it people lose it; and then they keep on searching for it and keep losing it after they have received it.

"My blessings are with you. You will achieve your goal in your lifetime, and those pure souls who have accepted you as a medium will definitely reach you, and you will achieve your goal in life. You are bound by your promise to these souls. You will experience in your life that efforts have no place because, even if you try, you won't be able to reach them; and they will reach you without any effort. Your life and the life of those pure souls will prove to be complementary for each other because liberation for both is not possible without reaching each other. Therefore, whatever efforts you put in will only be for your personal satisfaction, but your efforts won't bear any fruit. At the same time, you shouldn't put in efforts with the assumption that you won't achieve anything.

"You should always keep in mind that you are only a medium of Paramatma, and a medium doesn't have a separate identity. A medium is only a medium. Maintain your identity as an innocent, an empty, holy and pure medium. The more successful you are in maintaining this form, the more you'll be able to perform the duty as a medium. You'll be able to perform more in your capacity as a medium because performing that role is the goal of your life. A medium always has two ends—he receives through one end and gives through the other. The difference between us (Gurus) and you is: the end through which we give and the end through which we receive is one and the same. We don't have the collectivity of souls with us. For us, receiving from one soul and passing it on to another soul is our only role in life, but that is not the case with you. You have several souls who pass on knowledge to you, and several souls who receive it from you. The collectivity of these souls who pass on knowledge to you will be converted into a collectivity of souls who receive knowledge from you. And wherever collectivity exists, its identity will be merged, and that is why you won't do anything in life, but everything will take place through you as a medium; you won't pass on anything to anyone, but people will receive it through you as a medium. People will receive spiritual experiences through you.

"A Guru has several disciples, and you have several Gurus; you are the medium of several Gurus, and they'll be able to reach their disciples through you. Therefore, you will become the medium of several Guru-energies. Recognize yourself! And not only recognize yourself, but always remember your identity so that you will be able to continue to exist always in the form of a medium. The longer you remain a medium, the longer you aren't caught up in the dirt of feeling that you are a karta, and the more water will flow through your pipe. You have received a great treasure of knowledge in this birth, because of your desire for it, birth after birth. No one can receive all this in one birth. This knowledge has been collected over several births, but you are receiving it in this birth. You are the 'ocean' into which several rivers will merge, and it is the final goal of several rivers to reach you and merge into you. Several souls will dissolve their identity in your presence; you are the final destination of several souls.

"The sea is always calm and steady in one place. Similarly, you should also become quiet and wait in one place for those rivers that are yearning to meet you, those rivers that are eager to meet you, the rivers that have the goal of reaching you. These rivers have originated from their place, their only reason is to meet you, and they are advancing towards you with great eagerness so that they may end their existence. Once they reach you, their existence will come to an end, and you'll take on the identity of that collectivity which has no existence of its own.

"When a river merges in the ocean, the high tide in the ocean becomes a hindrance for the river. It is only when the tide ebbs that empty space is available for the river to enter the sea, and then the river enters the sea. The high tide wishes to embrace the river and invites it, and this invitation from the sea increases the speed of the river. Similarly, the more you try the more you'll be on the outside; and the more you are on the outside the more barriers you'll create in the medium's work. The quieter and more effortless you are, the more you'll turn inwards; and the more you are within, the more you'll be able to attract those souls who wish to meet you. Therefore, you should calm yourself, steady yourself, move inwards and create a space so that the souls may be able to enter that space. Several souls haven't been able to reach you because of your efforts, and several souls are wandering around.

"You are the lighthouse for souls. If the lighthouse is steady in one place and is lit up, then all its work is done. Several lost souls, like lost ships, will see the light of that lighthouse from a distance, and that light will prove helpful in guiding those ships to the shore. Thus, with the help of that small amount of light, the ship that is several souls will reach the shore that is liberation. I'm explaining all this to you so that you may understand the purpose of your life, because man is aware of his destination at the time of his birth. He remembers his destination after his death, and he keeps weeping, because when he remembers his destination he doesn't have the medium of his physical body anymore. Therefore, it is the duty of every Guru to remind his disciples of the purpose of his life, so that the disciple can fulfil his purpose in his lifetime. I'm performing my duty in reminding you. Now whether to accept it or not is your choice, not mine. I have performed my duty by explaining all this to you, and the rest is up to you."

I mentally thanked Gurudev for telling me about the purpose of my life, so that I could reach my destination during my lifetime.

My Gurudev is very compassionate, and it is because of his compassion, due to his grace, that I have woken from my sleep (come out of my ignorance) today. I'll remember to remain awake all the time because Gurudev has performed his duty by awakening me once. Now by remaining awake I'll fulfil my duty.

The next morning, I went from the jungle to the place where some days ago I had planted some seeds of the tree on which lai leaves grow. All around was a mountainous jungle area, and therefore I had to search for a place to plant the seeds where there were no stones and only soil, because it is useless to sow seeds on rocks. There were very few seeds available there, and I didn't want to waste them. Therefore, I had to walk around for miles in search of suitable soil. Secondly, one also required a place where the rainwater didn't collect, that is, on a slope. I searched for such suitable places and planted seeds every eight days so that I could always get good fresh leaves.

After walking for a few miles, I reached the place where I had once sowed some seeds. It was difficult to find it because so much grass had grown around there that I only recognized it with great difficulty. When I arrived there, I was overjoyed because a great crop of lai leaves had grown and was swaying there. Monkeys had eaten the leaves in some places, and I was happy to see this because I had found some companions who were eating the leaves with me. I was tired, and so I rested for some time and sat on a big rock. I started to think—I had only a few seeds with me and so I hadn't wanted to waste them, and I had walked for miles to sow them. Then I had searched for a place where there could be a good crop from those seeds; but man also takes birth on earth with a few moments, like the seeds, and then he wastes those moments, which are seeds, by sowing them in useless places. Then, when the seeds in the form of his life are used up, he accepts death. Man cries after his death; he feels that he has wasted his life. Actually, before he dies, when his physical body becomes useless in his old age, man gets inner peace only through the work he has done. The good works he has done give him peace of mind, and his mind feels peaceful because he has performed very good deeds in his life. These good deeds give him joy.

Man should therefore spend the seed-like moments of his life in places where a good crop can be grown. Man has come alone to this earth, and he'll return alone. In his old age, his body isn't able to move around, his contact with people decreases, and even the people who come to meet him only do so out of a sense of duty, as if to say that they are coming to meet him because he is still alive. When they see your bad state, they come and pray to Paramatma that you should die quickly. When you're lying in bed and waiting for death and you are alive only because death is not approaching, at such a time only the deeds you have performed in your lifetime give you happiness. You remember how many seeds you have sowed in good places and feel inner peace. Thus, at such a time when he is alone, man is with his soul, and it is only the soul that always stays with man, no matter what the condition of the body.

The leaves of the lai seeds I had planted had grown very big, and I picked and gathered them up. They would now be useful to me for a whole week. I broke off all the lai leaves, collected them, then sat on a big rock and started tying them into bundles. As I was tying the bundles, I was thinking that my ego is feeling so happy that I have created so many leaves, and that I was able to grow such a crop. It is because of me that such a crop could be grown, but in reality, could I have created even a single lai leaf in my life, let alone a whole crop? No, never. A small plant grows out of a seed, and a small shoot grows from the plant, and that small shoot opens into a leaf; then that small leaf grows into a big leaf—all this is created by Paramatma. The energy that makes the seed sprout is Paramatma; the energy that forms the shoot is Paramatma; and the energy that makes the shoot grow into a leaf is also Paramatma's energy. So why should my ego feel that I have created it? This ego I have is so useless. This ego was present inside me, and therefore I was happy that I had grown this crop. If the ego wasn't there inside, then I would have said that this is the grace of Paramatma, such a wonderful crop has grown by the grace of Paramatma! Paramatma is so compassionate! Paramatma has showered blessings on this harvest! But that didn't happen. I forgot Paramatma because of my ego; I forgot that even a leaf doesn't move without the desire of Paramatma, so how can a leaf be grown without Paramatma's wish?

I collected each leaf as a gift from Paramatma, tied it into a bundle and started walking towards the hut. I was thinking that this crop is a gift of the grace of Paramatma, and because I was thinking like this, I didn't feel the weight of the bundle I was carrying. I climbed the mountain with ease, and everything seemed to be very joyful. Now I had enough provisions for my meals to last me for a week. One seldom gets the chance to cook one's own meals and eat them on one's own. One prepares the meal according to one's desire. There's no tension of worrying about how it'll taste, who will eat it, whether the person who eats it will like it or not; that's why it doesn't matter how the food one has cooked turns out, but its taste gives a lot of pleasure. I was thinking like this and didn't notice when I arrived back at the hut.

It was evening; I hadn't eaten anything since the morning. Now I entered the hut, washed the lai leaves, and after having my bath sat down to clean them. I cleaned the mud from the leaves, separated the stems from the leaves and then cut the stems into small pieces. I also cut the leaves into small pieces, then stuffed them in the hollow of a big bamboo and filled it with water. There was a knot on one side of the bamboo, and I tied the other end with banana leaves and closed it. Then I placed it on the fire to be cooked. I allowed the leaves to boil in the water for some time. The juice of the bamboo mixed in with that of the leaves, and then I removed it from the fire and placed it on banana leaves and ate the leaves. This was my meal.

It wasn't possible to eat this type of meal more than was necessary. Man should eat to live and not live to eat. Sometimes, I used to add some ginger or bay leaves to the lai leaves, if I could find them. These leaves were tasty. They could also be cooked in different ways with different things. Sometimes, I would cook them with wild bananas. These bananas were bigger in size than ordinary bananas, but they didn't taste very good. There used to be big black seeds inside the bananas; these bananas could also be boiled and mashed and eaten.

After eating this kind of food, my tongue had lost all sense of taste. I would eat anything that was available. It's true that all my Gurus were vegetarians, and this Gurudev was also a pure vegetarian. There were several edible fish available in large numbers in the river; since there was no fishing there, they were present in large numbers, too. They were quite fearless, and they would come up to me on purpose when I was bathing and touch my body.

Suddenly, I remembered the day when Gurudev had said, "Look at these fish. They are present in such large numbers because there is no one to catch them here and it is not appropriate to catch them, either. These fish also have their own life and there is a portion of Paramatma in them, too. We should establish a sense of oneness with that portion. That is why having meat is not suitable for a person who undertakes spiritual practice. When a person undertakes spiritual practice, he awakens the living energies within himself; he brings his energies to life.

"Thus, while awakening that energy within himself, how can he awaken it through the medium of the bodies of animals that are outside, by eating the fish? How can he absorb the dead energy? It is not appropriate to eat non-vegetarian food. Man is not violent; that is not his basic nature. Violence is against man's pure nature. How appropriate is it to take someone's life in order to save one's own life? Man somewhere, at some place, kills the humanity within himself by killing these animals. Humanity is the energy within a human being, and whatever deeds we perform by killing that humanity will always be wrong.

"As man's spiritual level develops, the sphere of this non-violence also increases. In the beginning, the reference is to violence at the physical level when one refers to non-violence. But in the expanded sphere of non-violence, the mental form is also included. If someone is made unhappy because of you then that is also included in the sphere of violence. You shouldn't either knowingly or unknowingly say a single word that will cause hurt to someone, because that is violence, too. This is called verbal violence, and this verbal violence proves more deadly than physical violence. It often happens that a person is so hurt by our thoughts or by our words that he remains hurt throughout his life. This is deadly because the wound made on the body heals, but the wound on the mind will never heal, and he will remain unhappy throughout his life as a result of that hurt. This is also a big violence. Therefore, one should practise non-violence on a very large scale.

"Generally, those people who are wounded within themselves hurt other people. This means that they keep on opening their own wounds again and again by hurting others. Thus, they are violent towards themselves. How can a person who has no wounds within himself hurt others? To give something to others you should first have it within you. One can abuse another person only when he himself has been abused by someone else. A person who has never been abused in his life will not be aware of what abuse is. So, how can he abuse anyone when he doesn't have any abuses with him at all! Abuse is a form of violence, which someone uses against you. You remember that and use it against someone else.

"This is the reason why a person who has been abused keeps on abusing everyone. Abuse generates bad feelings. A person who doesn't have bad feelings will not be able to abuse anyone; and bad feelings are not the sign of a good and pure mind. When one's mind is polluted then it's possible to abuse someone, and those abusive words can cause hurt. Therefore, using abusive words in this way also comes within the sphere of violence. This action of abusing someone is also violent. Similarly, in contrast, I've seen several saints and sages being abusive; I have myself been abused by several Gurus, but I was never hurt by their abuses, I was never unhappy; instead, I experienced a lot of happiness after being abused by them. I felt this happiness because they had not abused me with any bad feelings, nor did they wish to hurt me through their abusive words. When their purpose wasn't to hurt me at all then how could I be hurt? That's why I was never hurt; instead, I was happy because my Gurus were abusing my faults. They were abusing me to break my ego. Just as iron is required to cut iron, this was a similar interaction, because the Guru doesn't possess anything that is bad. When he doesn't have anything bad, then how can he do anything bad to others through bad words?

"The Guru's arrows of words would be aimed at my faults; my ego would be destroyed, and my mind would be purified. Then, because of this pure mind, I would feel happy. In reality, the Guru is beyond social interaction. One can't realize this by observing his interactions, because his interaction appears different. We don't have an insight that is as comprehensive and complete as theirs. As a result, the interaction that we see is not actually present, and what is present can't be seen. Therefore, one can never understand the Guru's behaviour. If you pay attention to your feelings as a result of that interaction, then, no matter what the interaction, the vibrating energy will be showered on you continually. There are very few fortunate people who are able to enjoy this in their lifetime. One can't catch a Guru because of his behaviour. His behaviour is always the opposite of the usual interaction. So how can you catch a Guru because of his interaction?

"The Guru is not a spiritual acharya who can be recognized by his behaviour. The Guru is beyond interaction and behaviour. The Guru can only be experienced. His behaviour is misleading, and one should always stay away from that danger. We should only pay attention to what we are experiencing. These abusive words also come within the sphere of social interaction. Social interaction is for the ordinary human; it is at the physical level. How can there be any social interaction for someone who isn't a physical body at all? There can never be any interaction. One can't recognize a Guru by his interaction, and neither can one know him through his behaviour.

"The ordinary man can understand a person by his behaviour, but that behaviour can also be a pretence. Good behaviour and good interaction are at the physical level because one is aware that one shouldn't behave badly or have bad interaction with someone. This means that, somewhere at the subtle level, me and my interaction and me and my behaviour are connected to that 'I.' Thus the 'I' sense is present together with my behaviour and my interaction. One can also make a show of one's good behaviour and one's good interaction because, wherever there is a question of seeing something, the object that is visible can also be wrong; there is a danger of seeing it in the wrong way. The Satguru's level is above his behaviour and interaction because he doesn't want to show anything. He doesn't want to influence anyone either through good behaviour or good interaction. He appears exactly as he is. He won't make a show because that is external behaviour, and he doesn't possess anything that is external. He is within himself, and that's why he doesn't have any false appearances. He doesn't want to show anything in order to attract the person before him. People are attracted automatically because of the Satguru's Aura and are drawn towards him. When people are drawn just like that towards him, why should he make any effort? Instead, he always tries to save himself from people. The Satguru always behaves in a contrary manner and keeps behaving wrongly to avoid individuals approaching him.

"For example, there was a Satguru who had the habit of abusing people. He used very nasty abusive words. There was another Satguru who behaved as if he was insane and threw stones at anyone who came close to him; actually, till today, not a single stone has ever touched anyone. Another Satguru used to live in filth, in dirt, and no one would go near him because of the dirt. Thus, their behaviour would always be such that people would keep away from them. Just as a dancer sometimes creates a body language through her dance, similarly, while the vibrations of consciousness are flowing through the Satguru's body, he can accomplish interaction through the body. The Satguru doesn't have any interaction, but interaction takes place; and it isn't necessary that that interaction should be good, because he doesn't possess either good interaction or bad interaction—only interaction happens. Therefore, one's attention shouldn't be on the Satguru's behaviour but on the consciousness flowing out of that interaction. This behaviour by the Satguru is to distract our attention from the consciousness. That's why one should experience the Satguru; one should experience every aspect of the Satguru's behaviour. The Satguru is a medium of universal energy, and whatever he does is only for that energy.

"One should therefore experience the Satguru. The Satguru doesn't interact; interaction happens through him, and behaviour occurs through him. As a result, there is no feeling of being a doer; being or not being a doer are both interactions. There is 'interactive behaviour' with the doer and only 'behaviour' with the non-doer.

"As long as there is a feeling of being the doer, the process of any action doesn't start because where 'I' is present, 'He' is not present; and the moment 'He' arrives, 'I' will not remain. 'He' can never be present as long as 'I' exists. The behaviour and interaction that take place through 'I' has the influence of that individual. The influence can be either good or bad, but, in any situation, where behaviour and interaction take place without the 'I' being present, there are only vibrations and consciousness, which is not visible, but can be experienced. The Satguru is free from social interaction. He doesn't interact, but Paramatma gets some interaction accomplished through his medium. And in any interaction that is carried out through Him, Paramatma will definitely be present, in some form or other. Paramatma doesn't have any form, which is why He can't be seen. He is present in the form of energy, which is why He can only be experienced. Paramatma's energy keeps on flowing through every interaction of the Satguru, but we shouldn't keep our attention on his interaction; we should only experience it. This is a very difficult process because one is supposed to close one's eyes to what is visible and experience what is not visible, but this is exactly what needs to be practised, and if one learns how to practise this, be sure that he has learned everything.

"To experience what is not visible is one step forward towards Paramatma. Once you have reached this path, then the experience of Paramatma will commence everywhere, and then we'll realize that the whole universe is filled with Paramatma. I was the fool who couldn't experience that. The study of getting experiences takes place in the presence of the Satguru. Paramatma is present in every particle of the whole universe. We always exist with Paramatma and he always stays with us. It is we who are not present with him.

"We aren't always present with him because Paramatma exists in the present, and we either live in the past or keep on thinking about the future, so how can we experience Paramatma in the present era? It isn't possible to get that experience. We don't live in the present, and therefore our attention is not in the present, and as a result we are not able to get the experience of Paramatma in the present. Our attention is always on the unhappy events of the past; it is on the bad incidents and bad individuals, and when our attention is not in the present at all, how can we get the spiritual experience? The experience of Paramatma is a living process. We can acquire that in our lives only by remaining in the present. It is absolutely necessary to remain in the present in order to obtain the experience of Paramatma, and our attention should not stray anywhere else. We should be a complete void so that we are always ready to absorb that universal consciousness.

"The universal consciousness is ready to meet us in every moment. It is we who are not ready, and being ready in this way is meditation. Not doing anything either through the physical body or through the mind is meditation. Meditation is a very simple process and only the lack of proper guidance makes it seem difficult. That's why it appears so simple in the presence of the Satguru." I felt as if Gurudev was passing on all this knowledge to me in his presence.

He seemed to be telling me that once one learns to experience the consciousness of Paramatma at one place, then one can experience him anywhere in the universe. But this seemingly simple process is actually very difficult. This simple process appears to be difficult because it is we who are being difficult. We are present in one place and think about another place. This is an incongruous life; there is no balance between living and existing. When there is a balance between the body and the mind, and if we can be present physically where our mind is, then meditation will happen automatically. Meditation is not something to be done; it happens automatically. Meditation is a natural process, but for that it is necessary for us to be natural ourselves. As we become more and more natural, the energy of nature starts flowing through us, and our identity ceases to exist. Then we become mediums of the energies of nature, and then we don't perform deeds; they happen on their own. Meditation is the link between performing a deed and the deed happening on its own. Meditation, too, can't be done; it happens. It was so peaceful in this jungle that one could hear the rhythmic sound of that silence. Silence also has its own sound.

The sound could be heard even more clearly at night. Here in the jungle, there were a lot of fireflies, which were shining in the dark. It often seemed that the scene in the jungle was similar to that of a wedding procession. All night, the fireflies tried to remove the darkness with the light of their bodies; they seemed to be saying that as long as there is life, one should give light to others, and if possible, remove the darkness around us. We can't remove the darkness that is spread all over the world, but we can at least remove the darkness around us. We should do at least this much in our lives. The fireflies had become my friends, and every night they would come to my hut to meet me, and it appeared as if a procession of stars had entered my hut. They would light up the hut and say, "Don't see how far the darkness stretches, just light your own lamp."

I found their message to be quite true. Man's life is so short, and he wants to change the whole world in this short life. He wants to light up the whole universe; he wants to remove the darkness from the whole universe, and he keeps looking and trying to find out how far the darkness stretches in the world. While looking for darkness all his life, he himself doesn't realize when his life gets lost in the darkness. There is so much darkness and ignorance in this world that it isn't possible for any one person to remove it. The whole world is filled with the darkness of ignorance. Even if we search all our lives, we won't be able to reach its other end and find out how far that darkness stretches. We can never understand in our lives how far there is darkness in this world. Therefore, man should not search for darkness in this life. Yes, he should light his inner lamp; and if every human being in this world lights his inner lamp in this way, then it is possible that there won't be any darkness left in this world, and there will be light and brightness everywhere in the universe.

Similarly, man spends his entire life in searching for faults in other people—where something bad is happening, where something is not right—and even after observing the faults of others he isn't able to remove them. How will a person who isn't able to get rid of his own faults remove the faults of others? That's why man shouldn't spend his life trying to remove the faults of others. Man should be soul-oriented, and he should first of all search for his own faults, to try to remove the darkness within his own mind. Man can get rid of his own faults because those faults are close to him, they are within him, and therefore it is easy for him to remove them. Man should always try to remove his own faults instead of trying to get rid of the faults of others because man can't even do this much properly in his life. One can gauge how short man's life is through this fact. The day man realizes that he's wasting his precious time, he won't spend it looking for faults in others, and then like these fireflies he'll first remove his own faults—and then the light of knowledge, no matter how small, will remove the darkness from this world. He won't be bothered about this but will remove the darkness around him. Then there may be darkness in the world, but there will only be brightness around him.

In order to light his inner lamp, man first of all requires a peaceful atmosphere so that he can look within himself and make his soul aware and understand the importance of his soul. Then he can move closer to his soul. As he studies this process, he'll have a deeper connect with his soul, and as the closeness with his soul grows, man will realize the brightness of his soul. Then he'll start getting universal knowledge from within himself. I suddenly felt that the Satguru's presence is lit in every atom and every particle; its effects can be felt in every atom and every particle. Today, Gurudev explained a great mystery of the world to me through the medium of a firefly. Actually, my Gurudev is very compassionate. He keeps passing his messages through different mediums. He doesn't bother about how much I'm able to acquire or can't acquire, but continues with his task of giving, as if his life's work is only to give light, the only purpose of his life now. He had obtained everything in his life and now there was nothing left to be acquired. That is why he was happily distributing whatever he had received in his life. I was thinking in this way and I didn't realize when night fell. I didn't realize my eyes had closed, and I went to sleep. I didn't even know how long I was awake that night.

The next morning, there was a lot of noise made by several birds, and I looked outside to find out why they were making so much noise. I saw that Gurudev had come out of meditation and was sitting quietly under a tree on the opposite side, and all the birds had gathered around him. The birds seemed to be talking to him, and it was a highly captivating scene. I tried to understand what they were saying. They seemed to be asking him about something. When I came out and touched Gurudev's feet, he said, "All these birds are trying to learn about liberation from me, and I'm explaining to them that this is not the right time for them to receive this knowledge. What will they do with this knowledge in their present form as birds? They still have to undertake a long journey until they reach the human form. Then they'll have to undertake another long journey in the human form, but these birds are not ready to accept it!" Then Gurudev again started trying to explain it to the birds.

"Oh, my dears! The soul is separated from Paramatma because of its curiosity and as a result of moving outwards; and then the soul travels through thousands of forms like viruses, insects, birds and animals. The soul wishes to move towards Paramatma in every birth and wishes to separate itself from this cycle of life and death.

"The soul is a portion of Paramatma, who moves the wheel of life and death. Paramatma moves this wheel, but he is not a part of the cycle. Paramatma is not a part of this natural cycle of life.

"Thus, the soul finds itself caught up by mistake in this wheel of life, and unwillingly connects with this life. It continues to live; and this desire for life becomes the purpose of its life, and it keeps taking births again and again in different forms. It can't leave this cycle of life. It finds that the only way to get out this cycle is in the human form. The soul is aware of this, and that is why now all of you (birds) have only one goal—somehow, you need to reach the human form so that in future you will find the path to liberation. But you are not aware that even after reaching the human form you will not immediately reach liberation. Also, in the human form, you will have to take birth again and again. Thus, the soul once again finds itself caught in the human form. It goes through several different forms so that it may finally acquire the human form, but you are not aware that the human form is also a cycle. The soul gets caught up in the wheel of that form. The soul evolves in the human form in a slow but systematic manner because the soul reaches the human form together with a lot of intelligence; and then, once the intellect is present, then thoughts arrive; and then the soul slowly develops in the human form.

"The soul has to take seven births in the human form. The soul takes birth for the first time in a human form in the house of a poor person and wishes, in that birth, that it should at least get two square meals every day. In its second birth, its purpose again is to get proper meals. It has different desires in the next birth. Then it takes birth in a lower middle-class house. Its next birth is in some rich family, but it's not satisfied in spite of being rich. In this way, the soul takes seven births in the human form, and when the soul is not happy even after taking birth in a very rich person's house, it realizes that all this wealth and these material joys are not everlasting. Then the soul takes birth in search of eternal happiness and achieves self-realization. It achieves self-realization as a result of some Satguru's grace and compassion, and it gets the knowledge that it is a soul; and as it gets this knowledge, as it starts awakening, it starts to separate from the external material world. Then it gets joy only in obtaining inner knowledge. It starts meditating and attains a state of liberation in its lifetime. Then, in this state of liberation that it has achieved in its lifetime, the soul attains a total spiritual death; and as a result of achieving a total spiritual death, it attains liberation. The purpose of man's life is to achieve a total spiritual death, because spiritual death is the end of life of the human form. Spiritual 'death' is the total death of the human life. This means that now there is nothing left to be experienced.

"There are three types of death. The first type of death is adhi-bhautik. This is the death that takes place before its time, death that takes place suddenly because of some severe physical illness. The person's lifespan is not yet complete, and death occurs. Such a death is called adhi-bhautik death. If a person gets proper medical attention and facilities, he can be saved from this type of death. People mostly die through this type of death.

"The second type of death is adhi-daivik. This death is caused as a result of committing suicide or due to some accident. In this case, too, death takes place suddenly, whereas the person's lifespan still remains to be lived. The person still has a desire to continue living, but death occurs.

"The third type of death is adhyatmic (spiritual death). This type of death is the final death of the human form. A person attains liberation after this death because he has no desire to live any further, nor does he have a goal to attain; but man has to take several births in order to get this type of death. In this type of death, man's attraction for the physical body is also left behind. Several saints and mahatmas invite this type of death. They take their physical body to a stage when it becomes frail, so that the desire for one's physical body doesn't become a barrier on the path to their liberation, and then their soul leaves the physical body. They invite such a death so that they don't have to acquire another physical body. They distribute all their spiritual energy in different mediums and themselves become energy-less. Then they cure the sicknesses of others, and in the process, they take over that sickness in their own body. That is why these saints suffer from serious illnesses, or we can say that they keep on burning until their last moments like sandalwood incense sticks and spread fragrance to others, and also keep the surrounding atmosphere scented. Even after they leave, their fragrance lingers around their resting place.

"In this way, when the soul takes birth again and again with the pure wish of helping others, then helping others becomes its nature. As a result of this helping nature an Aura is formed around the physical body, and that always remains even after their death. This is why, even after several years, we experience waves of consciousness and vibrations around their shrine, because the body that has been kept there was connected to millions of souls in its lifetime, and millions of souls were connected to it. Our soul can always experience those vibrations. That is why millions of souls visit the shrines of such Gurus and acquire inner peace.

The soul can acquire inner peace because when it goes near the shrine, its identity becomes zero, and this happens because there is a collectivity of millions of souls around the samadhi. Thus, we can understand how much power there is in the collectivity of Paramatma. It is the goal of every soul to attain a complete, absolutely spiritual death, and to free itself from this cycle of life and death.

"According to the spiritual canons (principles), after man takes seven births, he can attain liberation. Man has to go through this full cycle; there is no other way out of it. Yes, if one meets a living Satguru in some birth, then because of his spiritual powers the Satguru can help man through the journey of seven births in one birth itself. But the question is: where will one be able to find such a Satguru and how will we be able to recognize him? How will we be able to believe and accept him? One can find such a Satguru in life only when one stays in the present and searches for him and finds him.

"Generally, one searches for the Satguru in the past because he himself lives in the past, and therefore he'll find a Satguru of the past in some Satguru's biography. Such a Guru of the past will be imaginary, and not the truth, because a biography of any Satguru is written several years after he passes away. We don't know how much of it is the truth and how much is imaginary, because the writer would be a devotee of the Satguru. Why should any devotee describe his Satguru's faults? He will always write only good things about his Satguru, and anyone who reads that Satguru's biography won't understand that a Satguru can also have faults. This is because, in any Satguru's biography, only his good qualities are praised and his virtues are extolled. His good qualities are magnified and narrated, and this exalted version that is written is not always the truth, and it appears unreal. A body can't exist without the process of excretion; when the body exists then excretion will also take place. Similarly, physical faults will also be present together with the physical body. Until today, no physical body has been created without faults, nor will it ever be created in the future. Even a statue can't be made without faults. Some fault or the other remains in every idol and every statue that is made. Thus, when a statue can't be made without faults, then how can the human body be without faults?

"A well-known sculptor has said, 'I have created 1065 statues, and in every idol some fault or other remains. Yes, if I make a new statue today then I can definitely say that that idol won't have a single fault that was present in those 1065 statues. But this new idol won't be flawless, either. I will create the 1066th fault in that new statue; it will definitely be created. This will happen because no statue can be created without faults.'

"How can the Satguru's body be without faults? Faults will definitely be present in the Satguru's body, too, and the Satguru in our books is free of faults. Therefore, he is imaginary, and then we start searching for the imaginary Satguru in the present. The beginning of our search goes in the wrong direction because no such Satguru exists, so how can one meet him! Man's faults are proof that he is alive, and then man searches for a Satguru without faults! He wanders from one Satguru to another, because when he surrenders before a Satguru and then notices his faults, he leaves him and surrenders before another Satguru; he notices faults in him, too, and leaves him. Then he surrenders before the third Satguru and, on finding faults in him, he leaves him, too. Thus, you keep searching all your life, but you yourself are not without faults, so how will you be able to find a Satguru who is free of faults? It is man's basic nature that, first of all, he notices faults easily. That's why he'll definitely find faults in any living Satguru and that is also the reason why he is not able to see faults in the biography of the Satguru in whom he believes, because that

Satguru is not present in the disciple's life. If this disciple had been present in the biographical Satguru's lifetime, then he would not have believed in him because he would have noticed the Satguru's faults. Faults are immediately noticeable in a physical body, just as one notices the skin that covers the physical body.

"The living Satguru doesn't want to attract anyone to himself, and that's why he won't hide his faults. Actually, the Satguru is a saint and is above any behaviour. On the other hand, his behaviour is an illusion that deceives us. These Satgurus make people aware of their faults so that people may see their faults and keep away from them. There is only one way of keeping oneself free of the Satguru's faults, and that is total surrender, because after total surrender one won't see any faults. Surrender is not always that of one body towards another physical body; it is surrender of one soul towards another soul. When you are at the soul level, and your attention is on the Satguru's soul, then you won't be able to see his faults because faults exist at the physical level. The soul is a portion of Paramatma. You will get a vision of Paramatma; you will get an experience of Paramatma. You will get the experience of consciousness, and then one won't see the living Satguru, one won't hear him, one will only experience his presence; one will fill every moment of his presence in his mind. One's attention won't stray to the fact that he is showering his grace; one won't notice what he is doing or what he's saying. In reality, the Satguru doesn't speak, nor is he seen. He only makes one experience him. That is why one should experience him when he is close to us. I, too, obtained the presence of several Satgurus in my lifetime, but I didn't find any Satguru who was without faults. It is true that my attention never went to their faults as a result of their flow of consciousness.

"This is the one and only path for man to attain liberation. The state of liberation means to get the inspiration of a Satguru from a book and to actually search for a living form of Satguru; to accept the Satguru with all his faults, and to surrender completely to him. In this way, one doesn't notice his faults, and achieves the experience of Paramatma, and continues to live in the proximity of that experience. Man can attain it in his lifetime while he exists in his physical body. One can accept the Satguru as Paramatma, but one should do so with the knowledge that he is a human being and not Paramatma; that he is a medium of Paramatma, that one can reach Paramatma through him, but he is not Paramatma. No physical body can be Paramatma because Paramatma is not a physical body. He is an all-pervading universal energy. So how can he be an individual? Satguru is a medium for attaining Paramatma. This type of quest for a Satguru who is without faults takes us far away from the Satguru. Despite being close to him, we are not able to recognize him. One's spiritual progress also happens together with the progress of one's soul. A spiritual state is created in a sadhak due to his spiritual progress, and it is that spiritual state which brings him close to a Satguru."

There were no signs on this isolated, thickly forested island that any human had ever come here. There were tall trees and there were creepers climbing upon them. Some tree had fallen and was stuck and couldn't fall to the ground as the jungle was so thick. Neither did there seem to be any possibility of coming across any human for several miles. Therefore, there was no question of pollution by man's thoughts. This island had purposely been chosen on the shore of the river for spiritual practice. It is true there were some mountains around here, and one had to use a stick to push aside the bushes and make a path in whichever direction one walked.

This place was a small world in itself, and insects were my only friends; some birds were my neighbours because Gurudev mostly stayed in deep meditation. I would cut the wild bananas into small pieces and place them close to the anthills. Ants have a great feeling of co-operation with each other. I never saw an ant eating the piece of banana that I had placed there. The ants would make tiny pieces of that piece and take them inside their home. They were very honest ants, and I would sit near their house and watch them for hours at a time. Sometimes, I would throw them a big piece, and then an ant would come and try to lift it; when it couldn't, it would go into the anthill and return with a long line of ants following it. They arrived in a line, and all the ants would try, and they would slowly lift the big piece and take it inside their home. They would face great difficulty in carrying it to their house. Then I asked for their forgiveness for giving them such a big piece. I was angry with myself that I wouldn't have lost anything if I had given them a smaller piece. I realized my mistake.

I was very happy with their sincerity towards the task. Sometimes, even a small ant would drag a piece that was several times larger than its own size. It would try constantly and would carry on with the task with great commitment and hard work. This, then, became a great attraction to me; I would watch the ants and I would observe them, but until today I haven't seen any ant eating those pieces. I have only seen them storing. There was an amazing mechanism of organization amongst them. I have never seen them fighting. On their return journey they would touch their mouth to that of the arriving ants, and they seemed to pass on some message and then continue moving. There was some communication, some kind of amazing conversation between them. I felt at that time that any organizational structure should be like that of these ants. Perhaps if every weak individual, every poor person, every support-less person who has no one to depend on, a person who is always busy with too many thoughts—all get together and understand, first of all, that they are all weak people in society who are distressed, then they will always remember that collective organization can make them strong. They'll realize that they are of no use by themselves and that staying together is a necessity for them. All weak people in society can come together through the power of this organization.

Similarly, one should leave alone those people in society who have found Paramatma, or those who don't want to reach Paramatma at all, and they should form an organization of such people who have the desire to find Paramatma but don't know how to. These are people who themselves don't possess the physical or mental state to do so. Such people should first realize their weakened state and come together to form a good organization for themselves. Then they will be able to attain liberation in collectivity because their ego that 'I can attain liberation on my own' will not be present in them; the ego that 'I can do meditation' won't be there because they'll realize that they can't do anything alone.

When they realize this, they'll start using words that are full of collectivity, such as 'we' are meditating, 'we' desire liberation, and they'll attain liberation in collectivity. Weak people are stronger when they are organized because they don't have any ego, and they are aware that only the organization is their strength. They know that organization is a necessity for them. If they wish to move forward in the spiritual field, they'll need to make organized efforts. The organized efforts of these people will bestow collectivity on the path to liberation, because now the time for developing the spiritual field has arrived; the treasure of spirituality that has been lying hidden should be distributed amongst all people, and spiritual progress can also happen in collectivity. But for this to happen, one will have to pray to the Guru-energies: "Oh Guru-energies! Please descend to earth and convey the blessings of these Guru-energies to each and every person!"

I mentally made the ants—who had provided me with this knowledge my Guru, that an organisation of small and weak people is stronger because their 'I' is not present in it. They are aware that they need to make an organized effort. Then, whenever I had time, I would go to the anthills and sit there. The next morning, I again went to the river to bathe with Gurudev. There was a different type of joy in being with Gurudev. I used to go to the river every day for my bath, but the joy of bathing with Gurudev was very different. The whole atmosphere would be filled with consciousness in the presence of Gurudev, and all the water in the river would vibrate, as if even the river became happy in Gurudev's presence. I always felt that this moment should stop, and my life should end then and there because I had nothing left to achieve. There was no need to continue living!

After his bath, Gurudev sat on the stones with me and started explaining, "There is a story about Bhagirath in our culture. The Sage Bhagirath had performed penance in order to bring down the river Ganga, which flows in heaven, and invited Ganga to descend after great penance, and then the river Ganga started flowing on earth. Similarly, there is a purpose in your life, that you have to convey the river of knowledge to the ordinary man; today, 'knowledge' is being conveyed from one soul to another soul. Now you have to perform the task of conveying this (inner knowledge) from one soul to millions of souls. You are thinking of ending your life in my presence. If you think like this, then that inner knowledge will stay just with you. It is the goal of your life to convey that inner knowledge to the ordinary man. The coming time is very difficult, and collective efforts are the need for this time.

"Inner knowledge is the only true knowledge in this world. Man has become so deluded that, instead of understanding this knowledge of experience as the (true) knowledge, he thinks that the knowledge of books is the (true) knowledge. He doesn't know that bookish knowledge is only informative. Information about something that has already happened will never give one any experience. Experience is the one and only knowledge that can never be acquired through books. For example, you have read a book about a cow; there will be information about cows in that book—a cow has four legs, a tail, two horns, the cow may be white or red or yellow or black in colour, the cow gives milk, the cow's milk is health-giving and white in colour. All this is information about the cow. It is true that with this information you can make a distinction between a cow and a horse, because you have received information about the cow through the book. Thus, books give this type of information. But books can never give knowledge because 'knowledge' is only 'inner knowledge.'

"Inner knowledge is a spiritual experience. A book can't give us the experience of cow's milk. Similarly, one can get knowledge from a book about what is inner knowledge, but one can't obtain it; and managing inner knowledge is very complicated. A person who has acquired inner knowledge is already immersed in it, so how can he make another person experience it? But because he is bound to pass on this knowledge to others, what he does is that, while giving up his physical body, he passes on that knowledge to someone. Until he passes on this knowledge, he can't free himself from his debt to the Guru. In order to free himself from the debt to his Guru, he has to bestow the knowledge on someone. Knowledge is a spiritual experience, and he bestows it so that he himself can attain liberation. I, too, am going to perform this duty today; I'm going to give you my inner knowledge so that I can attain my path to liberation and be free of my debt to my Guru. The biggest obligation in this world is the debt to one's Guru, and we can never repay it.

"I, too, won't be able to repay it, but I can at least offer a flower in the form of spiritual experience at my Guru-charan, and I'm going to do exactly that. I'm going to entrust you with the treasure of the knowledge of spiritual experience because this is necessary for me. I'm not obliging you in any way, I'm fulfilling my duty. I will be free of my duty, but your path is not as easy as mine. Your path is very difficult. You have to distribute inner knowledge to millions of souls. If a hungry person is given some fruits and asked to cut them into small pieces and distribute them amongst people, he'll find it very difficult because he has to control his hunger and distribute the fruits to others. Thus, this is possible only if one's desire to distribute is greater than one's hunger. You have to perform this difficult task.

"Every soul carries along with it a goal before arriving on earth, and your soul has taken birth again and again with the purpose of distributing. But you weren't able to complete your purpose of distributing, and you took another birth to complete that purpose. This wheel kept turning, and now this cycle is coming to an end because, in this birth, the Guru-energies are helping you to obtain that knowledge through me as a medium. But this knowledge that you are receiving after several births will also not be able to give you liberation because you are tied down by your promises. In your previous births, you had promised millions of souls that when you acquire the knowledge of liberation you will bestow it on them. Now you are stuck, having given this kind of difficult promise. You won't be able to attain liberation until you give them the knowledge. It has become a necessity for you to give them the knowledge. You were thinking just now in my presence, weren't you, that this life should end here itself? But your life's spiritual work still remains; you still have to fulfil your promises. My work was limited to myself, and my requirements were few. Therefore, whatever I obtained was related to my requirements. But your requirements are much greater, and you will receive more.

"Your level of receptivity has grown greater because of your desire to give. The purpose of your life is to deliver the river of inner knowledge, which had been flowing in isolation for several years, to the ordinary man. It is your duty to do so. The thirsty person who thirsts for liberation will cross seven oceans and will definitely come to you. Therefore, don't think of giving up your life with me. I had asked for this knowledge for myself, and I have received it; you have asked for it for others and you will have to convey it to others. This is the goal of your life."

I thanked Gurudev for enlightening me about the purpose of my life, and said, "Gurudev, I was hungry, and was going to find the fruit of inner knowledge and eat it. You reminded me that I have not received it for eating but for distributing. Gurudev, my condition is like that of a weak ant. I can't do anything without your blessings—I can neither receive any fruit, nor can I distribute it; and even if I distribute it, who will accept it? I am neither suitable for receiving nor for distributing it.

"Gurudev, only you have given me the fruit, now only you will have to get it distributed through me. I'm not in a state to do anything after reaching you. Every atom and particle of my body is being awakened, and my entire body is being filled with consciousness. I'm becoming as cold as ice, and now I can't even blink my eyes. How am I going to distribute the fruits of inner knowledge? Gurudev, please get it distributed through me. Gurudev, man has not tasted the fruit of inner knowledge; he is hungry and is still eating the soil, and he thinks that it is the fruit. He is so ignorant.

"Gurudev, because of his ignorance, man thinks that the information he has obtained through books is true knowledge, because he has never had the experience of knowledge. He is not aware that knowledge is an experience that can't be obtained through lifeless books. Gurudev, bless me and have compassion on me by getting this inner knowledge distributed through me to the ordinary man. I am like that weak ant; I can't do anything without your blessings." Saying this, I started crying, I started pleading, and suddenly went into a semi-conscious state.

Gurudev said, "You are aware that you can't perform this task. This means that your feeling of being a 'doer' has ended. Now, when you have realized that 'I' can't do it, then entrust it to me completely and stop your efforts towards this goal, because efforts and 'I' are both connected with each other. Now you should only become my medium. A pure and holy medium can neither receive anything nor give anything. This is the hallmark of a good medium. That medium does not have any identity of its own, but everything can be obtained through that medium. One can't obtain anything without a medium. A medium is only a medium. He is equal and the same for everyone. Now you become a medium. Your work will be easy depending on how good a medium you are, because the Guru-energies are going to make use of you in the form of a medium. When there will be millions who are going to receive from your medium, then there will be several Gurus who will be giving the receivers. You have my blessings that you will be a good medium through whom any human will be able to acquire inner knowledge."

I expressed my desire to Gurudev to allow me to perform puja of his lotus feet, and Gurudev gave me permission by nodding his head. Then I took Gurudev to a large rock on the riverbank and made him sit on it. I took water in my cupped hands and first washed his feet properly. The touch of those divine Feet itself was a divine spiritual experience. Then I slowly started massaging his feet and washing them at the same time. I don't know how long I continued doing it. Then I went to the nearby bushes, picked some flowers and placed them on each toe. I decorated the feet nicely, and then I prostrated myself before him and sat with my eyes closed. I prayed, "Oh, abode of mercy, I have neither seen Paramatma nor have I ever experienced him. Paramatma's energy is spread all over the universe, but I have experienced universal energy through you as a medium. You are the medium of Paramatma's energy. I am aware that you are an ordinary human being, but by making you the medium of extraordinary energies, Paramatma has made you extraordinary. You may be a medium from the viewpoint of Paramatma's energies, but for me you are Paramatma. My search for Paramatma has come to an end after meeting you; and any search comes to an end when one finds Paramatma. I have found my Paramatma. Now I have no desire to meet Paramatma because I have found Paramatma in my lifetime.

"I believe that Paramatma can't be a physical body because Paramatma is formless. He doesn't have any form, but he also acquires various forms in order to incarnate. His forms keep changing from time to time according to the needs of time. The form of Paramatma in the present will be of the present. We humans always live in the past, and that's why we hold on to the form of Paramatma of the past. But we never search for Paramatma of the present time in our lives. The form of Paramatma of the present time will be like that of the present; only then will he be of the present. My quest has ended in your presence; all my wandering is over. I am experiencing an inner peace myself. You are the form of Paramatma for me, and today I am taking this opportunity to worship your lotus feet. Please accept it. Gurudev, there is only one truth in this world. We can accept it anywhere, in any form. Wherever the soul is ready to accept it, where it gets the vision of truth, where the soul experiences the truth—that form is the truth. And that medium of the physical body which gave the vision of truth is also the truth, because there is no physical awareness left in that physical body as the body has merged with Paramatma.

"The body is alive, but there is no feeling of being a body because the body has merged into Paramatma. A body that has become one with Paramatma and has no more feeling of being a physical body, which has already become a medium of Paramatma, has become one with the supreme reality, and through whom Paramatma has incarnated. That body is the form of Paramatma for me. Today, I have realized the meaning of the phrase Guru Saakshaat Parabrahma: Guru is the supreme reality. If there is any supreme reality on this earth, then that is the Guru. One should meet such a Guru, after meeting whom one's quest for Paramatma comes to an end. Today, I am bowing before my Paramatma.

"A Guru is given the stature of Paramatma only if one believes in him. A person may see Paramatma in someone, and another person may find Paramatma in someone else. Actually, Paramatma is present in every physical body, but when one finds a physical body in which the awareness of being a physical body has ended, a body that has become one with Paramatma, then that physical body is the form of Paramatma. Today, my soul has accepted you completely as Paramatma, and this acceptance is a feeling of my mind. That is why I'm expressing my feelings before you and am accepting you as Paramatma. I have accepted you as the Paramatma of the present time, and I pray at your lotus feet with folded hands so you can make me your medium. Make me your medium just as you could become a pure and holy medium of Paramatma. I know that I am not qualified enough for this, but with your blessings even the impossible can become possible.

"Everything is possible in your presence. You are my Paramatma and Paramatma can accomplish everything. You have blessed me that I will become a medium, and I will always keep those blessings in mind. Let me never get any feelings of the physical body within me in my life; let the feelings of any physical body not overcome me in life and allow me to carry on doing your work all my life. My entire life should be spent with your grace and with your compassion. Please bless me that I should carry on with the work of inner knowledge all my life.

"Give me your blessings that, until the last breath of my life, I can continue doing your work; but this is not possible without your compassionate grace. One doesn't realize how time passes while performing Guru-karya. Guru-karya is just an excuse to be connected to you. I wish to get connected to you and wish to remain connected to you by performing Guru-karya all my life."

With these words, I once again prostrated myself before him. He lifted me very lovingly and made me sit beside him, and started explaining, "Paramatma is not a physical body. The one whom we consider as Paramatma was also a Guru of his time; and the one whom we accept as Paramatma has also believed in his Guru. This means that Paramatma has also been created by Gurus. Paramatma keeps on changing from time to time. Paramatma is a universal energy. It incarnates in the universe from time to time, and after incarnating it performs the task of balancing the universe. It manages the world through its different mediums. The physical body that has ended its feeling of 'I' becomes a medium of Paramatma. Each physical body is different depending on how long it is free from its ego.

"Every human has a strong chance of being a medium. Any person can remain a medium of Paramatma depending on the period of time that he can remain without his 'I' sense and the knowledge of 'I' in his body. It's not possible for an ordinary man to be free from body consciousness of 'I' all his life. But for some moments, at least somewhere or other, this feeling of the body consciousness leaves a person, and at that moment he becomes a medium of Paramatma. Performing work for the Guru means doing the work that we have accepted with our soul, that this is the Guru-karya. When one performs such work, one gets rid of one's physical 'I.' The work from which one's ego, that 'I have done the work,' is removed, is Guru-karya. Guru-karya is a tool through which we wish to forget the feeling of having a physical body and become the medium of Paramatma. Man chooses to do Guru-karya for this very reason so that he may progress spiritually. Actually, the Guru's complete attention is on work and on the person who takes up his work. The Guru automatically follows him. The easiest way to get connected to a Guru is to take up his work. When one does this work throughout one's life, then doing Guru-karya becomes one's nature.

"When one reaches that state, his physical body becomes a medium of Paramatma. The physical body keeps making us aware of its existence, and it is very difficult to have control and disregard that awareness. But it is possible to gain control through continual practice. You can also be totally free of physical awareness like me and spend the rest of your life in that state. All this is going to happen, but some time still remains before it can happen. Paramatma also has a definite plan, and he doesn't give anything before the due moment. Wait for that moment. I'm very happy to have met you. I can foresee the work that is going to take place through you as a medium. I'm truly blessed that I got the opportunity to offer my contribution in my lifetime for such a great work. Now the purpose of my life has come to an end.

"My body has also become weak now. This body has given me a lot of support in my spiritual practices. I am thankful to this body, because if this physical body was not present then I would neither have been able to reach my Gurudev, nor would I have been able to obtain the energies from him as a gift of his blessings; I would neither have been able to increase them, nor would I have been able to hand them over to you. All this has been possible only because of this body. Today, you have accepted this body as Paramatma and have also freed me from my debt to this physical body. Now I have become free of this physical body. I wish to thank this body before giving it up. Actually, I'm very thankful to this weak body of mine; this strong body has become weak as a result of helping me in my spiritual practices; it is tired. Now the body also wants to rest. I, too, wish to give up the body now; I, too, wish to go to my place of liberation. This body was my halting place, and one stays only for a few days at a halting place. This body was an inn where I stayed for a few days, but now I wish to return home. I wish to go to the world where all the Gurus dwell."

I started weeping when Gurudev said that, and I asked him not to leave me behind all alone. Gurudev replied, "Oh, you foolish child, I'm not going anywhere. Now I'm changing the covering of this body; I'll still remain alive in your form. Both of us have merged into one form. I have handed over my entire existence to you; rather, it would be more appropriate to say that you have taken it over. I'll stay alive with you in the form of work. Oh, my dear, I have surrendered my entire life's work (Guru-karya) and my life has ended long ago. The part of me that has remained alive is only for that Guru-karya. Now I have handed over even that Guru-karya to you. The body is perishable; the body can be destroyed, but the work remains alive. I'm alive with you in the form of the work. Whenever you perform Guru-karya, you'll realize that I'm with you.

"Now I'm bound to you because of the work, although nothing is happening at present. Come, it's getting dark. Let us go to the hut." Then Gurudev bowed before the setting sun, and we started walking towards the hut. Night had already fallen by the time we reached there. I remembered the red colour at the time of sunset, which had spread over the water, and due to the brightness of that red colour, it seemed as if there was a flow of red-coloured water. Deep in such thoughts, I didn't realize we had reached the hut. Then Gurudev left to take rest, and I also went to take some rest. It was already nighttime, and my body was tired. I didn't realize when I had fallen asleep.

Next morning, I woke up early, cleaned the whole hut and

also the courtyard, and then I waited for Gurudev to arrive. After a while, Gurudev came out and stood holding on to the door of the hut. I suddenly noticed that he had started looking very weak in just one day. There was a lot of difference in him in just one day. He was suddenly looking older and more tired.

Gurudev sat on a stone. I asked him why he looked so tired today. He replied, "I had prevented my body from becoming weak so that I could bestow the energies on you for performing Guru-karya. Yesterday, I handed over your treasure to you, and after that I was able to free this body. Now it is free to leave. Therefore, all the tiredness of those years has suddenly appeared. This weak body has given me a lot of support in my spiritual practice." Then it seemed to me that each day was affecting Gurudev's body like a year. In the last ten days, he appeared to have grown older by ten years. But he was very happy. Secondly, he didn't meditate anymore now, and always remained awake. That was why, nowadays, I had many chances to serve him. I was getting his living presence, and I was overjoyed. One beautiful evening, when I held Gurudev's hand and brought him outside, he said, "I had a great desire to attain liberation right from my childhood, and I had started making efforts for this right from then. I knew that liberation is a living state, and it can only be obtained through the medium of a living Guru. That is why I ran away from home as a child and found this path. Once, as a child, when I expressed a desire to walk on this path, everyone at home opposed it. Therefore, I left my home without telling anyone and wandered for twenty years. After twenty years, I could reach this uninhabited island. My Gurudev used to live here, and he brought me here.

"My Gurudev said to me—I have donated 'inner knowledge' to you, and you are indebted to me, and this debt can only be repaid when you donate this knowledge to someone else. Until then, you will obtain the state of liberation but won't be able to attain liberation. That is the Guru-dakshina that you have to pay me. As long as one doesn't give the offering to the Guru, the knowledge one has obtained can't fructify. Several souls are roaming around on this earth in order to offer Guru-dakshina. They manage to acquire inner knowledge from their Guru, but they are not able to give Guru-dakshina to their Guru. Thus, those souls acquire inner knowledge; but despite obtaining liberation, they are not able to attain liberation because their soul is held up in the Guru-dakshina. Every disciple has to surrender himself completely as Guru-dakshina, and in order to surrender themselves, some disciples use flowers, some disciples use fruits, some disciples use water and some take the support of their inner wealth. This means that some offer flowers at the Guru-charan and offer their good deeds as Guru-dakshina, some offer fruits as Guru-dakshina and surrender themselves, while some give up their soul as their offering. Thus, disciples offer Guru-dakshina according to their own wishes.

"I had offered my 'inner wealth' as my Guru-dakshina to my Guru, and later my Guru told me that in order to keep this fire of inner knowledge burning, he would send a medium to me, and that I should hand over to that medium all the treasure that he had passed on to me; and after that, I could give up my physical body. That is why I was doing penance in this place for several years and was waiting for you to arrive.

"Oh, my dear, every Guru feels that he should pass on whatever legacy of knowledge he has obtained to the next generation and that this lamp of inner knowledge should never stop burning. Therefore, every Guru entrusts someone or other with this knowledge. My Guru entrusted me with it, and I have entrusted you with it. You are the final resting place of inner knowledge, and you are the final stop, because millions of souls are connected to you, and you are connected with millions of souls. You have connected with millions of souls for the past 800 years, and you have taken them along with you and have promised to give those souls the knowledge of liberation. You are bound by the promise, and that's why you are 'one' at the physical level, but the ray of hope for millions of souls. I can clearly see an ocean of collectivity of millions of souls with you."

Gurudev was looking into space and speaking, and I got lost listening to him. Then, as I came back to the present, I asked Gurudev, "How did I reach so many millions of souls, and how will I fulfil my promises to them?"

Gurudev replied, "Those souls themselves are wandering around on a quest for you and are searching for you; and wherever they are in the world, they will definitely reach you. They will definitely find you, just as ants manage to find jaggery on their own.

"Oh, you fool, do you think that the jaggery goes to the ants? The jaggery is calm and steady and sits in one place with its sweetness. The ants keep searching and finally reach it. These millions of souls are also like ants. They take several births and will reach you in this birth. You don't have to do anything in this life. You are only the medium. Therefore, don't even think of doing anything, everything will happen in your life.

"My dear, my condition is like the water that rains down and is transformed into small springs; then the small streams are transformed into big rivers. All the water wishes to reach the ocean but is not able to do so. Somewhere on the way, it evaporates. I'm very fortunate to have seen the ocean. I was able to reach you in my life because you are an ocean of collectivity, and I am blessed that I could reach you. After this, the inner knowledge will now be distributed from 'one' to 'several.' Now after you, the inner knowledge will be distributed to the collectivity through you because this inner knowledge is going to acquire collectivity as a result of your promises. The decentralization of energies is going to happen. Whoever has obtained energies until today has done so with the desire to obtain them for himself, but you have not obtained them. The energies have been bestowed on you. You have been bestowed with these energies because you have made big promises, and to fulfil more promises you required more energy. You have received the energies in order to complete your purpose. Your goal is vast, and it is this vast goal that has been able to attract the energies.

"Your container has grown very large because of your desire to give in every birth. Your container is very large. This clearly indicates that a lot of water is going to be filled in it in the form of energies, and more and more people are going to drink this water. This can be seen very clearly.

"Man has limitless energy to give. One who develops his power of giving completely can give limitlessly, because his power of receptivity depends on his power to give. Just as water automatically flows towards the slope of a hill and one doesn't have to send the water, similarly, the energies themselves are attracted to the place where they are going to be utilized."

On that day my future had been described to me, and after hearing that, I started thinking that so much of my life had already passed. How will it happen in this birth, when I don't want to leave this heavenly place and go anywhere in this life? It doesn't seem to be possible in this birth.

Gurudev recognized my bemused condition and said, "I'm explaining these facts to you under difficult circumstances. But have faith in me; each and every word of mine will come true. In this birth itself, millions of souls will acquire inner knowledge through you as a medium. Oh, you fool! Why are you thinking about your next birth? You don't have a next birth at all! This is your final birth, and everything will happen in this birth. It is true that I don't know when it will take place, because whenever it happens it won't be through your efforts; it will happen due to the evolution of those souls. Whatever happens will happen because of the good spiritual state of those souls. You have no role to play in this; efforts have no place in your life. Then how can you put effort in this matter? Wait for the right time."

I told Gurudev, "That is enough for now. Come into the hut now, it has become dark." Then Gurudev nodded his head and gave his permission. I held his hand and took him inside the hut, made him sleep on his bed and started massaging his feet. Gurudev fell asleep, and I went to my hut. Gurudev's hut was quite old. It was broken in several places, and during the day, light used to come through the breaks. Compared with his, the condition of my hut was quite good.

I lay on my bed and thought: if many people come to me, then I won't have any isolation. If my Gurudev won't be with me, then what is the use if the whole world is with me? I don't wish to leave him at any cost. I so revered his physical body that I couldn't even imagine this world without him, because my whole world was my Gurudev.

The next morning, he again started explaining to me, "Oh, you fool! This body is meant to perish. This is the law of nature that whoever is born will also die. You were needlessly thinking during the night." I was startled! He knew what I was thinking even after he had fallen asleep! He was already sleeping, and later I had returned to my hut, so how did he come to know about my thoughts?

I was curious, and asked Gurudev, "You had already gone to sleep; how did you come to know the next day about my thoughts at night?"

Gurudev smiled and said, "My son, whenever we think, we release those thoughts into the atmosphere. No man has been here for the last several years, and today I experienced these thoughts in the atmosphere, and I immediately recognized them as all your thoughts.

"When a person thinks, those thoughts manifest around him. Our atmosphere gets polluted due to thoughts. We pollute the atmosphere through the pollution of thoughts. Thoughts continue to remain present in the atmosphere for a long time, and man pollutes the atmosphere through his thoughts. Man is not so sensitive as yet and therefore hasn't been able to understand about this pollution that occurs in nature. The more people there are, the more the thoughts; and the more thoughts there are in the atmosphere, the more polluted the atmosphere. The more polluted the atmosphere, the more fatal it is for man. But man doesn't see the dangers of this pollution. Actually, there are no thoughts at all in nature; man creates thought pollution, and these thoughts remain in the atmosphere. You were thinking about my body yesterday and were unhappy. Oh, my dear, I have done penance through the medium of this body, and all my life I have been wandering around with this body. Sometimes this body got food to eat and sometimes it did not; sometimes it got to sleep and sometimes not. So, I did not look after this body; but in spite of that, this body has served me.

"Now I wish to give rest to this body. I am bound to you now by making you my own. Now I can't give up my body even if I wish to do so until you wish for it. I am very thankful to this body. I didn't take care of it, but it always took care of me and helped me reach my goal in life. You are my final destination. By meeting you I have received everything. I will not be present to witness your life in collectivity, but I am blessed to have received your presence. I am extremely happy to see the vast ocean-like collectivity of souls who wish to receive inner knowledge. It is because of you that I could reach up to your collective energy, and

I feel blessed that I was able to meet this medium of collectivity and spend the final days of my life with it. My dear, the collectivity of souls is Paramatma. You are attached to the collectivity, and therefore you are Paramatma for me. I am very fortunate to have the opportunity of giving up my physical body in your proximity. My life has been fulfilled."

I couldn't understand what Gurudev was saying because he was speaking at a very high level, and I was not at that high level. That's why I couldn't understand what he was saying, and sometimes I felt that he was speaking out because of his love for me. Wherever man directs his love, the whole universe is contracted and gathers around that person, and I felt that Gurudev must have seen something similar around me.

I used to bathe him every morning. Nowadays, he had given me permission to bathe him. I was very happy in his presence. I used to go to the jungle and bring fruits for him. I used to cook leaves for his meals by boiling them and then serving him. But day by day, Gurudev's body was becoming weaker. He had kept control over his body through meditation. Now he had given up that control, and age was catching up very fast with him. He used to eat only a few fruits in the morning; that was his only diet.

He kept giving me information about what is to be found in which place, and where I should go at what time. The days passed, and he was becoming weaker and weaker. Now he had no desire to live anymore, and no matter how much I took care of him and how much I served him, he didn't wish to live. Then what more could be done? He used to say, "Now my body is tired and can't serve me anymore. The body also needs rest. I didn't take care of my body during my life, and still it took care of me."

One day, he was saying with closed eyes, "Oh, I have reached the world of gurus. The energies of all the Gurus are present here. All the energies that were created because of the spiritual practice undertaken by all the Gurus who had incarnated on earth are present in the world of Gurus. The physical bodies of Gurus are not present anymore, but their energies still continue to exist, and I, too, have joined that group.

"All the energies from the world of Gurus are watching—which human being continues to perform their work? Which human being is praying for the happiness and peace of the community? Which human being wishes to work for the welfare of society? Which human being is meditating? The person who is meditating is merging his existence in the meditation and is absorbed in it.

"These energies are performing work by making that person their medium. As long as man's ego is present, as long as the feeling of 'I' is present, he can't undertake any work for the Spiritual energies. Because of his ego, he can only undertake work that he sees and that he can show. He won't be able to perform work that gives a spiritual experience; nor will any spiritual work happen through him, because spiritual work can't be performed, it just happens. I have reached the world of Gurus, and I can clearly see my physical body. I feel ashamed to see my body from there—how negligible is my existence! And yet man has so much ego about himself. Like a frog in a well he thinks that the world around him is the whole world. Hey, the world is very big! The frog realized this when it reached the ocean. A human being's stature is as small as an insect, but man can't realize this stature when he is present in the physical body. What is the existence of one human being in this vast universe? It's nothing, but this fact can't be realized while one exists in the physical body.

"Man wastes his whole life by holding on to a small, tiny body. The Guru-energies keep on watching all of this with amusement from the world of Gurus—who is doing meditation and how much meditation he can get. Man should undertake only two types of work: firstly, to have the desire to perform good work, and secondly to meditate and to merge one's existence in the universe. One's ego is the last to merge in this process of merging.

"Man doesn't perform any work after his ego disappears, as the work happens on its own through him. It doesn't matter how close he has become to the Satguru. What is important is not proximity, but how much he understood him, how much he believed in him, how much he acquired from him, and how much he experienced from him, because the Satguru has to be experienced. That soul receives the presence of the Satguru because of the good deeds he has performed in his previous birth. His good deeds will end, and the presence will also come to an end, but first of all man needs to know himself. If man can get to know himself during his lifetime, then he will also understand what his stature is in this world; and when he realizes that his stature is not more than even a small insect, he'll stop being egoistical and give up his 'I' sense. Thus, he'll surrender to the Guru-energies. Just as a seed can't sprout without splitting, similarly, inner knowledge isn't possible without the breaking of man's ego. The sprouting of inner knowledge is not possible without the breaking of the covering of one's ego.

"In this world, knowing about one's soul is knowledge, and everything else that is written in books is information; it is knowledge about others. When man understands himself, he will also know his identity; how momentary his life is and how short it is. When he realizes that his life is short, then he'll make proper use of every moment of that short life; he'll realize the value of each breath.

"Man is needlessly egoistic: 'I' am doing everything. He'll realize that he can't even take an extra breath. Life is a string of some breaths, and each breath is important. Man takes ten positive breaths, and even one negative breath that he takes returns him to the same place from where he started. In this way, man goes through life, and when he dies, the ego of the physical body breaks, and then he repents—I wasted my whole life in useless thoughts; now I won't make the same mistake again. Thinking in this manner, he takes another birth, and thus this wheel of life and death never ends. One's ego is actually similar to the excreta of one's physical body. It can't be destroyed completely, but it can be controlled. Man realizes his stature after he comes to know himself. And he comes to know about his stature when he absorbs the magnitude. Thus, man can't realize his own identity without experiencing the magnitude.

"The path to free oneself from ego is the presence of the Satguru, because the Satguru will always hit one's ego. An egoistic person can't believe in or accept a Satguru; nor will he be able to stay in the Satguru's proximity. A Satguru and one's ego can't exist together because the Satguru is the overlord of one's soul. You accepted an ordinary person within your mind as Paramatma, despite knowing that he is not Paramatma, that he is a medium of Paramatma. Believing in someone is a feeling of one's soul. The feeling of one's soul will not appear until the feeling of one's body ends.

"The feeling of ego is a feeling of one's body, and as long as man has the feeling of one's body, the feeling of the soul can't appear. That's why an egoistic person will never accept anyone else as superior to him. It's very difficult to accept someone else as superior to oneself. This is the reason why egoistic people don't believe in the energies of Paramatma. They don't accept anyone else above themselves.

"No human being can completely wipe out his ego. The ego remains in a small form in man, and as soon as it finds a suitable atmosphere it appears. When man says: 'I do not have any ego,' that is also a type of ego. Man can control his ego only after recognizing his identity, and man understands his identity only in the presence of a Satguru. Then man's ego slowly starts reducing on its own.

"The energies of the Gurus exist in the Guru-world. They are always ready to find out which sadhak's body is ready to absorb them. The sadhak is not eager to accept those energies, but the energies are more eager to give him the energy. This happens because, whether the sadhak's nature is to accept or not, it is the nature of energies to keep on giving. It's their nature, and they're always eager to give.

"Man spends most of his time sleeping and thinking. He wastes it going here and there, performing useless deeds, and thinking ill about others. Man spends very little time in getting to know his own self. He spends his entire life in trying to understand others but never tries to know himself. It's very difficult to know oneself, and this becomes possible only after a long-devoted practice of meditation. The Guru-energies are eagerly waiting in the Guru-world. They are waiting to see which physical body, while remaining on earth, can reach the Guru-world through the practice of meditation. The Guru-energies will make such a person their medium, and through him they will incarnate on earth. Then, as a result of becoming a medium, a person having an ordinary physical body will also be able to carry out extraordinary tasks because that body could become the medium of the energies. It is possible to become a medium after long-devoted meditative practice of 800 years.

"I'm telling you all these things because I have reached the Guru-world in my lifetime, when I don't have much lifespan left. This means that I can't distribute this knowledge even if I want to. It is impossible to perform both these tasks in one birth. Life is very short, and spiritual practice takes a long time. In my lifetime, I have performed the task of making inner knowledge happen. Now, in your life, you must take up the task of distributing it; only then will this be possible. Man can't create anything new on his own to understand himself. That's why we will have to believe others in order to know ourselves; and believing is the pure feeling of one's soul."

I couldn't understand what Gurudev was saying. I was worried because of his condition, and he was enjoying himself. He was very happy in his own exalted state. He was present in his body, but he had given up physical desires. He suffered from several physical problems, but he appeared to be like a calm and deep ocean that maintains all its secrets within itself. When Gurudev stopped speaking, I asked him to rest, and I made him lie down and sat there massaging his feet; I fell asleep right there without realizing it. I had been sitting near Gurudev's bed for several nights, and I would go to sleep there. I didn't keep Gurudev away from my sight even for a moment. I was deeply worried about his health.

Gurudev's bed was made of leaves and grass, and he slept very comfortably on it. There were very few objects in his hut; there were no utensils, and there was a piece of bamboo that served as a glass to drink water, and banana leaves served as plates. He didn't have many objects in the hut. These days he found it difficult to move around, and I had to hold his hand to bring him out of the hut.

One morning, he was sitting outside, and on remembering something he suddenly said, "After my death you'll be left alone here. Then you'll get a lot of time to practice meditation. At present, all your time is wasted serving me. Continue to meditate until you reach a state when you can leave this place. You'll reach that state at the right time. Wait for that time and don't try to leave this place on your own."

I said, "Gurudev, I don't want to leave you and go anywhere. I'll always stay here." Gurudev said, "No, no, you will have to go, because you have the responsibility of a great task on your shoulders, and this is your final birth. You must carry out your responsibility in this very birth. Oh, my dear, it is the law of nature that one has to harvest what one has planted. You have promised millions of people, and you will have to fulfil the promises in this final birth. If you can't complete this final birth, then you will be stuck, and for that you'll have to take another birth again.

"Why do you want to get stuck for the next birth? Free yourself from your promises in this birth, complete your promise of giving inner knowledge, and then leave the rest to them. How long do you wish to stay here? Perform your duty, go into society and bestow the inner knowledge to society."

"Gurudev," I said, "there are so many religions in society, and so many old religions! People have been following them for many years; which people will leave those religions and listen to this talk of inner religion, and which people will accept this inner religion? This appears impossible to me. There are so many religious disputes in society. Why should anyone accept this new religion? Even if I go into society, who will listen to me? And Gurudev, I'm a poor speaker; I don't even know how to speak properly. An astrologer has told me that the effect of the planet Mercury is weak in my horoscope, and I'll always have difficulty in speaking. If I don't even know how to have an ordinary conversation, how will I be able to explain it to people?"

Gurudev looked out into space and said, "All this talk about planets and constellations is at the physical level. A person who is under the Guru's protective umbrella will not be affected by planets and constellations. My dear, do you think that a Guru is a person? He is an ocean of a great collectivity of people. When you merge into an ocean then you don't have a separate identity. Then how can any bad effect fall on you? You need to have a separate identity for any bad effect, don't you? But you don't have any separate identity at all. What you are talking about is related to your body, and what I am talking about is related to your soul.

"Your body may be weak as far as speech is concerned; you

may be physically weak, your body may be sick, your body may grow old, but your soul can never be weak. Your soul can never be sick, and it can never age because it is free from all these influences. Your soul is very powerful.

"Your soul has travelled through several births with the desire to reach Paramatma, and it is not possible to reach Paramatma without awakening one's inner religion. In the course of your journey through several births, you always performed the work of giving, and because of this you promised millions of souls that 'whenever I obtain Paramatma, and when I find the path to Him, I will definitely tell you about it.' You have given this assurance to millions of souls, and you are bound by those assurances. Therefore, return to society and fulfil your promises. Your work is only to show the path. Fulfil your promises. Your concern is not to decide whether to walk on that path or not, and when to walk on that path. That is the area of those souls. They will walk on it when they wish to. Therefore, you shouldn't expect them to do so in your presence; because in order to walk on your path, they should either have a high spiritual level or completely surrender to you. Until they choose any one of these two paths, even looking towards your path will prove to be difficult, let alone walking on it.

"Therefore, don't ever turn back and look to make sure if those souls are following the path indicated by you or not, because the path of inner knowledge is the path of pure and holy souls. Until the soul is free of the defects of the body, as long as it doesn't get pure, it cannot walk on this path of inner knowledge. One can reach this level only after crossing the physical level, the mental level, and the spiritual level. It's very difficult.

"A lot of effort is required to cross these levels, and the path is also very difficult. The second path is that of surrendering to one's Guru. This path is very easy, but surrender is very difficult because one must have faith in order to surrender. It is very difficult for us to accept a person, who is like us physically, as superior to us. Thus, the first path is easy in the beginning, but it's difficult to walk on the path; and on the second path, the journey is easy but the beginning itself is difficult. You should go into human society only after you understand all these facts.

"On the topic of religion, the most ancient and eternal religion is the inner religion. Inner religion is everlasting. This is the religion that is always present with the soul. Then the soul may take a birth in any form, but the inner religion will always be present in every form with the soul. Every soul has to go through the journey of evolution. After taking birth in all forms, the soul finally takes the human form in order to attain liberation. The soul obtains the human body after a long wait, and it thinks that obtaining the human body means attaining liberation. But it doesn't realize that defects are also present with this human body. The greater the body, the greater will be its defects. It is true that the human body has been structured to help it attain liberation. But just as the structure is great, so are its defects, which come along when one takes birth in the human form; and the greatest defect of the human birth is the ego.

"Man preserves his ego very carefully in his life. He doesn't allow that ego to be dented anywhere. That is why egoistic people don't believe in the Guru, because the Guru first hits out at the ego. One can't obtain the Guru's company with ego. In this journey of human births, man takes birth again and again in the human form, and his external religion keeps changing in every birth. Actually, what changes in every birth is not the religion, but the method of worshipping. Man's method of worship may be of any kind, but the purpose of every method is to awaken one's inner religion. These external religions are not the building (liberation) one wishes to enter; they are only ladders that lead to the building. All of them have the same destination. All religions reach the same place in the end, and the place they reach is 'inner knowledge.' Thus, you aren't going into society to explain some new religion to them; you are going to inform them about the destination of all religions. Therefore, you must go into society and tell them: 'I haven't come to change your religion, because all religions are one—inner religion. How can that be changed? You may follow any method of worship, but all methods of worship have been created only to awaken one's inner religion.'

"The method of worship keeps changing with every birth that man takes. Man follows the method of worship of the house in which he takes birth. Therefore, this method of worship is not religion. By religion we mean the religion of humanity—inner religion. This is the one complete religion of human society. Today, people think that the ladder of the method of worship is religion, whereas the method of worship is not religion. The method of worship is a path to reach up to religion. Go into society and give them knowledge of the eternal true religion, that what you're saying is the truth. Truth is always bitter. It takes time to understand the truth. Therefore, they will realize this truth someday, too. Leave it to them. You just do the work of telling them the truth. When you go into society and tell them about the truth, you'll become a medium for truth. When you become a medium for truth, then the energy will flow through you, and people will absorb that energy. Those who are not in a condition to bear the energy of truth will go to sleep, but they won't oppose it because their soul knows that you are speaking the truth. Now, coming to your weakness in speaking—when your soul starts speaking, then the effect of that strong soul will be felt through your speech, because you aren't aware of who you are, but the souls in the rest of the world know you. Those souls are waiting for you. Society has a great need of you; therefore, go into society. This place is not your place of work.

"Carry on with your work, whether they listen to you or not; whether they listen to you at the physical level or not, their soul will definitely hear it. And several great sages have chosen you as their medium and have entrusted you with the gift of their blessings for distribution.

"That prasad has been given for distribution, and you have to distribute the prasad, and that is your duty. Perform your duty, and the work will happen through their collectivity. A magnetic force has been created within you because of your powerful soul. This is the magnetism of a strong soul. Every soul knows this, and that's why they will be attracted towards you. Give up this useless thought that you are a poor speaker. Hey, this useless thought is that of the body, and this work is of the soul. Come out of this useless physical feeling and perform your work.

"The path will be created automatically, and the souls who have been searching for you for several births will definitely reach you. Today, you are my disciple, and that's why you are hidden in the shadow of the Guru's umbrella. Today, they aren't able to recognize you. Come out of my umbrella and become a Guru yourself. That is the final resting place of your soul. Those souls will recognize you when you go in the form of a Guru. You are the representative of spiritual Gurus. There is a level of spirituality; only a person who has reached that level will recognize him. It is possible to reach the state of spirituality through every method of worship; and after reaching there, it does not matter which method of worship has helped you to get there.

"Oh, my dear, a ladder is after all a ladder, and the destination is the building; and one can reach the building by climbing any ladder.

"When man succeeds in reaching his destination through some ladder, then he goes beyond that ladder; and a person who has gone beyond the ladder will speak about the destination, not about the ladder. No matter how many methods of worship exist, the final goal of all is to attain Paramatma. Therefore, whichever method of worship man follows, he'll reach only one destination. But man clings to the ladder as his method of worship and keeps sitting there; he doesn't think beyond it.

"Once man gets the spiritual experience of inner knowledge, he begins to understand all these facts automatically. For example, imagine that in a dark room I have mistakenly believed a snake to be a rope, and you are telling me from outside that what I'm holding is a snake and not a rope. But, due to my ignorance, I don't believe what you're telling me and say—no, this is not a snake but a rope. I sit there holding on to my own belief. But after some time, you open the door and enter the room and switch on the light; then, in the light of that lamp, I realize that you are right, I was wrong, and after that, even if you don't tell me, I will let go of the snake, I'll drop it. Similarly, there are several useless facts that man holds on to, thinking that it is religion. Once one obtains inner knowledge, all these facts are removed, and man finds inner peace. Then the process of man's hold on the ladder, his wandering, and his search comes to an end.

"You can obtain the experience of Paramatma through any medium. Paramatma's energy is spread throughout the world. It can be experienced through any medium—there is no difference, because Paramatma's energy has no form, and the form that is visible is only the form of the medium. Go into society and tell the people that the energy that manages the world is Paramatma, and the path to obtain that energy is inner knowledge. Human beings have only one religion—the religion of humanity, one's own inner religion; all the others are methods of worship. The methods can be different, but how can there be several religions when Paramatma is one, when man is one? All religions are also one. Inner religion will bestow this knowledge on man. But even though it takes him time to understand this, he'll definitely understand it. Go and tell them that it is the right of each and every human being to obtain inner knowledge. The language, the colour, the race, the gender, the country to which he belongs and the method of worship he follows may all be different, but all these are external factors; and in spite of that, man's inner religion is the same. Today, everything has been confined to books, but what is written in books is not knowledge. That is only information. Actually, there's only one 'knowledge,' and that's inner knowledge. After one obtains inner knowledge, there's no need to read the external information, because all the information that is given in books is obtained by man within himself through inner knowledge. Just as we see in nature that a plant slowly grows into a tree and then starts bearing fruits after a determined time, in the same way this plant of inner knowledge has taken 800 years to grow into a tree.

"Now it has borne the fruit of spiritual experience; but society doesn't have information about the fruit in the form of spiritual experience. Go into society and not only give information, but also make them eat the fruit of spiritual experience. Even if man doesn't recognize it, his soul is ripe for it because it is 800 years old. It will at once understand, though man's body may not, because it's still small and young, and doesn't have the knowledge of spiritual experience. As man starts getting spiritual experiences, he'll come to understand what is meant by Paramatma, what is meant by religion, what is meant by the medium of Paramatma, and what joy of the experience of Paramatma means! All this knowledge will be obtained only after getting just one spiritual experience. It is the wish of all sages that this knowledge of spiritual experience should reach human society, because now the time has arrived, and it is with the wish that it should reach the people, that all of them (sages/gurus) have poured their knowledge into you and entrusted you with it. Now it is your duty to convey this entrusted knowledge to society because the knowledge was given to you for this very purpose. You, too, won't be free of your obligations to your Gurus without distributing it in society. You, too, will have to distribute this knowledge and make a Guru-dakshina to your Guru."

Gurudev had been speaking for a long time and must have become tired. I took some water and gave it to him to drink, which he accepted. I requested Gurudev to take some rest. Gurudev said, "My dear, my time for rest is approaching, and I'm explaining all these facts to you so that I can rest without any worries. Once I pass on all the information that I have, I'll get a sense of satisfaction that I have handed it over to you. I'm doing all this for my own inner satisfaction. Whatever each person does is for his satisfaction and for his own inner peace. Actually, doing it is also a medium for obtaining satisfaction." And saying this, Gurudev got up and lay down to take rest.

I sat thinking that Gurudev is not present in society, but he has full information about what is happening in society today; and there is so much compassion in his mind for every human being. He desires that the inner knowledge should reach each human beings, and since that is his wish, he can definitely perform this task, and it will definitely take place; and I'll become the medium for this work. I don't know how this can be possible because I can't get out of this isolated, uninhabited place, and no man can reach here. It's Gurudev's work; let him worry about it. Why should I think about it needlessly? He wishes to get his work done, and he'll find some way or other out of it and get the work done.

The waiting was only for the right time. A tree can bear fruits only at the appropriate time. This means that both Gurudev and I had to wait until a determined period of time, and human society also had to wait because one always has to wait for Paramatma's grace; it can shower at any time!

Later on, Gurudev said, "We always have to be ready to accept grace, because grace is the fruit of Paramatma's compassion; only Paramatma knows when that grace and compassion will rain on us and how it will be showered. Everything depends on Him. I was bound by the promises I had given my Guru and was waiting on this deserted island for Paramatma's compassion. When Paramatma showered his grace, He sent you to me so that I could entrust you with the store of knowledge that had been given to me by my Guru. I had promised my Guru that I would hand it over to you. Your arrival here and being freed from my promise was a great event, which happened through Paramatma's blessings. When we meditate, we connect to Paramatma's energies; and we slowly start losing our identity in Paramatma's energies, and this process takes place in a very subtle form. This is not some physical process, which can be performed, which can be seen, or which can be shown. This is a subtle act that takes place when we remain close to nature. First of all, we gain control over our body because this is a process of moving within from outside. After we gain control over our body, the knowledge of our body and its awareness starts decreasing, and the body becomes suitable for spiritual practice. The body becomes ready for the practice of yoga, and the physical barriers of the yogic practice are removed.

"In yogic practice, the sacredness of one's body, its purity, and its cleanliness play a very important part. Then the body does exactly what it's supposed to do at that time. The body remains at that time in the state that it is supposed to be in; then, slowly, thoughts that are created in the mind through the body start getting controlled by the yogic practice. This happens because, just as we waste our energy in useless physical activities, we also use up a lot of our energy in unnecessary and uncontrolled thoughts.

"When we are successful in saving this energy through constant practice, then our mind starts getting controlled. When our mind is fully under control, we start attaining a meditative state. In all this, the more feelings of reverence we have towards our Guru, the more faith we have, the more easily this work will happen. This is because the Guru's body is a medium for Paramatma's energies. But we'll have to go and look beyond the illusory web of his body. We'll have to think about why we have accepted only him as a medium. We'll have to experience him at the level of spiritual experience and not think of him at the physical level because, while creating him as a medium, Paramatma only looks at his soul. The soul is an extremely subtle energy, which is not visible and can only be experienced. It can be accepted with faith, and to accept it is a feeling of the soul. We'll have to accept the Guru's body as a medium of Paramatma, and only then will we be able to get the experience of those energies, because whatever has to be obtained from the Guru can only be acquired if one believes in him. There's nothing in the visible physical body of the Guru. We have to go beyond it."

As Gurudev was telling me all this, my attention started going beyond his body, and I experienced a brilliant radiance around him. The scene was somewhat similar to the way golden rays come out from a rising sun, and that brilliance went on increasing. I slowly started realizing that in the whirlpool of that bright light Gurudev's body was looking hazy, and slowly the entire body vanished and became a great accumulation of bright light; and slowly that golden collection of light grew bigger. Now I can't definitely say whether that accumulation of light was growing bigger, or I was growing smaller, but something was happening, and I slowly became as small as a droplet, and that accumulated light of golden rays enveloped the whole world.

Then, in that all pervading accumulation of light, my existence became negligible. I wasn't able to see myself at all, and slowly I had no existence left. I also remained only as a portion of that accumulation of light. I had received the vision of Paramatma. In that moment I got the realization that the whole world is one with Paramatma, and Paramatma is an all-pervading universal energy that runs the universe. And the existence of the 'I' about which I was egoistic was nothing compared to this; my existence was smaller than even a small insect. I reached the realization in that moment—I'm so small, and Paramatma is so big.

Later, I saw that all the bright light had started stabilizing in one place; it started focusing in one place. It started collecting at one point, and that point slowly took the shape of my Gurudev; but even now it was very big. It took the shape of Gurudev's body, and as soon as I saw Gurudev I prostrated before him. He touched my head with the big toe of his right foot, and I experienced a lightning-like flow in my body. My whole body became like ice, and I remained in that state for three days.

After three days, Gurudev woke me, and then I felt as if I was waking up after so many years. He said, "A Guru is not a physical body. A Guru is the living medium of Paramatma. When we accept him as a medium, then our identity becomes smaller. The ego comes to an end, and then our level of spiritual experience increases. Then we're able to get the vision of those energies of Paramatma who are working behind the Guru's physical body. We are able to experience those energies, and we are able to undertake the spiritual practice of meditation through this medium. The more faith we have in the medium, the more trust we have in him; the more we will be able to go beyond the medium to that extent. The Guru's body is only a medium of Paramatma's energy. Through that medium we'll have to look into the future, and the sight of this future can only be experienced.

"That's why I thought it to be more appropriate to make you experience it rather than describe it, because one can't describe Paramatma at all. My dear, Paramatma is everywhere. So, how can we describe Paramatma while being present with Paramatma? Therefore, Paramatma can't be described at all. Paramatma can only be experienced. We can reach Paramatma only through a medium, because although 'Paramatma is present everywhere,' we won't be in a condition to see him. We can attain such a state through the Guru-krupa, so that we can get the experience of Paramatma. Paramatma is beyond our reach and only the medium is within our reach. We'll have to reach Paramatma through the ladder of the medium, and you have just experienced how that is possible. But it takes twelve years to undertake this meditative spiritual practice completely. A person can obtain this level after surrendering completely to a medium for twelve years and undertaking the spiritual practice of meditation through the same medium. All this is not easy at all, because to maintain one's faith, one's concentration, to maintain one's interest in meditation for such a long time is extremely difficult. That's why it is not possible for the ordinary man to do this, and neither is this like the fast-growing tree of lai leaves. This is a banyan tree, and one has to pass through a long process in order to create it. During these twelve years the sadhak must not lose his regularity and should maintain his faith. If he can do these two tasks, then the remaining spiritual practice will happen in life automatically.

"As the spiritual practice starts maturing, a person's ego starts coming to an end. First, he has control over his body, then his mind and then his chitta. But no Guru gives information about this twelve-year period because the disciple shouldn't get scared after hearing about such a long span of time. He'll always tell his disciple—do meditation, do meditation—so that he won't realize how much time has passed. One doesn't realize how slowly the twelve years pass, but twelve years is a very long period in one's lifetime.

"The physical body takes some time before it can form a habit of something, some rule or some spiritual practice; then it takes time to bring the mind under control, and then there is control over one's chitta. It takes some time to control the body, because the body has its own old habits and bad thoughts, which take time to get rid of; the mind is also very restless, and man takes a lot of time to control his bad habit of thinking. Then the work of purification of one's chitta commences, and the chitta is purified; it becomes holy, and then it becomes strong. A lot of importance is given to purity in the path of meditation. Purity is the life of this path. A sadhak should not only be pure physically and mentally but also through his chitta. This work can't begin at all without purity, because only a pure individual can be an authoritative Guru. By purity we don't mean purity at the physical level, but purity of one's chitta, which is the state even above the purity of thoughts.

"This purity of the chitta can only be obtained at the soul level, and it is obtained through faith. Faith is the most pure and holy feeling of man's soul, and only total faith in one's Guru can bestow this state on a sadhak.

"It's extremely difficult to have complete faith in a living person's physical body, and this faith is the most difficult thing on the path of meditation. For this, first of all, one will have to know the Guru and understand him. The Guru is a union of two things, a mixture of two things. One is the basic soul-element, which is very pure and is the same in every birth, and its life span is of 800 years. Over this period of 800 years, it acquires different physical bodies and moves forward towards its destination. He keeps adding new elements to his spiritual practice in every birth. In every birth this soul-element has to face the faults of the physical body of each birth. He is victorious over those faults, but after removing those faults in the next birth he absorbs new faults again. Thus, in simple language, it is impossible to acquire a physical body without faults. The body is a combined creation of the mother's and father's bodies, and the union of the mother's and father's combined faults takes place. One can find the faults of both parents in a person's physical body, because the effect of the parents' combined influence is formed before a person is born; and man takes birth with these combined faults. Thus, the soul-element is pure and holy and is 800 years old, but the body element is either sixty years or eighty years old. It is very difficult to see the inside of the fruit (soul) without looking at the skin of the fruit that is the physical body.

"This fact can be understood with the example of a coconut—the body element means the husk of the coconut, and the soul-element means the sweet pulp inside the coconut. But in order to eat the sweet, soft pulp of the coconut, it is necessary to first remove the husk. Similarly, man will have to go beyond the faults of the Guru's body and acquire the 'coconut' that is within, one will have to see the soul-element that is inside him.

"It is the law of nature that just as there can't be a coconut without its outer husk, a Guru's body similarly can't exist without faults of the body. This is because wherever living experiences are present, the physical body will also be present; and when the living body arrives, then faults of the living body will also arrive along with it. It's very difficult not to notice the faults and to have faith in the soul-element that is within the body. Every realized saint has also experienced this during the period of his spiritual practice.

"That's why he keeps his disciples a little away from his body, so that the disciple's attention doesn't go to the faults of the body element but remains on the soul-element that is within him. Thus, unless one surrenders totally to the Guru, the Guru's company may mislead the disciple. One's whole life comes to an end in trying to analyse what is right and what is wrong, whether this interaction taking place through the body is correct or whether the experience one had through one's soul is correct. This analysis can go on for several years, and because one's whole life passes in this analysis there is no time left for spiritual practice. Interaction at the physical level is always like that of an ordinary human being, and those ordinary interactions at the physical level can't be those of a Guru. An extraordinary soul is present in the ordinary physical body of a Guru, and that can only be experienced; it can't be seen.

"This is the reason why one should go near a Guru only when one is close to the Guru. If one is not close to the Guru, one shouldn't go near him. Here, by Guru, I'm referring to the Guru-element, and the second reference is to the Guru's body. Thus, only if you are close to the Guru-element, if you have proximity to it, you should go near the Guru's physical body. Then you'll be able to save yourself from the faults of the physical body, otherwise the body will mislead you because the Guru-element is bound in the frame of the physical body, and it will definitely interact like a physical body. There is a pure soul-element in the Guru's physical body, and because of that it influences the physical body, and a magnetic energy is created in the body. As a result of the influence of this magnetism in the body, an ordinary soul experiences that soul-element and is unknowingly attracted in that direction. The soul of every individual believes in the soul-element that is present in every Guru, and because of this the disciple is pulled towards his Guru. The Guru can attract the disciple towards himself, but he can't go to the disciple. Each one is bound to his limit. It is the law of nature that all external elements are the same. Just as if you look at the outer part of coconuts, they all appear similar, in the same way the Guru's body is also like that of an ordinary man. But it is under the influence of the soul-element, and therefore it has a kind of immense attraction. This attraction also can't be seen but can be experienced. Therefore, it is extremely difficult to recognize a living Guru. A living Guru is always recognized through spiritual experience.

"What one experiences in the presence of a Guru is more important than how he appears to you, what he is doing and what he is saying. The first spiritual experience that one gets is that one feels good in his presence. One senses that, in the desert of life, he has found a stream of cold water. One can involuntarily go close to the Guru, but one doesn't feel like leaving him. All thoughts stop. All thoughts stop because they have been created by the body, whereas once you become a soul the body doesn't exist anymore; the feeling of the physical body also ends, so how will one get feelings of the body? How will you think of going somewhere else from here, as that is also a thought, and if you don't get any thoughts, you won't be able to move away from the Guru. Man's soul rejoices after getting even a glimpse of the Guru, and the joy of that happy soul influences the whole body. vibrations start within one's body, and these vibrations can be felt more on the palms of one's hands and the soles of one's feet because these parts in the human body are more sensitive. One starts to experience the joy of the soul in the form of vibrations in the body. This is the first experience for the body because the soul has never before rejoiced in this way. The soul rejoices because the soul knows Paramatma.

"By Paramatma we mean the collectivity of millions of souls. This collectivity of millions of people is present with the Guru's aura, and as a result the soul in the Guru's physical body is a special soul. The Guru's soul is that soul which has no identity of its own. This is because there is a collectivity of souls, and the Guru's soul is distributed in that collectivity. This means that the Guru's soul is aligned to millions of souls and millions of souls that are attached to the Guru. It is this energy of souls that transforms the Guru's soul into Paramatma. The Guru's body is not unusual, the Guru is unusual. Due to his soul, which is distributed in millions of souls, the collectivity of those millions of souls attracts the souls of disciples to him. A soul will naturally be attracted towards a collection of millions of souls, and as a result of the collectivity of millions of souls, brahmanaad is created. One begins to hear this brahmanaad after going near the Guru.

"All this is possible only when you are in a humble state, when you are ready to bow down, because this humble state increases one's capacity to absorb. However, this bowing shouldn't be at the physical level but at the soul level. Your bowing will only have meaning if the soul bows, and that too before the collectivity of souls. If your body doesn't bow, I won't bow before the body, then it won't do. How can a soul's bowing before a collectivity of souls be possible without the soul having faith in it?

"Therefore, it is extremely necessary to have faith in the Guru, and this faith should not be blind faith. Others have faith in someone, and if we also imitate them and have faith, then that faith will be play-acting. It will be blind faith because we don't have spiritual experience, and despite that we have faith. This kind of faith won't last long. That's why the faith that is created when one gets spiritual experience is everlasting faith.

"Faith is a pure feeling of one's soul. This feeling should take place only after the soul gets a spiritual experience. That's why the foundation of faith should be spiritual experience. If one doesn't get a spiritual experience personally, one shouldn't just have faith. The basis of faith should be the experience of inner joy. Faith that is based on this pure feeling and spiritual experience will always keep us connected to the spiritual experience, and our attention will always remain on the spiritual experience. Then when we are in the presence of the Guru our attention will always remain on the spiritual experience; and if our attention is on the spiritual experience, our mind won't allow us to pay attention to ordinary interactions at the physical level. When you don't pay attention to the ordinary interactions at the physical level then you'll understand interactions at the soul level. Interaction at the soul level is pure joy. It is that joy which can be experienced at the soul level, and which is everlasting. Man can find such happiness only through complete faith. One will be able to obtain all this slowly through practice, and this practice should take place slowly. Physical activity can take place with speed, but spiritual work happens with spiritual experience, and that's why it doesn't have speed, and moves slowly at its natural pace.

"The spiritual field has a special quality. In this field there's no place for man's efforts because any effort that takes place will be at the physical level, and the spiritual progress happens at the soul level. Total spiritual progress depends on the grace of Paramatma. If one really thinks about it, one realizes the truth. Man can't take a single breath without Paramatma's wish. Man also obtains every breath through Paramatma's grace.

Man arrives on earth with some pre-determined breaths. He lives through those breaths and then he dies. He can't take even a single breath without Paramatma's blessings. Now the purpose of my life is also over, and I, too, am waiting for death. I'll take whatever breaths remain in my life, and then I'll take rest in the lap of death. But I have obtained everything in this short life. Now after handing over all these energies to you, I'm very happy and joyful. The spiritual energies I had kept safely all my life have now reached the right hands. No one can give a Guru the amount of inner joy that a sadhak who has surrendered can give him in his life, because it is the basic nature of a Guru to give, and it should be the basic nature of the disciple to receive. If a Guru finds such a disciple who receives from him then it is as if the Guru has found everything.

"I'm very happy to have found you; you are a strong medium

to reach millions of souls because you are the centre of the collectivity of souls. You only are Paramatma for me. You have come to bestow liberation on me during my final hours. It is my final wish that you should perform my last rites after my death and pray for my liberation."

I bowed before Gurudev and said, "You are my place of inspiration. I surrender myself; make whatever use you wish of this body. Let everything be according to your wish. Now come along; a lot of time has passed, and you should take rest."

After saying this, I made him lie on his bed, and he lay down peacefully. I was getting several thoughts in my mind about the moment of one's death; it can give man both happy and sad states, because during this time man's entire life passes before him, what he has done in his life. If he has performed good work, he'll get good experiences, and if he has performed bad work, he'll get bad experiences. He'll feel disgust and start weeping. My Gurudev has performed good deeds, and that's why he is happy and joyful. He is experiencing that he has made good use of his life, and now when it is time for him to leave, then due to his good deeds he feels inner satisfaction that he is leaving after performing good deeds. Everyone has to go; one has come in order to leave. But one should leave with self-satisfaction.

Man can neither give anyone life nor death. Everything is in the hands of the 'One' who is above us. Man makes a wrong assumption that 'this is my son, this is my daughter, I am this boy's father, I am this girl's mother!' In reality, all this is only an illusion. Neither can one produce a son, nor can one produce a daughter. A physical body is created as the result of a husband and wife's physical union, and only when a soul entered that body could it obtain an identity. That body is only a corpse without the soul. No one wants to keep a corpse in one's house.

The mother and father have only created a body; that, too,

hasn't been done by them, but has happened through them. The body that has been created through their medium is a perishable body; it isn't everlasting. Paramatma has bestowed a soul to that perishable body and made it alive for a short time. Therefore, what is important in that body is the soul, and parents have no hand in the creation of the soul. The soul hasn't been born through the medium of the parents; only the perishable physical body has been born through them. The parents haven't created anything, so how can they be called parents? They say that we have given birth to you, but in reality, the parents haven't created anything. What has been created through them is the body without the soul, and it is non-living. The energy that puts life in that non-living body is Paramatma. In reality, every human being has been created by Paramatma, and parents unnecessarily have the ego that they have produced the children, that they have given birth to children.

Actually, they can't do anything, and whatever they can do is all illusory. Due to this delusion, parents fall prey to confusion. Every child is a soul that has not been created by parents. It has its own identity. Allow him to create his own identity. Don't bind that soul by calling him 'my son' and 'my daughter.' You aren't anyone's parent, nor do you have any son or daughter. All this is the illusion of untruth. When you can't even put forward a thought of your own, how can you give birth to a child! Every soul has to endure the result of good or bad deeds, and similarly every child has to undergo the fruits of his karma. In this case, the parents can't even lend a helping hand to the child. That's why man should keep away from the confusion that this is 'my son' and 'my daughter.'

It's a good thing that my Gurudev was safe from all these confusions. He is experiencing so much peace in his final days! He hasn't created any confusion at all. Perhaps all this is delusion, which is why the Gurus always walk alone on the spiritual path.

It's better not to create a web of illusion, and keep away from it, rather than to create one and get caught in it, and then think that one has got caught in it and hold on to oneself and keep yelling, 'I've been caught, I've been caught!' Really, this life itself is a web of illusion. The spider spins a web around itself on its own and gets caught in that web. Then it cries, 'I've been caught, I've been caught'—all this when it has created that web for itself.

My Gurudev's body was tired; that was why, in order that he may get some strength, I cut two tender bamboos the next day; after picking their tender leaves, I cut them into small pieces. Then I stuffed them in the bamboo, added some water to it, put some bay leaves in it, some black peppercorns, some lai leaves; I also added some bananas, and then sealed the other end of the bamboo with some banana leaves. I sealed it tightly so that the steam inside the bamboo shouldn't come out. After that, I placed them in the fire and boiled them for a long time, and then I fed Gurudev with the cooked meal. I had to feed him with my hands because he had become so weak that he could neither sit properly nor eat on his own. I had to feed him, and later I had to fill the bamboo with water and help him to drink it. His eyesight had also become weak.

As the days passed, his body was becoming weaker, and by now he had stopped moving around, and when he stood up, his legs started trembling. He used to stay lying on the bed, and he had reached a stage where he would excrete and urinate on the bed itself. I remained there and served him. All through the day and night, at every moment my whole attention was on him. Now my spiritual practice had also stopped, and he, too, didn't sit for meditation. He used to lie with his eyes closed, and his body had become extremely weak, but the radiance of his body had not diminished at all. Even at present, the flow of radiance continued. Then one day I asked him, "Gurudev, your body has become so dilapidated, it has become so weak; even then your radiance has not decreased. What is the reason for that?"

Gurudev replied, "You foolish child! The state of this body has no connection with the state of that radiant energy. That is the radiance of the soul, and the effect of the radiance of that soul is falling on the physical body. The body may have become weak, but the radiance of the soul is just the same. The effect of this weak body will not be felt on that radiant energy. This body has become the medium of the radiant energy of that soul. It has been a medium for so many years that the radiant energy and the body are not separate from each other. The body has merged into the radiant energy. That is why this body is so weak, but it will still maintain the effect of its consciousness." I was looking foolishly at him because I couldn't understand what he was saying.

He understood my condition and said, "You foolish boy, you are not able to understand. I'll try to explain it to you through the example of sandalwood. When we take a small twig of the sandalwood tree and rub it, then sandalwood paste is produced, and we apply sandalwood paste on our foreheads so that our chitta remains pure, so that our agya chakra remains pure, and we are not affected by any bad influences. But doesn't the piece of sandalwood also wear out when we rub it? It slowly becomes smaller, and as we keep rubbing it, it becomes very small and thin; it becomes weak, but even that thin and weak small piece still gives the same amount of fragrance that the big piece used to give.

"It is the basic nature of sandalwood to give fragrance in this way. As long as it doesn't end, it'll keep giving out fragrance. My body is also similar; no matter how weak, how sick, how old it grows, it'll keep giving the consciousness because it has become its basic nature to make the consciousness flow.

"Therefore, whether the piece of sandalwood is with the tree or separate from the tree, it will keep on giving out fragrance.

Similarly, the physical body of realized saints may be in a living condition, or it may be dead; it will keep up the flow of consciousness. That's why the Satguru's body is not cremated. His body is enshrined so that even after the physical body dies, it will keep on spreading waves of consciousness into the atmosphere. Have you understood now why consciousness is flowing from my body? The consciousness will keep flowing even after I give up my body, but don't construct a samadhi for my body. Cremate my body, because now there is no work left for me, and it's my wish that all my consciousness should flow only through you as a medium. There shouldn't be two mediums in this world for my consciousness. That's why the second medium of my consciousness is this physical body. After my death, you should cremate this body and destroy it, and then you'll remain as the only medium for my consciousness. It is my wish that you should stay as the only medium of my consciousness in this world." And he fell silent after saying this; and I thought, he spoke such a profound fact so calmly and quietly.

Next morning, when he didn't wake up, I started wondering what could have happened! Has he given up his body? He didn't move at all, but I still felt a great support from him. My whole world had been only limited to him. When he opened his eyes, it was sunrise for me, and when he closed his eyes, it was night for me. All my attention was on Gurudev all the time; he was my whole universe.

I sat near his feet and waited for him to wake up. He was my whole life. I again wondered, has he given up his body? If he's dead, then I'll be left all alone in this world, and what is the use of living alone—I will also end my life. I'll cremate his body and jump on the fire and die. I'll also go up with him and serve him there if ever he needs me. I went outside and collected a lot of wood and thought—I'll prepare a huge pyre so that both our bodies can burn and turn to ashes. Thinking in this manner, I prepared a very large pyre and then returned to the hut. As soon as I entered the hut, I saw that Gurudev's eyes were open, my sun had risen. I started crying when I saw him, and he said, "Oh you fool, I have gone beyond life and death. Now I have no desire to live anymore, but I'm bound to you.

"If you don't give me permission I can't even die. Your power of consciousness has become so strong that I'll have to continue to live as long as you want. I don't want to live anymore, and you are not allowing me to die. Why are you creating a barrier on my path? Oh, you fool, let me go."

I said, "All right. You can give up your body—but give me this one permission and then take me along with you. I'll cremate your body, and then I want to die on the same pyre. I don't want to live without you. What will I do without you? You are my whole life. What will I say and do after you? I'm living with the support of your consciousness. After your consciousness ends, my support will also end. So how can I continue to live? Gurudev, please take me along with you. I want to go with you."

"Oh, you fool!" Gurudev replied. "My consciousness is not going to end after I die, or after my cremation. It will flow through you as a medium, and there can't be two mediums of consciousness, and that's why I wish to end this medium that is my body, through cremation. If you cremate your physical body, then how can the consciousness flow without a medium? All my penance of several years will be wasted and lost. Whatever I have handed over to you also is not mine. It's true that I have contributed to preserving that consciousness. But that is my Gurudev's prasad. Why are you destroying my Gurudev's gift?

"Oh, you fool! Instead of distributing to others what you have received in the form of a gift, you wish to destroy it! You have received the gift of consciousness for distribution, and it's your duty to distribute it. Why are you breaking their trust in you! You have no authority to destroy your physical body because you have surrendered it to me, and I have the right over your body. Now I'll make use of your physical body as I wish. Don't you dare destroy my wealth! Your body is not yours anymore. It has now become my wealth. The disciple is the Guru's wealth, and only the Guru has a right over that wealth.

Therefore, don't ever think of destroying your body after I die. This is my command. My dear, millions of souls are waiting for you, who wish to receive the gift of consciousness through your medium. They have been wandering for several births to receive the gift, and you have also given them an assurance and are tied by your promise to them. You have no right over your body. My son, as a father remains alive after his death in the form of his son, similarly, after his death, a Guru remains alive in the form of his disciple. I, too, wish to remain alive in your form after my death. I wish to perform the work of a Guru. Why aren't you allowing me to perform my duty? If you yourself don't remain, then I won't be able to do any of this even if I want to. Now, promise me that you'll remain alive after me and will carry on with my work."

I held his hand and assured him, "Gurudev, I'm not disregarding your command. I'll do everything according to your wishes."

I saw satisfaction on Gurudev's face. Nowadays, all my time passed in serving him, and I didn't notice if it was morning or night. I was always with him, and my whole universe was confined to that hut. These days, Gurudev's meals were irregular because he used to keep lying with his eyes closed and rarely opened them. He had difficulty in excreting, and even that was becoming irregular. When he lay with his eyes closed, I would stay sitting there waiting for him to open his eyes; but if his eyes were closed I had no courage to awaken him. I felt a strange kind of fear laced with respect for him. Now his stomach had also been pulled inside, and all the ribs in his chest were visible. His legs had become thin, and more wrinkles were visible on his arms. But in spite of such weakness, there was a terrific attractive energy in that body. Sandalwood fragrance emanated from his body all the time. I watched him for hours at a time while he slept. This had become my habit. The expression of innocence and purity one sees on a small sleeping child was visible on his face. My Gurudev was the master of a very peaceful mind. There was always a quiet satisfaction on his face. I had never experienced any foul odour while cleaning his excreta. Maybe this was because of my feeling that nothing impure can exist within a pure soul, or maybe it was due to his spiritual state. Secondly, he had given me an assurance that he would die only after telling me. That's why the thought, "Has he given up his body?" never crossed my mind.

While bathing him, I noticed that all his bones could be clearly seen, especially his spine. Both the bones of his buttocks could also be clearly seen. The whole body was just a skeleton, and there was no flesh visible anywhere. That's why I brought soft grass and placed him on it so that the stones below wouldn't prick him. Even if they pricked him, he would never tell me about it. I had no care for myself. My whole attention was only on him all the time. I used to keep observing his body and taking care of his entire body. Today, when I sat down to massage his feet, I saw that every vein on his leg was visible. His body was weak, so I was massaging his feet very lightly. I say that I was massaging his feet but I was actually just stroking them. This is how I stayed in his company through the day. Even at that time, I felt that Gurudev's body was performing some process on me and was binding me with the attraction of his body. Some process was definitely happening in that quiet atmosphere. When the wind started blowing fast outside the hut, the sound of leaves would break the silence.

Then, after some time, Gurudev opened his eyes and said, "My dear, man has to pay for these three things—debt, killing and enmity. Now watch how you have received energies through the medium of this body, and you have become indebted to it. And so even that debt shouldn't stay unpaid, I'm giving you the opportunity to repay it by staying alive, so that you may serve this body and get free of your debt to it. I don't want your obligation to my body to be kept pending with you, because you are a medium for millions of souls. Therefore, mediums should be free from obligations; the medium should be pure, it should be holy. As long as we take on debts, we'll have to repay them—if not in this birth, then in the next birth.

"This is because one can't attain liberation without repaying this debt, so why should I allow the debt of this weak body to remain with you? I want to allow it to end. Similarly, man's enmity is also a feeling that continues from one birth to the other. Someone has enmity with you, and you also have enmity with him, and this feeling won't allow your chitta to remain pure. If your chitta is not pure and holy, you'll never get the spiritual experience of Paramatma. Enmity is also a type of feeling that makes the mind dirty. The third thing is murder. If you kill someone, he'll kill you in the next birth. Then in his next birth you'll again kill him, and thus both the souls will be caught up in this cycle of killing. Both won't be able to find the path for years and years, and this won't end until the feeling of enmity is destroyed by some saint through his spiritual energy. This also becomes a big and long journey. In this way the give and take of debt, killing and enmity continues for several births. It's very easy to get caught in this but very difficult to come out of it.

"Man gets caught in this cycle through his own wish, but he can't come out of it on his own; this is a one-way path. That's why I am giving you the opportunity to serve this physical body and free yourself of your debt because now you and I don't have next births. We have to settle all our accounts in this birth. That's why man should save himself from this cycle of debt, killing and enmity."

I was thinking, Gurudev takes so much care of me; he keeps in mind even the smallest things and the smallest actions; he thinks so far into the future.

Gurudev said, "This talk is at the physical level, but the debt you owe the Guru-element will have to be repaid by performing work for the Guru. Whenever a sadhak obtains inner knowledge through the grace of the Guru-element, then the sadhak becomes indebted to the Guru-element, and he can't attain liberation without repaying and fulfilling that obligation. That is the reason why, in our scriptures, Guru-karya has been given so much importance. Guru-karya is work that isn't performed by a sadhak to show others. A sadhak performs Guru-karya to repay his debt to the Guru-element. I have repaid this debt by performing Guru-karya, and you, too, will have to repay it through your Guru work. We have to understand the importance of Guru-karya. We aren't obliging the Guru-element by performing it; we repay our debt to the Guru-element through Guru-karya so that not a single debt remains, and that obligation shouldn't become a barrier on the path of liberation. Everyone has to follow the same path—the path to liberation and attaining liberation—what else?

"This is not your field of work. You, too, are bound by karma. You, too, will have to go to your territory (of work). That area is waiting for you. Your work can't commence without reaching that place. The area for discharging knowledge is separate. This is your area for discharging knowledge. Your area of work is that territory, staying in which you had expressed a desire in your last birth, that the territory should achieve progress. You performed spiritual penance for that territory. Your work will begin only after reaching that region."

I asked out of ignorance, "How will I reach my area of work?"

Gurudev replied, "The Guru-energy of that place will give you the divine experience at that place—then you will understand that this is my 'place of work.'

"My dear, the 'place of work' is that place where the reservoirs of energies of the Guru-element are present for Guru-karya to be performed. But as there is no medium of the Guru-energies present there, they remain dormant. When their medium reaches them, they are activated through the medium. Thus, the medium and the place of energy complement each other. Work doesn't happen until the union of these two takes place. I can see this, and you can't, that's why I'm telling you about it. This (place) is not your 'place of work.' You are a divine soul who has arrived on earth because of your promises. Your duty is to fulfil those promises, and that task can't be performed in this place. You'll have to reach your 'place of Guru' because, until then, the purpose of your life can't be fulfilled. You'll have to leave this place, but don't try to leave this place on your own; everything will happen at the appropriate time.

"The place of work is that area where the work doesn't progress until one gets there. Man's 'area of knowledge' and 'area of work' are both separate. You created your area of work in your previous birth; there is work to be done in this life."

I was thinking that Gurudev indeed has knowledge of all three periods of time—he has information about the past, the future and the present. I said, "Gurudev, you have knowledge about all three periods of time, you know everything." He replied, "You, too, have knowledge of all three periods of time. But you will obtain this store of knowledge only after you reach your area of work. It is necessary to know 'who am I' in order to acquire this knowledge. When one has that knowledge, one also gets to know from where this 'I' has arrived. One also becomes aware where 'I' will be going. All this is based on the purity of one's mind; and the purer one's mind, the stronger it will be, and the stronger it is, the more sensitive it will be.

"It's impossible to live in society with a sensitive chitta, and that is the reason why ascetics don't wish to remain in society after their chitta becomes sensitive. They don't wish to remain in society, as they face a lot of problems there; as a result of extreme sensitivity, they have to maintain a lot of control over their chitta. If, because of extreme sensitivity, their attention goes to some person, then even if they don't pay attention to the faults of the person before them, they unknowingly acquire his faults. Too much of this effect is bad for the physical body of the yogis. That's why the yogis prefer to live in isolation in the jungle.

"They are safer in the jungle. Generally, yogis don't go into society at all, and if they do go, then they live with their eyes downcast. They do this because eyes are the media of the chitta, and the chitta gets polluted only through the eyes. If they stay with their eyes downcast, they won't be able to see anything; and if they don't see anything, then their attention won't be drawn there. Several yogis always speak with downcast eyes, and especially when they are speaking to a woman.

"They speak with their eyes downcast so that their attention shouldn't wander towards a woman, and their lust can't awaken, so that there shouldn't be any perversion; and they will especially never look into the eyes of a woman because eyes only are the medium of give and take.

"Several yogis who live in the jungle go and bathe continually in the river when their feeling of lust is aroused; several yogis lie down on the ice in the Himalayas when their feeling of lust is aroused, and several yogis bury themselves in the snow. They are yogis but they still possess a physical body; and when they possess a physical body then the body can't exist without the perversions of the body. The perversions of the physical body can be controlled in two ways—one is the control through one's chitta, and secondly by going through the experience of sexual pleasure. Thus, yogis resort to this path to control their minds. Feelings of lust are also a fault of the physical body. This is also a physical perversion. There are no women at all in the jungle, therefore keeping away from them becomes easy for these yogis. That's why they live in the jungle. But it's difficult to stay away from sexual passions when they live in society because women are present at every moment in society, and that can create the perversion of sexual pleasure.

"If thoughts of sexual pleasure are present in society, then it influences the yogis. It affects them more because their chitta is extremely pure and sensitive. Therefore, it is difficult for yogis to live in society. Only a yogi who is a family man can live in society—one who is present in everything and yet not present in anything.

"My dear, it's easy to wear white clothes and stay at home, but it's very difficult to wear white clothes and work in the coal mine of society, and to save oneself from the stains of that coal mine. That's why it is easy for yogis to live in the jungle but difficult to live in society. Society is domesticated and worldly. And if one wishes to convey the message of 'inner knowledge' to them, one will have to live with them. But it is difficult for a yogi to live with them. The Guru-energies have therefore chosen this path, and an ordinary person like you who is worldly yet not in society (mentally) has been made a medium by them. You can go close to ordinary people and ordinary people can come close to you, but the spread of inner knowledge is not possible without getting close to them."

I wanted to know from Gurudev the path through which one could be near women, stay close to them, and still avoid the perversion of lust. If such a path existed, then he should tell me about it. Gurudev said, "Your own feelings are the path for this. Keep only one feeling in your mind: that every woman is my mother; have a vision of a mother in every woman. Then the perversion of lust won't be created at all, and sexual feelings won't ever be awakened when you see a beautiful woman. The feeling of sexual perversion is awakened through our inner feelings.

"Woman in the form of Kundalini is present in our body. Always have a vision of the energy that is present in both men and women in the same form. When you see a woman, don't look at her body; look at her Kundalini Shakti, and after seeing her Kundalini Shakti, you'll see her in the form of a mother. Do you experience any feeling of lust when you see the idol of any beautiful Goddess? No, you don't, because you look at that beautiful woman as the form of Mother Goddess. Similarly, when you see a woman (as a mother) you won't have feelings of lust, but experience 'inner peace.' My dear, it's very easy to hide in these jungles out of fear of women; but to live in society in the midst of women and practise spiritual devotion, and to have control over one's chitta is very difficult. That can be practised only by a great yogi like you. Guru-energies have created you for this very purpose of going into society and performing this work. Therefore, go into society and perform your work; and while performing it, visualize Mother Kundalini in every woman. This is the only easy path for performing work in society.

"I'm telling you all these things, but my Gurudev had said the same things to me seventy years ago when I was a youth of twenty-five. Since then, I have lived here on this island for the past seventy years, and over these seventy years I haven't seen any other human except you. You are the first human to reach this island. But you, too, haven't come here on your own; my Guru has sent you here. Now I wish to handover all this knowledge that I have preserved for several years and leave empty-handed. I don't feel it is appropriate for me to carry anything at all with me.

"This knowledge is not mine; someone has given it to me, so why should I carry the knowledge that someone has given me? My dear, now I don't need the ropes whose support I took to climb the peak of Mandar Mountain (Heaven). I have reached the highest peak with their help. Now I can throw down the ropes in the form of knowledge (that I possess) with complete faith and experience, to the person who is going to climb that peak so that those ropes will be helpful to him. What will I do with the ropes on the peak? Now I don't have to climb anywhere, and these ropes are of no use to me.

"Hey! Every yogi who has reached the peak must have thrown down his ropes in the form of knowledge for other sadhaks. Now he shouldn't have the desire to hold on to his ropes. Actually, these ropes don't even belong to me. Some Satguru has thrown them down to me after reaching the peak, and I'm throwing down the same ropes. One can reach the peak of inner knowledge only in this way. These ropes in the form of knowledge are the repayment of my debt. You, too, will have to repay the debt when your life comes to an end. Whom do you have to throw these ropes to? That is not known. Who will catch them? That is not known. Who will catch hold of them and climb up? That, too, is not known. The only thing that is known is that whoever it is will be a sadhak who'll climb up to this highest peak, and this is how knowledge is spread. For whom is this knowledge being spread? That is not known. The one who walks on this path takes advantage of it. We, too, have searched for ropes in the form of knowledge and caught hold of them and climbed up with their help. Some similar seekers will catch hold of them and will climb up with the help of these ropes in the form of knowledge and reach the peak, too.

"All this is the wheel of time, and everything keeps on moving with this wheel of time. Now I, too, have very little time left, and this is my final wish—I wish to go to the peak of that mountain where there is a big flat stone like a platform. That is the place of my Guru, and my Guru died there. Take me to that place. I, too, wish to die in the presence of my Guru." I nodded my head, but very unwillingly, and started making preparations for the next day's 'Great Journey.'

I thought—it's impossible for Gurudev to climb such a high mountain. He can't even stand properly in his hut. How is he going to climb the mountain when he can't even stand? Which is the path he can take to climb the mountain, what do we do? I couldn't understand what to do. At first, I thought that I should prepare a bamboo basket and make him sit in it and pull it slowly up the mountain. But this didn't seem possible, because there was no proper path to climb the mountain, nor was there any level land. One had to move aside bushes and thorns and creepers to make a path. The jungle was so thick that it was also difficult to maintain the right direction. I didn't know what I could do to reach that 'place of Guru' in a good condition. I realized that Gurudev had taken me on the journey to that place some days back for this reason. Secondly, this time it was his final journey, and I had to return alone. As I thought about it, I had no enthusiasm for it. But I only had to obey my Guru's order, and I followed it.

It was difficult to make him sit in a basket and pull him up the mountain, because it's difficult to pull any burden upwards. After thinking for some time, I cut some green bamboos, and after skinning them I prepared a throne-like basket and lined it completely with leaves. After that, I also arranged flowers in it, and prepared two loops with creepers that I could slide and hang on my shoulders. I decided to make him sit in it and carry the basket on my back and travel the next day.

I tried to sleep that night, but I couldn't sleep. Then, when I got up in the morning, I saw that Gurudev had opened his eyes. I made him sit up. He meditated for some time in the morning and bowed before Mother Earth. Gurudev bowed before the deity of his hut in whose proximity he had been living for the past seventy years. He glanced around the hut once and then made a sign to me and said, "Let's go." I brought the basket that I had made into the hut.

I told him, "I have prepared a plan. Please sit in this basket, and I'll carry you on my back. You have to hold on to my neck with both your hands from behind, and when you have any trouble on the way, tell me and I'll stop."

Gurudev said, "Now I'm surrendering my body to your care. You may do what you please. My Guru has put his trust in you, therefore I, too, trust you completely. I have full faith that whatever you think will be right. I'm ready to co-operate with you on this journey." Then I lifted Gurudev, made him sit on the seat, placed it on my back, and Gurudev's great journey commenced. He had become so weak that I could not feel his weight. Or maybe because of his affection for me, I didn't feel any weight at all.

Both of us came out of the hut, and we felt that all the trees were waiting to welcome us. All the birds were sitting there but they were silent. All the flowers were blooming but seemed bowed down, as if the whole earth was standing to wish farewell to Gurudev. The trees that Gurudev had planted with his own hands were spectators today for his great journey. Those birds that had been born in Gurudev's presence had grown up, and they were also standing with their young ones for the final sight of Gurudev. We took leave of everyone with a heavy heart. It seemed as if the trees were saying—if only we could walk, today we would have joined you on this great journey. We were moving forward very slowly, and I went straight to the place where the ascent began and decided to climb up the mountain by following a circuitous path. This path was longer, but it was safer and also easier. I took the two bamboo sticks that I had sharpened in the front portion in both my hands. I was cutting the bushes with them and moving forward because I had to make the path.

We moved slowly ahead, and from time to time I asked Gurudev if he had any problems, and he would reply—nothing, everything is fine, move on—and I would walk ahead. We slowly moved forward. We had been moving since morning, and now the sun had climbed much higher. I stopped for some rest and helped Gurudev to step down on a high, flat surface and helped him to sit there. I sat at his feet and relaxed. I was drenched in perspiration. I had taken off all my clothes in the hut and wrapped only two banana leaves around my waist and hadn't worn anything else. My feeling was—why should I take part in this great journey wearing cotton clothes! I remembered my childhood when my maternal grandmother used to ask me to perform puja without wearing any clothes, and I did the same today. When I looked at Gurudev, I noticed that the bamboo strips were hurting him under his arm. There was a red mark at the spot. So, I picked some leaves and placed them near the bamboo strips so that they couldn't hurt Gurudev's body. He wasn't even aware that they were hurting him because he had no awareness left in his body.

That's why I had to take greater care of him. I asked him—didn't you realize that it was hurting? He said, "When one meditates, one is not aware of one's thoughts. Then afterwards one loses awareness of the body, too. One's attention doesn't go to one's body, so how will anyone be aware of it? As the body becomes very subtle and sensitive it also becomes very delicate. The physical body that is in the best state is also very delicate. This state is exactly like that of roses. The rose is the best part of the rose plant. But the rose flower is the most delicate part of the plant. Even a mild breeze makes the rose petals fall, whereas the same breeze doesn't affect the rose plant or the thorns on it. As the rose flower is very delicate, there's always a danger of it breaking and shedding petals. That's why we have to pay special attention to rose flowers. There's no need to pick the flower and hold it in one's hands to get its fragrance. The fragrance of the rose flower can be experienced even from a distance. The rose emits fragrance only after reaching a state of its 'soul form.' That's why it is also extremely sensitive.

"Now I have no attraction for the physical body. This body has supported me a lot, and now it needs to rest. This body is a tool to achieve liberation. One can attain liberation through this perishable body, but it requires practice to do so without being aware of the body. This happens only through constant study."

I once again placed Gurudev on my shoulders and started climbing the mountain. By now we had reached the steep slope, and my speed had slowed down. On one hand, there was the problem of climbing the slope, and on the other hand, there was no proper road. I had to make way and move forward. I would clear the bushes and then move forward. I would put my weight on the stick in my left hand and cut the bushes with the stick in my right hand; and then I would slowly move ahead. I wasn't doing anything with any jerks and was taking great care so that Gurudev shouldn't feel a jerk. I always took great care because I remembered that I was walking with a body that was as delicate as a rose, and I was aware of that body due to the fragrance of sandalwood. The fragrance of sandalwood was pervasive all the time. That fragrance of sandalwood was with me all the way. It was going to be evening and the sun was slowly setting. It was growing dark, and we decided to rest for the night. I made Gurudev get down from my back.

Gurudev said, "Man's life is like this mountain. He has to put in so much effort to perform good and positive deeds in his life, but he doesn't need to make any effort to fall down. One can fall in an instant, but one can't climb back in an instant as more time and effort are required for that.

"It is the same for the spiritual state. In order to reach newer heights at the spiritual level, it is necessary to continually put in more efforts. The higher the level, the more spiritual practice one needs to put in. Like I have entrusted myself to you and am sitting here carefree, with the belief that you will take me to the peak of this mountain one day, in the same way you entrust yourself to a person who is going to climb the mountain or climb the mountain on you own. One can reach the highest peak of the mountain both ways. I could entrust myself to you because of the weakness of my body. Similarly, man is also troubled in his life due to the problems he has to face. He finds himself incapable of solving those problems, and then he takes refuge at Paramatma's feet and entrusts himself to the Guru to receive Paramatma's help. But man's problems become the reason why he entrusts himself. If there is no such situation, then the question of entrusting oneself doesn't arise at all. This means that the bad situations that man faces in life act as a bridge between man and his surrender. Then, after some time, it becomes man's nature to remain in a state of surrender.

"Some individuals often think that to surrender means not to make any efforts to perform deeds. Actually, surrender doesn't mean that one shouldn't make any effort; it means that one should make a collective effort. When one surrenders, efforts take place in collectivity, and the attempt is made at a collective level. And when the attempt is made after connecting with collectivity, then that can't be seen, as that effort isn't made by a single person, but is made by a collectivity of people. Man's identity doesn't exist anymore in this, and that's why there is no question of ego, that 'I' have done something in this.

"Everything happens in collectivity. We can say that samarpan meditation is an effort to reach Paramatma through collectivity, which is not performed but happens."

I picked up some herbs in the jungle and ate them. These days, Gurudev had stopped eating, but I needed to eat the herbs so that I would get good energy to climb the mountain the next morning. After that, we slept.

When we woke, it was already morning. The whole sky had reddened with the crimson rays of the rising sun that had spread everywhere. Then sunrise took place, and both of us bowed before the sun God, and I once again tied the basket on my back and started on the journey. Gurudev was also sitting silently with his eyes closed, as if he wasn't present in this world at all and was roaming in some other world. During that journey, I started getting several divine experiences in every moment.

I was slowly moving forward; I had decided on a definite path this morning, and I was walking and trying to complete this journey in the least possible time so that Gurudev would have to bear less difficulty. My attention was always on Gurudev, and therefore I always thought about his comfort.

I suddenly hurt myself on a stone, and blood started flowing from the big toe on my right foot. I had started on this journey with bare feet, and that is how it happened. I immediately crushed some leaves and applied them to that spot, and it stopped bleeding. Then I again started walking. In the jungle, I usually tied my feet with the bark of some special trees that resembled banana plants. But on this journey in Gurudev's presence, I had thought of walking barefoot, and that was why I got hurt.

I could feel that Paramatma is present in every living creature, and that the Paramatma who is with human beings is closer to me; that I am a human being and therefore I am able to establish oneness more quickly with Paramatma who is within man. We can obtain more collectivity of energy depending on the number of people with whom we establish oneness, and that much more will we establish connection with Paramatma. I'll require collectivity in the form of Paramatma to remove my ego, and the more I connect with the collectivity, the more my own identity will start to decrease, and after reaching such a stage, my existence will merge into that collectivity. But one requires collectivity to merge into it, and surrender is not possible without collectivity. Where can one surrender, and where can one find so much collectivity?

This means that one will have to establish an inner relationship with each human being, one will have to connect with each human being, and one will have to connect with so many human beings that one's own identity becomes zero. All this is not possible in this thick forest. Therefore, I'll have to leave from here, go into the human settlements, and go into human society.

If I have learned how to swim and wish to swim, if I have a desire to swim, and I'm in a state to do so, and I actually want to swim—but one can't swim on this mountain—then I'll have to go to the ocean. If I don't go near the ocean and don't jump into that ocean, how can I swim? Just as one needs the ocean to learn how to swim, similarly, I need collectivity in order to end my identity. And just as the ocean can't be brought up this mountain, similarly, the collectivity can't be brought to this mountain. If you want to dissolve your identity, then go into collectivity and merge yourself after going into it. Leave this mountain and go into collectivity; that's where your 'place of work' exists. Then distribute the spiritual experiences you have received in the form of a gift after going into human society. This gift of experience is the only path on which someone can join, and you, too, can connect with someone. This living knowledge is really ancient knowledge, but it isn't public knowledge. Until now, it was used only at an individual level; until now, one Guru has given this to his own disciple. Carry the secret of this living knowledge to the entire society.

Get up! Go!! Now an atmosphere of disquiet is going to be created in society. Just as a period of intense activity is followed by a period of inactivity, a similar situation is going to arise. There will be a glut of physical resources in this material world, and the attention of people will be too focused on the material world. As a result, affinity will cease to exist, the feeling of closeness will end, and society will become completely arid and withered. Man's inner peace will end completely due to this dryness and disturbance, and dissatisfaction will arise within oneself; one will lose patience completely, and the growing dissatisfaction in society will take the form of violence on small things.

In the times to come, it is essential to take care of one's chitta. The chitta will go towards external situations and get destroyed more. The entire human community will suffer from the disease of dissatisfaction. People will collectively acquire faults; and once faults reach collectivity, a person will lose his own identity. Man will try to understand everyone without understanding himself, and his chitta will go outside in this effort and will get destroyed. If you wish to know this world, then first of all it is necessary to know oneself, because man is a component of the world. It is impossible without knowing oneself; thought pollution will take place due to this wrong effort. The balance of nature will be disturbed in this thought pollution, and man will try to take the human race away from this thought pollution. Man's efforts will be of various types. But at such a time, a simple and successful effort will be necessary, and society won't have knowledge of such an effort.

At such a time, Samarpan Meditation is the only such path that can bestow the completeness of meditation, because self-realization will be attained through this path of surrender. First of all, man will understand who he is, and when he comes to understand himself, then he will also understand the whole world. After he knows himself, man will have information about the entire world.

Man has a storehouse of infinite knowledge within himself. All that knowledge will start awakening, and in the light of that inner knowledge man will acquire a new insight, and in the coming night of thought pollution there will be a need for the sun of inner knowledge. Such a sun will arise not from outside but from within man. The sun of inner knowledge will rise within man, and then man's inner religion will be awakened, because only inner religion is the true religion of humanity. Go into society at such a time, become the medium of the grace of Paramatma and perform the task of removing the darkness of ignorance that has spread in society. This only is my Guru-dakshina.

I too was tired after climbing the slope and decided to take some rest. Now it was getting dark, and my feet were also swollen as a result of walking the whole day. Despite that, there was a sense of satisfaction that now we had come close to the mountain peak. I had some lai leaves with me, which I ate; I then drank some water and decided to stop and rest there. I prepared a bed for Gurudev with some leaves and I, too, slept next to him below the rock. Night had fallen, moonlight had spread everywhere, and the moon was also visible. The full moon night was approaching, and that was why the light of the moon was spreading out everywhere.

The moonlight appeared like a calm sheet of radiant light spread out on earth. Some wild animals were excitedly sending out different cries. It was a very peaceful atmosphere, and one could *hear* the jungle in this quiet atmosphere.

There is a different type of music in the solitude of the jungle. When you are quiet, this music of the jungle can be heard. This quiet music also makes our mind peaceful from within, and while listening to that quiet jungle music, the music within oneself begins to play, and before a person realizes it, he becomes one with the jungle. A stream of inner peace starts flowing inside, and one's soul bathes in the spring and reaches a state of satisfaction. One's inner religion is awakened through that feeling of satisfaction, and man acquires all the knowledge of his life, and then he doesn't need to know anything or to find anything. That's why ascetics always take refuge in the jungle for their spiritual practice.

The next morning, I went to a nearby stream to get water. This stream had come from the mountains and carried water from there. I had a piece of bamboo with me to carry the water. The water in the stream was shining and moonlight was reflected on it. I went and bathed there and brought water for Gurudev. When I approached Gurudev, I saw that there was an aura of a golden light around him, and it was light golden-yellow at the centre. On its outer edge, there was a deep golden band that kept increasing and decreasing. This band spread or decreased depending on the pulsations of Gurudev's breath, and within that golden whirlpool Gurudev's body had become invisible. This was his true form. His physical body didn't exist anymore and had completely merged with nature. When I crossed that whirlpool of light and reached him, only then his body became visible. I washed his feet, bathed him with the water and cleaned him. He also looked very happy.

I said to him, "Now when I was coming towards you, I saw your very powerful aura, which appeared to be like a great whirlpool in golden yellow light."

He replied, "As man starts meditating, his ego starts reducing, and he starts losing his own identity. Then man starts merging with nature, and this becomes possible only after twelve years of continual spiritual practice. Then, around him, a bright light like a physical body is created. The aura of this body is present as long as the physical body is present. This is the aura of the physical body, and thus one can gauge the extent of that person's spiritual practice through his aura. A realized saint can recognize another realized saint through this aura. This aura is created as a result of man's spiritual practice, but after the physical body is cremated, this aura is destroyed.

"This body of light (aura) is present around every living individual, but it is made up of different colours, and one can understand the personality of that individual through those colours. This body of light is different for every human being. The body of every human who exists in this world is different and it can be known and experienced from any corner of the world. I don't have this knowledge, but it is my desire that you should possess it, and I am fully confident that you will acquire this knowledge because you have the power of the collectivity of souls with you. The collectivity is connected with you. That's why, if you express a desire, you can sit in any part of the world and experience this body of light of any person. All that is required is that you should have the desire to obtain the knowledge.

"My subtle body will be created some years after my body is cremated; and whoever undertakes my remaining work will be helped by this subtle body that has been formed with this energy. But one more progressive development of Guru-energy will happen in your lifetime. Your subtle body will be created when you are still alive, and because of this, you will be able to witness the spread of your work in your lifetime. After this spread of your work, your body won't have any existence, because the subtle body will be formed; this means the existence of the physical body will end. In general, the subtle body is created twenty-five years after the physical body ends.

"Your subtle body will also develop twenty-five years after your physical body loses its identity; then this subtle body will be your medium, and through this medium you'll know about the light of any physical body in the world.

"When your body itself becomes a medium, then no work will happen through it because all the work will be performed by the subtle body, and there's no limit to the subtle body's area of work. The creation of that subtle body in your lifetime means that your work is destined to be on a very large scale and your lifespan is comparatively less. You have to perform the work of several lives in one lifetime. You will receive several experiences in life as a result of your subtle body. I know that you won't understand all these things now, but I won't be around when all these things happen. But when they happen, you'll remember that I gave you advance warning about all these things.

"This creation of the subtle body is a rare event. It always remains present in man's life for several years. The subtle body of people who have the power of collectivity with them, or those who are connected to millions of souls, is created. This subtle body can't be seen, but it gives one spiritual experiences. Spiritual progress is dependent on the fact that it can be experienced. The whole spiritual state is dependent on how many souls are connected to you or how many souls you are connected with. This means that the secret of spiritual progress is hidden in collectivity.

"My being connected to you actually means that I have remained connected to collectivity through your medium. My dear, every human is like a drop of water and man's life is like a bubble of water, and man is aware of it. That's why the final destination of every drop is the ocean. All drops have to finally reach the ocean.

"But this journey is very long. During the long journey of the drop, it has to make several rivers, several great rivers as its mediums. I'm doing the same thing. To perform a good deed and to co-operate in the performance of a good deed are one and the same. I have neither the energy nor the life to perform the work. That is why I wish to do all this through your medium, and you have been authorized as a medium. This authorization has great importance in the spiritual field, and the authorized person has no identity of his own, he is only a medium. He is beyond doing anything, but he is a very powerful medium through whom everything can be done. You have been authorized by the Guru-energies, and you yourself are not aware of this. But those who know you also accept you as a medium and wish to pass on to society whatever knowledge they have through you. They wish to be free of their debt after passing it on to society, and I, too, am doing the same work. I, too, am opening my own path by handing over my knowledge and my energies to you. What does it matter that I couldn't perform the work! It's enough that I could give it my support.

"A man as an authorized medium can't be created on his own. He is also created by someone else. This means that he has not been created through his own wish, and neither has he been born through his own wish. He has taken birth for someone else's wish. This means that even taking birth is not through his personal desire.

"A medium is always created for collectivity, because millions of souls will benefit through that medium. Your area of work will be less during your lifetime but will develop more after your lifetime. People will recognize you only after your lifetime because the illusion of the physical body won't allow them to recognize you in your lifetime. After giving up your physical body, the covering layer of illusion will also be broken, and it will be easy to recognize you.

"You should never have an expectation that people will know you or recognize you. No one will be able to recognize you in your lifetime, and this isn't happening only with you but has happened with all mediums. Whoever has come as a medium with messages from Paramatma, whichever messengers have come here have always done so with a covering layer. It's only because of that covering layer that they could perform the work, and they couldn't be recognized in their lifetime due to that. Hiding their identity is Paramatma's protective armour for them, so that they may be safe from bad influences and carry on with their duties. This is because the work is very important in the spiritual field. Great work will happen through your medium; it'll be less during your life and much more after it.

"All the energies that were tied up in the physical body will become free after your life, and when the energies themselves perform the work then there won't be any limit to the work performed by the energies. I'm very happy that I was able to get the presence of the medium for such a great work in my life and that I could join in such a great work."

I asked Gurudev whether we could move on, and he gave his assent by nodding his head. Radiance was showered even when he nodded his head. Even his smallest act would create consciousness. His eyes gave a lot of energy even without asking, and I felt very peaceful just by looking at him. The sun had climbed higher by now, and I placed him on my shoulders and started climbing the mountain. There were thick bushes near the foot of the mountain, but they weren't so thick on the upper part. This was because the rainwater didn't remain on the mountain peak but flowed down. It was a steep climb, and that's why it was taking some time. In my childhood, I used to visit the wrestling arena. I would dig up the entire area of the wrestling pit with a spade, and then level the ground by pulling a big log of wood tied with a rope. Then I would again start digging. This gave me a lot of exercise and the soil in the pit used to become soft for the wrestlers. Then, I was also very fond of playing kabaddi and that's why today I could climb up the mountain with Gurudev. Man should keep his body strong. One never knows when and where this strong body may be needed in life.

By now we had reached quite high, near the mountain peak. After some time, that flat platform-like stone could be seen. That big slab was easily noticeable because it was made of a different type of stone. We slowly approached it. I lowered Gurudev and made him sit properly with the support of the stone. I told him that it was due to his wish that this journey was possible, otherwise I had been very tired on the previous journey even when I had climbed it alone (without carrying Gurudev). Gurudev informed me, "This is a 'living stone.' If you touch this stone, you'll experience consciousness, and that is because several Gurus have sat here and undertaken spiritual practice on it. This stone has absorbed their radiant energy, and later they gave up their life on this very stone.

※

"Actually, at the time of giving up one's life, it is necessary to have a special energized place so that the soul can free itself easily from its physical body, and there is no desire left for the soul towards the physical body. That's why it was said in the olden days that if a person went to Kashi and died there, he would attain liberation. This is because one's soul is separate and one's body is separate. When the physical body is created, the soul is not present. It later arrives in the body according to the state of the body. The physical body is created as a result of the physical interaction between parents, and during their physical intercourse the environment and the level of thoughts influences the foetus. That's why the time of conception was also decided in the olden days. There should be a good environment at the time of conception.

"There should be good thoughts and a good state of mind. Conception also happens at three levels; the first is at the physical level. In this type of conception, the physical body is given importance. A feeling of lust arises in man, and in the excitement of that lust he has intercourse with his wife and doesn't bother about his wife's feelings; he doesn't even bother to find out whether she is interested in it or not; he crushes her feelings and thinks of the woman's body only as a tool to satisfy his lust, and he satisfies himself. The man has enjoyed this physical relationship, but the woman has not, and this is clearly a type of rape. The man indulged in the act without the woman's consent only to satisfy his lust, and this physical relationship took place only to satisfy his physical hunger; thus, physical lust will naturally be important in this act. Then the foetus that is created through this type of physical relationship will also be lust-centred and physically or body-centred. Such a foetus will not be able to attract a higher soul energy; souls of a good level will never arrive in such a foetus because that foetus doesn't have the capacity to absorb consciousness. That's why, through this type of relationship, a foetus that is of an inferior physical level will be created, which will be able to absorb only a lower level of energy. The mental effect of the level of the parents' thoughts at the time of intercourse will affect this foetus, and the chakras of this foetus will also remain undeveloped due to these thoughts. Even birds and animals don't like to sit at bad places, and the soul that arrives in such a foetus will also be of an inferior level, though actually a soul is not of a high or low level.

"The karma that is connected to that soul carries its records along with it in the form of Kundalini Shakti. This karma decides the future of the next birth; thus, the foetus that takes birth, because of the importance given to lust, is connected only to its physical body. It is body-centred and creates a similar body with a body-centred mentality. Thus, a bad low-level chain is formed. The entire secret of creation of human society is hidden in this process of conception. It is this process that gives birth both to Gods and demons. This process is actually a holy process, but at the physical level it becomes an inferior relationship, and then an inferior society is created. The bad level of society today is because people think that this process is only confined to a physical relationship. A society is therefore being created that gives importance to the physical body. When you sow the seeds of the babool tree (a thorny tree) then only babool trees will grow; mango trees can't grow out of babool seeds. And to sow babool seeds and expect mango trees, one can only imagine mangoes, not get them. Similarly, if one wishes to create a good society, then one has to first of all understand the importance of this holy process. There is no other way. The foetus that is created as a result of the parents' physical relationship is affected by its own aura, and the arrival of the soul depends on its capacity to absorb energy; or we can understand it in this way—the arrival of a soul depends on the situation at the time of intercourse.

"The second level is the relationship that takes place at the soul level. Both the husband and wife love each other: both have a good emotional relationship, and both have a soul feeling towards each other. Both become one at the soul level; there is a loving relationship between the two, both come together passionately, and a physical interaction takes place in a loving atmosphere. Thus, the assent of both is present in this act, both co-operate similarly. There is no importance to the physical body in this interaction, and there is more importance given to feelings. There is more importance given to love, and the intercourse takes place in a loving environment. Then the result of this intercourse is the creation of a foetus whose focus is on feelings. There will be a similar influence around this foetus, and the chakras of this foetus will also develop up to the heart chakra. This means that this foetus will attract the energy of some soul, which is mainly at the soul level, and then a love-centred human being will grow out of the foetus that is created. This person won't be emotionally barren; this person will be full of emotions and will be sensitive.

"As a result of being sensitive, he'll have the capacity to recognize good and bad vibrations in this world. Generally, such people can understand the difference between a good environment and a bad environment. The result is that they will be attracted towards good vibrant places, towards good people filled with consciousness, and will stay in good company in their lives. They'll progress in life, and if souls with such physical bodies get good company, they progress spiritually. Such souls are good sadhaks.

"These sadhaks can establish a soul relationship with some medium in the form of a Guru at a soul level. They are aware right from their birth that the physical body is not everything in one's life. Therefore, they don't get happiness out of the joys and comforts at the physical level, or in talking about physically related things. They have faith in such things, they have faith in being humble, in accepting everything; they observe less and experience more. But their attention is always on the level of their soul. They keep experiencing inner joy in their lives and are not attracted to material and perishable things. They wish to progress spiritually and are aware that a soul is present within them, which is a form that is close to Paramatma. They have a close relationship with their souls, and their soul guides them on what they should and shouldn't do in life. All they require is for a Satguru to arrive in their lives who can lead them to self-realization, so that they can turn inwards. Once they turn inwards then they set out on their inner journey because they have been born for this inner journey. They generally have a good relationship with everyone, and such people are good in society right from their birth. The energies lying dormant within them get awakened when they find a suitable environment, and they start experiencing them in their lives.

"Such people progress spiritually in life and ultimately attain a state of liberation. All they require is a suitable atmosphere, and they obtain a collectivity of good souls when they connect themselves with a Satguru who has a good collectivity with him. Through his medium, one can receive a good collectivity, and once they receive such a collectivity, then they'll progress spiritually. Such people are very sensitive; if some bad deed is committed at their hands, they carry the guilt for several years. Therefore, these kinds of people should be careful that they don't commit a bad deed.

"They also have a very good soulful relationship with their wives, and they prove successful in giving birth to a person who has good inner feelings. Thus, these people also contribute towards the creation of a chain of people in society who have good relationships at the soul level. They believe in Paramatma because they believe in the soul. This believing is their special quality, they are gentle and polite because of their belief, and they are humble as a result of their belief. They have an increased capacity to absorb everything because of their humility. Today, society has great need of such people because everyone can see whatever is visible; but these people obtain the insight to see even what is not visible because of their belief.

"A peace-loving, non-violent society is created when such people are present in greater numbers. Today, there is a great need to bring together such people in a collective form because they won't be able to do anything in isolation. They won't be able to recognize their own identity in a large, populated society of physically conscious people. They will have to be made aware of their level of knowledge. They are different from the body-conscious people, and this knowledge will have to be given to them. As soon as they become aware of their level, their whole life will be transformed. The body is ready and waiting like camphor; it just needs to be touched by a flame to flare up. But they will keep sleeping until they find someone to awaken them, as they can't awake on their own.

"These are people who are above the physical level, and there is yet another level above this soul level. And that is the spiritual level. There are very few people at this level in society because they are not present in society. This is the reason why spiritual progress is not taking place. A particular physical level has to be present, and if the parents come together at that physical level, at that spiritual time, with a spiritual purpose, and wish that a pious soul should be born to them, then such a foetus is created. This foetus will attract a soul of a high spiritual level, and that soul will be of the highest level.

"Three types of souls take birth—if the sexual intercourse has happened at the level of lust, then a soul of the 'demonic' level will take birth. If the sexual intercourse has happened at a loving and Soulful level, then a soul at the human level will take birth. If this soul finds a collectivity of demonic souls, then it will become a demonic soul, and if it finds a collectivity of pious souls, then it will become a pious soul. The third level is when physical intercourse happens at a very high spiritual level. Then the sexual act in this high spiritual state will give birth to divine souls. Everything depends on the state of the mother and father at that time. That is the reason why children of the same parents and brought up with the same values at home may be either divine souls, or human souls or demonic souls.

"Man is an important portion of this world because the world has been created for man. 'The universe exists in the body and the body exists in the universe'—this means that whatever is present in the universe is also present in the body, and similarly, what is present in the body is also present in the universe. If you wish to change the universe, then change the body, and the universe will also become all right. If you desire to have peace in the universe, then first of all you'll have to begin that 'world peace' with 'inner peace.' Inner peace will happen with the arrival of suitable souls. World peace depends on the kind of souls that will take birth.

"Souls can't take birth by themselves. In order to incarnate on earth, they require a medium in the form of a physical body. If the bad souls don't find a bad physical body as a medium, then they won't be able to descend to earth at all. And when they don't descend at all, then disturbances and disquiet won't enter this world, and peace will be established in the world.

"One will have to stop the demonic souls from arriving on earth in order to have peace in the world. If one wishes to stop them from reaching the world, then the present younger generation will have to be given the knowledge of the 'conception ceremony' before their marriage. A good spiritual state will have to be created both in the mother and the father. This goal appears to be impossible. But man will slowly have to try to move towards this goal in his life, and each and every person should contribute to this endeavour. It is possible that this goal may not be achieved in his lifetime, but the coming generation will at least get a loving and peaceful world! And you'll have the good fortune of giving your co-operation to a great work and will experience inner peace. Today, there is disquiet in the world due to ignorance about this 'conception ceremony.' This is a ceremony that creates the world. It has lost its importance in the present-day world because man doesn't have knowledge of it anymore. This living knowledge will have to be conveyed to society, and through its medium man will obtain spiritual experiences, and after obtaining spiritual experiences, he'll reach a good spiritual state.

"The spiritual state has no connection with religion. Every

religion has shown the path to acquire a spiritual state. Man can move forward with the help of any religion and reach the same place. This is similar to a city having several approach roads, but all roads come to an end on reaching it. All the religious roads also end when one reaches a spiritual state like the city. That's why it isn't important which road of religion one takes. What is important is the city, and everything is encompassed in it. Every religion has an equal potential to reach the spiritual state. The question that arises is whether you are holding on to your religion and sitting in one place or have reached the city on the path of religion. Generally, man is ignorant and thinks that the path of religion is the city. Thus, his whole life ends while sitting on the path. That's why it makes no difference what religion man has been born into. What is important is the religion of humanity through which man has reached the city that is the state of spirituality. That's why all human society is wandering around in the darkness today. We (Gurus) are aware of this; but we are not able to go into society because of our extremely sensitive condition, even though we want to. This is similar to the fact that one can't enter a coal mine wearing white clothes, but we don't have any lifespan left, either. Our whole life was spent in preserving what we had obtained.

"We could only perform the work of keeping our 'living knowledge' safe in our lives. We couldn't distribute it in society even though we wished to do so, because it wasn't our work to distribute it. Our work was only to preserve it, and so we took care of it. Now it is your work to distribute it and distribute it in your life. It is easy to acquire knowledge but very difficult to distribute it. One requires a very sensitive heart to distribute, and one requires a container that can contain the entire human race within itself. Our container is not so big, but your container is! That's why we have given our contribution to your container. We have performed our work; now you perform yours."

I once again expressed my doubts. "I have never distributed anything in my life, and I don't know how to distribute. I can't even speak properly to anyone; and when I can't give it properly, who will accept this knowledge from me? What will they accept from me? I myself am ignorant; I haven't read any scriptures or any religious texts. I haven't acquired any knowledge. I have neither taken up any spiritual practice, nor do I have any special energy or knowledge. What will I do all alone? And now you, too, are not going to remain with me. What can I do all alone? I won't be able to do this; please choose some other medium. Don't give up your body now. Acquire a good medium first; wait until then. Hand over your knowledge to some scholarly person, and then give up your body. I'm not fit for the responsibility you are placing on me."

Gurudev replied very seriously, "The decision of suitability or non-suitability is not mine. You have been chosen by my Gurus. Their spiritual practice of the past 800 years reaches you and then it ends. When your end comes, it will bring with it the end of an era of spiritual practice; and if that knowledge of 800 years is not distributed, then that spiritual practice will be meaningless.

"This 'living knowledge' is not bookish knowledge; it is the knowledge of spiritual experience. Books contain only information, but through living knowledge one gets all the information from within. Then there is no need to read any books. You yourself are a 'book' and people will read you—and books don't read other books! Therefore, recognize yourself! And when you recognize yourself, then all the misunderstandings will be removed. My dear! Even serving a meal is an art, and everyone doesn't possess it. And it isn't necessary that a person who is serving food should be able to cook it. There can be several cooks, but there is only one person who serves it. You are the person who serves the meal and not the one who cooks it. Therefore, there's no need to obtain that knowledge. That will come to you with the Guru's blessings. Just do the work of distributing it; that work only is your concern. Start doing the work that has been entrusted to you, and the work will start happening. Don't think about how you will perform the work. Does a bird ever think—the sky is so vast, so how can I fly?

"It just starts flying, because a bird has been born to fly. Similarly, the spiritual practice of 800 years will end at your hands. The final offering in this yagya will be offered through you. All this has been predestined, and this is the only purpose of your life. Then when you say, 'how can I perform this work?' it is a feeling of ego of your body. Put aside that 'I' sense and everything will be clear. You are not going to perform this work; it will take place through your medium.

"My dear! How can you distribute this vast storehouse of 800 years of knowledge? It will be distributed through you. Give up your sense of 'I' and surrender yourself; all the work will happen in your life. You are only a medium; think of yourself only as a medium. Whenever there is more work to be done, remind yourself that you are a medium, and the medium will do the work easily and automatically. I am leaving after completing the work that my Gurudev entrusted to me. Thinking about 'how will I do this work?' is not your lookout. You will experience this. This is not your area of work. That's why I'm telling you that one day you'll have to leave this place. But stay happy until then, and don't try to leave this place. You'll leave on your own when the right time comes. I, too, had felt like you when my Gurudev entrusted me with the storehouse of this living knowledge and said that I should keep it safe until you arrived here. I, too, used to feel that I hadn't received anything, so what should I preserve! But when I handed it over to you, then at the time of giving I realized what a vast store of knowledge it was!

"When the knowledge came to me, it wasn't through my own

efforts but through my Guru-krupa. That's why I didn't even realize when it arrived. But when I handed it over to you, then I realized what it was. Similarly, when work takes place through you as a medium on a very vast scale, then you'll realize that the knowledge you received was on such a vast scale." It had started growing dark, and we decided to halt for the night. I didn't realize how the time passed in Gurudev's presence.

Early next morning, I woke up because of the cold breeze. As we were on the mountain peak, the air was very cold, and we had no sheets to spread on the ground or cover ourselves. Gurudev was sleeping peacefully. When he slept, it seemed as if a small child was asleep. It was a different experience to see him lying asleep. Then he also awoke after some time, and said, "Now I have very little time left. Today, I'll give you knowledge about the evolution of human life. The human body is the best example of Paramatma's creation. One obtains the human birth after taking birth in several yonis. This evolution is possible only after taking birth in several forms. Several people experience the effect of their previous births; there are effects from their previous forms even after taking birth in the human form. After taking birth in the human form, man starts developing systematically, and all his development depends on the proximity he receives, the way in which he receives the company, and the type of parents he receives. All these facts are helpful in man's evolution. An ordinary soul first of all takes birth in the home of an extremely poor person, and all his time is spent in arranging for his two meals of the day.

"At such a time, man wishes that he should at least get two meals a day, and only then can he do something further. Then, in his next birth, he gets a slightly better family where the problem of his daily meals is not present. But he needs clothes, a house and education. Then his attention goes to all these facilities, and in his next birth the soul takes birth in a middle-class family, and in this birth all these facilities are available.

"But he keeps getting thoughts that he should get more opportunities, more wealth. As a result of getting more thoughts, he is able to perform less work, and his whole life is spent in these thoughts. Then, in his next birth, he is born into some rich family, and this time he has enough wealth to fulfil all his needs. Even then the physical needs are limitless, and as a result, he wishes that he should find material happiness and more facilities for material happiness; and he wishes that he should have more and more wealth to fulfil that desire, and he dies with all these desires still present. He takes birth in an extremely rich home in his next birth where he has all the happiness and facilities right from his birth, and then man is extremely rich and obtains unlimited material happiness and facilities. Then, even after obtaining unlimited wealth and unlimited material happiness and facilities, he realizes in his old age that he has gone through his entire life unhappy; but he had thought that he would be able to obtain more happiness through more wealth.

"Every material instrument bestows happiness for a short time, and at that time one thinks that this is happiness. But later, one realizes that it was only momentary happiness, and again feels emptiness and again searches for that new happiness. Thus, man realizes that these material instruments can't give everlasting happiness, that these are physical joys, and they are momentary.

"But by the time one realizes this, that birth also ends. But the desire to obtain inner happiness still remains; after obtaining this, no desire remains for anything else. Then he dies. The desire to obtain that joy still remains, but death takes place. Then he takes the next birth, and that birth is only to obtain that inner happiness. Then, right from his childhood, he starts walking in that direction; and in that birth, he catches hold of the religion of the house in which he has taken birth as a tool to obtain happiness, and then all through his life he holds on to that religion. He is called a staunch religious person. Those people who walk all their lives on the religious path are very religious right from their birth. They have great faith in religion. They hold on to their religion even through great difficulties and keep searching for everlasting happiness. Then they perform several rituals, which are part of that religion, in search of happiness. Some people perform puja, some pray, some chant mantras and some perform yagya.

"All these rituals give him some happiness; then it seems to him that he has reached his goal—but the search for the soul still remains. Thus, the physical body says you have got there, and the soul says, no—more happiness still remains to be found at the soul level. Thus, even after following his religion all his life, something still remains to be acquired in his life. Then what remains is— inner happiness. Then he starts desiring inner happiness, and then death happens.

"In his next birth, he stays with his experience. The religion of the house in which he takes birth is different this time, and he realizes that this is not religion. This is a method of worship that keeps changing with each birth. Then he makes the method of worship of that house his foundation, and he moves forward. But he doesn't hold on to that method of worship; and finally, he reaches some living Guru in search of inner happiness and obtains inner experience through the grace of that living Guru. Later, he experiences inner happiness and, after finding it, all his desires come to an end. He feels that he has obtained everything in human life, and in such a satisfied state he finds inner satisfaction. He obtains a state of liberation in his lifetime, and then his physical death may take place later. After this death he doesn't take birth again, because now there is no desire left, no reason left to take birth again, and his evolutionary cycle ends. Every man has to go beyond this long cycle.

"Man achieves these cycles of life sooner or later according to the company he keeps. Everything depends on the proximity in which the soul stays because one can obtain this path of inner happiness earlier through a good proximity. But the journey takes place in this way in the ordinary human form. Man keeps taking birth again and again to fulfil his wish, but when there is no wish left, there is no purpose left in taking another birth; and such a state is liberation.

"Now my final time has arrived, and I explained this to you because I don't want to take any knowledge with me. I wish to empty myself before I go. I will give up my physical body tomorrow morning with the sunrise, and you should cremate my body before the sun sets." Gurudev was saying all this very easily; on the other hand, I was trembling with the thought of staying behind in this world without him. There was no activity happening with his body, and he would lie still, but even then, he was a great support to me. He was my only support on such a lonely island, and that, too, would be gone tomorrow; I started feeling uneasy while thinking about it.

He told me, "Stay here in this place for three days after my death, and then go to the hut and stay there. I'll stay in this place for three days after my death because, after a person dies, the soul takes three days to be free of the influence of the physical body. After three days, the soul is freed and attains the next state. This was also my final birth, and now you have to fulfil the duties of your final birth.

"It was my final wish that my cremation should happen at your hands. You are going to be instrumental in my attainment of liberation after my death. I have acquired everything through this path of meditation. Now nothing remains to be acquired, and you, too, will acquire everything on this path." Gurudev bowed before the setting sun with folded hands and said, "This is my final sunset. I won't be able to witness the sunset tomorrow; the sunset bestows a lot of peace on the soul."

It was really a very beautiful scene. After sunset, the whole sky had turned red, and there was a splendid deep-red colour at the place where the sun had set. In the rest of the sky, there was a light yellow and golden reddish hue. All the birds were returning to their homes. There were thick bushes under the peak, and those birds had returned to their nests. Their young ones were also happy to have them back and were uttering beautiful cries of pleasure. Then a slight breeze started blowing, and the whole sky turned golden. Down below, the bank of the river Brahmaputra where I used to bathe with Gurudev was visible. Everything was peaceful today, as if everywhere nature was wishing Gurudev farewell. Slowly, the voices of the birds also faded away, and it started becoming dark. I selected and picked some leaves, cut them into small pieces, crushed them on the stone and offered them to Gurudev as a meal. But Gurudev smiled and refused them and returned them to me as a prasad and asked me to eat them.

He said, "I'm very pleased with your reverent feelings towards me. You can eat these leaves as a prasad." By then it was growing dark, and the sun had set completely.

Gurudev said, "To acquire inner knowledge and to distribute it are two separate activities; and man's life proves to be very short for performing both these activities. You have surrendered completely to me, but that surrender is not before an individual; it is towards a Guru-energy. You haven't been able to fulfil the duties of a son, a husband, or a father; now I have to complete them. The special quality of the Guru-element is that the feeling and emotions you offer are multiplied thousands of times and returned to you. The Guru doesn't keep anything with him, and it's your wish, isn't it, that this knowledge should reach the ordinary people? You'll have to return to society to fulfil this desire. You'll have to bring about a spiritual revolution in society, and you'll have to do so by living in society in an ordinary form. Today, an external quest is going on in society. This quest can bestow man with material happiness, but it can't give him inner peace. And one will have to go inwards for inner peace; he'll have to travel inwards. One can never obtain inner happiness and inner peace externally. One will have to undertake the inner journey together with the external journey; and only then can man retain his balance. Otherwise, while searching externally, man's chitta will go so much towards the outside that there won't be any balance left at all.

"An imbalanced society will be without any restraint, and once it loses control over itself, it will destroy itself. Today, society is creating instruments through the external quest to destroy itself. Whatever is created through man's efforts is perishable. Man can never create anything that is everlasting and abiding, and man's chitta is unstable because of the creation of unstable things.

"It's essential to always maintain a balance in society. If only speed (of activity) increases in society, it'll make society unstable. Balance is also required along with speed, and balance is not possible externally. Inner balance is the balance that can keep society balanced, and that is possible only if one stays in society. This is very difficult—I, too, am aware of it. But you'll have to live and perform this work. You have to perform only this one work in society. The energies that will get this work done are different. You don't have to get the work done; you just have to do it. You are only a medium, because the work is so vast that no one can perform it; you, too, can't do it. You won't be able to do it because the work will get done through you. This means that you'll be the medium for it, but you won't perform it. You won't perform it means that you won't do anything, because whenever a person does something, then that work happens within a defined limit; when the work happens through him (as a medium), there is no defined limit for that work. It happens at an infinite level. Today also several pious souls who can help in this work are present in society, but at present they themselves are going in the wrong direction. Those souls are wandering aimlessly. They are searching for inner peace in books, and that inner peace can never be found in books. My dear! How can lifeless books give active inner peace!

"What is found in books is the past, and the past can never create the present. The past can only give information, not knowledge. One can't obtain knowledge through books; knowledge is a living spiritual experience that can only be obtained through a living Guru. These days man wishes to acquire inner peace by reading books. Books only give information about what has happened in the past. If knowledge can be obtained through books, then there's no need to have teachers in the field of education, whereas the entire method of education is dependent on teachers. Teachers are the pillars of society. In this world, only the teacher knows the art of conveying facts into the brains of others. That's why the entire foundation is in the hands of the teacher. The teacher can create a good society if he wishes, and he can create a bad society if he wishes. Lifeless books can't bring about a revolution in anyone's life. An active revolution can be brought about only through the medium of the teacher. You also go into society and do the work of a spiritual teacher. A Guru is hidden in every teacher. If you wish to obtain something special from a teacher, then you'll have to bow specially before the teacher. And when you bow before the teacher, it won't be physically but through your soul. Only that teacher's soul will be able to give you something special.

"Go into society wearing the robes of an ordinary person. You are an ordinary person anyway. Go into society in your real form because society consists of ordinary people. You will have to go to its level in order to make contact. You will have to become like it and perform work like it. Only then will you be able to come close to man, as human society is a creation of man.

"Every human being acts as a mirror to society. Man is the mirror-image of society. If man wishes to understand society, then he'll have to understand 'man' first. Man will give him the information about society. Man is a social animal. He always prefers to live in society, and he thinks in the same way that the society around him thinks. Therefore, he has got lost while living in society. He has lost his identity and what is left is the ordinary man. In reality, one can only reach the ordinary man by becoming like him. Once you succeed in reaching there, then the Great soul that is within you will definitely make the soul before it aware of its own Greatness. What is present within you is an extraordinary Power, an Inner energy, because this soul energy is present in collectivity; a collective energy of millions of souls who have joined together in the past 800 years. That collective energy is a magnetic energy through which the soul in front of you will be attracted. But a soul will be able to get the knowledge of this collective energy, the spiritual experience of this collective energy only when that person, no matter how ordinary he is, stays in your proximity. That soul should obtain the proximity of the collectivity, and once he gets it, then spiritual experience will happen on its own. Spiritual experience is a process to reach from one soul to another. It happens naturally, and one doesn't have to do anything for it.

"Go into society as an ordinary person, and the pious souls in society will recognize who you are; they'll recognize the collectivity of souls within you. The collectivity within you is your special quality. You don't have to do anything. Just take your physical body, just carry this physical body, transport it and reach into society, and the work ahead will be performed by the energies themselves. The energies will perform their work. They will provide a new direction to those people who are searching for internal peace externally, in books. Then man will search in that inward direction. Man is not aware today that the knowledge of inner peace is to be found internally. Man doesn't possess this knowledge. But once he obtains it, he'll definitely obtain inner peace, because man desires inner peace, and is also searching for it. But the search for inner peace is taking place externally. It only needs to be guided in the right direction."

Even after Gurudev explained so much to me, my attraction for his body was not decreasing. I said, "If you are going to die, then why are you leaving me? Take me along with you. Why are you leaving me in this darkness? Please give me permission to die with you. I can't stay without you. I, too, wish to give up my body with you. I can't even imagine this world without you, so why should I stay at all? As far as society is concerned, about showing them the way—someone else will come to guide them in the right direction. I wish to die with you. Please permit me to do so and take me along with you. Please don't leave me alone here. Does a mother leave her child halfway? Why are you displeased with me, why are you leaving me? I wish to die with you."

Gurudev smiled and gave me his permission to die. He said, "All right, I give you permission to die on my pyre." On hearing this, I became very happy, and teardrops started falling one by one from my eyes. I was mad with joy that now Gurudev wouldn't leave me alone and go away. I would be going along with him. I closed my eyes and mentally started thanking Gurudev.

He said, "You have expressed a desire to die with me on my pyre tomorrow; thus, your physical existence will definitely end tomorrow. Destroy your feeling for the physical body tomorrow; once you give up the feeling for the physical body, it is as good as giving up your body. Give up your awareness of the physical body tomorrow on my pyre. Tomorrow, your feeling for the physical body will also be burned and get destroyed. Then, after giving up your awareness of the body, what remains will be your soul. Now live as a pure, holy and serene soul. Then nothing will remain to be accomplished. The soul is a pure form of Paramatma. Become such a pure and holy soul and perform your work as a soul and offer your body-awareness to me. And coming to the point about staying with me—my soul will always stay with you."

I kept on weeping and said, "No! I really want to die with you."

Gurudev said, "All right, think that tomorrow you have died at sunrise, and not me. The one who has stayed alive is not you but me. Now just understand this. All this is a play of understanding. Whatever you understand will be all right. After today, put me in your place and perform the work. When you are not performing the work at all, and I am going to perform it, then this whole affair is closed. Now come on, go to sleep and allow me to rest also."

Gurudev went to sleep very peacefully, but I didn't get any sleep all night. I kept on staring at the stars all night and thinking: "Gurudev is going to die tomorrow, and even then, he is sleeping peacefully, as if he's taking rest for the journey tomorrow. He's so calm and so much at peace; he's sleeping like an innocent child." I loved to watch him when he was sleeping.

I found that night to be very short. The moon was moving rapidly, every moment was slipping away out of reach. I felt that this night should continue endlessly, and the sun shouldn't rise at all, and Gurudev shouldn't die at all. Then, as the night passed, I found a change taking place inside me. As the night passed, I found that my darkness was also slowly receding, and I started getting the feeling, "What I am thinking are my thoughts. What Gurudev is saying is his command, and his command is supreme. Now everything should take place according to his command.

Sunrise should also take place, and according to Gurudev's wish he should also give up his body with the sunrise, and I should perform the work after Gurudev passes away. My Gurudev is immortal. He can never die, what can die is only the physical body. The soul is immortal, and that is with me. Gurudev will stay alive in the form of work." I decided to perform Gurudev's work all my life. I wished to stay connected to Gurudev in the form of his work, by performing his work.

The time was passing by at its own speed, the sun was about to rise and the brightness before sunrise was slowly becoming visible. I had been awake all night, but now Gurudev had woken up.

Gurudev signalled to me and called me, and I went and bowed at his feet. Gurudev was smiling quietly and said, "Now wish me farewell with joy. I have attained whatever I wished for, and you will also attain it just through spiritual practice. Don't ever give up this spiritual practice. It will help you until your last breath, because this spiritual practice is a collective energy. Now go and bow before the sun, which is rising in the East, then turn your back to it and go and sit on that high stone and meditate." I went and sat on that stone, and then Gurudev sat in front of me. What happened after that was an extremely divine spiritual experience, which can only be experienced. It can't be written in words. A flow of consciousness came out of his crown chakra and started showering on my crown chakra, and I experienced that I was watching the sun rising; that day, I saw the sun rising in the west.

Gurudev's body wasn't visible at all; there was only a great brilliance of energy as if sunrise was taking place and thousands of rays were showering on me from that sun, and consciousness was filling me from within. Every particle of my body was awakened, and after some time, I felt as if the ring of brightness in front of me was increasing, and I was losing my existence in the storehouse of that light. I was slowly experiencing an extraordinary radiance, and there was bright light everywhere. I experienced a lightning-like flash, and after that, I lost consciousness. When I opened my eyes after some time, I saw that Gurudev was sitting below me and bowing to me. At first, I thought that he was bowing to the sun behind me. Then I saw that the sun had climbed much higher and was above me. My Gurudev said to me, "Gurudev, I offer you my heartfelt thanks, because you gave me the good fortune to perform your work." And then, after bowing with folded hands, he passed away.

I couldn't understand at all why he addressed me as Gurudev and why he did it. So, who am I? And as soon as I tried to find out 'who am I,' a state of void was created, and then I slowly came out of that state of void. I laid out Gurudev's body on the stone, and after bowing before him, I started making further preparations. I selected and collected good sticks from the neighbouring area and prepared an asana of sticks for Gurudev. Then I bowed before those sticks also with reverence—you are very fortunate to go along with my Gurudev on his final Great Journey—you are so fortunate that you are getting the presence of Gurudev! It was already noon by the time I finished all this.

After that, I went to a stream that was flowing near the peak, and I brought water from it in the bamboo sticks, and I bathed Gurudev's body. He appeared very calm and peaceful, as if he would wake up soon.

I brought some flowers from the jungle and placed them on his feet. Then I bowed before him with folded hands and prayed to Gurudev's body. "Only you are my Gurudev. Please bless me that I may be able to perform work according to your wishes." I stood up and placed Gurudev's body on the pyre. I took one last look, and then placed some more wood on his body. I created a spark by rubbing two bamboos vigorously and lit some grass, and with that grass I lit the pyre. I had to work hard to create the spark;

it was as if the fire also didn't want to light today and was afraid of the sunset. Gurudev had commanded that his body should be cremated before sunset. Then the sun started setting and the wind started to blow before the sun set, and the act of lighting the pyre was performed. The pyre was burning, and my Gurudev's body was being dissolved into the five basic elements. I bowed before the sun and got Gurudev's darshan in the sun. He appeared to be very happy and seemed very calm and peaceful.

Slowly, it started getting dark, and I sat there for some time, and then I went into deep meditation before I could realize it. I had the string of beads given to me by Gurudev, in which there were two beads of rudraksh and two crystal beads. Now that rosary was my support.

According to his wishes, I cremated him on that same flat slab of stone where his Guru's cremation had also taken place. The whole night passed, and next morning again I went down to the stream near the peak and bathed there for a long time. Now I didn't have to go anywhere and didn't even have to go to anyone. I was getting thoughts that this body is like an inn, in which the soul arrives to spend some time, and later returns home; and the soul that returns home after achieving completion remains happy because it isn't afraid of death. It feels happy with death, now that the soul is getting the chance to go home. Even now I could experience Gurudev's presence in the surrounding atmosphere. It is said that the soul remains present in the atmosphere for three days after death occurs. It takes the soul three days to come out of the environment of the body. That's why I felt now as if he was lying near me. I could feel his presence there. I bathed for a long time, and then, when the sun rose, I cupped my palms and offered water to the sun, and I prayed for my Gurudev's soul that it should easily move forward on the path to liberation. Then I came out of the stream, I had a creeper around my waist, and I removed that, too.

I also removed the two leaves that were attached to the rope-like creeper. They had also withered in the last two to three days. I used to wear them in place of clothes. I wore the string of rudraksh and crystal beads that Gurudev had gifted me, and then I sat naked on the bank of the stream and meditated. Now everything felt very light. While caring for Gurudev's body I had neglected my own body. My toe had healed by now, but it was still a little swollen. Again, I sat down to meditate, and the same questions arose in my mind: Why did Gurudev address me as 'Gurudev', and Who am I? These questions were arising again and again. I prayed to Gurudev that he had created this puzzle by bowing before me with folded hands, and he should do me the favour of solving it, and I felt as if Gurudev was guiding me and explaining to me that I was born as an ordinary human being. Therefore, there was no difference between me and an ordinary individual. Then I came in the presence of Gurudev, and in my Gurudev's presence I experienced the collectivity of several souls who were awakened souls, and in the proximity of the collectivity of those awakened souls my soul also received the inspiration to awaken. And when my soul also awakened, I realized that my Gurudev was not only an individual but an ordinary-looking individual in whom an extraordinary energy of a collectivity of souls was hidden. This energy is hidden, and therefore it can't be seen; it can only be experienced, but it can't be displayed.

This energy can only be experienced depending on one's belief in Him. Seeing is a physical, bodily feeling and believing is a feeling of the soul. But this believing should take place only through a pure and clear emotion. The body is not required to believe—this means that one should not believe it at the physical level, otherwise that depth won't be present.

Believing occurs between one soul and another soul, and only then can one experience the collectivity that is present with the soul. The soul is alone, but Paramatma is a vast assemblage, and the soul that connects with such a vast assemblage doesn't have any separate feeling of its own. This is only possible when it becomes free from the physical feeling. After this happens, Paramatma is reflected through the medium of that soul, and Paramatma can be experienced in the presence of that one soul. That's why such pure souls have been called 'Guru'—a Guru who is beyond the physical body, who is in the body and yet not in it. He himself can't perform any physical activity, nor does he have any identity of his own. He has merged into Paramatma, and Paramatma keeps giving indications through him as a medium. He becomes the medium of Paramatma. Paramatma always keeps manifesting on earth through such mediums. We can't understand the meaning of his activities because the activity takes place at his level, and the influence of what is going to happen is present in that activity. Those mediums always keep on giving indications about the future, and that is why 'Guru' is an element. It would be a pretence to believe that the physical body, which has lost its identity completely, is a physical body.

'Guru' is not a physical body. It is a large collective energy of souls, which is called the Guru-element. These physical bodies have merged so much in collectivity that, with every breath that they take, the collective energy can be experienced. My Gurudev was also the same. Whatever different activities he performed appeared to be different; but they were not separate activities. If one looked at the physical level, they appeared to be different, they appeared to be separate. But if one experienced them within oneself, these activities were not separate, and neither were the interactions that took place through the body. They looked separate, but only one work was being experienced from within—he was sending out a flow of consciousness. Or one can instead say that consciousness was always flowing through his body. But this consciousness could only be experienced by the soul and not through the body, because soul consciousness can only be experienced through the soul. Whether Gurudev was observing silence or whether he was speaking, whether he was scolding someone or praising someone, even if he only blinked, the flow of consciousness would begin. consciousness was present when he walked, it was present when he sat down, and it was present when he slept. Even his smallest activity was filled with consciousness. If he just moved his hand casually, a flood of consciousness would be experienced as something would start awakening just with the casual wave of his hand. One can't explain this awakening, but it seemed as if the sun was rising within oneself; dharma was being awakened.

Then, due to this, one's soul would start blooming in his presence. My soul loved his proximity and never wished to move away from him. It loved being close to him, and my body couldn't understand the reason for it. But in spite of that, it used to stay in his presence. All this happened because Gurudev's body didn't have any existence, and the whole body had become a medium for universal consciousness. For the same reason the body didn't have any activity of its own, and everything was happening through the consciousness. Every activity was pleasing because of that, and when he abused me, it seemed as if nectar was being showered. Therefore, whenever he shouted at someone, one felt like listening to it continually. Paramatma's supremacy was always present over his body, and this is only possible when one loses his identity over his body. Let alone the presence of such a body, even if one gets a darshan of such a body, his soul will receive so much energy from it that it'll be able to find the path to liberation. Such an event can happen just with one glimpse, and only pious souls can get such vision, only pious souls can come before him. That's why one should always experience a Guru; then that experience will always be the same.

There will be only one spiritual experience—that the flow of Paramatma's consciousness is always continuous. I got the proximity of such a Guru in my life, and he started the flow within me and asked me to entrust you with this flow of the Guru-element. I preserved that Guru-element in the remaining part of my life for you, and later I made it flow through you. The Guru-element is a stream; I bowed with folded hands before that flow and addressed that flow of Guru-element as 'Gurudev.' When it was present within me, it wasn't visible to me, but when it was present in my Gurudev's physical body, I could get its darshan. And then when I poured it into your physical body, it was visible to me. I got a vision of my Gurudev in your body, and I bowed before him with folded hands. That act of bowing indicates that the relationship at the physical level has ended and now meditation has also ended.

Now I understood why I was so attracted to my Gurudev's physical body. This was because I could experience the same stream of consciousness that was flowing through him. Now I realized why I used to like every act of his, why I kept hovering around him like a wasp. It was because I could get Paramatma's fragrance from him, and that fragrance can also be described. Sometimes, it seemed like the scent of sandalwood, and sometimes it seemed like the fragrance of a rose; and sometimes it seemed like a mixture of both the fragrances. Sometimes, it seemed that this wasn't an earthly fragrance at all.

This is not a created fragrance; this is Paramatma's fragrance, and the soul is filled with joy on acquiring it. This fragrance can only be understood through spiritual experience.

Now Gurudev has poured this fragrance into me; otherwise, how can I experience this fragrance that is within me now? This fragrance can only be experienced when some soul obtains it. Then the desire to meet those souls who would acquire this fragrance was awakened. It is true that no matter how much of a prasad one has, it is always meant to be distributed, and it can be distributed only when someone is present to accept it. There may be many gifts, but if no one is present to accept them, then to whom will you distribute them and who will accept it? If no one will accept it, then how will you distribute it? Thus, Gurudev had thrown me into a whirlpool where collectivity was necessary. He had given me gifts for distribution but no one else was present in this place, which meant that Guru-karya could never be carried out on this deserted island. This meant that the work of distribution couldn't take place on this island, on the banks of this river Brahmaputra. Now I would have to leave this place—but how could I? Gurudev had said I shouldn't try to leave this place as it would happen automatically at the right time. I got up and went into the jungle. I searched for a fresh creeper and tied it around my waist like a rope. Then I took two banana leaves and bent them to make a loincloth and tied them tightly around me.

Then I went and sat near that stone platform. I could still experience Gurudev's presence there. It was evening, and I bowed before Gurudev. There was a hollow place on the slope between three stones, and I decided to sleep there.

It was quite cold throughout the night, and so I couldn't sleep. Next morning, I again went to the stream. This stream was flowing down from quite a height, and as a result it was flowing very fast, and the water was also quite cold and very clear. I bathed very leisurely as there was no work left for me now. I didn't have to go anywhere, nor was anyone waiting for me. After my bath, I looked around for a creeper and tied it tightly around my waist. Then I took two pieces of long banana leaves and wore them like a loincloth. This was my clothing now, and after some time I went near Gurudev's pyre and started meditating. As I meditated, I experienced Gurudev's energy. He was saying, "According to the tradition of our Indian culture, people have been working for everlasting peace. Every saint and mahatma has contributed to the quest for it and obtained 'inner knowledge' while searching for this 'inner peace.' After obtaining inner knowledge, they enquired about what man should do and what he shouldn't do and, based on this, based on his inner knowledge, they prepared some rules and karma for man's way of living. They developed the karma that should be performed, and decided which karma shouldn't be performed.

"The experiences of karma that had to be performed through them were explained to them, and they were given the name of holy karma and good karma, and the bad karma was called a sin. In this way, the karma was divided, and sins and the soul were considered separate from these.

"A soul that performs good karma is known as a holy soul. This soul possesses a storehouse of good karma. Similarly, a soul having a storehouse of bad karma became a bad or sinful soul. This means that the soul was called a pious soul or a sinful soul according to his karma, and then karma was given importance. Some religions or methods of worship were created due to the importance given to karma, and in the process, the existence of Paramatma was negated. If you performed good karma, you would get good rewards, and if you performed bad karma or sins you would get bad returns. Thus, the importance of Paramatma disappeared, and one's whole life was constructed based on one's karma. Karma was given so much importance that no one realized that some energy exists that performs the karma. Karma was considered to be everything. But the fact that there is an energy that helps one in performing one's work was forgotten; for several years, when the importance of karma was mentioned, all these rules and regulations stayed confined to books—'these are sacred karma and they have to be performed' became the rule; 'this is bad karma and should not be performed' became the rule—and man became entangled in these rules. So, if he desired liberation, he would have to obey all these rules.

"These rules formed the foundation for developing human society. Some new scriptures were also created on the basis of this 'warp and woof,' but Paramatma went further away. Then all the living knowledge that was based on spiritual experience, the knowledge due to which one could understand what should be done and what should not be done, that living knowledge was also lost, and the lifeless knowledge that was written in books got publicized in society. The main reason for this was that it was easy to read books, and one could read books and tell others about it.

"Reading books and listening to what was written, and then telling others about it—all these were physical acts that could be performed easily by any human being. Man is lazy by nature, and he quickly catches hold of whatever is easily available. That's why he caught hold of these books, and then scriptures were created on this basis; and those who performed the work of reading shastras were called shastris or scholars. All this was easy, therefore it spread easily, and people caught hold of the rules mentioned in scriptures. The scholars and pundits who were well-versed in these rules were respected in society. They were highly esteemed in society, and due to this reason, they departed from the living knowledge of spiritual experience. Now, because of the respect they received in society, they became arrogant. They were egoistic about their knowledge, about the scriptures, and about the lifeless knowledge. But knowledge can never be acquired from books. Inner knowledge is a spiritual experience that can only be acquired through the medium of a living Guru.

"The living knowledge of spiritual experience slowly started moving away from society. In reality, this knowledge was the true religion of mankind—what one should do and what one should not—this knowledge would come from within oneself.

This process of spiritual experience was difficult because no Satguru was present here in the form of a medium to help one to obtain spiritual experience. Satgurus used to go into the jungle and practice meditation, and they would acquire knowledge in that jungle. But after that, they didn't go into society at all, and therefore living knowledge based on spiritual experience wasn't spread. It remained hidden in the jungle, and this was the most important reason for it. If such Satgurus had come into society, then after seeing them, man would have been influenced even more in this direction in their presence. But this didn't happen.

"The second reason was that this was the path of devoted spiritual practice, that is, it was necessary to do penance for twelve years in order to obtain the experience of inner knowledge. This was a path that was superior but also difficult, and whatever is superior is rare. Just as we see that one can easily find crows in large numbers, but peacocks are rare and can't even be easily seen, something similar happened there, too. The experiences of the great sages and their preaching were based on spiritual experience. People ignored that spiritual experience and caught hold of the preaching and experience; and various religions started to establish themselves based on their preaching. Then the entire religion was confined only to books. Thus, religion became devoid of spiritual experience. Books are lifeless; they can never give the experience of living knowledge.

"Books can only give knowledge about events that have happened in the past. Therefore, we can only obtain information from lifeless books and not the spiritual experience of inner knowledge. This is similar to seeing a cow's picture in a book and getting information about a cow—about its colour, that a cow has four legs, that it has two horns, a tail, that the cow gives milk and that the milk tastes sweet. We can obtain all this information through a book, but we won't be able to drink the milk. If we wish to taste the milk, then we'll have to go to a living cow as the cow in the book can't give us milk.

"Similarly, one can never obtain the spiritual experience of inner knowledge through books. But these books contain a description of the Satgurus that can give a spiritual experience, and a Satguru can be recognized through this bookish knowledge. A desire to meet the Satguru can also be created after reading these books. Thus, one can get information about a Satguru, and this is what actually happens. Lifeless books can only give information, and this information is of the past; spiritual experience is of the present time, and there is a vast difference between the two. One is the truth and the other is only a shadow of that truth. One can get an idea and shape of truth through the shadow, but one can't obtain the truth. Human society held on to these books and scriptures because it was easy but forgot about the 'Eminent Sages' who had created these scriptures.

"The result was that man used this bookish knowledge according to his needs and for personal selfish reasons. Then these books started being used to establish one's supremacy. Books are lifeless. Man can use them both positively or negatively according to his desires, just as a knife can be used for a good act and also for a bad act as it is lifeless. Books are similarly lifeless, and their knowledge can be used for a good or a bad purpose. Once inner knowledge based on spiritual experience moved away from mankind, the inner peace was also gone. Then man started searching for inner peace and the basis through which he could acquire it. The medium for inner peace, which is the Satguru, was beyond his reach. Therefore, he started depending on the lifeless support of books. He started to search for inner peace. Thus, after moving in the wrong direction, he also moved away from the living knowledge of spiritual experience. He caught hold of the wrong direction, and so a double ditch was created between human society and living knowledge, which has never been bridged. The experience of inner knowledge through which the saints and mahatmas preached has remained imaginary and only in the present. A great divide has been created over the years between that inner knowledge and society, and spirituality is coming to an end due to this. One will have to cross that ditch in order to revive spirituality, and this work isn't possible in a short span of time.

"This is going to take quite a long time. But one can at least make an effort towards it. This effort may not bring about a great revolution, but it can at least lay the foundation-stone for that revolution. Someone will have to act as the stone for that foundation, and I want you to undertake this work. I couldn't do it, despite my desire to do so, as my life was coming to an end. Every Guru wishes that his disciple should complete his unfinished work, and this Guru-dakshina in the real sense. It is my desire that you should go into society and preach about the living knowledge. It is possible that people will find what you tell them to be new or even strange, but they can at least get the spiritual experience of this living knowledge; they can at least observe it. Someone will have to make a beginning!

"It's easy to live here in the jungle and think about transforming society, but you'll have to go into society to bring about a change. One can't obtain coal without going to a coal mine. If you wish to wipe out the ignorance from society, you'll have to go into human society. Destiny has a pre-determined time for every work that needs to be completed, and the work can't happen until that time arrives. Now, after 800 years of devoted spiritual practice, the time has arrived to descend into the field of karma for (another) 800 years. Now the time has arrived to begin this great work. At present, all the management of religions is based on books. All knowledge about good deeds and sins is based only on books.

"Religions are based on scriptures, and books have become scriptures. It is the scriptures that define good deeds and bad deeds. But books are lifeless; they can describe what is meant by good deeds and sinful deeds. However, they can neither inspire people to perform good deeds nor give energy for that purpose; they can't establish any regulation by which sins can be prevented from being performed. Thus, just giving information about good deeds and sins is incomplete knowledge. Total and complete knowledge is one in which good deeds happen at your hands and sins are not committed at all. But this type of regulation is not present in society, and that regulation is inner knowledge. Once the lamp of inner knowledge has been lit within man, then he'll begin to receive all knowledge from inside. However, inner knowledge can't be acquired without obtaining inner experience. After obtaining inner knowledge, one's inner religion or dharma is awakened. By this inner religion, we mean that knowledge about what karma should or shouldn't be done by man. After this inner religion has been awakened, man acquires inner happiness; after obtaining inner happiness, he'll obtain inner satisfaction; and after obtaining inner satisfaction, man obtains inner peace. This is the peace for which man has taken birth, and no other desire remains after achieving it.

"After obtaining inner peace, man automatically reaches a state of inner liberation. This is the state where man's own identity and existence come to an end. After reaching this state, he merges with Paramatma. A maanav is transformed into a mahamanav. After this soul merges into Paramatma, man exists only as a medium of Paramatma's boundless energies. By medium, we mean a person who has a physical body and yet has no existence. He is only a medium, and Paramatma manifests through him because he doesn't have any physical identity. One experiences Paramatma in the form of consciousness in his presence. What is special about this spiritual experience is that it always happens at the soul level. Therefore, it can only be experienced and is not visible at the physical level. The creation of such a medium that has lost his existence but continues to interact at the physical level is a very difficult problem, because one who has reached the state of being a medium can't even blink with his eyes, so how will he go into society and explain everything to the people? It isn't possible for him to live in society and explain it because he had left society and reached the jungle before obtaining the state of a medium. Thus, it just wasn't possible for him to go into society after reaching that level. He'll be cut off from society. This means that those who attain this spiritual experience are no longer in a state to tell anyone about anything.

"Those who are living in society and giving information are doing so without any spiritual experience, and only on the basis of books. The basis of books is lifeless; one can talk at that level but one can't make someone else experience it. Books can't give spiritual experiences to anyone as they are lifeless.

"The problem before the Guru-energies of the past 800 years was how to convey this water in the form of consciousness to society. This was because whenever it was poured into some medium, that container would start to overflow. This meant that, even after the container was filled with consciousness, it couldn't be taken from one place to another. That's why now the container is kept in society, and then consciousness has been poured into it separately. This means that a medium whose vessel is very large has been chosen, and consciousness has been poured into it in collectivity. You are therefore only a large container; you aren't Paramatma's consciousness. Always remember that.

"You are the consciousness for society, as the consciousness has reached society through you as a medium. But for you, Paramatma, who has filled you with consciousness, is everything.

Therefore, you are the medium with one container, which contains the consciousness of several Gurus. Don't spend time staying here and absorbing consciousness, because if you stay here and acquire consciousness, you won't be capable of leaving from here, and then your condition will be similar to mine. Go into society and perform the duty of acting as a bridge between the devotee and Paramatma. Without the bridge, Paramatma can't reach his devotee, and neither can the devotee reach Paramatma. Both can look at each other but can't touch each other. Therefore, don't sit here and merge into Paramatma, because if that happens, then the one who is supposed to go will not exist anymore. So, who will go into society?

"Don't become Paramatma; become Paramatma's bridge so that Paramatma can reach his devotees through you as a medium. It's very easy to eat sweets, but it's very difficult to remain hungry yourself and feed others with sweets. But you have only been born to perform this difficult task; and your only goal is to perform this work. Recognize the purpose of your life and perform work according to your life's purpose. Convey spiritual experiences to people in society; this will awaken their inner religion, and they'll acquire inner knowledge. It's possible that this work may prove to be new and difficult, but a beginning will have to be made. You'll have to face great difficulties; you'll have to explain it to people whose minds have become dull. You'll have to awaken man's understanding. You'll have to wake up people, and society doesn't like the person who awakens people because he shakes everyone up. That's why people won't like you. It's possible that there is a delay in obtaining results, but you'll definitely get them. My dear! The farmer sows the same seeds in his field, but the seeds that go deeper stay pressed down. They take longer to grow but they'll definitely grow. Similarly, everyone will acquire spiritual experience, but everything depends on how deeply ignorant the person who stands in front of you is. Everything depends on that. But this is not your area of work. Your concern is not to see how deeply the seed is embedded. Your concern is to sow the seed. You just perform your work and don't pay attention to other things.

"A huge container was required to take this water in the form of consciousness, and you are that container. You have an eternal energy of 'giving' within yourself, and you have spent 800 years in developing and increasing that capacity. Therefore, you shouldn't reduce your capacity to give, even if you feel that the person before you isn't absorbing it. Keep on giving, as 'giving' is your work, and accepting it is his work. He'll accept it if he wants to and won't if he doesn't want to. That is not your area of work. You just carry on with your work. The receiver's job is to preserve the consciousness, and you just maintain your part of giving. That's why I say that your container is very big."

I suddenly remembered my previous Gurus. All these Gurus appear different in shape, size and colour of their bodies. But that is only their external covering. All the Guru-element is the same from within. Therefore, we shouldn't look at these Gurus as we can be confused by looking. We'll start looking for what is different in them and then we won't be able to see what is similar in them. What is common in all of them is Paramatma, who keeps flowing equally through all of them. Our attention should always be on that flow, and one's attention can remain on it only through the soul. One's attention can only rest at the physical level through one's body. That's why it is said that the Guru is not a physical body; you should neither think of him as a physical body nor see him as one.

Although they appear different externally, they are the same from within. That's why they all say the same thing. Secondly, it seems as if all these Gurus are taking me in the same direction and all of them are aware of what that direction is. I'm the only one who doesn't know it. Every Guru that has come into my life has held my hand. He has taken me on his lap and carried me in a determined direction. He has walked with me to a determined place, and then handed me over to someone else. Thus, I'm like a boat that is moving forward in a determined direction; it is moving in a determined time, at a determined speed. It is moving in a determined direction, but from time to time the navigator changes. It seems like that, but actually all the navigators are one and the same.

I don't know what that direction is; I, too, have given up and allowed my boat to move in that direction, thinking that no matter how big the river is, it will finally reach the sea. Similarly, it doesn't matter which direction I follow, as going there is my work; but the final goal is Paramatma. What difference does it make which path one follows? Now I have surrendered everything to Him, and I'll allow whatever happens to take place and look at what is happening from a distance. I won't be static and be attached to any place, nor will I stay in any one place. I'll keep on flowing, and just be swept along in the flow that goes to the ocean.

I stayed sitting there and didn't even realize that darkness had fallen. By now, it was quite dark, and all the birds had returned to their homes, and the sun had also set. Again, I slept between the three stones and spent the night there. It was quite windy even at night, but it was very pleasant there in the moonlight, and also very peaceful. Sometimes the cry of some animal would disturb the silence. I couldn't sleep because of the cold, and the stones on which I was sleeping had also become very cold. But I was aware of some change taking place inside. I can't explain what that change was, but something was happening from within.

Early next morning, I started to meditate, and today again I made contact with my Gurudev's consciousness. Gurudev was telling me about his experience. He said, "When man acquires a human body, he confines himself to a small physical body. That small body has a small boundary, and he has to exist within that boundary and get to know everything—through touch, through sight, and through his ears by listening to sounds. Thus, he requires physical proof to understand each fact, and he asks for evidence of every fact; he can't understand it without proof. This means that the medium to understand the physical body is its proof. He'll come to understand it and accept it only if the proof is present. Outside the limit of the physical body is the vast boundary of the soul, and one attains spiritual experience through it. There's no proof of this because one experiences every fact, and spiritual experience can neither be seen nor shown; it can only be experienced.

"When that spiritual experience of the soul takes place in the physical body, it happens in the form of subtle waves and pulsations. But it is so subtle that it can't be seen, and those waves of consciousness are experienced only by the body. Secondly, the soul starts having control over the body, and as a result, whether the body desires it or not, whether the body is attracted or not, the soul is attracted towards Paramatma.

"Whatever I have given you when I existed in my physical body has been given following the Guru's orders. I hadn't known you for long, and there wasn't any need to know more, either. It was my Guru's wish, he asked me to give you knowledge, and therefore I gave it. But only after leaving the physical body have I realized why he asked me to give it to you. I got the opportunity to know you and understand you.

"First, the knowledge that you acquired; to acquire that knowledge was the purpose of your life, because your soul has been taking births for the past 800 years only for this purpose. Over these 800 years, the soul came in contact with other souls and gave them the assurance that, when I find inner knowledge, I'll show you the path to obtain it, too. Now, in this birth, all those souls are going to get connected to you, and this physical body of yours is going to be the medium for fulfilling the desire of millions of souls. You are the medium for millions of people, and that's why your container is very large. Millions of souls are going to partake of that nectar of inner knowledge, and all your past births are also clearly visible. It's very difficult to have the same wish for so many years in so many births, and to take a birth with only one wish.

"The direction keeps changing due to the karma in each birth, but in all these births you have followed only one direction. As a result, you have obtained inner knowledge, and for this reason this is your last birth. Now the purpose of your soul has ended, and your life is the end of an era for millions of souls. A spiritual balance has been created with your life, and that foundation will end with your life because the collective energy of pure souls will also come to an end, and the future path will be very difficult.

"You have the power of the desire of millions of souls with you. The collectivity of millions of souls is clearly visible. Even after your life, this effect will continue for another 800 years, which means that your life is the mid-point between 1600 years. Just as the fragrance of sandalwood remains for a long time after the wood has been completely used up, similarly, even after your life, your fragrance will be experienced for 800 years. The light of the karma you have performed will guide future generations. You have the collectivity of mind power with you, and you can accomplish whatever you wish. Whatever you pray for will bear fruit. You are Paramatma's pure medium, and Paramatma will manifest through you and can be experienced through you. But a proper spiritual level of the soul will be needed to reach the medium of Paramatma. The soul also can't reach you until it reaches a high state. The souls who can get the opportunity to perform work with you, who get the opportunity to be in your presence, to know you and to understand you, will be really blessed.

"Those souls will be fortunate to be present in their physical bodies and to accept you, because to accept is a feeling of the soul. Acceptance at the soul level is a great event, because while one exists at the physical level, the faults of the physical body definitely intrude; and the chitta of the soul, which is covered by the body, is always focused on the physical body and not on Paramatma. Those souls will be blessed souls who will be present in the physical body and still rise above it and reach the soul level; they'll recognize Paramatma within you and accept him. Acceptance is also connected to recognition, and recognition is not at the physical level but at the level of spiritual experience.

"Once the soul understands at the level of spiritual experience, it accepts it because acceptance is the purest feeling of the soul. The reward of recognition is acceptance, but this acceptance will be very difficult for souls that exist in the physical body. The soul will come to understand everything after giving up the body, but it's very difficult while being present in the physical body. Therefore, very few people will recognize you completely while you are present in the physical body. Your work will commence only after you give up your physical body, because the covering of the physical layer will come to an end. Everything will be clearly visible and clearly experienced. Therefore, don't expect all souls to recognize you in your lifetime and acquire inner knowledge. Your area of work will commence with your death, because then your physical body, which is the biggest barrier, will not remain.

"You are the flower that will give fragrance only after it withers. There's one more reason for that—the dormant energies that had been shut up in a collective form within the boundary of the physical body will be free after your death. My work also ended when I gave up my body, but it is different for you. Your work will begin only after you give up your body, because your work will happen through the medium of the soul and not through the medium of the body.

"Your body is a web of illusion, and the further one stays away from it the better. But work will also happen only through this illusory web. Otherwise, the crowds of people won't allow it to perform the work. The body has to be free to perform work. You should therefore thank your body that its web of illusion, the web of delusion, has kept you free, and the body can perform work through it. Sunrise will take place after this illusory web is removed, and then everything will be clear. Therefore, as long as you exist in the physical body, you are covered with a layer of the deluding web; and a soul is covered with the physical body, which is its personal covering. Thus, it's difficult to recognize you under the double covering layers. It will be possible to accept you only when one of these covering layers breaks away, i.e., after a man dies, he'll be able to recognize you, or he'll recognize you when you give up your physical body. This process appears to be difficult while both physical bodies are present. That's why I'm telling you that your work will commence only after your death.

"Now the feeling of my physical body, too, has ended completely, and that's why I have been able to recognize you completely today. I'm blessed to be cremated at your hands. Now it is my wish that my bones should be discharged into the river Brahmaputra. I was very attached to this river Brahmaputra as I have lived near it for so many years. Now just discharge my bones, but I'll always remain with you in the form of energies. You have taken up my work, and therefore my energies are firmly behind the work. I'm with you in your work."

The sun was about to rise, and the redness before Sunrise had spread all over the sky; and Gurudev's soul was also moving towards liberation. It seemed to be waiting to get a vision of the sun. Then I went to the stream and bathed and changed my clothes of banana leaves. I picked four banana leaves and went up to Gurudev's pyre and saw that only bones remained there; all the ashes had been blown away by the strong winds. Then I realized why Gurudev had asked me to discharge only his bones in the river Brahmaputra, as only those remained. I collected the bones in the banana leaves and tied them into a big bundle. I lifted it, then bowed and started walking towards the hut. Now Gurudev was present with me in the form of his bones. I could descend very fast on this journey. I reached a stream in the evening and decided to spend the night there, and I stayed there.

I woke up next morning, and again started walking towards the river Brahmaputra. The sun had already risen by the time I reached the river. I bathed and meditated there and then offered the flowers (collected from the nearby jungles) to the bones. After that, I went up to the river and, with great reverence, discharged Gurudev's bones; then I walked towards my hut. Now I don't know why, but I suddenly realized that I was all alone.

Gurudev's bones had been with me all this time, and that was a support for me. Now that too, was no more. When I bowed to Gurudev, I felt as if Gurudev's soul was moving towards liberation like a white, cloud-like shape, and then, slowly, its existence ended. Now there was complete silence in the hut. There had been only Gurudev's presence in such a thick jungle, on such an isolated island. Now even that didn't exist anymore. I kept thinking about him; even when he maintained silence, when he couldn't be seen, or he was inside his hut, his presence could be felt everywhere, that someone is present. Now I kept feeling that I was alone everywhere. I couldn't sleep at night, and there was no relief during the day, either. It had turned into a very strange situation. There was desolation everywhere outside. I couldn't understand what to do. I passed the night somehow, and then again sat for meditation in the morning. The desolation outside helped me to prepare a stable atmosphere to stay inside. Now I started experiencing joy in meditation. The advantage of meditation was that, although there was a sorrowful feeling in the atmosphere, it was not experienced when I turned inwards.

Soon, I started feeling better inside. I could feel activities happening in the body during meditation; I could feel the control of my breathing, and I became aware of what I should and shouldn't do with inner knowledge. I wouldn't only get knowledge of this, but energy like that began to be created. Two types of events occur through meditation—first of all, the bad energy, which has been created around the body through bad thoughts, stops; and then, slowly, the bad energy that has collected also ends.

The second influence is that, after all the bad energy ends, good, pure and positive energy is created. Then, slowly, that positive and good energy is collected and creates an aura of good energy around our body. After the aura is created, one doesn't get negative thoughts. The body may stay in any place; it may stay in a bad collectivity or at a place that has bad, polluted energy, but the effect of that place can't reach us. In this way, man is always safe from bad influences. Thus, inner knowledge doesn't only give us knowledge of good and bad karma, but it also saves us from bad deeds. In reality, one requires energy to perform any deed. When bad energy isn't present around a person, how can bad deeds take place? Meditation is the only path to save oneself from bad deeds. But how will this path reach mankind? I have acquired this knowledge, but how will it reach all humanity?

This was the question before me now. I can't convey this knowledge to all humanity just by wishing it, but even if I can convey it to some humans, I will get an inner happiness that I could at least give it to some people. Then I bowed before the Guru-elements and said, "I surrender myself completely before you. Please get this work of spreading inner knowledge done through me and give the knowledge to those blessed souls who wish to receive it and to whom you wish to give it." I prayed in this way and then experienced a lot of inner peace. First of all, the thought that 'I' had to perform the work ended.

Then the feeling that the work would happen when he wished for it saved me from the sense of urgency to perform it. Therefore, this made it easy for me to merge in the surrounding atmosphere. I thought that so many laws have been made to reform man; that these laws have been formulated by man, and man himself breaks them, and then he searches for ways to save himself from them. Thus, laws that have been made by man are not effective in improving him. Man can't change as long as he doesn't want to reform himself, and man will improve on his own when he submits to his soul; and he'll be submissive when his soul becomes strong. The soul can become strong when it acquires inner knowledge. I realized that all paths to peace and happiness come to an end at inner knowledge. I understood that this inner knowledge would have to reach every human being; it should at least reach those human beings who have a pure desire to obtain it.

I started praying for this every day, and at that time I found a lot of support through prayers. When you have the desire to do something for others, and don't have suitable tools to do so, then at such a time the way to convey your good intentions to others is to pray. On one hand, it creates a path for you, and on the other it also bestows on you the satisfaction that you could do something. When one has a desire to do something and is unable to do so due to a lack of devoted spiritual practice, it creates a kind of quest that gives rise to dissatisfaction, and this prayer saves man from that dissatisfaction. That's why prayer is the support for those who don't have any tools or support. Sometimes, a situation is created in life where there's no way out, and at that time, too, this act of praying balances you. Prayers give man inner peace and inner satisfaction. At this time in my life, too, prayers bestowed me with a lot of inner peace.

I was thinking that some people must have had a similar desire to mine in this jungle, and they actually did have the desire, but stopped at that point. They must not have been able to return to society, and as a result the knowledge couldn't reach humanity; or maybe the right time hasn't arrived as yet for human society to get this knowledge, because this doesn't always depend on a person's desire to give. It depends more on the receiver's desire because the receiver has a pure desire and can pull the energy. It's easy to receive, but giving seems difficult. It's easier to receive because one can reach that level just by wishing for it, wherever it's available. While giving, both the receiver's desire and the receiver's suitable state are necessary.

Man can prepare his own state for giving but he can't create a proper state for the receiver, as that state is the desire of his soul. Whether he accepts it or not depends on the receiver. For example, if someone abuses us, he can do so, but accepting that abuse or not accepting it depends on us. If we accept the abuse, it can create a disturbance; but if we don't accept, it nothing will happen. People abuse saints and mahatmas, but they don't accept the abuses. That's why realized people always remain happy.

Today, in the morning, I made up my mind to go and pick some lai leaves. I hadn't been there for several days. Now a lot of bushes had grown over the path, and I had to clear them to create a way. As it was several days since I had been there, I found that several lai leaves had grown bigger in size and turned yellow, and some had become extra-large. I picked some leaves, put them in banana leaves and tied them into bundles. Then, after preparing such bundles, I carried them and returned to the hut. Then I put those leaves in pieces of bamboo, added bay leaves to them, and cooked and ate them. Now I started to enjoy this food. There wasn't much choice in this place, and I ate whatever was available. Then I slept at night. I had been walking throughout the day and fell asleep immediately. The next day, when I woke up, I don't know why, but I felt that Gurudev was present in the hut. I felt that it was an illusion. Actually, he was not present at all. I used to think about him a lot because I was aware of signs of his presence at every place.

Today, I decided to clean Gurudev's hut. I cleaned the hut and then bowed before Gurudev's bed, and suddenly remembered the last time I had picked the lai leaves, and how I had bowed before him. I had said to him, "Gurudev, I wish to bow before you," and he had nodded his head and given his assent, and I had bowed.

Then he had said, "You are calling me 'Gurudev!' Do you know the meaning of the word? There is a great meaning hidden in this one word.

"There are three main channels in the human body. One is on the left, which is the Chandra Nadi; Surya Nadi on the right, and the Madhya Nadi in the centre. Man is either in the right channel or the left channel, and both these channels are under the influence of the sun and the moon, and like night and day, man also stays in the Surya Nadi or Chandra Nadi. The Madhya Nadi relates to the present time, but man never stays in it. As a result of the influence of these channels, he stays at an extreme level, and nothing that is at an extreme level is good. When man remains in the right channel, he believes in Paramatma and wishes to attain him. Then he immediately desires liberation. This is an extreme state on the spiritual path. If one desires to reach Paramatma, then nothing will happen by going into the past; one will have to come to the present. An aura is formed with whatever work man performs, and as time passes, this aura starts moving away from man. In reality, all this happens in the form of energies, and is actually beyond man's reach. That aura can't be caught at all.

"For example, a Satguru arrived on this earth and gave some messages; he narrated his spiritual experiences, and Paramatma manifested on earth through him, because he was Paramatma's medium; later, he died, and people started thinking of him as Paramatma when he was not Paramatma, but a medium of Paramatma. Actually, Paramatma is not a person at all; Paramatma is an eternal energy, which is always present, and which keeps manifesting from time to time through different mediums.

"The medium through which it manifests is only a medium; he is not Paramatma. But the Satguru's energy goes up to such a high level that it reaches the 'Paramatma' level and merges into Paramatma. Then man considers the Satguru to be Paramatma and tries to catch hold of him; at that time, he was a medium, but isn't one now. And secondly, he is not Paramatma. It's essential to understand both these mysteries to progress spiritually. The first is that Paramatma is a universal eternal energy and not a human being, not someone in a human form. Secondly, he was a medium of the past and is not a medium of the present. That's why it's easy to catch hold of a medium of present time rather than a medium of the past. The one whom we accept as Paramatma was a Satguru of his time. As time passed, he became Paramatma (for people). Secondly, Paramatma is present at all times and will also be present in the present time. Now who is the Paramatma of present time? Who is his medium? One will have to remain in the present and only search for him in the present.

"When man goes into the sun channel, he'll immediately wish to attain Paramatma but not the medium. He will immediately wish to attain liberation, but not the state of liberation. The search for Paramatma in the past is a search in the wrong direction, because you wish to attain something that is beyond your grasp. Man has a short lifespan; how can he catch hold of the medium of Paramatma, who is thousands of years away in the past, in his (present) life?

"All these are very unbalanced factors. How can the person

who is not in the present go back into the past and catch hold of him? How can a person who can't catch hold of someone who is near, catch hold of the Paramatma who is thousands of years away? This means that attaining Paramatma itself is going the wrong way, because Paramatma doesn't possess any shape; one will only know the shape having caught him. If someone doesn't possess a shape at all, how will you catch him? If you can't catch him, it means that it isn't something one can catch. Therefore, this kind of running around is useless.

"Paramatma is an entity in whom one can have a belief, a feeling. You can't catch hold of energy through this feeling; you can make your existence void in energy through the help of feelings. Therefore, to lose your identity in universal energy is to attain Paramatma, and this attainment is a living process. This means that to believe in something, to have feelings, are all processes at the physical level, and without a physical body we won't be able to merge our identity in universal consciousness. Oh, my dear! First of all, you need to have the existence of a living physical body in order to dissolve it! Thus, it is obvious that all this can only happen while one is alive.

"This means that liberation is also not some object that can be given to you by someone, and which can be obtained by you from somewhere. Man will have to attain liberation by himself. Liberation is the state in which man becomes one with Paramatma in the form of universal consciousness, and he loses his own identity.

"One cannot obtain Paramatma in this way by going to an extreme level. One will have to remain in the present to obtain Paramatma and accept Paramatma through some medium of present time; he'll have to surrender his existence through the medium of the present. When one tries to catch hold of Paramatma of the past, then that also is an extreme level, and the other extreme is that they don't believe in Paramatma. They say that Paramatma doesn't exist at all; this is the second extreme state. This is a hyper-negative state. They catch hold of the other end (by being extreme) and believe that there is nothing like an entity named Paramatma or any energy. That is the second end of the spectrum. It doesn't make any difference to that energy whether you believe in Paramatma or not. Its state is the same in its interaction with you in both situations. Paramatma was present yesterday, is present today, and will remain present tomorrow, too. But we are present only today, and therefore we'll have to search for the medium of the present Paramatma. By the present medium we mean that individual of the present who has dissolved his identity in Paramatma, and Paramatma flows through the medium of that physical body. That medium is the Satguru. That's why, when we accept the Satguru completely, and when we bow before him by accepting him as a medium, we are not really bowing before him but before the energies that he has obtained from within. That's why we address the Satguru as Guru + Dev = Guru + Paramatma. To address him as Gurudev is like saying: I accept the medium of the present Paramatma; everything is included in the word 'Gurudev'.

"Man believes in the Paramatma of the past, whereas history indicates that the same form has never returned, which means that Paramatma also keeps on changing his form; he keeps changing mediums. The present form will be according to the present situation, and it will be according to the present situation because that medium is in the present. The characteristic of that present medium is that one can easily catch hold of him. Any person, because of being near and in the present, can easily be caught hold of, and faults are present in him because he is of the present, and not according to your imagination. He isn't according to your imagination and is therefore difficult to catch. One can easily catch the medium of the present time, but one can't believe in him, whereas the older medium can be accepted but can't be caught as he is outside one's reach. A middle path will have to be found out of this situation; one will have to remain in the centre and one will have to move forward and take both the characteristics along in order to stay in the middle (channel). The characteristic of the medium is that it is always in the present and therefore can be easily caught. So, catch hold of the medium. Secondly, forget about catching hold of Paramatma, and start believing in him. This means that to catch hold of the medium and to believe in him is the path to obtain Paramatma. I have done the same thing in my life. I considered my Gurudev as a medium of Paramatma and caught hold of him and believed in him, and this is the reason that I could obtain the state of liberation in my lifetime.

※

"This is my personal spiritual experience, and you may consider this spiritual experience as my teaching. Start accepting Paramatma through the medium of your Satguru. It is easy to accept the medium of a Satguru because the Satguru has obtained it and there is a large collectivity with him, and therefore this acceptance becomes easier. Paramatma is an eternal energy that is easy to obtain through its present medium, and it keeps changing its form according to the situation. That's why our attention should not be on its form. Paramatma always manifests through the medium. The medium of Paramatma itself is not created by Paramatma. A soul that has wiped out its existence while it is present in the physical body and has merged the existence of its physical body in Paramatma, such a soul becomes the medium of Paramatma, and one can reach Paramatma through such a soul. The path to reach such a pure soul is his physical body. If you catch the physical body in which that soul exists, then you'll be able to catch that soul.

That soul is hidden in that physical body, and because it is hidden it can be caught. After death, the arena of the soul is enlarged, and then it'll be difficult to catch it but will be easy to believe in it. Now, it is difficult to believe, but easy to catch hold of it. This is the reason why it's difficult to catch the pure soul while it exists in the physical body, and that's why we call the Satguru 'Gurudev,' which actually means catching the Satguru's physical body and accepting it as Paramatma. In reality, even the Satguru's physical body is not Paramatma.

"To believe any medium to be Paramatma is a feeling of our mind. You can believe anyone to be Paramatma. But if the medium whom we believe to be Paramatma is close to us, then it is easier to believe in him. That's why I accepted my Gurudev as Paramatma; and I accepted him knowing that he is an ordinary human being, but that the energies of Paramatma made his body a medium so that they could reach me. I received divine experiences through his medium, and that is why he became Paramatma for me, and I accepted him as Paramatma. In reality, there is only one Paramatma in this world, and he is spread out everywhere in the form of energy. But we are not able to recognize his all-encompassing form in our short lives; and for that reason, if we accept any one medium with unbounded feelings, then our inner journey commences, and we obtain inner knowledge.

"By inner knowledge we mean knowing oneself. A person who knows himself also recognizes Paramatma, because knowing oneself is possible only at the soul level. When you become a soul, you'll realize that 'I am a soul,' and this is my body that I have assumed, but I am not this body. Then all the attraction and desire for the body will come to an end; you will be separated from the body and attain the spiritual experience of being a soul, and you'll go beyond all the faults of the body. Thus, you'll be free of the illusory web of the physical body, and this freedom is liberation.

Man has to obtain this while he is alive, and you can obtain such a state of liberation when you surrender before a human being who has obtained such a state of liberation. Then you'll be able to obtain such a state of liberation in his presence.

"Paramatma keeps manifesting from time to time in different forms through human beings who have obtained soulfulness, and then dissolved their existence in Paramatma while existing in their physical bodies. Then nothing that is separate or their own remains; and as a result of the end of their existence they become Paramatma's mediums. Paramatma keeps on manifesting in a different way through them, and our soul is filled with joy just by getting their vision. The soul knows in whose presence it is standing. Paramatma keeps manifesting even through the speech of such a medium. What that medium is saying, the language he uses, and the subject he's talking about—all that doesn't matter at all. What matters is that he is speaking, and Paramatma is manifesting through the words of that medium. Then the soul gets control over the physical body, and even if the body wishes to leave that place, the soul won't allow it to move away. There is a great power even in the medium's name. Just through his name or mantra the energies in a person's body can be awakened; and the dormant energies in man's physical body start awakening. Several dormant energies are present in man's body, which lie dormant and hidden, and these energies begin to manifest.

"Then even an ordinary man starts performing extraordinary work; and all this is possible only when he merges his identity with that of the universe. By identity we mean existence of the body. It means to give up the existence of the body and go to the level of the soul, and when he exists at the soul level, he attains a very subtle level. The subtle energies that exist within the body are awakened only after one achieves this subtle level. There is a storehouse of positive energies within man's body, and man goes through his entire life with such a large storehouse. Man's life comes to an end, but he isn't even aware of this store of energies within him, and he's unaware because no Satguru who can awaken them has entered his life. This happens exactly like a lamp that is filled to the brim with oil—there's a wick in it, too, but there's no one to light the lamp. This lamp is man's body, the wick is the soul that is ready to be lit, but someone is required to light it; and the oil in the lamp represents the energies within man, which are useless until the wick has been lit. Until another lamp, which is already lit, doesn't come near it, it is of no use even though all the other factors are present. It's all useless in spite of everything being ready. There is darkness, and the lamp that is lying in such darkness keeps looking at the darkness around it. He keeps on searching and thinking—how far does that darkness extend? His attention is on searching through the darkness. He can only see darkness everywhere, and there's no light to be seen anywhere. It's not as if light isn't present! But he can't see it.

"He can't see the light because his attention is not on the light at all. He doesn't wish to search for the light at all. He's not aware at all that light is present in this world. When your chitta is not on the light, then what is being searched for is just the darkness; what one is looking for is only darkness. Your search itself is not for the light. Light exists but you are not able to find it because you don't wish to receive. You are searching for the darkness. You're trying to find out how far it extends. You're happy to see darkness at every place and are happy to think that there's darkness everywhere in the world, so how will you be able to see the light? If you want to be enlightened, then change your search. Don't look at how far the darkness stretches, because your whole life will be used up in that search, but the darkness will not end. If you wish to move from darkness towards light, then the light is right within you. You are the flow, the stream of light. First of all, go within yourself, express a desire to obtain the light within, and keep your attention on the light. Then, as a result of your inner desire for light, a lighted lamp will one day come near your lamp, and you'll feel that the lamp has come close to you. But what actually happens is that as a result of your inner desire for light, you yourself have entered a class of lighted lamps, and after going close to that lighted lamp, its wick will bump into your wick. Then that lamp won't light your lamp, but your lamp will get lit in its proximity.

"It is the basic nature of that lamp to burn. It can't light up any other lamp. But other lamps get lit automatically in its proximity. Your desire is above everything in this process because it is due to this desire that your chitta went to the light; and because your attention went to the light, it reached the light. The lighted lamp was burning; it was lighted right from the beginning. It didn't light up especially for us as it was already burning. It is we who got lit up in its proximity; and when our lamp is lit in the proximity of another lighted lamp, only then is the light visible all around our lamp.

"After one's own lamp has been lighted, one experiences light everywhere. This doesn't mean that the whole world has been lit up. If there is darkness in the whole world and there is brightness around you, then why should you bother about that dark world? So many lamps were lit and came into this world and then left; they, too, couldn't remove the darkness of this world because there are some that don't wish to remove the darkness at all. Therefore, you should never see in this life how far the darkness stretches. Just light your own lamp! If every lamp lights itself, then it's possible that all the darkness in this world may end. But if one desires to remove the darkness from this world, then a beginning will have to be made with one's own self, and it's impossible to light up the world, but it's easiest to light up oneself because the size of your lamp is smaller, and there's only a little oil in it. The oil isn't so much that it can light up the world; there's only enough oil to light up one's own self.

"Paramatma also wants the same thing, that every lamp should be lit and enlighten itself and remove the surrounding darkness. That's why Paramatma has created every lamp in a smaller size, and every lamp has to begin by lighting up itself. If every lamp fully lights up on its own, then it is possible that one day there may be a lot of brightness everywhere. But we'll have to start this process of lighting up on our own. That is why, first of all, the lamp must have a desire to light itself up, so that its attention will go towards the light. When it goes to the light, then it will reach the light, and one day it will enlighten itself.

"Man's size is also small, like this lamp. Man's energies are limited. Just as there is a limited amount of oil in a lamp and there is a wick in it, similarly, there is a soul within man, and around him there are negativities. These negativities are spread all over the world like darkness, and no one can remove them even if they want to. If we keep our attention on the faults of every person, then our whole life will come to an end, but the negativities of this world will not end. That's why we'll have to change the direction of our search. We'll have to search for the good qualities in the person before us and will always have to keep our chitta on them. Then, one day, the virtues within us will be awakened. First of all, we'll have to express a desire to light up ourselves, and only then will we be able to reach some enlightened Satguru. Then we'll be enlightened just by going in his presence. That Satguru will not enlighten us because he has gone beyond any action. But it has become his basic nature to enlighten. His proximity is so pure and holy that we get enlightened just by going near him.

"Similarly, one can't undertake self-realization, because this is a divine process, and no one can perform it. It happens automatically. This process happens on its own in the presence of a Self-Realized Satguru. This self-realization is attained due to your pure wish because, first of all, you express the desire, then your attention goes to it, and then you go into the presence of a Self-Realized Satguru, and just by being in his presence you attain self-realization. After achieving self-realization, the lamp of the soul is lit and in its light, there is brightness in all directions and the darkness is removed. If you want to remove the darkness around you, you'll have to enlighten yourself, and your lifespan is just long enough for you to enlighten yourself. Therefore, don't waste this short life in trying to find out how far the darkness stretches in this world. Just light your own lamp. Instead of improving himself, man tries to change the world. How can there be light in the world when there is darkness around him? He just can't do it. Similarly, one can't receive good qualities by looking at the bad qualities of the others, because our chitta is not on good qualities. We need to change the direction of our chitta, and everything will happen just by changing the direction.

"But first of all, we must have the desire to do so; desire is the first step. Always have the desire to enlighten yourself, and this is a wish that can only be completed in your lifetime. Don't have the wish to change the world; your life will come to an end in that process, but the world will not improve; it won't improve. Just light your own lamp.

"Millions of lamps come into this world with oil and wick and leave this world without being lit up because they don't find anyone to light them up. Don't be like those millions of lamps that couldn't get lit. If you are not enlightened, then Paramatma will also be unhappy. He has sent you to be enlightened; he had sent you with the wick and the oil. Paramatma gave you the blessings that he wanted to give. Paramatma gave everyone an equal opportunity to light up, but the desire to light up is your own. Paramatma can't put that desire into you. You'll have to create that yourself. Paramatma can do everything, but he can't make you have this desire. You yourself will have to express that desire. The purpose of this human life of yours is to be enlightened, and the shape of the lamp in the form of man's body is in the upward direction. Perhaps that is the reason why man's spine is straight, so that he can move the energies within himself in an upward direction. But in spite of man's structure being suitable, if he doesn't express a desire to be enlightened, then he spends his life just looking at the darkness.

"You must become a lamp that has the desire to be enlightened; a lamp, which has a large container, and is a lamp in which there is a large quantity of oil."

Now I just have to light up, I have to be enlightened; and I don't have to search for the lamps that will be enlightened through me. I just have to keep on burning. It is Gurudev's work to light lamps. He'll perform his work and send those who wish to be enlightened to me so that they can be lit, and until then I'll have to keep on burning. It is this duty to burn that Gurudev has entrusted to me. I'll keep on burning until my last breath and continue to perform the work that has been entrusted to me. Gurudev will send those who wish to be enlightened to me, and I just have to perform my work. Then I prayed to Gurudev, "Gurudev, please bless me that I may continue to burn all my life with the oil in the form of energies that you have poured into me."

I was alone on this island, but I never felt alone as I kept experiencing Gurudev's presence. He stayed on this island for so many years; once he arrived here, he never left. It was a very peaceful atmosphere. Several birds considered this place to be safe and had built nests here. Sometimes, during the rains, the low-lying areas would get flooded; but I never felt unsafe because of the peaceful conscious energy in the place, and neither did the birds and animals. All of us always stayed there very happily, and now the birds had become my friends. I used to talk to the trees. There were several varieties of birds and their different colours looked very attractive. The chicks would try to fly from tree to tree even when their parents were not there.

All the activities of nature went on—creation, then destruction, and then again creation. The wheel was moving properly on both sides, and I watched all this like a spectator. Today, when I went to the river for a bath, I was searching for a place to get down into the water from a large rock. I happened to see my reflection in the calm water, and I was startled, as I couldn't recognize myself. My face resembled that of some tribal jungle-man, my beard had grown long, and my hair had also grown. I hadn't combed my hair for a number of days, and it was now knotted. The hair in my beard had also become entangled. I hadn't seen myself for a long time. I felt that my soul had taken charge of the instrument that is my body, and I had brought that instrument to such a miserable state! I had brought to such misery the medium of the physical body through which I could reach Gurudev after so much toil and hard work!

My mind was filled with disgust; first, I asked my body for forgiveness: "I couldn't take care of you due to my involvement with other things. I wouldn't have been able to reach this place at all without you. I could only serve my Guru with your help. You are my companion, who wordlessly keeps on doing all the work and never complains about anything. I could obtain my Guru's gift only through your help, but now you'll have to help me in distributing this gift, because I have obtained it only for distribution. Both performing good deeds and helping to do them is one and the same. I'm going to perform the work of distributing my Guru's gift of inner knowledge, and I want you to help me in this work.

"Gurudev has said that the work will happen through this very body. This means that you, too, are going to get the opportunity to help in this great work. I'm invisible but you are visible; people can see you. You will be called the medium of my Guru-karya. People will know you and not me. You can easily be seen, but I'm not easily visible to everyone. Special eyes are required to see me. You have seen such highs and lows in my life, you have seen the changing circumstances; you have seen so many different 'Gurudevs' and you have taken me to so many different places and roamed there with me. You have never bothered about physical comforts and facilities and have always supported me even in the worst situations. You have grown so much, but I'm still the same.

"Gurudev says that your container is very big; that millions of people will be able to receive inner knowledge through your medium. Gurudev is telling me about taking this inner knowledge to the people, but it's you who will convey it to them and it's you whom they'll recognize and accept. People will take care of your comforts and facilities; they'll serve you because people will think that 'Guru' means a physical body. They'll garland you and decorate you and offer you gifts. They'll keep moving around you and listen to you because people will understand the language you speak. My language is 'silence,' and no one wishes to hear that language. My language can only be experienced; and how many people will be able to experience it! How many people have knowledge of it? Gurudev was telling me that my work would begin only after my death. That's good, because you won't have to perform much work; you'll get a lot of rest. Now you work hard, and I'll take rest; later on, I'll do all the work and give you a lot of rest. It's my duty to give you rest as you have suffered a lot.

"Pure and holy souls have always undergone a lot of suffering, and they have to do so. Sufferings and difficulties harden the body and strengthen it. All this suffering is to help one to form the habit of suffering for some big programme or for some great work; this is the beginning of some great work. You should consider yourself to be only a medium of Paramatma. Paramatma gets his work done through his energies; we are only the mediums. But that medium has to bear the pain of all the happiness that others are going to obtain. So, you have to bear all this hardship and pain. But this means that so many people are going to obtain happiness through your medium. This is a law of nature, and nothing can be done about it. Therefore, all the mediums in this spiritual field have been worshipped, but they have borne a lot of sorrow in their lifetime. You'll have to absorb the afflictions of other people, and only then will you be able to give happiness to others. The sicknesses of others will be cured through your medium, and therefore you'll have to absorb those sicknesses. This is the law of nature; nothing is destroyed, it is only transformed. The sicknesses of people will also be transformed in you, and you'll have to get ready for all this.

"My dear! Sandalwood paste gives fragrance to others, but in the process, it has to destroy itself. This is the destiny of the sandal paste, and your destiny is to wear yourself out for others. You are my final physical body, and after this I won't take on any other body. You have received the opportunity of being the final physical body. You'll stay here and I'll go away. Even after I go away, I'll be known through your medium; it is you who'll be recognized. Oh, my dear! A seed has to wipe out its existence in order to grow into a tree, and you, too, will have to wipe out your identity. You are the physical body that has been with me until my final journey. Everyone will reach you. There will be very few people to reach me, but these same few people will prepare a new path for liberation, on which the coming generations will complete their journey. It's easy to reach you, but very difficult to reach me. At the same time, it's not possible to reach me, either, without you. You are the gate to my path; you are the great gateway to liberation through which millions of souls are going to pass."

I then went into the river water and bathed for a long time. Today, there was no hurry to go anywhere, nor did I have to get to anyone. I don't know why, but now physical activities had slowed down, and a sort of pause had occurred within me. There was peace within me, and the universe suddenly seemed to become insignificant. I had started finding great meanings even in small incidents, as if I had obtained a great depth and was observing the whole atmosphere through that depth. I was observing everything very minutely. I could experience the consciousness that was spread around the surrounding atmosphere, and a kind of joy was arising within. I still couldn't understand whether I had really obtained something, or the surrounding atmosphere was making me experience it.

I could feel a lot of vibrations in the small, rounded stones lying around the river. These small stones had remained in the river for thousands of years, and while rolling around they had formed into a small shape. As a result of staying in the water in collectivity for thousands of years, they had developed a magnetic force within them. The first effect of consciousness is these magnetic waves, which pull our soul towards it. Then, whether the body desires it or not, the soul knowingly or unknowingly takes the body in that direction. The soul does this because though the physical body doesn't experience the consciousness, the soul does so immediately. consciousness is Paramatma's energy, and the soul recognizes this Paramatma's energy, and that is why it is attracted towards Paramatma's energy. Secondly, the soul's control happens over the body. Man is enamoured of the soul and comes under its control. Then, because it is controlled by the soul, it only performs the work that its soul desires. That's why the soul takes the body again and again near the consciousness. In the same way, the magnetic element was created in those small stones, and such stones are called "Shaligram." They are black in colour and have faint lines on them. These stones also have a small hole in the centre, and one can find gold in these holes.

There is a lot of conscious energy in these stones, and that's why some people place them in their puja room. They prepare a silver stand and place them on it. As a result of remaining in the water for thousands of years, these stones keep on rolling around; and in this way a kind of energy is created, and this can be experienced when one goes near them. These stones are placed in the puja room so that man can remain near them with the excuse of performing worship and can absorb good Radiant energy. consciousness can't be seen; it can only be experienced.

These stones are not very attractive to look at, but they appear to be different from other stones, and this difference is their consciousness. The activity of inhaling and exhaling becomes very controlled in their presence. My heart also experienced an inner peace.

These stones could be recognized by their vibrations, and if one went to the spot in the water where these stones were lying, the pulsations of the body increased; as soon as one went near those stones, one could feel vibrations in one's palms and soles of the feet. There are millions of pores in our bodies, but they are present in larger numbers in the palms of the hand and the soles of the feet. And this is the reason why man's hands and feet are so sensitive, and this is also the reason why the vibrations of these stones could immediately be felt. When a man's hands and feet absorb these vibrations and spread them throughout the body, and when the entire body becomes full of vibrations, then man starts feeling them on his sahasrara.

If these stones are held in one's hands, then the whole

body starts pulsating with those vibrations. Then I, too, started experiencing those vibrations on my sahasrara. I collected ten such stones and came out of the water, and then I tried out an experiment. I lay down on the sand near the river facing downwards. I didn't even wipe my body as I hadn't brought any leaves today for that; otherwise, I used to bring leaves from a special tree every day. I wiped my body with them after my bath, and the juice of those leaves would make my body very sensitive and pure. After lying down, I lifted one stone and placed it between my buttocks. I lifted another stone and placed it on the part behind my waist. Then I lifted the third stone and placed it on my spine at the place behind my navel. The fourth stone that I lifted I placed behind the heart chakra on the spine. I lifted the fifth stone and placed it at the spot where the neck begins. I took the sixth stone and placed it behind my head, and the seventh stone I placed close to my head on the sand. Later, I started experiencing the effect of the vibrations of those stones on my body. I slowly realized that vibrations were coming out of every stone, and every stone was vibrating in the place where it had been put. The vibrations coming out of those stones spread all over the body, and the effect of energy could slowly be felt from one stone to another stone, and a shiver passed through the body, which felt very cold but still felt very good.

I was experiencing a lot of joy, and I experienced something hot on my sahasrara that was coming from within, and after it came out, I could feel a cool wave of consciousness. The same wave that was coming out in the form of consciousness then entered the body from the muladhar chakra, and after passing through all the chakras it again came out of the sahasrara from the top of my head. Then again it would return through the muladhar chakra. It appeared as if a circle had been formed with the consciousness of nature.

Every day, after my bath, I used to tie a creeper around my waist like a string and tie two banana leaves to protect my private parts, but today I hadn't tied the leaves, and my whole body was free of any encumbrance. As a result, I could experience even the smallest sensation. We are told to wear fewer clothes, lighter clothes, cotton clothes during meditation, and the body should also not be bound in any way, so that we may experience even the minutest sensation. The clothes should not be bound, and they shouldn't be knotted anywhere because this knot can also be a hindrance for the consciousness. That's why the dhoti is not tied with a knot while meditating, and only wrapped around the body. The sensations that take place on the body are minute, and the body has to be free of encumbrances to experience them.

The entire aura expands when the body is free of encumbrances. Today, I was free of the bondage of clothes, and I could feel the vibrations of these stones very deeply, and in this I didn't realize that I had gone into deep meditation. Performing this experiment became a part of my daily routine.

One day, I carried out another experiment. From the stones I had brought (out of the river) I wanted to place one stone on the top of my head, but it wasn't staying there. Then I placed it on a leaf, and during meditation I placed it on my sahasrara and had a similar experience of consciousness flowing through my whole body. First of all, due to the weight of the stone on my crown, my chitta quickly stabilized on the sahasrara, and then I experienced a radiant energy all over my body.

This experiment seemed very good for those who have newly learned to meditate because the sadhak's attention will stabilize with the weight of the stone on his sahasrara. Then he'll automatically go into meditation, because during meditation practice a wandering chitta is a major problem, and the chitta wanders more towards the weaker link. For example, if a man is not satisfied at the sexual level, then his sexual desire will awaken when his chitta becomes subtle; if a person is not satisfied at the material level, then his attention will desire material things—I want this thing, I want that thing—such feelings will be awakened. If there is a feeling of guilt or disgust in the body, then the chitta will wander to the feeling that one should receive respect, one should receive praise. Thus the link that is weak when you are meditating will open, and your meditation will break at that point. That's why one should never do meditation with a weak link because that weak link proves to be fatal for us.

It has therefore been said that the first step to meditation is satisfaction. There can't be progress in meditation until one acquires total satisfaction. Man keeps swinging between satisfaction and dissatisfaction. Both these activities are equal in man, and therefore he cannot be completely satisfied. He'll be a completely satisfied person when he obtains the collectivity of completely satisfied people. Thus, complete satisfaction can also only be obtained in collectivity. If man is not satisfied, then dissatisfaction will be present; if dissatisfaction is present then his attention will go towards satisfaction; and he will get thoughts relating to his dissatisfaction. Then his chitta will keep wandering amongst those thoughts; and how can he get meditation when the chitta is not stable? Therefore, because satisfaction and dissatisfaction are present in equal parts, no man can do meditation. Meditation takes place in the collectivity of satisfied people.

Then the question that arises is: From where do you get a collectivity of satisfied people? We can get that collectivity at the Guru-charan. This is the place where a great collectivity of satisfied, contented souls is present. This is the place where one can connect oneself to the Guru's energies. Now there is going to be so much thought pollution in society that no individual will be able to meditate alone. At such a time the need for collective meditation will be apparent, and when this need is felt, then collective meditation will become necessary. When the need for collective meditation is experienced, then the tradition of inner knowledge, which a Guru used to pass on only to one disciple in his lifetime, will also have to be done at a collective level.

A collectivity of people who have attained inner knowledge can't be created without making the spiritual experience collective. When I understood the need of the hour, I started praying to my Gurus during meditation, "Gurudev, you wish, don't you, that the gift of this inner knowledge should reach each and every person? Then show me the way by which it can reach them! The ordinary man can't come to this island, this desolate island in the middle of this river Brahmaputra, and I can't leave from here. So, will the knowledge end with me in this place? Will I not be able to distribute my spiritual experience to others? Gurudev, my very purpose of obtaining inner knowledge was to distribute it to others. If that doesn't take place, then the purpose of my life is over; and if the purpose is over, why should I remain alive? Why didn't you allow me to burn on your pyre? Gurudev, I accept that some people are religious and believe in Paramatma and sincerely wish to attain Paramatma. But those who really wish to attain him have already attained his spiritual experience.

"Many people are atheists, they don't believe in Paramatma, but they've also been created by Paramatma, and they, too, have a portion of Paramatma within them. Gurudev, have pity on everyone. They are ignorant and are therefore non-believers. Give them good counsel and they, too, will realize through spiritual experience that the portion of Paramatma within them is the soul, and that soul will recognize Paramatma. The soul can never be religious or non-religious. Gurudev, please bless everyone, give the gift of spiritual experience to everyone, either through methods of worship or through presumptions. It's possible that some people may have been indifferent to methods of worship. But that would only be for some time as everything has been created by Paramatma and everything is related to Paramatma. Paramatma can give good counsel to everyone. Gurudev, I haven't seen Paramatma; and I neither know him nor wish to know him. You are my Paramatma and I have attained Paramatma through your medium. He may be Paramatma for you, but for me only you are Paramatma. That's why I'm telling you, a child will go first of all to its mother for its needs. Only you are my mother, only you have compassion for me; find some path, some way out of this, so that I can distribute the gift of your spiritual experience in my life. I won't even be able to die until this has been distributed, and I will neither be able to live, nor to die. I'll face such a strange situation.

"Will you like all this? You won't, right? Then find a way out. At present man is divided in the name of his race, in the name of religion, in the name of his country, his language, colour, intelligence, wealth and appearance.

"This divisible human society is alive, and because it is alive it can understand the living experience of consciousness. This spiritual experience of consciousness will be experienced by their souls, and all the souls will be awakened. Then they will give up all distinctions and become one in the name of one spiritual experience, and the whole universe will come together in the name of spiritual experiences. Then a beautiful and peaceful universe will be created where all will have equal opportunities, where a society devoid of wars will be created.

"Gurudev, I accept that this is a very big goal. It's possible that I won't be able to see it in my lifetime, but at least I can begin it in my lifetime. It's possible that I may not be able to reach the destination of such a beneficial universe in my life. But I will get the satisfaction that I went some distance towards such a destination. Awakening the soul is the only solution through which all truth will be experienced in the light of the soul. The sunrise of truth will take place, and the darkness of ignorance that has been spread will be removed. All these distinctions are only due to one reason—ignorance. When man attains self-realization, then ignorance will be automatically removed, and the whole universe will be a benevolent universe. All this can't happen without your blessings."

It had now become my daily routine to start with the spiritual practice that Gurudev had taught me. Every evening at sunset, I would start my spiritual practice by pouring water before the setting sun. Then I would keep on standing all night in the river and carry on with the spiritual practice until sunrise. I faced some difficulty for the first three days, and then I found a good place in the river.

Now the spiritual progress was regular. Starting this spiritual practice gave me an inner satisfaction that I was offering some service to this work. Due to standing for a long time in water the skin of my feet had become very soft, and I had to walk with great care as even small stones would prick my feet. I felt a lot of inner peace through this spiritual practice; I obtained satisfaction that I, too, was able to do something. I didn't know how successful or otherwise my spiritual practice was, but I got a lot of happiness out of it; and I knew that the tradition that has been going on for several years—that of passing consciousness from one to one—would have to be made public. However, this was not an easy task. The task was like conveying a river to the ocean. But I was practising devotedly, and I thought that if I was successful through the spiritual practice, then the entire human society would receive the inner knowledge of spiritual experience; and if it didn't happen, then I would have the satisfaction that I spent my life in performing good deeds. Even if I were to die while performing Guru-karya, then one couldn't have a better death. I thought both ways and felt that my decision was correct, and I continued with my spiritual practice.

I faced a lot of difficulty in my spiritual practice. The river water used to be very cold, and I would be very stiff when I came out of the water in the morning. I thought that my body may be troubled, but man would be so happy if I could convey the spiritual experiences to him! I would have to give up the comforts of my body to see the happiness in society. Even otherwise, what else would I do after obtaining the knowledge of spiritual experience? It would be much better if I could distribute it.

Every evening, when I left my home, I would meet all the trees, all the creepers, all the birds and especially their chicks, as I didn't know whether that night would be the final night of my life. Now I had become very emotional. The trees, stones and bushes on the way had also become my friends, and I would meet them as I went along. Every evening, I would stand in the river Brahmaputra and see the sunset. I would remember that scene. I would offer water to the sun and pray, and then I would turn my face towards the East and start the spiritual practice of meditation, which would only end at sunrise. The water would splash against me all night, and as the flow of water was very fast, there was a real danger of drowning in it. However, I never felt afraid; if I was washed away, then so be it, and if I drowned, then let me drown. What more had I to do now by staying alive? Now there was no attraction for life and there was only one goal—to convey inner knowledge to each and every human being. At that time, my model was Bhagirath Maharaj. I had heard that he had undergone a very severe penance in order to bring the river Ganga to the earth. I had accepted this great ascetic of Indian culture as my role model, and I, too, was performing penance.

It was my wish that this Ganga of inner knowledge should reach the most ordinary of ordinary men, and this had been going on from one person to another for several years. It was a great task for one man to convey it to millions of people, and it was a difficult task, too, because the hindrances of those millions of souls who were going to receive this benefit were creating a barrier in this work, and therefore problems were arising.

However, I had full faith in my Gurus. They had given me blessings for this sacred work, and my spiritual practice may not be suitable, but the energy of my Gurus' spiritual practice was definitely suitable. I had the energy of the spiritual practice of my several Gurus behind me, which was guiding me in this difficult spiritual practice. This was not my effort, as I was only a medium of several Gurus, and all the Guru-energies were making the medium perform the spiritual practice. They had shown me the path of how to perform this spiritual practice, and they were going to guide me on the future path. I had been made a medium through the efforts of several Gurus to reach several people, and I kept doing whatever they commanded me. I just kept praying continually to them, "Gurudev, they are ignorant children. They can't even pray. I am praying on their behalf, so please show them the path of truth. It shouldn't happen that your spiritual practice should stay limited to me when that was not the purpose of your spiritual practice. Your purpose was that the spiritual experience of self-realization should reach the ordinary man."

It will reach them too, but I will have to bear the difficulties on behalf of those souls. I was aware of that, but I didn't know how many more difficulties I would have to bear. I was just involved in spiritual practice. Every sunrise brought a new ray of hope for me. I was involved in spiritual practice in the proximity of my Gurudev. I, too, was experiencing why the efforts of the Sage Bhagirath are called 'Bhagirath Efforts'. While starting the spiritual practice, there must have been some feeling as to whether it would be completed or not. Thus, I was between the two ends of success and failure, but I couldn't see any other way out of it except to carry on with the spiritual practice. The 'I' sense was present; that is, somewhere there was a subtle feeling of 'I.'

As I continued with spiritual practice, I started getting my Guru's presence, and then only the spiritual practice remained, and the feeling of success or failure of that spiritual practice came to an end. This means that the feeling of 'I' ended. Even a seed can't sprout until it destroys itself. This is a natural process, but the secret of all regeneration is hidden in this one event. This is the cycle of nature, and everyone will have to cross this cycle. Now only the spiritual practice remained, but I didn't do it, either, since it happened on its own.

Now all my time was being spent in this meditative practice, and I didn't even realize it. I myself became immersed in the spiritual practice.

Today, as it was my daily practice, I came out of the river Brahmaputra after sunrise and went towards my hut on the mountain. This had become my daily path, and I didn't even realize when I reached the hut.

*To be continued...*

# Glossary

**Acharya**
Teacher

**Adhi-bhautik**
Untimely

**Adhi-daivik**
Supernatural

**Amavasya**
Moonless night

**Anubhuti**
Spiritual experience, perception, feeling, knowledge

**Arghya**
Pouring of water as an offering before the sun

**Asana, Aasan**
Seat, yogic posture, a small carpet/mat for sitting while worshipping, praying or meditating

**Atmalok**
Where souls reside

**Ashram**
Hermitage, monastery, a place where spiritual discipline is practised

**Ashwamedh Yagya**
Horse sacrifice Yagya; performed in the ancient times by kings. A sacrificial horse would be let loose after the fire ceremony, and the

territory he covered without being stopped would belong to that king. If any other king caught that horse, it would lead to war with the king who performed the Yagya.

**Assam**
Name of a north-Indian state

**Atma**
Soul

**Atma-dharma**
Inner-religion, religion of one's Soul

**Aatmic**
Of the Soul

**Ayurveda**
Ancient science of medicine (written in Sanskrit) in India

**Bhagirath**
An ancient king of the solar race (Suryavanshi) who, by his austere devotion, brought the river Ganga to earth from heaven; the river Ganga is also called the Bhagirathi. Therefore, 'Bhagirath prayatn' means effort or performance of a mammoth or Herculean task.

**Brahmanaad**
Celestial music

**Chaitanya**
Divine consciousness, radiant energy, vibrations

**Chandra Nadi**
Left (Moon) channel

**Chitta**
Inner-mind, attention, psyche, the lens of the mind.

**Chitta-shakti**
Power of Consciousness

**Dakshina**
donation, fee, honorarium.

**Darshan**
Divine audience, sight, glimpse, vision

**Dharma**
Religion, duty, attribute, nature, justice, righteousness, law, function

**Dhoti**
A garment for the lower body tied around the waist

**Dhyan**
Meditation

**Dronacharya**
Royal Guru of the five sons of King Pandu, an expert who taught archery especially to Arjuna, in the epic Mahabharata.

**Eklavya**
A poor tribal boy who wished to learn archery from Dronacharya and was refused by him; Eklavya then made a mud statue of Dronacharya and absorbed the knowledge and energy after connecting to him through the statue.

**Ghat**
Stairs or a passage leading down to a river; in this case landing area of river Ganga near Howrah Bridge

**Guru-charan**
Guru's feet

**Guru-dakshina**
Repaying the Guru for the knowledge received by offering either money or gifts or by offering one's services

**Gurudev**
Guru as God

**Guru-krupa**
Guru's grace

**Guru-sthan**
Guru's place

**Guru–Shishya parampara**
Guru–Disciple tradition

**Guru-tattva**
Guru's element

**Havan**
Fire ceremony, oblation

**Kabaddi**
An outdoor game played with two teams where each member takes turn to touch the member of the opposing team without being captured

**Karma**
Action, tasks

**Karya**
Work, deed, task

**Kashi**
The ancient name for the city of Benaras, now known as Varanasi in the state of Uttar Pradesh where people went to die because they believed that it would give them liberation

**Kutir**
A small cottage

**Lai**
Mustard leaves found in the jungle

**Lungi**
A long piece of cloth wrapped around the waist; a kind of loincloth worn by Indian men

**Madhya Nadi**
Central channel

**Mahamanav**
Superhuman being

**Mahatma**
Lofty-minded, high-minded sage or great soul

**Manas-putra**
According to scriptures, the son born by wish and not coition

**Manav**
Human being

**Mantra**
Incantation, a Vedic text or hymn

**Maya**
Illusion, delusion

**Moksha**
Salvation, liberation

**Muladhar Chakra**
The root chakra, situated at the base of the spinal column and considered to be the base or foundation chakra

**Nabhi Chakra**
Navel Chakra

**Namaskar**
Greeting or bowing or salutations with folded hands

**Nani**
Maternal grandmother

**Ojha**
Witch-doctor

**Paramatma**
Universal Consciousness, Supreme Soul, God

**Purnima**
Full-moon night

**Prasad**
Offering made to God and distributed to devotees as a gift (blessed food), boon, blessing

**Puja**
Worship

**Roti**
Unleavened Indian bread, also called chapati

**Rudraksh**
Dried seeds of the tree Eleocarpus ganitrus, which are used in rosaries

**Sadhak**
One who does sadhana and is engaged in regular spiritual practice; devotee; one who meditates

**Sadhana**
Spiritual practice, meditation

**Sahasrara**
Crown Chakra

**Saint Gnyaneshwar (Jnaneshwar)**
Foremost among poet–saints of Maharashtra during the Bhakti movement. Gnyaneshwar's (1275–1296) verse commentary 'Jnaneshwari' on the Bhagavad Gita, is acknowledged as one of the world's greatest spiritual works.

**Samadhi**
A state of meditative union with the Absolute, tomb or shrine of an entombed saint

**Samarpan**
Complete surrender

**Sansar**
The mundane existence, the world, domestic life

**Satguru**
The True Guru

**Surya Nadi**
Right (Sun) channel or meridian

**Shakti**
Energy, power

**Shaligram**
Small, black and smooth rounded stones; these stones are worshipped as a symbol of Lord Vishnu according to Indian mythology

**Shastri**
One who is acquainted with scriptures (shastras), a scholar

**Vajrasan**
A yogic asana, the 'Thunderbolt' or 'Diamond' pose in Hatha Yoga

**Vastu Shastra**
Science of building a house

**Yagya**
Oblation, fire ceremony, religious sacrifice

**Yagya Shala**
Special place for fire ceremony

**Yoni**
Source, origin, place from which a thing originates; form; class into which animate things are divided (there are 84,00,000 yonis in Hinduism)

**Yug-purush**
Man of the age

# HarperCollins *Publishers* India

At HarperCollins India, we believe in telling the best stories and finding the widest readership for our books in every format possible. We started publishing in 1992; a great deal has changed since then, but what has remained constant is the passion with which our authors write their books, the love with which readers receive them, and the sheer joy and excitement that we as publishers feel in being a part of the publishing process.

Over the years, we've had the pleasure of publishing some of the finest writing from the subcontinent and around the world, including several award-winning titles and some of the biggest bestsellers in India's publishing history. But nothing has meant more to us than the fact that millions of people have read the books we published, and that somewhere, a book of ours might have made a difference.

As we look to the future, we go back to that one word—a word which has been a driving force for us all these years.

Read.

Harper Collins | 4th | HARPER FICTION | HARPER NON-FICTION | HARPER BUSINESS | HarperCollins *Children's Books*

HARPER DESIGN | Harper Sport | HARPER PERENNIAL | HARPER VANTAGE | हार्पर हिन्दी